INDUSTRIAL
MARKETING

INDUSTRIAL MARKETING

H. ROBERT DODGE, PH.D.
Professor of Marketing
Memphis State University

**McGRAW-HILL
BOOK COMPANY**
NEW YORK   ST. LOUIS
SAN FRANCISCO
DÜSSELDORF   LONDON
MEXICO   PANAMA
SYDNEY   TORONTO

**INDUSTRIAL
MARKETING**

Library of Congress Catalog Card Number 72-108562

ISBN 07-017301-X

67890 KPKP 79876

**FOR DONNA JEAN
AND MELODY JEAN**

PREFACE

This book is designed for both the student and the businessman. One objective is to supply the reader with a better understanding of the workings of the industrial marketing complex and its role in the national economy. Another objective is to present the reader with data, techniques, and ideas that represent current thinking in each of the major functional areas. Still another objective is to describe the industrial marketing environment as it exists by specific examples taken from actual business experience.

The main focus of this book is on the structuring of the proper management organization for the most effective planning, organizing, and control of industrial marketing activities. The author places special emphasis on the concept that all marketing activities should be controlled and measured. The book is decision-oriented in that it puts the reader in the position of examining each of the major functional areas in terms of the pertinent decisions that have to be made by management. Only in the last two chapters is there a shift to the more traditional descriptive approach. Although written substantially from the standpoint of the manufacturer, the material nonetheless has application throughout the industrial marketing complex.

The primary audience for this book is the student with upper-division or graduate standing who has completed at least the basic course in marketing. For businessmen, the book is intended to serve as a comprehensive guide to management thinking. Nowhere in the book does the author presume to provide the answers to problems confronting the practitioner.

The organization of this book is thought to be fairly logical. In Part I, two chapters describe the competitive environment of industrial marketing. Chapter 1 answers three questions: What is industrial marketing? What are the general types of industrial goods and services? and What is the quantitative size of the industrial market? Chapter 2 is an analysis of the general characteristics of industrial demand and the industrial marketplace. Part II is concerned with marketing management. Chapter 3 introduces the subject by considering the marketing management concept. Planning and control are covered in Chapters 4 and 5 respectively, and Chapter 6 discusses marketing research.

Part III, entitled "Product Formulation," comprises Chapters 7 through 9. Chapter 7 discusses the general considerations in product development, and Chapter 8 deals with pricing. The subject matter of Chapter 9 is customer financing. Although it might appear more logical to position this subject elsewhere in the text, the author is of the opinion that customer financing, much like pricing, is an important attribute of the total product offering. Part IV is concerned with the distribution of products. Chapter 10 sets forth what is involved in managing channels. Moving on to Chapters 11 and 12, the discussion centers on the various types of marketing channels to be found in the United States as well as other nations.

The functional areas of sales and service, advertising and sales promotion, and logistics are developed in Chapters 13 through 15, which are comprised in Part V. Part VI offers some insight into three selected industrial markets. Agriculture, one of the oldest markets, and oceanology, one of the newest markets, are described in Chapter 16. Chapter 17 covers the immensely important defense market.

The author wishes to acknowledge the significant contribution of Professor Steuart Henderson Britt of Northwestern University, who reviewed the entire manuscript and made innumerable valuable suggestions. Two other persons I would like to thank are Emeritus Professor Clyde William Phelps of the University of Southern California for taking the time to provide additional information for the chapter on customer financing, and Miss "Corki" Nelson, who typed the final draft of the manuscript. In addition, I would like to express my appreciation to the many publishers, business firms, consultants, and associations who granted me permission to cite their materials.

H. ROBERT DODGE

CONTENTS

Preface   vii

PART ONE **BASIC CONCEPTS**
Chapter
1   Nature of Industrial Marketing   3
2   Characteristics of Industrial Marketing   20

PART TWO **MANAGEMENT OF MARKETING ACTIVITIES**
Chapter
3   Management of the Marketing Task   45
4   Managerial Action—Planning   63
5   Managerial Action—Control   88
6   Marketing Research   111

PART THREE **PRODUCT FORMULATION**
Chapter
7   Product Development—General Consideration   147
8   Product Development—Pricing Decisions   185
9   Product Development—Customer Financing   215

PART FOUR **PRODUCT DISTRIBUTION**
Chapter
10 Marketing Channels—Management   235
11 Marketing Channels—United States   261
12 Marketing Channels—In Other Nations   274

PART FIVE **FUNCTIONAL AREAS**
Chapter
    13 Sales and Service   301
    14 Advertising and Sales Promotion   328
    15 Marketing Logistics   364

PART SIX   **SELECTED MARKET STUDIES**
Chapter
    16 Agricultural and Oceanology Markets   397
    17 The Defense Market   423

    Index   459

1

basic concepts

nature
of industrial
marketing

We fail to realize the presence of the industrial market because it is partially hidden from our view by the retailing structure. It is, as some have said, the market behind the market.

Despite this obscurity, the impact of the industrial market on our everyday lives is noteworthy. For consumers or users, the performance of the industrial market will have an important bearing on such questions as what products are available, how suitable these products are in relation to the needs of users, and what the prices will be for these products. Our concerns as taxpayers center around the utilization of tax dollars and prospective tax rates. These in turn are affected to a great extent by governmental spending for goods and services, a major segment of the industrial market. The actions of the industrial market and its members can have economic and social implications for our particular community or state as well as the nation as a whole. These may range from the benefits of economic developments to the problems associated with pollution.

DEFINITION OF INDUSTRIAL MARKETING

What is industrial marketing? The first step in answering this question is to define marketing. While there are about as many definitions of marketing as there are writers, the one adopted by the American Marketing Association is appropriate for our purposes. This definition interprets marketing as the performance of business activities that direct the flow of goods and services from the producer to the consumer or user.[1]

With this in mind, we next divide the subject matter of marketing, goods and services, into two broad categories. The basis of this division is the intended purpose in purchasing the particular good or service. Goods and services of a consumer nature are purchased for the personal satisfaction of the purchaser and/or his family. The physical form of consumer goods is such that no further commercial processing is necessary.[2]

Industrial goods and services, on the other hand, are destined to produce or become parts of other goods and services, or to facilitate the operations of business, public, and nonprofit enterprises. Goods which can be included in the production category are machinery, materials, and components. Paper, a seemingly indispensable

---

[1] Ralph S. Alexander and the Committee on Definitions, *Marketing Definitions,* Chicago: American Marketing Association, 1961, p. 15.

[2] *Ibid.,* p. 11.

supply item, is an example of a good which is utilized in the operation of all types of enterprises.

It follows then that a particular good may be either consumer or industrial, depending upon how the purchaser intends to use it. The nature of the good, while appropriate for some commodities, is not always a valid basis for making a distinction. The following examples will help to illustrate this:

1   Automobile batteries are purchased by both automobile manufacturers and car owners. In fact, the use of a particular brand of battery by the manufacturer as original equipment is perhaps its strongest selling appeal in the replacement market.
2   Office furnishings, such as a desk or lamp, are frequently indistinquishable from those found in homes. Often a store will number among its clientele both types of purchasers.
3   Trucks, until a few years ago, were considered as strictly industrial goods. This view has changed substantially with the development of the camper market.

Thus, the most workable definition of industrial marketing is based on the intended use of the particular good or service in question. Accordingly, *industrial marketing is the performance of business activities that direct the flow from producer to user of goods and services which produce or become part of other goods and services, or facilitate the operation of an enterprise, either business, public, or nonprofit.* Stated more succinctly, it is the marketing of industrial goods and services.

TYPES OF GOODS AND SERVICES

For purposes of convenience in studying, both goods and services can be classified into more definitive groupings. The use of classifications, however, is subject to several qualifications, the most significant of which is the lack of mutually exclusive categories. As a result, it is not possible to classify all goods and services; some will be of a borderline nature. Industrial chemicals, for example, can be a fabricated material or supply, depending upon the exact situation. The same ambiguity is encountered among some items of accessory equipment. Such items tend to exhaust their utility through use and are frequently discarded rather than repaired. Thus, these items of equipment could be easily confused with operating supplies. Another qualification is that specific use of a good may change over a period of time. Thus, its current classification may not be applicable a few years from now. Goods in the research category, when adopted, present a situation requiring reclassification.

Before proceeding with the descriptions of the various goods, consideration is given to the area of services. There are only two distinct types of industrial services: physical and advisory. Application of a physical service results in a change of form or composition. Wrecking or demolition is a service which brings about a very evident change. Other examples include electroplating, the polishing of metals, and the acid treatment of oil wells. Most of the firms performing this type of service are relatively small. An effort is usually made to locate as near the potential customer as possible.

Advisory services include geological and oceanology surveys, the x-raying of castings for flaws, and R&D contract programs for the government. They are performed by businesses, nonprofit organizations, foundations, and universities. Firms engaged in providing this type of service are frequently international in scope. Under contract from the United Nations, Aero Service made a comprehensive inventory of Surinam's mineral resources. Their most significant discovery has been a bauxite deposit valued at $350 million.

A recent development in advisory service is that provided by such nonprofit research corporations as Systems Development, Mitre, and Aerospace. What the Mitre Corporation does was briefly outlined by their officials:[3]

1 Dispensing technical advice in evaluating concepts, proposals, and hardware for the Air Force
2 Coordinating the projects of military contractors and holding proprietary information the various companies will not share among themselves

Machinery and Equipment

Examples of machinery and equipment can be found almost anywhere. In the plant such goods as lathes, grinders, and stamping mills manufacture other goods and services without becoming part of the final products themselves. Machinery and equipment of a more administrative nature include such items as typewriters, postage meters, copying machines, and electronic data processing equipment.

Major equipment comprises those items of a high unit price which appear in the balance sheet as capital assets. Usually this type of good is marketed directly to the customer by the manufacturer. The

[3]"Controversy Warms over Non-profit Labs," *Business Week*, Dec. 16, 1961, p. 67.

feasibility of a direct approach is enhanced by the high unit price and the infrequency of purchase. Some use is made of functional middlemen by smaller firms who find themselves a considerable distance from the market.

Major equipment of a significant size, such as a blast furnace or a crude-oil distillation tower, is referred to as an installation. As part of the fixed plant, installations are closely allied with construction. Therefore, a more extensive market is involved because contacts must be maintained with architects, engineering firms, and consultants. By way of illustration, an engineering and contracting firm was given complete responsibility for the engineering, purchasing, and construction of a liquid-fertilizer plant. In another situation, consulting engineers designed an oil refinery in conjunction with engineers from the oil company and then constructed the facility.

Accessory equipment is lower in unit price and is charged off to current operating expense or depreciated over a short span of years. Almost every conceivable marketing channel is utilized to distribute such equipment. If the marketer is large enough and has a fairly extensive line, he may even have his own sales branches. A part of any industrial distributor's line is accessory equipment.

Machinery and equipment can be further categorized as special-purpose or multipurpose. A special-purpose machine is designed to perform a single operation. Often as not, it is built to customer specification, as is usual in the case of coal-mining equipment. The market for special-purpose machinery and equipment is ordinarily limited to a single industry or trade.

When machinery and equipment can be utilized with little or no modification by different industries, they are generally referred to as multipurpose. Among the items which can be classified thus are hoists, power wrenches, lift trucks, and hydraulic presses. Industrial distributors occasionally maintain a market for used goods of a multipurpose character. They may be forced to do this because of trade-ins. In many areas, however, local demand will far exceed the supply resulting from trade-ins. As a consequence, distributors have had to seek out sellers in other areas to replenish their inventories.

Raw Materials
Raw materials can be defined as the unprocessed goods which come from mines, oil wells, forests, fisheries, and farms. In getting raw materials to market, two vitally important functions are transportation and storage. Transportation is important because raw materials

often have to be shipped great distances. The following examples illustrate the shipping distances for two raw materials—lumber and copper. The Douglas fir region in the Pacific Northwest, which accounts for about 30 percent of the softwood consumed by the nation, is a considerable distance from all of the major urban areas with the exception of those in California. Forty-five percent of the copper in the United States is mined in southern Arizona, but a large part of the nation's refining capacity is situated around New York. Raw materials are also bulky, so economical means must be found for moving vast quantities of the commodity. As an example, boats and pipelines, two of the lowest-cost forms of transportation, carry over 92 percent of the crude petroleum obtained from fields in the United States.

The bulkiness of raw materials also necessitates provision of extensive as well as economical facilities for storing raw materials. Buying and selling of raw materials are facilitated by the extensive application of standards. In the United States, the federal government through its various agencies has assumed much of the responsibility for control of standards. Agricultural materials have been standardized under the direction of the U.S. Department of Agriculture. The Commodity Standards Division of the U.S. Department of Commerce is interested in the development and control of standards for other types of goods.

The marketing of raw materials is not limited to the United States. American industry depends upon a number of foreign countries to supply its raw-material needs. Pakistan for jute, Katanga for cobalt, and Canada for uranium ore are but a few. Some of the major imports of raw materials are presented in Table 1.1.

The United States also exports raw materials, partly in conjunction with foreign-assistance programs. It can be seen in Table 1.2 that agricultural materials predominate.

The flow of goods from the raw-material source through the various production and marketing levels or stages to its final destination can be described as a vertical chain. Absorption or control of one level by another is called vertical integration. For the manufacturer of industrial goods, vertical integration may be backward toward the raw-material source or forward toward the end user. It is fairly common to find industrial-good manufacturers integrating vertically in the direction of the raw-material source. Among the major advantages sought through integrating the extraction of raw materials into a company are assured supply, desired quality, and lower costs. Examples of this form of vertical integration are the iron-ore

TABLE 1.1 Imports of Selected Raw Materials, United States, 1965 (in thousands of dollars)

RAW MATERIAL	VALUE
Petroleum	1,187,741.9
Iron ore	443,806.6
Sugar	440,502.0
Wool	278,480.6
Rubber	194,124.6
Bauxite	148,557.8
Cocoa	137,455.2
Tobacco	129,812.6
Maganese ore	110,280.9
Crude asbestos	70,457.2
Zinc ore	54,417.1
Lead	26,923.1
Cotton	26,734.4

Source: *United States Import Statistics, Commodity by Country,* Washington: U.S. Department of Commerce, 1966.

mines, oil wells, and timberlands owned and operated by steel, oil, and lumber companies respectively.

Even in agriculture, some tendency toward integration is noted. Poultry processors in the South have extended their operation to the raising of chickens, and canners of frozen juice own their own citrus groves. However, such integration is not without its disadvantages, one of the most significant being the reduced ability to adjust when changes occur in the demand for the consumer product.

Functional middlemen who do not take title to the goods in which

TABLE 1.2 Exports of Selected Raw Materials, United States, 1965 (in thousands of dollars)

RAW MATERIAL	VALUE
Wheat	1,063,630.8
Corn or maize	832,739.5
Cotton	506,236.6
Tobacco	382,686.3
Wood	243,922.1
Cereals, unmilled	210,273.6
Barley	76,383.7
Natural phosphates	66,557.5
Sulfur	65,324.4

Source: *United States Export Statistics, Commodity by Country,* Washington: U.S. Department of Commerce, 1966.

they deal play an important role in the marketing of raw materials which are not controlled by firms that have integrated. For nonagricultural commodities, the two most important types are brokers and selling agents. Brokers are also involved in the marketing of agricultural raw materials. The selling of grain and livestock at terminal markets is usually handled by commission merchants.

Commodity exchanges provide markets for various raw materials, generally agricultural . The most prominent exchange is the Chicago Board of Trade, whose annual volume is normally in excess of $25 million. Cash and futures markets are maintained in wheat, oats, rye , cotton, corn, soybeans, soybean oil and meal, and lard. Other exchanges and commodities traded include:

> Commodity Exchange, Inc., in New York: burlap, copper, hides, rubber, tin, and zinc
> Kansas City Board of Trade: corn, oats, millfeeds, sorghum, wheat, and rye
> Minneapolis Grain Exchange: wheat, corn, rye, oats, and flaxseed
> New York Cocoa Exchange: cocoa beans
> New York Coffee and Sugar Exchange: coffee and sugar

Fabricated Materials

Fabricated materials are those goods which have received some processing but will require even more before becoming part of the finished product. They frequently lose their identity in the finished product. Examples are tinplate, glass, plastics, corn syrup, cold- and hot-rolled strip (steel), and plywood. In the aluminum industry, both alumina and metallic aluminum can be classified as fabricated materials.

The physical properties of fabricated materials provide a wide range of application. The markets for certain industrial chemicals, commodities used by nearly every industry, are probably the most extensive. For some fabricated materials, such as aluminum, the range of possible uses is still expanding. In this stage of development, labeled "imitation" by Schumpeter, research is undertaken largely to discover new-product applications.

Marketing of fabricated materials which possess few unique features is highly competitive. Take, for example, the competition that exists between steel and aluminum. Steel, the more traditional material, is being actively challenged by aluminum in canning, automobiles, construction, and many other markets. The high degree of competition is evidenced by the advertising campaigns both types of industries have undertaken to get the ultimate consumer to appreciate and select those consumer goods made of their particular material. An important part of this has been the development of trademarks to assist in identification.

Large-scale marketers sell all or a large portion of their output directly to users through sales branches. Metallurgists and architectural engineers as technical specialists support the sales force when and wherever needed. In the metals industry, there has been a tendency on the part of certain large firms to utilize fabricated materials in making consumer products such as foil wrappings, kitchenware, and furniture.

Direct sales, for the most part, are in large quantities. In the steel industry a carload lot is usual. Two thousand five hundred steel distributors are relied upon to take care of customers who need less than a carload.[4] This channel accounts for 16 percent of the total steel shipped. The major products handled are cold- and hot-rolled sheets, standard pipe, and plates. Steel distributors tend to concentrate in those areas which have a preponderance of small manufacturers. A good example is Los Angeles, California.

Small-scale marketers may locate near customers to facilitate direct selling. Textiles, as an example of a fabricated material which is produced at some distance from its markets, are distributed by various types of middlemen. These include selling agents, brokers, and converters. From the standpoint of functions performed, selling agents can be considered the most important. In addition to selling, they provide their principals with advice on merchandising, prices, and future trends. Among the extra services offered are research, inventory control, designing, and credit and collections. Commission rates range from 2 to 5 percent.

Component Parts

Products which perform a specific function and do not require further modifications to be installed as part of the final product are classified as component parts. Vacuum tubes, diesel engines, automobile batteries, transistors, and ball bearings are but a few examples of what can be called component parts.

There are two markets for parts: original-equipment manufactur-

---

[4] *Charting Steel's Progress in 1967*, New York: American Iron and Steel Institute, 1968, p. 29.

ers (OEM) and replacement or aftermath. Original-equipment manufacturers, after deciding on purchasing rather than producing the part, buy components for two reasons. The first and more compelling one is that the part is essential to the operation of the finished product. Examples would be a torque convertor and a clutch in the power-shifting transmission for an earth scraper.

The second reason is that the part enhances the finished product from an engineering or a marketing standpoint. In neither case, however, will the part be absolutely necessary to the operation of the final product. The addition of a counter to certain types of machinery and equipment is a good illustration of an engineering enhancement. A counter will allow the positioning of a table on a milling machine or similar equipment by digital readout instead of vernier dial The quantitative output of a punch press can be measured with a counter. It should be noted, too, that improvements such as these which are basically engineering in nature are used as marketing features.

Components are frequently added to increase the marketability of a product. This is the situation in the automobile industry. Power steering, air conditioners, radios, and countless other components have been added to cars for marketing reasons. Even in the truck industry, one company has designed a new driver's seat to improve the riding qualities of the heavy-duty truck. Most of the time, however, marketing components are used to heighten the attractiveness of consumer goods.

Many component parts are marketed directly to OEM accounts. In the automobile and aerospace industries, component suppliers have a tendency to locate their manufacturing facilities near major buyers. Much of the industry in the Detroit and Los Angeles areas is of this satellite nature.

Large marketers have their own sales forces, whereas small firms, if they are geographically close, rely upon an owner, partner, or executive. A common arrangement is a partnership in which one partner sells and the other manages the plant. An unusual situation develops when the buyer franchises out the production of component parts to still another company. An example of this is found in the television industry. One West Coast firm pays a royalty under a licensing agreement for every part they have made by a Chicago manufacturer.

Both functional and merchant middlemen are retained by small marketers. Manufacturing agents or reps are used when there is no need for intensive coverage, the agents' established contacts are desired, technical knowledge is required in selling, and there is little need for warehouse or service facilities. Agents are also ideal for supplementing other methods of distribution. Industrial distributors handle more of the standardized parts, such as valves and fasteners, which are frequently purchased by the wide variety of manufacturers.

Two basic distribution systems are used to reach the replacement market. The first consists of channels controlled by the original-equipment manufacturer. The second, established by the part manufacturer, involves all the middlemen who normally sell a particular part. Ideally, maximum use is made of both systems.

The replacement market for automotive components provides a good example. Briefly, more than 1,000 manufacturers distribute over $7 billion worth of parts through two channels.[5] The first is labeled the manufacturer channel and is composed of franchised dealers and service organizations like the General Motors' United Motor Service Division. The second is an independent channel which contains autonomous warehouse distributors, jobbers, garages, and repair shops.

Research Goods

Research goods are the tangible results of government- or industry-contracted R&D programs. Accordingly, goods in this category are closely related to the advisory service provided by R&D, and are most often found in highly technical industries such as electronics and aerospace. It is estimated that 83 percent of R&D monies are concentrated in the aircraft and electrical-equipment industries.

From a marketing standpoint, research goods differ considerably from other types. First of all, it is not the goods themselves which are being marketed, but rather the abilities and experience of the firm doing the R&D work. Secondly, many research goods are models, prototypes, or mock-ups. A third factor is that most R&D programs are heavily dependent upon government financing. Government expenditures account for about two of every three dollars spent annually for R&D. Finally, research goods are frequently employed in promotional campaigns directed at the ultimate consumer. All automobile manufacturers exhibit experimental cars from time to time to obtain some indication of public opinion.

Salvage Goods

Material objects which are extracted from wreckage, destruction, or the like, and have further value and usefulness can be classified as salvage goods. Much of what is considered salvage has metallic

[5] Freeman Lincoln, "The $7 Billion Aftermarket Gets an Overhaul," *Fortune*, March, 1962, pp. 82 +.

content. Copper, gold, lead, iron, and aluminum are all reusable commodities.

Many salvage goods supplement the supply of new materials. The world's copper resources represent only fifty years' supply at the present rate of usage.[6] This is not significant, however, when it is estimated that 60 percent of the copper put into use eventually returns as scrap. Almost one-third of all newly made steel in the world comes from scrap. The exact percentage will vary, depending upon the type of furnace used and the nation in which the furnace is located. Bessemer converters accept almost no scrap, but there is ready utilization by open-hearth furnaces. Among the various nations, the amounts vary between Belgium, which depends on very little, to Italy, which uses over 80 percent scrap.[7]

Supply and demand considerations play important roles in pricing salvage goods. The drop in price of steel scrap between 1956 and 1968 is a good illustration. In 1956, the average price per ton was $53.50. On September 25, 1968, the quotation for a ton, Chicago, was $23.50. The contributing factors were a reduction in the amounts of steel scrap required in existing furnaces, the erection of new steel facilities with basic oxygen furnaces which use only 25 percent scrap, and the availability of more new ore from the exploitation of mines in other parts of the world.

The inability to supply the demand for used brick frequently results in its being priced higher than the new. An attractive product for home construction, used brick, in any appreciable amount, is difficult to extract from wrecking operations.

Salvage goods are marketed through two channels. In terms of number and sales volume, merchant wholesalers are the more significant.[8] These middlemen, often criticized in the past for their high profit margins, are predominant in the distribution of iron and steel scrap. The Ogden Corporation of New York City is considered the world's largest, with 30 percent of its annual sales derived from scrap.

The other channel is made up of wrecking and salvage companies that obtain salvage goods in the course of their service operations. These wrecking firms vary in size from international corporations to proprietorships with no more than one or two employees. Many of the larger firms also handle new products to supplement salvage sales.

[6] *Copper*, Mineral Facts and Problems, Bulletin 556, Washington: U.S. Bureau of Mines, 1956, p. 16.

[7] Richard S. Thoman, *The Geography of Economic Activity*, New York: McGraw-Hill Book Company, 1962, pp. 462-465.

[8] For scrap and waste materials, merchant wholesalers constitute 98.6 percent of the total establishments and 94.1 percent of the total sales. *U.S. Census of Business: 1963—Wholesale Trade*, Washington: U.S. Department of Commerce, 1965, table 1, p. 1-72.

The largest wrecking company in the United States has added such lines as new kitchen equipment.

Operating Supplies

Supplies are goods that exhaust their utility or are used up in the production process or the operation of any enterprise. What purchasing agents refer to as MRO items are included in this category. Lubricants, drills, cleaning solvents, and abrasives are production supplies. In the operation of any business or public organization, paper in its various forms is undoubtedly the most necessary supply item. Other administrative supplies include ink, pencils, paper clips, fuels, and maintenance products. The use of supplies by many different industries results in their markets being more widespread than is normal for other types of industrial goods. In this respect, there is some resemblance to the marketing of consumer goods.

Supplies have a relatively low unit value and are usually purchased in small quantities. Wherever practical, the routine reordering of supplies has been automated with electronic data processing equipment. Some buyers, in an effort to reduce the frequency of purchase, have entered into a contract for specified quantities to be delivered during a given period of time, generally a year.

Price is the dominant buying influence to the extent that supplies are standardized. Other factors governing the choice of a vendor include the convenience of his location, his capacity to fill orders completely, and his reputation for reliability.

Supplies are distributed through almost every possible channel. The practice of manufacturers of machinery and equipment is to market supplies through the outlets used for their primary products. Such is the case with electronic data processing equipment and office machines. Very often more than one channel is employed to reach an extensive market. Paper is a good example of multiple-channel distribution. Manufacturers' sales branches, merchant wholesalers, and functional middlemen are all employed.

Wholesale sales of paper and paper products (not including wallpaper) in 1963 were as follows:

	NUMBER OF ESTABLISHMENTS	SALES (IN THOUSANDS)
Merchant wholesalers	7,046	$4,714,610
Manufacturers' sales branches	2,646	8,562,090
Merchandise agents and brokers	443	835,033

Source: *U.S. Census of Business: 1963—Wholesale Trade* (Washington: U.S. Department of Commerce, 1965, table 3, pp. 1-13, 1-15, 1-17.

TABLE 1.3 Expressed Buying Sources for Various Cutting Tools

TYPE OF CUTTING TOOL	PERCENTAGE OF ALL PLANTS	
	BUY FROM AN INDUSTRIAL DISTRIBUTOR	BUY ONLY FROM AN INDUSTRIAL DISTRIBUTOR
Coated abrasives	95.3	91.5
Files	98.6	98.6
Grinding wheels	96.4	84.1
Hacksaw blades	99.3	99.3
Saws, band and circular	99.3	95.3
Taps, dies, and reamers	98.6	89.9
Twist drills	97.1	92.7
Wire brush wheels	95.3	92.5

Source: *Industrial Distribution*, May 1958, p. 124.

Probably the most important middleman in the marketing of sup-plies is the industrial distributor. A survey of manufacturing plants disclosed that industrial distributors are the preferred source for many supply items. Table 1.3 summarizes the findings on cutting tools.

SIZE OF THE INDUSTRIAL MARKET

Up to the present time, there have been no concerted attempts to measure, either in terms of the value of goods marketed or the vol-ume of trade, the magnitude of the industrial market. A number of authors have estimated that the industrial market accounts for ap-proximately one-half the value of manufacturing shipments. There are a number of reasons which can account for the failure to take a measurement:

1   A consensus that demand which is derived rather than direct is not an indicator of economic activity. This, of course, complete-ly ignores the multiplier effect of derived demand.
2   A lack of agreement as to the definition of industrial marketing.
3   A number of practical difficulties that would have to be overcome in the collection of data. One severe limitation is imposed by the fact that very few industries maintain records of shipments by class of consumer.

Some idea of the dollar volume of industrial transactions can be obtained by the statistics on cost of materials to manufacturers, capital expenditures for the various forms of private enterprise, and government purchases of goods and services. Data for the years 1961 through 1965 are presented in Table 1.4.

Two major conclusions can be drawn from the data presented in Table 1.4. The first relates to the quantitative significance of the industrial market. For purely comparative purposes, the dollar volume of transactions in both 1964 and 1965 is equal to roughly two-thirds of the valuation placed on Gross National Product. Another impression of size can be gained from the fact that the industrial market very nearly approximates the combination sales of retail and merchant wholesale establishments. [9]

A second conclusion is the impressive rate of growth experienced by the industrial market between 1961 and 1965. The yearly rate of growth for the industrial market exceeds that reported for GNP during the same periods. The sharp rise between 1961 and 1962 would distort any average for the period 1961 to 1965.

TABLE 1.4   Industrial Marketing Transactions, United States, 1961 through 1965 (in billions of dollars)

TYPE OF TRANSACTION	YEAR				
	1961	1962	1963	1964	1965
Cost of materials, manufacturers*	176.8	221.5	229.4	243.8	266.3
Government purchases†	107.4	117.1	122.5	128.9	136.2
Federal	57.0	63.4	64.2	65.2	66.8
National defense	48.3	51.6	50.8	50.0	50.1
Other	8.7	11.8	13.5	15.2	16.7
State and local	50.4	53.7	58.2	63.7	69.4
Capital expenditures	34.4	37.3	39.2	44.9	52.0
Manufacturing	13.7	14.7	15.7	18.6	22.5
All other ‡	20.7	22.6	23.5	26.3	29.5
Total	318.6	375.9	391.1	417.6	454.5
Yearly growth rate	....	18.0%	4.0%	6.8%	8.8%

* Some precaution should be observed in interpreting the cost of materials. The total amount is overstated in that it includes materials taken from inventories and transfers from other establishments belonging to the same company.

† To arrive at this total, government sales were subtracted from purchases.

‡ Includes mining, railroad, transportation other than rail, public utilities, communication. trade, service, finance, and construction.

Source: *1963 Census of Manufactures,* Washington: U.S. Department of Commerce, 1965; *Annual Survey of Manufactures,* Washington: U.S. Department of Commerce, appropriate years; *Survey of Current Business,* appropriate *National Income Numbers* and quarterly issues.

[9] In 1964 retail sales were $261.6 billion and merchant wholesale sales were $174.3 billion. *Survey of Current Business—National Income Number,* July, 1966.

SUMMARY

Industrial marketing is defined as the marketing of goods and services which enter into the production of other goods and services or facilitate the operation of any enterprise. Through its functioning, this system affects everyone in the roles of consumer, taxpayer, and resident. Furthermore, an estimate of the volume of transactions shows that quantitatively the industrial market is of major significance in the nation's economic structure.

To facilitate the study of industrial marketing, both goods and services can be classified. There are two types of services: physical and advisory. Physical services through application bring about a desired alteration or change in the recipient. Services of an advisory nature provide information, often exploratory in nature.

Industrial goods are categorized as machinery and equipment, raw materials, fabricated materials, component parts, research goods, salvage goods, and operating supplies. Machinery and equipment produce goods and services. They are also to be found in various operations of the enterprise. Raw materials, fabricated materials, and component parts all become part of the final product. The models which result from engineering and scientific projects are referred to as research goods. Salvage goods are still useful commodities that are extracted from wreckage, destruction, and the like. As a machine or business functions, it uses up or wears out so-called operating supplies.

DISCUSSION QUESTIONS

1   In what ways are ultimate consumers affected by the functioning of the industrial market?
2   Why is the nature of a good a poor basis for determining whether it is categorized as consumer or industrial?
3   Advisory services are performed by what types of organizations?
4   How does an installation differ from other forms of machinery? Does this require a different marketing approach?
5   Contrast the markets for special-purpose and multipurpose machinery.
6   Why is transportation an important consideration in the marketing of raw materials?
7   What support can be given to the statement that the market for raw materials is international in scope?

8 To obtain ultimate consumer awareness of the fabricated material used in the final product, what have manufacturers resorted to?

9 Explain the ways a component part can enhance the value of a final product.

10 The replacement or aftermath market for components has received a great deal of attention lately. What channels are utilized to reach this market?

11 Both research and salvage goods are related to the performance of industrial services. Explain these relationships.

12 What are the marketing similarities between operating supplies and consumer goods?

13 What difficulties are encountered in measuring the size of an industrial market?

SUPPLEMENTARY READINGS

Alexander, Ralph S., James S. Cross, and Richard M. Hill, *Industrial Marketing,* 3d ed., Chicago: Richard D. Irwin, Inc., 1967, chap. 2.

Beckman, Theodore N., and William R. Davidson, *Marketing,* 8th ed., New York: The Ronald Press Company, 1967, chap. 8.

Beckman, Theodore N., Nathanael H. Engle, and Robert D. Buzzell, *Wholesaling,* 3d ed., New York: The Ronald Press Company, 1959, chaps. 6 and 9.

Davidson, Charles N., *The Marketing of Automotive Parts,* Ann Arbor: Bureau of Business Research, University of Michigan, 1954.

Highsmith, Richard N., and J. Granville Jensen, *Geography of Commodity Production,* Philadelphia: J. B. Lippincott Company, 1958.

Lincoln, Freeman, "The $7 Billion Aftermarket Gets an Overhaul," *Fortune,* March, 1962, pp. 82 +.

Phillips, Charles F., and Delbert J. Duncan, *Principles and Methods of Marketing,* 5th ed., Chicago: Richard D. Irwin, Inc., 1960, chap. 17.

Thoman, Richard S., Edgar C. Conkling, and Maurice H. Yeater, *The Geography of Economic Activity,* 2d ed., New York: McGraw-Hill Book Company, 1968.

characteristics of industrial marketing

In the previous chapter, the distinction between industrial and consumer marketing was based on the intended utilization of the particular good or service. The two marketing systems differ in a number of other important respects—the nature of demand, market characteristics, and the various roles of government.

DEMAND FOR INDUSTRIAL GOODS AND SERVICES

Demand is not inherent in industrial marketing as it is in consumer marketing. Rather, it is derived from the demand for consumer goods and services as well as the purchasing of governmental units at all levels. Industrial demand can also be distinguished as showing a wide degree of fluctuation, an acute sensitivity to buyer inventory policy, and a tendency to exhibit counter price elasticity initially.

Derived Demand

The demand for industrial goods and services, being derived, is activated by ultimate consumer and government purchasing. The level of such transactions is translated into marketing activity not only for the firms making these products, but for their numerous suppliers as well. For example, a manufacturer of consumer products will buy industrial goods and services to implement and sustain his operation only if his own products are selling. Likewise, the suppliers of consumer-product manufacturers will in turn base their buying on what is sold. As this chain of sale and purchase lengthens, the influencing effect of derived demand weakens. Automobiles represent a product for which changes in ultimate consumer demand generate repercussions throughout much of the industrial market. According to the Automobile Manufacturers Association, the auto industry consumes over 20 percent of the nation's steel, about 60 percent of its rubber, almost 60 percent of its malleable iron, and over a third of its zinc.[1]

Another way of looking at the industrial market is in terms of input-output data or the interindustry flow of dollar transactions for a period of time. Analysis of such data necessitates the arrangement of production and consumption statistics in tabular form. A hypothetical example is shown in Table 2.1.

It can be seen in Table 2.1 that total purchases or inputs equal total

---

[1] *Automobile Facts and Figures,* Detroit: Automobile Manufacturers Association, 1965, p. 14.

TABLE 2.1   Hypothetical Input-output Data (in millions of dollars)

INDUSTRIES PRODUCING	INDUSTRIES PURCHASING				TOTAL OUTPUT (SALES)
	A	B	C	OTHER	
A	10	8	5	2	25
B	6	2	6	4	18
C	7	4	1	0	12
Other	2	4	0	10	16
Total input (purchases)	25	18	12	16	71

sales or outputs. This is a basic assumption of input-output analysis. The rows of the table show how the output of one industry is distributed to other industry segments. The columns reflect the purchasing patterns of the industries. Thus, each statistic in the table is both an input and an output for an industry segment.

Using input-output analysis, a manufacturer obtains a general picture of the market segments for the products of his industry—a general picture because the various market segments are defined as heterogeneous SIC groupings. This has resulted in some rather surprising findings, as witness the fact that the food and kindred products industry has been shown to consume almost 2 percent of the communications industry output. Even so, input-output analysis contributes valuable information to the industrial-good manufacturer in planning market strategy.

The derived nature of demand causes it to have a multiplying effect on the volume of industrial trade. The following hypothetical example will help to illustrate this phenomenon. Suppose that Company ABC, a manufacturer of consumer products, has a yearly sales volume of $1 million. Since it is essentially an assembler, suppose its cost of material amounts to 80 percent, or $800,000. Further assume that suppliers are arranged in three levels with each firm's purchases divided up among four vendors. Computation of the total volume of industrial trade arising from this given amount of consumer sales is shown in Figure 2.1.

The total volume of industrial trade, as indicated in Figure 2.1, is 36 percent greater than the consumer demand from which it is derived. A still greater increase would have been noted if the allotted capital and supply expenditures for the eighty-five firms had been included. It is also noticeable that the extent of the increase has a direct relationship to the number of supplier levels and the relative costs incurred by individual suppliers for materials and capital.

The multiplier effect also increases the initial contract outlays made

FIGURE 2.1   Multiplier Effect of Industrial Demand.

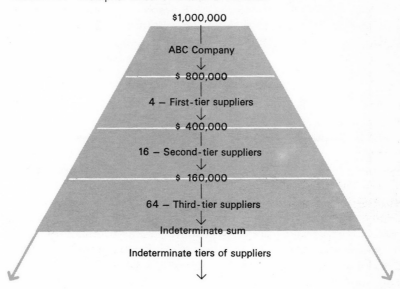

$1,000,000
|
ABC Company
↓
$ 800,000
|
4 — First-tier suppliers
↓
$ 400,000
|
16 — Second-tier suppliers
↓
$ 160,000
|
64 — Third-tier suppliers
↓
Indeterminate sum
|
Indeterminate tiers of suppliers
↓

by the government to meet its obligations. In the aerospace industry, for example, about 100 prime contractors are supplied by over
100,000 "first-tier" subcontractors and some 200,000 "vendors."[2]

Widely Fluctuating Demand

The derived nature of demand for industrial products causes it to
experience a wide degree of fluctuation. Frequently, it can be said
that industrial demand takes on the appearance of what might be
described as a "boom or bust" cycle. This can be understood by looking at the market during prosperity as well as depression. During
prosperous times, the manufacturers of consumer goods increase
production. This accelerates the purchase of industrial goods and
services. Industrial goods which become part of the final product
are absorbed at a greater rate to meet current requirements and expectations of still further growth. Firms speed up the replacement
and addition of capital items. Then, too, the amount of overall business activity causes an increase in the consumption of supplies. Dur-

[2] An excellent discussion of the supplier levels in the military market is contained in Harry
Williams, "Marketing Military Components and Equipment," *Effective Marketing Coordination.* A reprint of the article is to be found in *Reprints on the Subject of Defense Marketing,* Chicago: American Marketing Association, 1962, pp. 93-99.

ing this time the market gravitates toward the seller. Many of the buying considerations such as price and quality are outweighed by shorter delivery dates. If the seller's output is relatively limited, his problem is how to allocate it between old and new customers. New firms will spring up in those portions of the industrial market where entry costs are not formidable. One of the best examples of such a market is the one for gray-iron castings.

When consumer-goods demand slackens, the opposite situation develops with deceleration rather than acceleration and pessimism replacing optimism. Production of consumer goods is at a lower level, inventories of both consumer and industrial goods are reduced, and no new capital expenditures are made. Often, too, expense-cutting programs are initiated to lessen such costs as those incurred by the use of operating supplies. Some retrenchment is also noted among consumer-goods manufacturers. Goods and services which were formerly purchased are now produced so as to sustain as nearly as possible the levels of employment. This, in effect, abolishes much of the supplier spectrum. The indirect suppliers in the lower strata are most acutely affected, often having to cease operations.

Some indications of retrenchment in recent years have been observed in the auto industry. A division whose sales are down will change over to the production of components for other more successful divisions. Another example is found in the military market today. The failure to obtain a contract or a cutback of a current project has brought more serious consequences for the subcontractors than for the major contractor.

Sensitivity to Inventory Policy

The demand for industrial goods and services is highly responsive to changes in customer inventories. These changes may be effected to adjust to new sales patterns or to modifications in general company policy. What happens may best be explained by the following hypothetical situation. A company operates on a two-month inventory of a component part, one part going into each final product. If there is a constant flow without time lags that occur under actual conditions, balance is maintained by purchasing the same amount as is sold every month. Suppose that sales increase 25 percent. To satisfy the expansion of both sales and inventory, purchases of the component part will have to be increased 75 percent—25 percent to allow for current sales growth and 25 percent for each of the two months of inventory. With future sales expectations bright, the amount of inventory might also be increased. If another month's supply were added, three times as many components as before would have to be purchased. Inventory buildups, for the most part, are gradual with purchases spread out over a number of months.

Now, suppose that sales have fallen off by some 25 percent. An immediate inventory adjustment will mean that the firm will need to purchase only twenty-five percent of the original order for the next thirty days. If a decrease in inventory requirements, say to a month's supply, accompanies the drop in sales, nothing more need be purchased until the third month. Changes that occur in a declining market have a sense of urgency about them and tend to be abrupt.

Initial Counter Price Elasticity

Elasticity is the responsiveness of demand to changes in price. Normally, the demand curve is pictured as downward-sloping. That is, as the price is lowered, demand increases. Conversely, demand will decline with a raising of price. Demand is elastic if the percentage change in quantity demanded is greater than the percentage change in price. For example, a 5 percent decline in price results in a 10 percent increase in demand. If in the preceding situation the increase in demand is less than 5 percent, demand is said to be inelastic.

Initially, the elasticity of demand for industrial goods and services runs counter to this. A price increment brings about a growth in demand, whereas a drop in price is attended by a shrinking of demand. The reasoning behind such a response by industrial consumers is that any price change foretells greater movement in the same direction. An increase, therefore, will signify that prices will go still higher. In order to avoid even greater material costs, users commence to "load up," as it is usually termed in industry. The extent of the commitment depends on three factors—the relative cost of the material, the degree of price competition for the final product, and the financial capabilities of the purchaser.

When the price is cut, purchasers will surmise that it will fall even farther and will consequently refrain as much as possible from entering the market. How much they will have to purchase depends upon their inventory position at the time of the price decline and their present rate of consumption.

This abstaining action, if taken collectively by a major portion of the market, will in effect drive the price even lower. This is especially true when the suppliers have a relatively high and unavoidable fixed-cost burden. In recent years, remarkable progress has been attained in alleviating such marketing hindrances. Much of this can be attributed to increased accuracy in sales forecasting and market analysis. A notable example is a West Coast cement company whose research objectives are slanted toward the prediction of long-range sales trends. Sometimes, not only the buying requirements of immediate customers are studied, but those of their customers as well. One steel company states with a great deal of pride that its research department forecasted a slump in automobile sales much before the automobile manufacturers themselves.

Another approach that has been used successfully by some firms is the attainment of greater manufacturing flexibility. One major steel firm can operate profitably at a much lower rate of capacity than was ever thought possible. Facing the rigidity of vertical integration, another firm has found it profitable to channel off some of its unneeded iron ore to Japanese concerns.

MARKET CHARACTERISTICS

Generally speaking, there are two types of industrial markets—*vertical* and *horizontal.* Narrow markets which involve a particular trade or industry are referred to as vertical. Distribution tends to be intensive in that almost every market segment will possess a need for a particular good or service. The limited number of potential customers in a given vertical market is apparent from the data shown in Table 2.2. Notice, too, that the market represented by what is defined as mineral industries is even more restricted when only mining establishments with twenty or more employees are considered.

Horizontal markets involve those goods and services whose use is not confined but rather extends to all kinds of firms in many different industries. Most multipurpose equipment and operating supplies fall into this category. A good example is sulfuric acid, the market for which is so extensive that its rate of consumption has often been used as an indicator of general industrial activity.

The number of manufacturing establishments itemized by geographical census division in Table 2.3 indicates how vast a horizontal market can be. It is also apparent that in all but two of the geographical divisions there are more manufacturing establishments with twenty or more employees than the total reported for all establishments of this same size in the mineral industries.

Other distinctions that can be made between the industrial- and consumer-goods markets are the geographic location of customers and the process of arriving at a purchasing decision. How the industrial market tends to localize is considered first.

TABLE 2.2 Number of Mineral-industry Establishments, by Geographical Division, United States, 1963

GEOGRAPHIC DIVISION	INDUSTRY*		OIL AND GAS EXTRACTION	
	TOTAL	20 OR MORE EMPLOYEES	TOTAL	20 OR MORE EMPLOYEES
New England	349	57		
Middle Atlantic	4,072	516	932	40
East North Central	4,743	574	2,230	124
West North Central	3,547	398	1,877	175
South Atlantic	4,433	807	1,080	39
East South Central	3,336	569	1,051	101
West South Central	12,131	1,726	11,362	1,552
Mountain	3,656	511	1,820	254
Pacific	2,370	332	885	155
Total	38,637	5,490	21,237	2,440

* Included in mineral industries are metal mining, anthracite mining, bituminous coal and lignite mining, oil and gas extraction, and nonmetallic metals mining.
Source: *1963 Census of Mineral Industries—Area Statistics,* Washington: U.S. Department of Commerce, 1965, table 2.

Geographical Concentration

In following the same geographical pattern as its largest customer, the manufacturer, the industrial market gravitates toward urban areas and certain regions of the United States. Its density is highest in and around major metropolitan areas. Measured in terms of value added by manufacturing, the degree of urbanization is vividly demonstrated by the following:[3]

	PERCENTAGE OF THE TOTAL VALUE ADDED FOR THE STATE
Arizona:	
Phoenix	69.5
California:	
Los Angeles - Long Beach	53.5 ⎫
Orange County	⎬ 75.4
San Francisco - Oakland	21.9 ⎭
San Jose	
Michigan:	
Detroit	51.1
Texas:	
Dallas - Fort Worth	25.1 ⎫ 52.2
Houston - Galveston	27.1 ⎭
Wisconsin:	
Milwaukee	41.7.

[3] Derived and computed from statistics for standard metropolitan areas, *1966 Survey of Manufacturers,* Washington: U.S. Department of Commerce, 1967.

TABLE 2.3 Number of Manufacturing Establishments, by Geographical Division, United States, 1963

| | ESTABLISHMENTS | |
GEOGRAPHICAL DIVISION	TOTAL	20 OR MORE EMPLOYEES
New England	24,650	8,677
Middle Atlantic	81,707	28,526
East North Central	63,092	22,320
West North Central	20,668	6,257
South Atlantic	35,546	11,809
East South Central	14,196	4,939
West South Central	20,237	5,920
Mountain	8,527	2,022
Pacific	43,307	11,813
Total	311,930	102,283

Source: *1963 Census of Manufactures—General Summary,* Washington: U.S. Department of Commerce, 1966.

Probably the most important industrial region is the one which extends from Pittsburgh to Chicago and from Cincinnati to Milwaukee and Detroit. The value added in the Chicago-northwestern Indiana area alone is greater than that recorded by 45 states.[4] The largest single concentration in terms of value added is the New York-northeastern New Jersey area with over $19 billion.

Additional evidence of the high degree of geographical concentration in the industrial market is provided by comparing for five states the shipments of gray iron and the number of foundries with the number and the sales of retail establishments. This is presented in Table 2.4.

The trend toward industrial decentralization may have only limited disruptive effects on the time-established patterns of concentration. The auto and meat-packing industries provide two examples which seem to support this observation. In neither case have a substantial number of suppliers moved to be geographically decentralized with their customers. Much of this apparent inertia may be attributable to there being no reason for the marketer to be convenient. Another explanation may be the deep-rooted relationship suppliers have with those firms who in turn provide them with goods and services. The experience of a manufacturer of speciality lacquers and

---

[4] This area's value added of $14.6 billion is exceeded by only California, Illinois, New York, Ohio, and Pennsylvania.

TABLE 2.4   Comparison of Gray-iron Foundries and Shipments with Retail Establishments and Sales, Five East North Central States, 1963

STATE	PERCENTAGE OF TOTAL			
	GRAY-IRON FOUNDRIES	VALUE OF SHIPMENTS	RETAIL ESTABLISH-MENTS	RETAIL ESTABLISHMENT SALES
Michigan	8.1	21.4	4.1	4.4
Ohio	10.1	16.5	4.9	5.3
Indiana	5.6	5.7	2.5	1.8
Illinois	6.6	5.5	5.4	6.2
Wisconsin	4.9	5.2	2.6	2.1
Total	35.3	54.3	19.5	19.8

Source: *1963 Census of Manufacturers—Industry Statistics,* Washington: U.S. Department of Commerce, 1965, table 2; and *1963 Census of Business, Retail Trade—United States Summary,* Washington: U.S. Department of Commerce, 1965, table 4.

varnishes is contrary to this. To retain the volume of business they had been doing with the automobile firms, they were forced to locate near the assembly plants. Special orders, it seems, are the rule rather than the exception for this group of products.

Rational Buying Motives

Industrial buying is substantially rational in nature. A careful and frequently exhaustive study of all the objective factors is the basis for buying a product from a particular vendor. This should not be interpreted to mean, however, that emotional motives involving the images of the salesman and his company do not influence the final decision. They most assuredly do, particularly among products and vendors that are fairly competitive in price and quality. One major detriment to a favorable image in the eyes of most buyers is the supplier's small size.[5] At the risk of overgeneralizing, it can be surmised that emotional buying motives become more important as the degree of similarity of quantifiable factors among products and vendors increases.

The industrial buying process starts with the anticipation or recognition of a need and ends with the placement of an order with a vendor. The buying process may be new in that it represents the initial purchase of the item in question, or it may be a repurchase to

[5] A survey of 208 companies revealed that one of the reasons most often offered for thinking of a supplier first was the "large size" of the company. Bertrand Klass, "What Factors Affect Industrial Buying Decisions?" *Industrial Marketing,* May, 1961, p. 34.

replenish inventory or replace equipment. Informational requirements of the purchasing influences will vary in direct relation to the newness of the purchase. The newer the item is in regard to purchasing experience, the greater the extent of the need for information.

The informational dimensions of the industrial purchasing decision are quality, price, and vendor. While the definition and the relative influence of quality and price will vary from situation to situation, the usual approach is to obtain the lowest price consistent with minimum quality standards. This was aptly and succinctly expressed by the chief design engineer for a manufacturer of portable industrial equipment. Reflecting his company's interests in both cost and weight, he said, "Our rule of thumb is a dollar a pound."

Since the early sixties, the technique of value analysis has played a prominent role in the cost-reduction programs of industrial buyers.[6] The organized approach to cost reduction is a systematic way of determining the most economical means of reliably performing a function. This is called the value of the function. The crux of value analysis is the evaluation of an item's function or use parameters.

The concept of value analysis is particularly applicable in purchasing components because it implies that the minimum standard of one vital part determines the maximum for all those related to it. For example, there would be no need for transistors which have a longer life than the system of which they are a component. Value analysis has also encouraged the expanded use of materials which are lower in cost and perhaps more suitable than the more traditional ones. One company, by way of illustration, was able to achieve substantial cost savings and a reduction in weight by substituting anodized aluminum for stainless steel.

Industrial consumers conceive of quality in terms of their products and manufacturing processes. How will it affect performance? Does it extend the life of the final product? Is servicing made any easier? These are but a few of the questions which might be asked about goods and services which become part of the final product. For machinery, equipment, and supplies, the considerations include possible savings in labor costs, improvement in output performance,[7] and reductions in maintenance expense.

The importance of price for goods and services which become part

[6] Nearly 50 percent of the companies with centralized purchasing report the use of value analysis. H. Jay Bullen, "Value Analysis—Marketing Men Take Notice," *Industrial Marketing*, August, 1963, p. 87.

[7] Performance factors such as reliability, accuracy, and maintainability often determine the selection of one machine rather than another "How Controls Get Bought for a New Machine Tool-Case History," reprint from *Control Engineering*, New York: McGraw-Hill Book Company, 1962.

of another product is relative to their position in that product's cost structure and the degree of price competition confronting the product. If the cost position is proportionately high, purchasing will tend to be highly specialized and concerted efforts will be made to minimize the market risks incurred by unfavorable price fluctuations. As an example, a flour miller will have a separate department that purchases nothing but wheat. The head of this department may be as high in the company's hierarchy as a vice-president.

Three basic approaches are taken to secure added protection against unfavorable price fluctuations of a major component or material. The first is exhaustive study of the market. With adequate information the reactions of the market can be predicted with more surety. A second approach is to integrate vertically in the direction of the supplier. All too often, however, this will reduce the flexibility of the firm to adjust to changes in demand. One more obstacle to integration is the substantial amount of capital that has to be committed for such an undertaking. Hedging, the third approach, is often resorted to when commodity exchanges furnish continuous cash and futures markets in the particular commodity. Briefly, what happens is that the purchaser takes positions in both the cash and futures markets to assure his operating profit regardless of future price fluctuations.

The more competitive the market is for the final product, the greater will be the pressures on all suppliers for price reductions. Purchasers will apply pressure in an effort to gain more leeway in their own pricing or to maintain a specified profit position. Even those who supply goods and services which constitute a relatively insignificant part of the cost structure are subjected to some form of stress. The reasoning is that collectively such reductions may be noteworthy and the purchaser's bargaining position is usually more formidable to many of these suppliers.

For machinery, equipment, and supplies, the question of price revolves around the attainability of savings—how significant and when. Today's purchasers are also concerned with their capital position. The present burden, which would necessarily be increased, as well as their status in regard to depreciation, is carefully reviewed. Such considerations may have been the major cause for the soft-drink bottlers' postponing or at least slowing down the changeover to canning, an operation which has countless product and process advantages.[8]

---

[8] A capital investment of up to $300,000 may be required to install high-speed canning lines. In contrast, the investment for a nonreturnable bottle line is only $50,000. "How Do You Pick a Winner?" *Dun's Review*, November, 1961, p. 66.

The third informational approach to the purchasing decision is an appraisal of all potential suppliers or a vendor analysis. This appraisal is divided into two parts. One part has to do with rating vendor performance. Although the definition of vendor performance may vary from firm to firm, most plans rely on three factors—quality, delivery, and supplier relations. Once ratings are arrived at for each performance factor, they are combined into a composite index for the individual supplier.

The quality rating depends on the relative number of defective items received from a supplier. This, in turn, is weighted by the disposition of the defectives. If the defectives can be used as they are, the weighting is not as adverse as it would be if the cost of reworking the defectives had to be absorbed. The delivery rating is determined by comparing the promised delivery date with the actual delivery date. The resultant rating may be modified by a quantity factor and/or an expediting factor. The purpose of the quantity factor is to penalize the supplier for failure to deliver the exact quantity specified. It is felt that the supplier who makes several smaller and unscheduled shipments is not doing as good a job as the one who delivers the specified quantity as promised. The expediting factor penalizes the supplier for more than a routine number of contacts by the purchaser. The greater the number of excessive contacts by the purchaser, the higher the affixed penalty.

Supplier relations are services other than quality and delivery. Among the services considered are before- and after-sales service, technical counseling, prompt supply of requested documents, salesman calls, and cooperation. Needless to say, supplier relations are difficult to quantify.

The other part of the vendor analysis is the evaluation of vendor capabilities. All potential suppliers are appraised in terms of their R&D, manufacturing, service, financial, and management capabilities. One very large aerospace firm has specifically assigned this responsibility to the purchasing department. Initial evaluation is performed by survey teams, which are composed of an engineer, cost analyst, and representatives from manufacturing, reliability, quality control, and purchasing. The person from purchasing is charged with the administrative function. All reports on experience with the suppliers are filed for future reference in a library maintained within the company.

Among the more significant factors influencing the selection of a supplier are:

1   Price including transportation charges

2   Terms of sales
3   Maintaining quality standards[9]
4   Dependability, particularly in meeting delivery schedules
5   Reputation for integrity
6   Availability of servicing facilities
7   Keeping customers informed
8   Efficient handling of requests

Businesses and governmental units, in ever-increasing numbers, are utilizing computers in the purchasing process. There appear to be three broad levels of application. Undoubtedly the widest application has been in automating the repetitive, routine clerical tasks such as those found in placing the purchase order. Another application has been in the repurchasing of such items as operating supplies at regular intervals. In such situations the purchasing decision rests with the purchasing department and the requirement for new information is minimal. The third application is in supplying purchasing information. In addition to providing up-to-date and comprehensive data, the computer can provide new facts never before available to the purchaser.

Other factors which have to be considered in the buying process are testing and design cycle. For a new product, the buyer relies initially upon the laboratory and field testing the marketer has done. The results of these tests are usually contained in a specification sheet. Credence is placed on past experience for more mature goods and services. After deciding on the basis of the evidence thus presented that the good or service is worth further appraisal, the buyer requests samples so that he can proceed with his own testing. This may take anywhere from a few weeks to a year. Small firms have a tendency to accomplish the necessary testing in a shorter period of time. Their lack of complexity often facilitates faster action. This is demonstrated by a small manufacturer of cement mixers who field-tests with customer permission a component in the final product less than a month after receiving the samples. Too, the good or service may be of greater significance to the small firm; for example, a quarry operator, with a large impending gravel order, had to test a number of loaders during a two-week period.

Design cycle, the other factor, is defined as a sequence of events necessary before a fabricated material or component part appears in the final products which roll off the assembly line. The cycle start-

[9] The findings of one study indicate that maintaining quality consistent with specification is the most important product factor in selecting a supplier. Bertrand Klass, *op. cit.*, p. 35.

ing with testing runs about a year in most industries. When the final product has a yearly model changeover, the design cycle can extend over an even longer period of time. In the automobile industry, production of parts starts about ten months before the introduction of new models. In a twelve-month design cycle, testing would have to commence almost two years before the part appears in the final product. Complete redesign of the final product is effected in stages and stretches over a considerable number of years. A manufacturer of industrial equipment estimates that it takes about ten years to accomplish this in his line.

Two of the more commonly found general purchasing policies are order splitting and reciprocity. Many companies divide up their purchases among all approved suppliers.[10] There are at least three reasons for such a policy. In the first place it prevents any one vendor from becoming too important. Secondly, this policy has been found to be a highly effective method of creating goodwill. A third reason is that a greater diffusion of reciprocal influentialness can be obtained.

Reciprocity, almost a standard operating procedure in many portions of the industrial market, is another policy that plays an important role in supplier selection.[11] Its significance tends to be greatest for large firms and for buyers and sellers who are able to use each other's products in worthwhile quantities.[12]

Reciprocity

Reciprocity, or in less maligned terms trade relations, is the practice of extending purchasing preference to those suppliers who are also customers. So-called primary reciprocity involves a direct arrangement between a buyer and a seller who have reciprocal product needs. A simple illustration of this is as follows: Company B, a manufacturer of office equipment, agrees to buy steel from Company S if the steel producer, in turn, purchases its equipment. If Com-

---

[10] A survey of 208 industrial companies revealed that 56 percent follow this policy. *Ibid.*

[11] The findings of a study of 300 purchasing agents showed that all of those in the iron and steel, chemical, petroleum, and other process industries cited reciprocity as a major factor in buyer-seller relationships. On the other hand, only 36 percent of the purchasing agents in consumer-goods firms mentioned it as a factor. Leonard Sloane, "Reciprocity: Where Does the P. A. Stand?" *Purchasing,* Nov. 20, 1961, pp. 76-77.

[12] Reciprocity as a major factor takes on greater importance as the size of the firm increases. Seventy-eight percent of the purchasing agents in firms having over $50 million in sales said it was a factor; in companies within the $10 million to $50 million sales range, the figure dropped to 62 percent, and only 47 percent noted it in companies with less than $10 million in sales. *Ibid.*

pany S represents a fairly small potential for office equipment, Company B may decide to divide up its purchases among other firms (S_1, S_2, and S_3). The amount purchased from each will be in proportion to the business done with him. One of the basic tasks of the purchasing agent is to compile summaries of the business done with each supplier.

Often as not, however, reciporcity is more indirect. Through integration and diversification industry has become increasingly complex. An inevitable result has been the ampliation of possibilities for reciprocity requests. Such arrangements are usually referred to as secondary and may involve any of the myriad subsidiaries, divisions, customers, and suppliers who are associated with either the buyer or seller. As an example, a glass-container corporation will exert pressures upon those chemical companies from whom it purchases soda ash to buy corrugated cartons from its paper-box subsidiary.

Enforcement of reciprocity agreements takes two forms. One is reprisal in the form of a decrease or discontinuance of orders as soon as it is practical. The other is more casual in nature and not quite as drastic. The purchasing agent or a salesman from the firm contacts the supplier to express the company's displeasure over the recent action. Such a tactic is generally reserved for small suppliers and those which do not represent much of a potential market for the buyer's products.

Purchasing Influences

Most industrial purchasing decisions are influenced by a number of persons within the organization.[13] Specifically who is involved will depend upon the good or service being considered and company policy. Only rarely will one person make a decision without consulting others. It is hard to imagine even the owner of a small machine shop not seeking the advice of his employees before purchasing a new item of equipment. The usual role assigned the purchasing agent is a facilitating one. What influence he seems to have is confined to the selection of suppliers, especially for highly standardized items. It is generally conceded, however, that to ignore him in making the sales contact is a serious tactical error.

---

[13] A study of 465 plants which manufacture motor-driven machines, appliances, and equipment showed that over eighty different engineering titles were listed as specifying influences for both machine drive and electrical control components. *The Original Equipment for Machine Drive Components in the Field of Electrically Operated Products,* New York: *Electrical Manufacturing,* Market Research Department, August, 1959, p. 6.

This multiplicity of influence creates a major problem for the marketer. He must ascertain who are the most influential individuals concerned with his product. While some reliance can be placed on past experience, much of the evaluation will have to be accomplished through trial and error. This is further complicated by the ambiguity of title nomenclature. It is little wonder that the selling process is apt to be lengthy.

To help in understanding the influences on purchasing, a number of periodicals have undertaken studies of a particular industry or product. One such study by University Research Associates for *Electronic Design* surveyed the purchasing influences in 133 electronic companies for 24 product categories.[14] To indicate clearly the nature of a person's influence, the purchasing task was broken down into specific actions as follows:

1 Establish need for product type
2 Develop specifications or standards
3 Locate potential suppliers
4 Evaluate suppliers' products for performance and reliability
5 Select and specify brand
6 Approve purchase expenditure
7 Place the purchase order

Table 2.5 summarizes the findings on the actions of establishing product need and brand selection for three selected electronic-product categories. As might be expected, engineering exercises the greatest purchasing influence in the technically oriented electronics industry. The influence of both administrative and marketing officials is more apparent in establishing need than it is in brand selection. The purchasing agent's influence appears to increase as the products become more standarized.

INFLUENCE OF THE GOVERNMENT

Government's participation in the economy has a tremendous impact on the functioning of the industrial market. To understand this more readily, it is necessary to consider both the direct and indirect relationships between the industrial market and the complex of local, state, and federal governmental units.

[14] *How the Electronics Industry Buys,* New York: Hayden Publishing Company, Inc., 1963.

TABLE 2.5 Percentage of Respondents Influencing Two Specific Actions in the Purchasing Process, Three Selected Products, Electronics Industry, 1963

JOB FUNCTION LEVEL	PRODUCT NEED			BRAND SELECTION		
	MICRO-WAVE COM-PONENTS	PRODUCTION MACHINERY AND EQUIPMENT	WIRE AND CABLE	MICRO-WAVE COM-PONENTS	PRODUCTION MACHINERY AND EQUIPMENT	WIRE AND CABLE
Administrative management	2.5	4.4	1.2	1.0	3.8	1.4
Engineering management	49.6	40.3	40.7	44.2	35.1	32.5
Engineer	41.2	25.2	51.8	45.2	22.9	51.2
Purchasing agent	0.0	1.3	0.9	7.7	6.1	10.8
Production plant manager	0.0	24.5	3.6	0.0	29.0	3.1
Marketing, advertising	2.5	1.9	1.2	0.0	0.0	0.3
Research management scientist	4.2	2.5	0.6	1.9	3.1	0.7

Source: *How the Electronics Industry Buys,* New York: Hayden Publishing Company, Inc., 1963, pp. 15, 17, and 23.

Direct Relationships

The buyer-seller relationships where industrial marketers and the government deal directly with each other are undoubtedly the most significant. Government represents the biggest single customer. In 1967, federal, state, and local expenditures for goods and services amounted to about $139 billion.[15] The rate of growth of government spending since 1958 nearly parallels that attained by the Gross National Product during the same period of time.

Of greater import, however, is the appropriation of total government monies. Many decisions have political overtones. Witness the controversy over the awarding of the TFX contract,[16] the basing of numerous political campaigns on the theme of more government spending in a given area, and the direct appeals to Congress when it is felt that a designated share of business has not been forthcom-

[15] *Survey of Current Business,* March, 1968.

[16] A very interesting and informative article on the TFX contract is contained in Richard Austin Smith, "The $7 Billion Contract That Changed the Rules," *Fortune,* March and April, 1963.

ing.[17] Other relationships that have a direct effect are government doctrines on antitrust and pricing. To gain economies of scale, industrial marketers frequently resort to the merger process. Today, such economic reasoning is viewed as irrelevant by the courts.[18] Even conglomerate mergers (between parties that are neither competitors nor related as supplier and customer) have not escaped legal challenge. An injunction was entered against Ingersoll-Rand restraining the contemplated acquisition of three manufacturers of underground coal-mining machinery and equipment.

In setting prices, industrial marketers must operate within an enforceable framework of government regulations and scrutiny. The most important and at the same time most heatedly debated statute is the Robinson-Patman Act. This law prohibits price discrimination between buyers of commodities of like grade and quality. The government can also bring action under its antitrust powers when pricing policies are used to restrain competition. This was dramatically demonstrated in the 1961 suit against seven manufacturers of electrical equipment.

Another factor which has a measurable effect on pricing is the mindfulness of government regarding the industry to which the firm belongs. Industries which produce basic commodities are particularly susceptible to this form of possible intervention. This was made apparent by the pressure placed on twelve steel producers to rescind their 1961 price increase.[19] Finally, firms should realize that in all direct relationships, the government can utilize public indignation to strengthen its position. The glare of adverse publicity was quite harmful to the public images of the electrical and steel companies involved in the situations cited previously.

Indirect Relationships
Included within this group are foreign policy, taxation rulings, depreciation allowances, and government subsidization of special in-

---

[17] As an example, the Western Shipbuilders Association, concerned over the loss of contracts under the government-subsidized ship replacement program, appealed directly to Congress.

[18] For an informative review of merger litigation, see Charles F. Phillips, Jr., and George R. Hall, "Economic and Legal Aspects of Merger Litigation, 1951-1952," *University of Houston Business Review*, Fall, 1963.

[19] For a discussion of the presidential action taken against the steel companies, see Charles F. Phillips, Jr. and Harmon H. Haymes, "Psychological Price Control: Meddling or Masterstroke?" *Business Horizons*, Summer, 1962, pp. 99-106.

terests such as small business. They may or may not affect a particular firm's operating environment.

One relationship industrial marketers are not fully aware of is their role in the nation's foreign-policy commitment. For example, business has been made a full partner in the Alliance for Progress program for Latin America. The goods and services required by these needy nations at their stage of economic development will be predominantly industrial in nature. Then, too, trade is becoming increasingly important as a tool of foreign policy. Businesses are being called upon more and more to make short-run sacrifices, such as an unfavorable tariff position, to further international cooperation and respond to the economic challenge of the communistic world.

Another indirect relationship for marketers of machinery and equipment is the possible acceleration in sales from liberalized depreciation allowances and the tax credits for capital investment. The effect of these will vary from firm to firm and from industry to industry, the greatest sales increases occurring where customers now are able to fully utilize their present capital and a speedup in cash flow is imperative.

SUMMARY

Industrial demand is derived from the demand of the ultimate consumer and the government for goods and services. This primal demand is translated into marketing activity for the firms directly involved as well as their suppliers. The total amount of trade generated often exceeds the value of the consumer product. This multiplier effect is directly related to the number of supplier levels and the material and capital burdens incurred by the various suppliers.

Industrial demand's derived nature and responsiveness to customer inventory policy causes it to fluctuate widely. It can be characterized as having more of a "boom or bust" cycle than consumer demand has. The initial reaction of industrial demand to changes in price runs counter to the normally conceived inverse relationship. Instead, purchasers will abstain from the market when the price is lowered and increase their activities when the price is raised. The reasoning behind such actions is that any change foretells continued movement in the same direction.

Industrial markets, showing a high degree of geographical concentration, are of two types—vertical and horizontal. Narrow in scope, vertical markets are confined to the members of a single industry or trade that have a common product need. Horizontal markets involve products such as supplies that can be used by many kinds of customers in different industries.

In contrast to consumer marketing, buying motives are substantially rational in nature. Price and quality are the primary considerations in selecting a product, whereas suppliers are usually thought of in terms of their ability to maintain quality standards, prompt delivery, and purchaser-supplier relationships. Value analysis, vendor analysis, and computer technology play vital roles in the industrial-purchasing process.

Extensive technical testing by both the buyer and vendor is relied upon to determine the quality specifications of the product offerings. Starting with buyer testing, the design cycle for a component or material is the time that elapses until it becomes part of an assembly-line unit. The sophisticated technique of value analysis is being used more and more in an effort to reduce purchasing costs.

Two general purchasing policies that play important roles in supplier selection are order splitting and reciprocity. Now commonly referred to as trade relations, reciprocity has become more intricate through the ever-continuing integration and diversification of industry.

More often than not, industrial purchasing decisions are influenced by a number of persons within an organization. Specifically who is involved will depend upon what is being considered and company policy. Usually assigned a facilitating role, purchasing agents will exert their greatest influence in selecting suppliers for highly standardized items.

Government participation in the economy has a tremendous impact on the structure of the industrial market. The most significant reason for this is the dominant customer position. Also directly affecting the functioning of the market are government antitrust and pricing doctrines. Included among the relationships that have an indirect or semimeasurable effect are foreign policy, taxation rulings, and subsidization of special-interest groups.

DISCUSSION QUESTIONS

1 How would knowledge of the multiplier effect assist in formulating plans for bolstering the economy?

2 Why will industrial demand fall faster and farther than customer demand during depressed times?

3   What is the purpose of retrenchment by consumer-goods manu-
    facturers? How does it affect the industrial marketing structure?
4   One of Mr. Jones's accounts has experienced a 10 percent sales
    increase. As the sole supplier of a component, he figures that
    orders from this firm will also increase 10 percent. Has Mr. Jones
    reasoned correctly? Explain your answer.
5   An industrial marketer wishing to stimulate sales has decided
    to cut the price of his product. What will be the immediate re-
    action of the market?
6   Distinguish between vertical and horizontal markets.
7   Why have industrial marketers not followed the geographic de-
    centralization of their customers?
8   Why would it be important to know the design cycles for poten-
    tial users of a new product?
9   Why are purchases divided up among approved suppliers?
10 When do emotional motives become important in the industri-
    al-purchasing process?
11 How does the multiplicity of purchasing influence complicate
    the job of the industrial marketer?
12 What effect does the general public have on the direct relation-
    ships between the government and the industrial market?

SUPPLEMENTARY READINGS

Aitken, Thomas, Jr., "Can Business Carry the Flag?" *Business Horizons,* Winter, 1962, pp. 101-107.

Ammer, Dean S., "Realistic Reciprocity," *Harvard Business Review,*
January-February, 1962, pp. 116-124.

Beckman, Theodore N., and William R. Davidson, *Marketing,* 8th
ed., New York: The Ronald Press Company, 1967, chap. 28.

Buggie, Frederick D., "Lawful Discrimination in Marketing," *Journal of Marketing,* April, 1962, pp. 1-8.

Clee, Gilbert H., "The Appointment Book of J. Edward Ellis," *Harvard
Business Review,* November-December, 1962, pp. 79-92.

May, Todd, and Sanford S. Parker, "The Market behind the Markets,"
Fortune, December, 1959, pp. 110+.

Phillips, Charles F. Jr., and Harmon H. Haymes, "Psychological
Price Control: Meddling or Masterstroke?" *Business Horizons,* Summer, 1962, pp. 99-106.

Van Cise, Jerrold G., "How to Live with Anti-Trust," *Harvard Business Review,* November-December, 1962, pp. 119-126.

2

management
of marketing
activities

management
of the marketing
task

A great deal has been said and written in the last decade or so about the concept of marketing action known as either the marketing concept or the marketing management concept. This amount of current attention, however, should not delude anyone into thinking that what is being proposed is entirely new or revolutionary. On the contrary, the precept of consumer orientation shows marked resemblance to earlier viewpoints of theorist and practioner alike.

What is new is the apparent willingness of business to consider and accept such an ideology. There are two possible explanations for this. One is the search for approaches to offset the increased risks of decision making brought about by the rapid technological advances in both production and distribution. The other is the growing awareness of the unsuitability of other approaches in predicting the ever-increasing capriciousness of the consumer.

INTERPRETATION OF THE MARKETING MANAGEMENT CONCEPT

While some disagreement exists on what is implied by the marketing management concept, substantial agreement has been reached on at least three of the basic components. These in essence are:

1   Orientation of all the firm's activities to the interests of the consumer rather than to the interests of the firm
2   Emphasis on the profits returned by sales rather than the magnitude of sales as depicted by volume or share of market
3   Development of strategies that coordinate all marketing activities and not just the more traditional ones

Consumer Orientation

If any of the marketing actions which are comprised in the concept is more important than the others, it is the focusing of attention on the consumer. Drucker has gone so far as to say that the exclusive purpose of a business is to create a customer and it is this force which in turn determines what a business is.[1] The consumer was considered the focal point of business activity also by many of the early economists. Adam Smith, credited as being the first to synthesize economic

[1] Peter F. Drucker, *The Practice of Management,* New York: Harper & Row, Inc., 1954, p. 37.

thought, held that the producer should be considered only insofar as necessary in promoting the interests of the consumer. Another early economist, John Stuart Mill, pointed out that changes in consumption tend to modify the direction of production as well as distribution.

Business under the sales concept, to be sure, is concerned with consumer interests, but only as an end rather than a means to an end. Formation of a product starts with the design engineers. When they are completely satisfied with the technical proficiency of the product, it is turned over to production. Here certain changes are instituted to facilitate manufacturing processes. The finished product is now ready to be sold. The sales force is charged with the responsibility of developing tactics that will induce the consumer to buy the product. All too frequently these tactics revolve around pricing with the result that production must bear the brunt of achieving further economies. The whole process can be visualized as progressing from the engineer's drawing board to the consumer.

The first step under the marketing management concept is the determination of the actual and potential needs of the consumer. This information is then relayed to design and manufacturing engineers. The sales force, buoyed up by the knowledge that their product is the right one, can do a better job of creating demand. The effect of adopting the marketing management concept, as described in the foregoing, is to focus on consumer satisfaction throughout the entire development of a product.

No firm can bring about complete consumer orientation without market segmentation. The reason for this is that the aggregate market for a product is usually heterogeneous. A continuous policy of seeking out differences provides a greater knowledge of the consumer in terms of needs and wants. Then, too, such differences can be exploited by the use of unique selling appeals and marketing mechanisms.

Livestock chemicals offer a good example of an aggregate market that was successfully segmented into definite subsections. These subsections can be briefly described as follows:

Licensed Veterinarians. These individuals operate on an economic rationale in purchasing drugs to be administered to livestock. They appear especially "touchy" about their professional status.

Feed Industry. Manufacturers who buy drugs in bulk for mixing with their registered or custom feeds. More than half of the manufactured feed volume is accounted for by 5,000 small firms.

Over-the-counter Packaged Products. This segment is composed of drugstores, feedstores and mills, country elevators, hatcheries, cooperatives, farm-to-farm salesmen, and other retailers who number close to 25,000. Their resale of livestock chemicals in both feed and nonfeed forms is to the farmer.[2]

Profit Emphasis

Traditionally business has relied upon sales volume in dollars or physical units to measure both short- and long-run economic performance. Invariably, initiated sales action will have as its sole purpose a percentage increase in sales or a greater share of the market. Virtually obscured is the effect this will have on the firm's profit position. The marketing management concept emphasizes profit as the primary objective of sales effort.

For the firm with only one product, an objective based on sales alone completely ignores the life cycle of the product. The product may be in the saturation phase, in which efforts to increase or maintain sales can be accomplished only by raising selling costs appreciably, thus squeezing the profit margin. For the firm with a line of products, sales-volume goals may often be obtained by selling the less profitable items. The more profitable will not comprise a large enough portion to sustain an adequate total profit margin.

Adopting the marketing management concept does not mean that a firm discards sales volume. What it does mean is that sales volume becomes a means to an end rather than an end in itself. A marketer, for example, might increase sales volume without a corresponding increase in marketing cost, thus enhancing profits.

Marketing-strategy Development

Implementation of the marketing management concept implies coordinated direction of all marketing activities toward one common objective—the needs and wants of the consumer. To accomplish this, it is necessary to formulate interrelated strategies primarily directed toward this goal. There are essentially two types of marketing strategies—product and market. Product strategy is concerned most with the creation of products to meet the ever-changing needs of pres-

---

[2] Alan A. Roberts, "Applying the Strategy of Market Segmentation," *Business Horizons,* Fall, 1961, pp. 91-92.

ent customers and/or to attract new customers. It includes among other activities the planning of new products, functional obsolescence, pricing, and credit arrangements.

Market strategy involves two creative decisions. The first is to select the segment or segments that appear to be the best target for the firm to exploit. Companies can no longer beguile themselves into thinking that their product can satisfy everyone—the risk is just too great. Trying to sell to the entire market is like trying to bring down an elephant with a shotgun. The best that can be done is wound him. A segment, on the other hand, represents a clearly defined task for management, and though it may not replace the shotgun with a rifle, most certainly it will improve the aim of the shotgun.

The second decision is to select the composition or mix for promotion and distribution of the product to the predesignated segments. The selection of a marketing channel is crucial. Management must also determine the relative roles to be played by personal selling, advertising, servicing arrangements, and other marketing functions that might be used to induce prospective consumers to purchase the product. In a simplified illustration suppose a marketer of machine tools has decided that small machine shops (properly defined) in the geographical region where the plant is located offer the most lucrative potential for his products. Next it must be determined how to reach this submarket. The more traditional approach would be to use middlemen such as industrial distributors. They regularly fulfill the needs of such customers and are a conveniently located supply point. On the other hand, there are certain competitive advantages in having the firm's own salesmen sell the machines directly. Once a selection of distribution channels has been made, the marketer will be faced with decisions on the concomitant inducements to be instituted.

In developing marketing strategies, emphasis should be directed toward effectiveness rather than efficiency. The implication is that it is better to take the right action even though it cannot be performed at present as proficiently as the wrong action. Management should be guided solely by long-run profit opportunities in their search for innovations in products and marketing methods.[3] Strategies as opposed to tactics are long-run commitments of means to achieve consumer-oriented objectives. In formulating strategies, utmost use should be

---

[3] A good case for a marketing-development department to seek out new marketing methods is presented in Theodore Levitt, *Innovation in Marketing*, New York: McGraw-Hill Book Company, 1962, chaps. 5 through 8.

made of the scientific method as applicable to business decision making.

IMPLEMENTATION OF THE MARKETING MANAGEMENT CONCEPT

A number of approaches have been taken by firms in attempting to adopt the marketing management concept. One of the commonest can be called a semantic transition. The term "sales" is discarded and organizational charts are relabeled, but no fundamental changes in philosophy or organization take place. To quote the oft-used phrase, "Only the names have been changed." Such a change may evoke some imagined prestige for the firm, but much of this can be more properly attributed to narcissistic reflections.

Another form of transition is the one that seeks a solution. With a tremendous number of testimonials on its behalf, the marketing management concept comes to be regarded by many marketers as the elixir for all their sales problems. To incorporate this concept into their firm, they hire outsiders for such newly created positions as marketing director and manager of marketing research. But as no other changes are effected, these men are virtually powerless. One manufacturer of technical products changes marketing directors every four to six months. This hardly allows the director time enough to acclimate himself to his new position and company, let alone commencing to solve existing problems.

From the experiences of more successful firms, it appears that there are at least four requirements for complete integration of the concept into the firm. These are (1) total commitment to consumer orientation, (2) coordination-directed structuring of marketing functions, (3) unity of action in terms of marketing programs, and (4) gradualism in the integration process. Foremost is a consumer-focused mindfulness on the part of everyone in the firm. In the initial stages of adoption it is imperative that higher-level management, particularly the board of directors and the chief executive, recognize this and foster its development in a convincing manner.

A second requirement is to structure the organization so that all the marketing functions are mutually supporting. By formally grouping on the same organizational level product development, field sales, advertising combined with sales promotion, marketing research, logistics, and possibly credit under a principal marketing executive, the work can be coordinated far more effectively because it is geared to a single objective. This is shown in skeleton form in Figure 3.1.

However, granting other marketing functions the same organizational status as field sales will cause resentment among the members of the sales force and erosion of the formal organizational structure. To prevent this, all of the marketing functions with the exception of field sales could be positioned as staff agencies. Another variation would be to have four line functions—field sales, advertising and sales promotion, product development, and logistics. Marketing research and credit, possibly enlarged to handle other financial matters related to marketing, would be designated as staff. The latter variation is preferable for several reasons.

1   It emphasizes the importance of functions other than sales in the marketing effort.
2   It facilitates recruitment for these other areas of marketing.
3   It facilitates allocation of responsibility and authority.

The development of executives who think in terms of the entire marketing program and possess competence in the skills of scientific management is a third requirement. The fourth and final one is that the process of integration be gradual. The underlying reason is that some of the members of the organization will find it difficult to accept this new approach. Therefore, it will be necessary to make personnel changes, which is apt to be a lengthy operation. It has been suggested that integration be phased out over a period of from three to five years.

ACCEPTANCE OF THE MARKETING MANAGEMENT CONCEPT

The marketing management concept has seemingly gained its greatest foothold in the consumer-goods field. There are a number of explanations for this phenomenon. One is that for many markets, such as white goods, competition has been intensified through the entry of more and more sellers. Another is that consumers' ever-changing desires are probably more keenly felt by manufacturers of consumer goods. A good example of this has been the inroad on American car sales made by the popular European economy car. Still another explanation is the mistaken impression of many smaller marketers which typify the industrial market that the concept is practical only

FIGURE 3.1   Skeleton Organizational Chart for Marketing Department.

insofar as large corporations are concerned, say General Electric, U.S. Steel, or IBM.

A final stumbling block to acceptance is the failure of industrial marketers to appreciate the significance of these new ideas. The thinking of many marketers tends to be regimented along the lines of product, production, and current operations.

Product

Since the cessation of hostilities in World War II, producers of industrial goods have been enamored of the "better mousetrap" or quality-product philosophy. Rather than directing their efforts toward the consumer, they have devoted themselves to developing a technically superior product through research and engineering. The electronics industry provides a good example of the attainment of growth through such an emphasis.

The perils of competing solely on such a basis exist even for electronics companies. The predicament one company found itself in bears this out. The principal product for a small but prosperous firm had for the last few years shown a steadily declining market position. Sales analysis by geographic region revealed sizable losses in two districts which represented about 60 percent of the potential for the product. Further investigation disclosed that their major competitor had altered his marketing approach some time ago in these two areas and was now selling directly through his own salesman. Faced with this overwhelming evidence that a change in marketing channels was in order, the president stubbornly clung to the belief that an entirely new product or a technical change in the old one would

FIGURE 3.2   Skeleton Organizational Chart for Marketing Department.

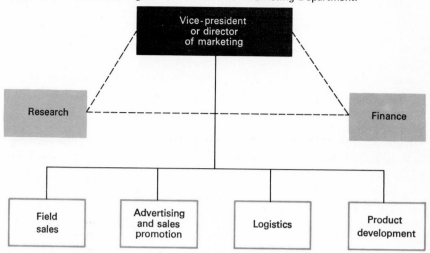

solve the problem. His contention was that he and his technical staff would just have to apply their efforts more diligently.

Product bias also encourages innovations that lend themselves to scientific experimentation and control. The chief engineer for an industrial-equipment manufacturer made the statement that the only new components he is concerned with are those that will make the equipment more proficient from an engineering point of view. The following direct quotation from his comments shows how positive he was on this subject: "My engineering department's objective is to create an item of smooth running efficiency. If this means a little more increase in price, the sales department will just have to try harder to sell it."

Production

A number of industrial-good manufacturers, more specifically those that have high fixed-cost ratios such as steel and cement, are biased toward products that lend themselves to the techniques of mass production. The lure, obviously, is the possibility of greater profits from lower per unit costs. If the market can be characterized as a sellers', the entire output can be disposed of with little or no effort. The only problem that may arise is allocation. A good example of this was the

position of Weirton Steel as the only major steel mill still functioning during the strike of 1959. The sales department was charged with
the responsibility of devising methods by which they could remain
loyal to old customers while at the same time attracting new ones.
When the market tends toward the buyer, more and more stress is
placed on getting rid of it. Selling tactics become aggressive in an
attempt to maintain a fairly good balance between production rates
and market absorption. If the consumer is thought of at all, it is in
terms of price adjustments.

Individual firms, without resorting to collusion, find that the answer
to how to sell for less does not lie entirely in large-scale economies
because the market will rarely accept the production quantity. Consequently, many have focused their attention on developing production technology innovations. For example, steelmaking has come
up with oxygen furnaces, continuous casting lines, vacuum degassers,
and pelletized ores. Continuous castings, called the most important
advance since the advent of the continuous hot-rolling mill in the late
1920s, promises to cut costs by as much as $5 to $10 a ton.

For a production-oriented firm, it is the consumer who tends to
stimulate the flow of new product ideas. To illustrate, the upsurge
in sales of galvanized sheet steel is attributable not to the marketing efforts of steel producers, but rather to the auto makers and build-
ers who were able to find new uses for the rust-resistant material.
Likewise, petroleum companies have prospered from changes that
consumers such as the auto industry have brought about in their product. As an example, the work on antiknock fuels which led to the development of leaded (ethyl) gasoline and high-octane fuels was done
by Charles Kettering of General Motors.

Current Operation
Far too many marketers, industrial or otherwise, are completely absorbed in the concreteness of day-to-day happenings. Managements
move from crisis to crisis, often dissipating many of their resources. In justifying this, executives can cite numerous projects that just
have to be dealt with agggessively. It is as if they are on a treadmill,
always trying to catch up with what should have been done yesterday.

This attitude presents a formidable roadblock to successful implementation of the marketing management concept, the implication
being that planned action is inherent in the concept. Too, the emphasis on current operations tends to obscure many of the recent de-

velopments in the industrial market. Some of the more crucial developments which can be noted are:

1   Foreign competition
2   Alternate-product competition
3   Complexity of consumer markets
4   Cost-reduction pressures

Although foreign products have invaded almost every segment of the industrial market, nowhere is this competitive force demonstrated as dramatically as it is in steel. Figure 3.3 shows that with the exception of 1959, when a prolonged strike shortened supplies of United States-made steel, foreign imports have progressively mounted. Further evidence of the snowballing effect of steel imports is the statement made to the Federal Trade Commission by a representative of the steel industry that in a period of three years foreign firms were able to capture 24 percent of the West Coast market for hot-rolled sheet.

While there is little doubt that price is the strongest appeal for foreign products, it would be a serious mistake to regard it as the only one. Most of the current agitation on pricing is over the practice of "dumping" or selling for less in the United States than in the coun-

FIGURE 3.3   Imports of Steel-mill Products, United States, 1958–1967.

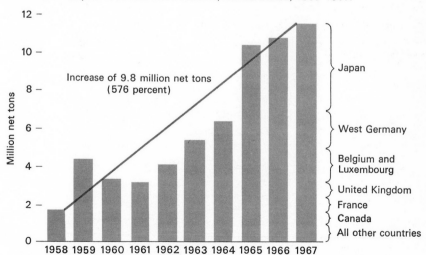

Source: U.S. Department of Commerce. Reported in *Foreign Trade Trends* (New York: American Iron and Steel Institute, 1963) table 4, p. 56; and *Charting Steel's Progress During 1967* (New York: American Iron and Steel Institute, 1968), p. 39.

try of origin. If dumping is proved and the Tariff Commission rules it has hurt American firms, a special tariff can be levied.

Many imports are of equal or even superior quality. One example is in the oilseed industry, where there exists a decided preference for flaking rolls made from German chilled iron. Other examples are the quality refinements of foreign manufacturers in such products as business machines, grinding mills, electronics, and nonelectrical machinery.[4] Then, too, importers are adopting more sophisticated marketing tactics. Evidence of this is the attention that is now being given to locating convenient warehouse and service facilities.

While the growing array of alternate products has intensified competition throughout the industrial market, the greatest impact seems to be occurring in fabricated materials. Possessing great versatility, such products as aluminum, glass fiber, and plastics are making sizable penetrations into the more traditional material markets. Aluminum is strongly asserting itself in the hitherto steel-dominated markets for autos and containers. Tonnage in cans alone for 1964 was about double that of 1963.[5] New uses are being found for glass fiber in truck production. The Molded Fiber Glass Body Company of Ashtabula, Ohio, long the supplier for Corvette bodies, has diversified into parts and bodies for trucks. Some of the glass-fiber items produced for trucks are:

1   Entire body
2   Full cab
3   Sleeper cab attachment
4   Lower body panels and grille for conventional steel cab
5   Fenders
6   Liner panels for refrigerated trailer interiors[6]

Tonnage sales of plastics during 1963 were about equal to the combined total recorded by aluminum, copper, and zinc. The use of plastics, concentrated in the area between the front seat and the windshield, is estimated to be 28.2 pounds per car with excellent prospects of an increase to 55 pounds by 1970.[7] Among the wide range of jobs

[4] For a discussion of Japan's position in world export markets, see John Davenport, "Japan's Competitive Cutting Edge," *Fortune,* Sept. 1, 1968, pp. 90+.

[5] This increase is even more significant when it is figured that a ton of aluminum displaces two to three tons of tinplate.

[6] Joseph Gescelelin, "Making Corvette and Avanti Bodies of Fiber Glass Reinforced Plastic," *Automotive Industries,* Jan. 15, 1963, pp. 78-79.

[7] Joel Frados, "Automotive Uses on the Upswing," *Modern Plastics,* November, 1963, p. 74.

plastics have won for themselves are oil-field piping, beverage cases, and forming blocks for construction.

The consumer-goods market is rapidly becoming more complex. The opportunities generated by its dynamism will go for naught with a misplaced emphasis on current operations. A good example of these changes is what has been happening in shoe materials. Today shoes may be animal, vegetable, or mineral. Calf leather, alone, can be finished in six different surfaces. There are twelve dyeable fabrics that are woven into material strong enough for shoes from primarily natural fibers. A rainbow of colors is available from such newly developed synthetics as Pattina and Patenlite. All told, there are seven man-made materials now used in shoes.[8]

Pressures to reduce the costs of what is purchased are coming from every portion of the industrial market. The reason for this is the growing realization of firms everywhere that such efforts can make significant contributions to profits. What is spent on industrial goods and services constitutes about 50 percent of the sales dollar.[9] The average company can increase its profits 15 percent by merely reducing supply costs 2 percent.[10] Johns-Manville during one year saved more than $1.3 million on purchases of $144 million. Another giant, Union Carbide, saved about 1 percent on yearly purchases of $625 million.[11]

Three major approaches are being used to attack the problems of cost improvement. The first is to install a scientific purchasing process with such techniques as value analysis, supplier rating, and economic order valuation. A tactic Singer Manufacturing has used to achieve its greatest savings is negotiation, usually for annual contracts. The second approach is to broaden the scope of the purchasing department to facilitate coordination of all the activities related to the movement of materials. The third is to automate as fully as possible all paper work. Monsanto Chemical has automated purchasing at their Texas City plant to such an extent that 20 percent of the 5,000 items regularly stocked are automatically reordered.

[8] Information on shoe materials extracted from a fashion bulletin distributed by the Wohl Shoe Company, St. Louis, Mo. Spring, 1965.

[9] A 1964 survey by the First National City Bank showed that the 100 largest United States manufacturers spend an average of 51.1 percent of their sales dollar on goods and services.

[10] Derived from assuming a pretax profit of 10 percent and a purchasing department that returns four times its cost in profits.

[11] "Purchasing: From Rags to Riches," *Dun's Review,* May, 1963, p. 55.

TOP MARKETING MANAGEMENT

Whether he is called a vice-president, manager, or director, the chief marketing executive is the key to successful marketing. Evidence of this is the trend toward positioning the executive organizationally in order to increase emphasis on the broad aspects of marketing as contrasted with sales administration. In addition, the chief marketing executive is assuming a more significant role in the overall management of the firm.

Explicit Responsibilities

Although no two job descriptions are exactly the same, various studies have revealed only situational differences in the principal responsibilities of planning, direction, coordination, and control. Key executives are having to spend an ever-increasing amount of time in the planning function. To anticipate more adequately the seemingly inevitable changes, much of the planning is necessarily long-range. Answers are sought for questions about the future: What products will be sold? Who will comprise the market? How much will the sales volume be?

The chief executive is also called upon to participate actively in the direction of all marketing-related activities. In line with this is the requirement that the executive gain a broad enough understanding of each speciality area to evaluate both its potential and actual contribution to the total marketing effort. The executive may also be required in his direction to interject and maintain enthusiasm throughout the entire marketing organization.

Another and very important responsibility is coordination. Firms recognize that only with internal coordination can the full potential of all the available marketing tools be utilized.[12] The traditional separation of field sales and advertising, with each pursuing its own purposes, is perhaps the most crucial coordination problem the chief executive will face. Externally it is the responsibility of the chief executive to coordinate the functioning of the marketing department with the rest of the firm, particularly production. An example of this might be a planning committee whose representatives of marketing, production, and finance meet periodically for the avowed purpose of synchronizing production, inventories, and sales.

[12] Ninety-five percent of the chief executives in industrial marketing firms indicated field sales, advertising, sales promotion, market research, and new-product planning as primary activities in the marketing department. Fewer, 82 percent, also included public relations. Bud Reese, "The Marketing Boss—Does He or Doesn't He?" *Industrial Marketing*, August, 1963, p. 77.

Finally, the key executive is responsible for controlling the operations of the marketing department so that a satisfactory return is earned on investment. Many industrial marketers enumerate advertising and physical distribution as two activities which offer the greatest profit possibilities through the application of control.

Implicit Responsibilities

The chief marketing executive has a number of other responsibilities that are not spelled out in any job description. First, and perhaps the most significant of these, is the responsibility to make decisions rationally, using the generally accepted process. The second is to understand and utilize where applicable in decision making the various systems of quantitative methodology. Concomitant with this responsibility is the necessity of knowing how data processing equipment can facilitate such an approach. A third responsibility is to encourage innovation not only in products but in marketing methods as well. The fourth responsibility is to conform to high social and ethical standards even though immediate circumstances appear to dictate otherwise.

Backgrounds of Chief Executives

Field sales management provides the largest number of chief marketing executives. The results of a survey conducted among top industrial marketing executives revealed that over 60 percent list a sales-management job as their previous organizational title. Twenty-eight percent were sales managers, 17 percent general sales managers, 11 percent vice-presidents of sales, and 5 percent sales directors.[13] Another study of backgrounds reported that the proportion of top marketing men with field sales experience is holding steady or is expanding.[14] This would seem to indicate that such experience is an essential prerequisite for the upper echelons of marketing management.

Formal and informal training in engineering plus field sales experience is common for chief executives in firms selling highly technical lines. For firms that establish a marketing organization after using the services of a middleman for many years, it is not uncommon to find a chief executive whose entire background has been in

---

[13] *Ibid.,* p. 78.

[14] Henry Bund and James W. Carroll, *The Changing Role of the Marketing Function,* Marketing for Executive Series, no. 3, Chicago: American Marketing Association, 1957, pp. 24-25.

production usually with the same company. Only occasionally will staff experience qualify a man for a top marketing management position.

SUMMARY

The essentials of what has come to be called the marketing management concept are (1) consumer orientation, (2) profitable sales volume, and (3) coordinated marketing effort. Undoubtedly the most important is the focusing of attention on the actual and potential needs of the consumer. For consumer orientation to be complete, it is necessary to segment the market, the reason being that an aggregate market is rarely if ever homogeneous.

The emphasis on profits means that sales-volume goals should be sought with an eye toward profits. Too often, it seems, a marketer sacrifices profits in an attempt to increase or maintain sales or share of market. To achieve coordinated direction of all marketing activities, it is necessary to formulate interrelated strategies directed toward consumer needs and wants as a common objective. These strategies can be categorized broadly as either product or market.

Neither semantic nor cure-all transitions have led to successful implementation of the marketing management concept. Experience has shown that there are four requirements to successful implementation.

1   Consumer-focused mindfulness on the part of everyone in the firm
2   Organizational structuring that tends to ensure mutually supporting marketing functions
3   Executives who think in terms of the entire marketing program and possess competence in the skills of scientific management
4   Integration which is gradual in nature, perhaps from three to five years

One of the major stumbling blocks to the acceptance of new ideas such as the marketing management concept is the regimentation of industrial-marketer thinking. This regimentation is along the lines of product, production, and the imperativeness of current operations. Absorption in current operations is especially perilous because it obscures such developments as (1) foreign competition, (2) alternate-product competition, (3) the growing complexity of consumer-good markets, and (4) pressures for cost reduction.

The key to successful marketing is the chief executive, whatever his formal title. Study of job descriptions shows only situational differences in the principal explicit responsibilities of planning, direction, coordination, and control. Similarly, chief marketing executives display very little difference in background. A majority list field sales management as their previous job designation.

DISCUSSION QUESTIONS

1   What evidence can be cited to show that consumer orientation is not a relatively new theory?
2   Why might market segmentation be referred to as "divide and conquer"?
3   How should sales volume be sought under the marketing management concept?
4   Describe the evolution of a product under the marketing management concept.
5   Distinguish between market and product strategies.
6   Define semantic and solution transitions. Explain why they have not met with much success.
7   Why have marketers of consumer goods been more willing to adopt the marketing management concept?
8   The implementation of the concept should be gradual. Why?
9   How does product emphasis conflict with a philosophy of consumer orientation?
10   What limitation is there on increasing production to lower costs?
11   Define the developments an industrial marketer might overlook in stressing current operations.
12   What is perhaps the most serious problem the chief executive faces in coordinating marketing effort?
13   The chief marketing executive has a number of responsibilities other than those listed in his job description. What might they be?

SUPPLEMENTARY READINGS

Bund, Henry, and James W. Carroll, *The Changing Role of the Marketing Function,* Marketing for Executive Series, no. 3, Chicago: American Marketing Association, 1957.

Calkins, Robert D., "The Decision Process in Administration." *Business Horizons,* Fall, 1959, pp. 19-25.

Felton, Arthur P., "Making the Marketing Concept Work," *Harvard Business Review,* July-August, 1959, pp. 55-65.

Lear, Robert W., "No Easy Road to Market Orientation," *Harvard Business Review,* September-October, 1963, pp. 53-60.

McKitterick, J. B., "What Is the Marketing Management Concept?" in Frank M. Bass (ed.), *Frontiers of Marketing Thought and Science,* Chicago: American Marketing Association, 1957, pp. 71-82.

McLean, John G., "The New Responsibilities of Marketing Management," *Journal of Marketing,* July, 1958, pp. 1-8.

Oxenfeldt, Alfred R., "The Formulation of a Market Strategy," in William Lazer and Eugene J. Kelley (eds.), *Managerial Marketing: Perspectives and Viewpoints,* rev. ed., Chicago: Richard D. Irwin, Inc., 1962, pp. 34-44.

Roberts, Alan R., "Applying the Strategy of Market Segmentation," *Business Horizons,* Fall, 1961, pp. 65-72.

**managerial
action –
planning**

Planning is the process of projecting a course of action into the future to bring about a desired state in the business organization or a portion thereof. This desired state is termed an objective; courses of action can be broadly conceived of as strategies and tactics.

OBJECTIVES

Objectives, the core of managerial action, provide direction to the planner by defining the goals, aims, results, or targets of the organization. By asking where he wants his operation to be at some future date, the planner can determine the objectives for the particular operation. Some of the questions an industrial marketer will want to know the answers to are:

1 What should be our annual rate of sales and/or profit growth?
2 What should be our return on the dollar invested in marketing?
3 What market share do we want next year, several years from now?
4 What key differentials in the market can we take advantage of next year or at some specified future time?
5 What should be the composition and breadth of our product mix at specified future dates?
6 What should be our image in regard to technological advancement and/or capability?
7 What degree of diversification do we want in our present product offering?
8 What position do we want in our industry?
9 What position do we want in our society?
10 What should be the status of our resources in terms of manpower and equipment?

Classification of objectives may be in terms of time, a designated area of the firm, or scope. The time dimension distinguishes between long-run and short-run objectives. Frequently, to prevent confusion, the latter type of objective is referred to as either an operational goal or a target. Objectives may be expressed for any functioning area or organizational level deemed important as well as for the firm itself.

To add meaning to the vast complex which results, particularly in a large firm, a hierarchy should be developed. The usual basis for this hierarchy is the organizational structure of the firm. The logical approach to this difficult task is to proceed from the broad to the specific. Thus, the starting point is a statement of the nature of the business from which will flow the broad company objectives. Generally, these broad company objectives can be categorized as economic, service, or social. Ideally, the answer to which is the most important is spelled out in the statement of the nature of the business. It should be noted that acceptance of the marketing management concept would seem to suggest the dominance of service to the consumer through the provision of product value.

Next, the broad company objectives are translated into key result areas. Key result areas can be defined as those areas in which success is vital to the firm and success is conducive to objective measurement. Market penetration and the growth rate of sales are examples of possible key result areas for the broad company objective of business expansion.

The third step is the derivation of the subobjectives necessary to accomplish the broad source objective. In the case of marketing, these include higher sales-volume goals, a broader customer base, and geographical expansion of the market. The designation of key result areas to serve as yardsticks for the subobjectives thus determined is the fourth step. The process outlined in steps three and four is repeated again and again until specific objectives have been created for the lowest level of management, both line and staff. At each succeeding level of management, subobjectives are checked horizontally with the subobjectives of other departments and vertically with the broader source objective for inconsistencies and conflicts. Development of a hierarchy of objectives is facilitated by the construction of a flow diagram.

The general sales manager, for example, will want to check out his objectives with the marketing subobjectives which are for him the source objective as well as the subobjectives for other functional areas of marketing and the other relevant areas of the firm. A sales subobjective which calls for expansion of the sales force would appear to be consistent with the earlier-cited subobjectives for marketing. Horizontally, conflicts or inconsistencies may develop with advertising over the division of the selling task and the provision of sales aids, and with personnel in regard to recruitment. In the event that conflicts or inconsistencies do arise, the problem should be referred to the next higher organizational level, which in this case is the head of marketing.

STRATEGIES AND TACTICS

The concept embracing strategies and tactics emerges when the dimension of time is considered in planning. Strategies are plans created to accomplish long-run objectives and as such are likely to bring about major changes in the relationship between the firm and its competitive environment. Capital budgeting is an important part of strategic planning. Tactics, on the other hand, are plans directed toward the accomplishment of short-run objectives. More often than not tactics will deal with either implementation of strategies or problem situations. The planning of these respective missions constitutes what has come to be called strategies and tactics. These definitions are similar to those encountered in military terminology. The Strategic Air Command and the Tactical Air Command of the Air Force provide an excellent analogy. The missions of the former, for example, are directed toward targets, the destruction of which might lead to the capitulation of the enemy at some future date. A factory making roller bearings, which are found in practically every moving item of warfare, would be such a target. On the other hand, a typical target for the Tactical Air Command would be a recent development such as a concentration of the enemy massing for a battle.

Similarly, marketing has its strategies and tactics. Marketing strategies may be grouped under two general headings—product and market. Included under the head of product strategies are:

1 Market segmentation and product differentiation
2 Product-line simplification
3 Product-line diversification
4 Product obsolescence
5 Product customization
6 Inter-line product competition
7 Product pricing
8 Customer financing

Market strategies are concerned with maintaining market contact for established products and securing markets for new products. For established products, a blend of market strategies might be based on a classification of customers. Such strategies might be an exclusion of marginal accounts and the concentration on key accounts. For new products, market strategies in the introductory phase are concerned with market development. This may involve selling the new product to present customers and/or new customers.

Because it is done almost continuously, tactical or operational planning occupies much more of management's time than does the planning of strategies. Tactical planning also differs in that the planner will usually have a deadline, the results of his efforts are more apparent, and he must keep ever alert to competitor actions and reactions.

A crucial problem for the tactician is raised by the requirement for maintenance of consistency with overall strategies. The issue is whether the starting point should be long-term objectives and hence strategies or, in planning tactics, adjustments should be made in objectives in light of reality. The latter approach, although less popular in actual practice, is nonetheless the more rational because it establishes attainable objectives. The marketing climate will necessarily change and therefore so must objectives.

BENEFITS FROM PLANNING

Planning does not ensure success; rather it helps to prepare an organization for the future. The basic assumption in planning is that changes are inevitable. Thus, despite the admitted inability to gauge these changes precisely, planning helps to identify the range of possibilities and prepare for them. This is not to say that planning eliminates or reduces future risks. Rather, planning can be visualized as the determination of what can be done about forecasted changes to maximize the favorable effects and minimize the adverse effects.

Included among the other benefits which may accrue as a result of planning are:

1   The establishment of standards by which the course of the organization can be measured, evaluated, and controlled
2   The achievement of greater coordination between the individuals, formalized components, and functions of the organization
3   The realization of more effective resource allocation
4   The anticipation rather than the correction of problems, thus directing management effort to more productive areas
5   The changeover in management's attitude from a mood of hesistancy to one of readiness for the future
6   The precaution against hasty countermeasures in reaction to moves made by competitors
7   The integration of current information about the organization and its economic environment

8   The framework for developing the planning capabilities of management

9   The synthesis of management experience in planning

STEPS IN PLANNING

Regardless of the course of action, all planning should follow the conceptual framework set forth by the scientific method. The fundamental steps involved are as follows:[1]

STATEMENT OF OBJECTIVES   For planning to have meaning, it must be directed toward some definite objective or goal. Logically, then, the setting up of objectives or goals is the first step in planning. Some opposition to this can be found among those who hold that in order to have realistic goals, the first step should be a critical self-audit to gain awareness of company strengths and weaknesses. There are even some who would go so far as to relegate the establishment of objectives to the third step after self-audit and forecasting. However, establishing objectives first provides an excellent starting point because in essence it is planning to plan, and as stated previously, realistic objectives can be developed gradually through adjustments during the course of planning.

In setting up objectives, the planner must keep in mind what an objective should accomplish. A list of criteria to test the validity of an objective is as follows:[2]

1   Does it, generally speaking, guide decision making by assisting management in the selection of the most desirable course of action?

2   Is it explicit enough to suggest definite action?

3   Does it suggest tools for measuring and controlling effectiveness?

4   Is it ambitious enough to present a challenge?

5   Does it recognize both external and internal constraints?

6   Can it be related to both the broader and the more specific objectives at higher and lower organizational levels?

---

[1] The discussion which follows is adopted in part from Harold Koontz, "The Rationale of Planning," in Donald M. Bowman and Frances M. Fillerup (eds.), *Management: Organization and Planning*, New York: McGraw-Hill Book Company, 1963, pp. 72-74.

[2] Charles H. Granger, "The Hierarchy of Objectives," *Harvard Business Review*, May-June, 1964, p. 65.

DEFINITION OF PREMISES Planning premises or assumptions standardize the environment for making decisions. Their importance is such that they should be available in writing to all planners. Broadly speaking, premises can be grouped into either of two major categories: forecasts and management philosophy. Clearly, a planner will need to know what has been forecasted for the major environmental factors. These will probably include general economic conditions, changes in the market and competitive climate, as well as contemplated changes in the firm itself such as increases in R&D, marketing capabilities, and productive capacity. Policies and top-management attitudes are the major ingredients of management philosophy.

Consistency, hence coordination, is an obvious advantage of the utilization of planning premises. A not so obvious advantage is the assistance given to the evaluation of planning. Having all the managers use the same assumptions in formulating their plans helps to control many of the variables, and this in turn provides a more objective basis, for comparisons of planning performance will lead to improvement in an intellectual activity which can only be described as arduous.

SETTING UP ALTERNATIVE COURSES OF ACTION This third step involves seeking out the alternatives which appear promising in light of the objective sought. Such a task can be called truly the essence of creativity in planning. It is also here that marketing has yet to be heard from in countless firms. Too often, management feels intuitively that there is only one way to market a product, or to perform any of the countless tasks associated with marketing. Innovation is limited strictly to new products and productive processes.

Competing through the use of pricing policy is characteristic of situations where marketing management feels there is no alternative. A president of a plywood corporation expressed his philosophy of relying exclusively on price:

> With a product like plywood you don't sell it, you price it. For that, all you need is a few clerks on long distance lines, not a sales force. To keep these telephone people on their toes, get the head of your mill to produce more stock than you can reasonably expect to sell.

That there is an alternative to lowering the price, even for a highly standardized product, is shown by the experience of International Minerals and Chemicals Corporation. To their principal customer for raw materials, the small fertilizer company, the only ostensible difference among suppliers was the price quoted at a particular time. Realizing this, International studied the small customer in an effort to come up with something its competitors did not have and could not duplicate quickly. The result was a consulting service to help the fertilizer company with its own marketing problems.

EVALUATING ALTERNATIVE COURSES OF ACTION   Once all possible alternatives have been listed, the next step is to evaluate their advantages and disadvantages in light of the objective.

As an example, suppose an industrial-good manufacturer wishes to improve both the quantity and the speed of market information from the field sales force. In oversimplified terms, the following alternatives are developed:

1   A more comprehensive reporting system for salesmen
2   A major revision in primary duties whereby the district sales manager spends a majority of his time in the field with his various salesmen
3   A nesting of district offices for each region

The first alternative is advantageous in that it involves little additional cash outlay, thus preserving present profit margins. However, the additional burden on the salesman will tend to have an adverse effect on his morale. This can lead to the salesman's doing less than his best in completing reports and spending selling time on reporting.

Having the district sales manager spend all of his time in the field might increase market knowledge, but an administrative assistant would have to be hired to take up the slack at each district office. Then, too, it is doubtful whether it is advisable to assign such a task to a member of management. The most costly alternative would be the relocation of salesmen into regional nuclei. The advantages are that there will be no realignment of duties or assignment of additional duties. Moving to a larger city and the opportunity to associate with other members of the sales force may contribute to improved morale. Quantitative decision making attempts to weigh mathematically the advantages and disadvantages of each alternative course of action. Rarely, however, is it possible to quantify all the relevant factors.

SELECTING A COURSE OF ACTION   At this, the point of decision making, the planner decides upon a course of action which is closest to an optimum adjustment of effort to opportunity. In doing this, he follows more or less a routinized thought process. An outline of this process is as follows:

1   Each course of action is summarized in terms of favorable and unfavorable effects.
2   A subconclusion is reached based upon each alternative's summary.
3   An overall conclusion is made as to the course of action offering the most promise of success. If several courses of action offer equal prospects, the planner should select the alternative which offers the best basis for future planning. A statement of minimum expectations is useful to the planner in weighing subconclusions.

In selecting an alternative, the planner will be bound by his perception of alternatives and their consequences, rather than how the alternatives are given. This influence of perception has come to be known as the principle of bounded rationality.[3] This theory maintains that behavior such as exhibited in decision making is rational within limits. The limits are basically the capacity of the individual planner and the exceedingly complex environment confronting him in reaching a planning decision.

A planner may use one or a combination of approaches in coming to a planning decision. One popular approach among marketing executives is to rely heavily on intuitive judgment. Many courses of action are adopted simply because an executive feels this is the way something should be done. To reach this decision, he has not involved himself in any conscious reasoning nor has he made any attempt to sort out the facts.

Somewhat allied to an intuitive approach is to come to a decision relying almost exclusively on past experiences, the assumption being that if it worked once, it should work again. This approach can be criticized on two points. In the first place, the chances are remote that any situational environment will repeat itself. Basing a decision exclusively on past experience, the planner is saying in effect that nothing has changed. The very nature of marketing would dispute this. Secondly, this approach tends to stagnate creative planning. Exclusive reliance on past experience develops frequently an abiding bias toward one course of action.

Experimentation is an approach which is generally quite costly but possibly unavoidable in certain circumstances. The market test-

[3] John A. Howard, *Marketing Theory,* Boston: Allyn and Bacon, 1965, p. 27.

ing of a new product is a good example of selecting a course of action by trying it. If any type of marketer were more apt to use experimentation, it would be one with large financial resources.

A "trial balloon" is a variation of the experimentation approach with less costly consequences. The trial balloon used by one marketer was to test the feasibility of a preventive maintenance program sometime in the future. Customers were asked to give their opinion rather than to accept or reject the proposal. Thus, a negative reaction did not saddle the marketer with a service he could not sell and a blemish on his reputation. Additionally, the only out-of-pocket expenditures were the traveling expenses incurred by the personal query and the costs of the sales aid which explained the salient features of the program.

The most productive approach would seem to be one based on the principle of the limiting factor. Succinctly stated, this approach places primary emphasis on the factors which are limiting to the solution of the problem involved. Following this principle, the planner concentrates on the limiting factors in evaluating the various courses of action. Application of this principle helps the planner focus on the crucial variables without becoming lost in the countless ramifications of the problem. The importance of these limiting factors was expressed by Chester Barnard as follows:

> The limiting (strategic) factor is the one whose control, in the right form, at the right place and time, will establish a new system or set of conditions which meets the purpose.[4]

In formulating a market strategy for a new product, the limiting factor might be competitive status, marketing capabilities, or financial resources. If a marketer lacks competitive status in a new market, it is logical to design a strategy which focuses on selling the new product in established markets. The recognition that the new product would overburden the marketing organization and field sales in particular would suggest a strategy of utilizing middlemen. A lack of financial resources could limit the scope of market strategies from the standpoints of marketing effort, geographical coverage, and type of customer target.

ACTIVATION OF PLANS   The mere act of planning is not sufficient; plans must be put into action. Usually this will mean such derivative

---

[4] Chester Barnard, *Functions of the Executive*, Cambridge, Mass.: Harvard University Press, 1938, pp. 202-203.

plans as programs, budgets, and control reports. The over-riding consideration in derivative planning is, of course, the objectives for each particular organizational level. With a sales-volume objective and a static market position, a general sales manager might implement a strategy of greater return on investment by a program to motivate salesmen toward the higher-profit items in the product line. This may entail, in turn, the planning of financial rewards, sales-performance reports, and supervisory procedures for field sales managers.

Lower down on the organizational ladder, the field sales manager will have to make derivative plans to implement those of his superior as well as the overall general strategy. Continuing the example, suppose the general sales manager decides upon a compensation plan for salesmen in which gross profits rather than sales volume are the basis for an incentive bonus. The field sales manager must decide upon a plan whereby he can achieve his assigned market penetration and at the same time ensure a fair chance to each and every salesman to attain his respective gross-profit quota. In essence, then, the purpose of derivative planning is to translate plans into meaningful assignments for the parts and the individuals making up the organization.

ADDITIONAL CONSIDERATIONS IN PLANNING

Besides the planning sequence, planners must recognize certain other considerations relative to the task of planning. The first of these is the features which characterize a sound plan. A second is the question of how far into the future a plan should commit a marketer. A third consideration is the relationship between planning, planners, and the organizational structure.

Features of a Sound Plan

To be useful, a plan must have certain features, such as those prescribed by Henri Fayol, a noted management theorist. He lists four general features of a good plan: unity, continuity, flexibility, and precision.[5] By unity, it is meant that only one plan at a time should be put into action. More than one plan would generate confusion and dilution of a firm's resources. Continuity implies the generation of

[5] Henri Fayol, *General and Industrial Administration*, New York: Pitman Publishing Corporation, 1949, pp. 43-44.

one strategy after the other and the meshing of strategies and tactics without disruptive effects. As previously stated, the hierachy of objectives should ensure the absence of conflict in goal seeking. However, seeking the same goal is not sufficient. A pairing of tactics or for that matter succeeding strategies directed toward the same objective can be incongruous. For example, in directing his efforts toward the market segment typified by customers of rather limited financial resources, a marketer might find the sales force stressing the tactic of price cutting while advertising is using credit as its basic theme. Incongruity in strategies arises from "180 degree" alterations in succeeding plans, say from price to nonprice competition or vice versa.

Flexibility permits adjustments to bring a plan into accord with unforeseen circumstances, the introduction of new information, or rethinking of the problem. Inflexibility adds another rigidity to a marketing organization which must function in an environment which is anything but static. Precision in the forecasting marketing activity is what differentiates a business concern from a venture. Today it is possible through the proper utilization of marketing-research tools to attain a fairly accurate degree of forecasting accuracy.

Other features a good plan should possess are relevance, measurability, and compulsoriness. A good plan should have a definite bearing on the matters at hand. Accordingly, it is necessary to develop criteria for use in judging the relative importance of plans. These criteria might be grouped under one of the following major headings:

1 Defects in current marketing system. Current defects should be weighed in relation to their individual and collective contributions to possible system breakdown.
2 Changes in market structure.
3 Changes in market requirements. Typically, these changes take on the nature of technological advances among users.
4 Changes in economic environment. These include changes in monetary policy, government relationships, and general business attitudes.
5 Changes desired in the institution. These are synonymous with both long- and short-range objectives.

Plans are not statements of intentions. Rather plans are selected courses of action, the results of which can be measured. Being measurable, a plan becomes operational and can be controlled. Thus, the trait of measurability is a vital connecting link between planning and control. Finally, a good plan must be compulsory. It must evoke the full support of all who have a role in the selected course of action. Much support for a plan can be generated during the planning stages. Through the utilization of affected personnel in the planning stages, the planner can create a feeling of participation. This feeling can be translated into full support.

Planning Commitment

A question which must be asked is how far into the future a plan should commit the marketer. Commonly, the period of time for strategies is five years whereas tactics are thought of in terms of one year or less. The reason for according strategies a span of five years is obscure. Perhaps, the five-year plans of the communistic nations have been an influence.

Nevertheless, the two basic determinants of the time period are the nature of the marketer's business and the type of plan. A maker and seller of installations, for example, will be able to plan farther in advance than, say, a component manufacturer who supplies the automobile industry. Likewise, a new-product plan will entail more years than a plan to upgrade the selling skills of the field sales force.

One author cites four factors that lead to the selection of the proper planning time span. These are (1) lead time necessary for action, (2) amortization period for capital invested, (3) future market prospects, and (4) future availability of raw materials and components.[6] The first three factors are particularly applicable to the planning of the marketing operation. The planning of a new airliner is a case in point. Suppose an aircraft firm wishes to build a small jetliner to land at airfields heretofore barred to jet aircraft. The length of the planning time span is to be determined by:

1 The time lapse between the concept of a new-product idea and a production unit. This will correspond roughly to the product evolutionary cycle up to the final or commercialization phase.
2 The time period necessary for the recovery of the capital investment in plant, equipment, and manpower.
3 The time lapse until the primary customer—small regionalized airlines—will be in the market actively for such an aircraft. This can be expected when present aircraft are obsolete and/or customer traffic has reached certain volume levels.

---

[6] Reprinted by permission of the publisher from Stewart Thompson, *How Companies Plan*, AMA Research Study No. 54 © 1962 by the American Management Association, Inc.

In the sense that a plan commits a marketer to certain obligations, the logical length of time for a plan is directly related to the discharge of those obligations.[7] If all obligations can be said to be financial in nature, this line of reasoning would result in a time span nearly identical with that necessary for capital amortization. Use of the term "obligations," however, signifies much more than the recovery of investment. The best example for marketing is the obligation to the customer. There are also the nonfinancial obligations to marketing personnel and to retained middlemen.

Planners and Organizational Structure

Two basic problems associated with planning are who should do the strategic planning and what their organizational status will be. Who does the planning is subject to different interpretations in individual organizations. At one extreme are those marketers who feel that planners must be separated from doers. Under such a concept, the planning function might be assigned to the board of directors. It is not practical, however, for directors to give continuous attention to this task. This is especially true of boards containing outside members.

Another alternative is to have the board chairman assume the responsibility for planning. In his position the chairman is above the day-to-day, crisis-to-crisis responsibilities for operation. This alternative also ensures that planning will be supported by top management, thus guarding against a significant contributor to planning failure. Still another organizational alternative is the creation of a separate planning department. In actual practice, however, this alternative appears to be limited to very large marketers, those who can sustain the added financial burden. In setting up a separate department, one very large marketer has gone so far as to physically disassociate planners from the rest of the firm's activities.

At the other extreme are the marketers who adhere to the principle that planning is a pervasive management activity. As such it is the job of every manager to plan and no changes need to be made in the structure of the organization. A compromise between the two viewpoints is the integration of all the concerned portions of the firm into a committee, team, or task force. The advantages of this approach

[7] Harold Koontz, "A Preliminary Statement of Principles of Planning and Control," *Journal of the Academy of Management,* April, 1958, pp. 45-60. Reprinted in Paul M. Dauten, Jr. (ed.), *Current Issues and Emerging Concepts in Management,* Boston: Houghton Mifflin Company, 1962, pp. 116-135.

are collective thinking and participation. To fix planning responsibility, the head of the team can be given a permanent position, as a planning manager or director. It is his job to assemble, coordinate, and evaluate the the planning efforts of team members so that one final plan evolves for submission to the chief marketing executive for approval. When the marketer's financial resources are limited, the job of planning manager is frequently assigned to the head of marketing research as an additional duty. The basic qualifications of the person appointed to the position of planning should be:

1 Close rapport with top management
2 Working familiarity with the various functional areas of the marketing organization
3 Creative imagination
4 Firm belief in the philosophy of change
5 Independence of close affiliation with any one functional area

When a firm is organized into operating divisions such as a chemical company, each division can have an assistant to the general manager for planning. At the corporate level, a separate department on the president's staff can handle consolidation of division plans and development of corporate strategy.

SELECTED AREAS OF STRATEGY

In the previous chapter it was stated that generally strategies are either product or market. At least two strategies defy classification as either major type. These are diversification and research and development.

Diversification

There is hardly a manufacturer of industrial goods who has not considered diversification. The lure, of course, is enhanced profits. Frequently diversification has a defensive trait. The marketer in question faces stagnation in his present business. Diversification, however, offers obvious opportunities in a growth area. The closer the growth area to present markets and technology, the more attractive the acquisition. Baldwin-Lima-Hamilton, an outgrowth of defensive diversification, expressed its philosophy as seeking out companies that make products which are profitable enough to support the tremendous engineering reserves and promise a reasonably steady market.

What starts out as defensive can evolve into an offensive strategy. Offensive diversification as distinguished from defensive utilizes acquisitions as means or steps to an end, rather than ends in themselves. A useful classification of offensive-minded firms is the one employed by *Forbes*. This publication divides the major diversifying companies into two major groupings—corporate collectives and diversified manufacturers.

Corporate collectives are a wide-reaching array of businesses. Litton Industries, one example, turns out some 6,000 different products from 146 plants and laboratories. Another corporate collective, Textron, is a conglomerate of 40 different firms making a wide range of products. More strait-laced, diversified manufacturers tend to keep to products related to each other by technology, productive techniques, or markets. Allis-Chalmers, for example, makes electrical equipment, tractors, and miscellaneous machinery—different products, but related by engineering and production. The sales growth and profitability of selected corporate collectives and diversified manufacturers are shown in Table 4.1.

Industrial marketers face formidable obstacles in attempting to diversify. The most formidable is perhaps the increase in rivals in what appears to be a sellers' market. Another obstacle is the growing concern of government antitrust agencies. Conglomerates today

TABLE 4.1   Industrial-good Manufacturers Prominent in Diversification

	PERFORMANCE (PERCENT)	
MANUFACTURER	GROWTH*	PROFITABILITY†
Corporate Collectives:		
Litton Industries	27.0	24.1
Textron	17.9	14.0
Kaiser Industries	9.9	0.6
AVCO	5.7	13.9
Olin Mathieson	4.7	9.1
Diversified Manufacturers:		
FMC	16.1	15.5
Midland Ross	10.8	8.7
TRW, Inc.	7.9	10.8
American Machine & Foundry	5.7	14.5
Borg-Warner	4.5	9.8
Allis-Chalmers	4.2	3.4
Westinghouse Air Brake	3.4	8.4

* Seven-year compounded growth rate in sales volume.
† Five-year average return on equity.
Source: *Forbes,* Jan. 1, 1967, p. 160.

as never before are being scrutinized for possible harmful effects on competition. Still another obstacle is the inherent risks attendant upon any acquisition. An executive from a firm which is quite active in acquisitions has gone so far as to say these inherent risks are such that one out of every three mergers will fail.

In fashioning a diversification strategy, an industrial marketer would do well to take a look at the leaders in this field. Leaders appear to have three major operational characteristics in common.[8] The first is the direct personal involvement of the chief executive officer of the company from beginning to end in planning and negotiations. Second is a firm commitment to the belief that acquisitions are not ends but means to an end. Litton expresses this offensive philosophy as filling out a plan. The third basis of similarity is the critical financial audit each prospect is subjected to before the initiation of negotiations. The two most important financial aspects of acquisition appear to be the asking price and the potential return on investment.

The usual approach to determining whether the asking price is reasonable is to relate the ability to earn a return on investment to the price. This necessitates in turn an in-depth or, as it is sometimes called, a no-kidding audit of the prospect. Quite often a firm will establish a minimum return on investment. Textron, for example, has set up a requirement that the prospect must possess the ability to earn a 25 percent pretax return on investment.

Diversifying companies, however, should not become obsessed with the financial aspects of acquisitions. A broader approach is suggested by the rules adopted by Litton. The first question that is asked is whether the prospective firm fits in with Litton's product and market planning. The next question concerns the strength of the prospect's management. In assessing management strengths, the diversifying company might find useful the following listing of what one author calls "core" skills.[9]

1 The ability to deal with tough unions
2 The talent of being able to live with a market characterized by unstable prices
3 The sensitivity to customer needs
4 The ability to develop commercially successful new products
5 The ability to administer marketing channels

[8]"The Perilous Quest for Acquisitions," *Dun's Review,* July, 1965, p. 34.

[9]Gordon R. Conrad, "Unexplored Assets for Diversification," *Harvard Business Review,* September-October, 1963, pp. 69-71.

6 The talent to collect accurate marketing information
7 The ability to set up an effective organization particularly in regard to the delegation of responsibility and authority
8 The ability to make remarkable intuitive decisions
9 The ability to manipulate successfully customer-service programs
10 The conscious awareness of logistics implications

Only after affirmative answers to the first two questions will Litton management consider the financial aspects of the acquisition. The decision and resulting action based on the answers to questions such as those prescribed by Litton signal the end of the selection process but not the diversification strategy. Diversification strategy should contain a clear statement of the organizational relationship between the acquisition and the parent firm. The purpose of this statement is to facilitate the merger by communicating explicitly to all concerned their respective roles during and after the merging of the business units.

Research and Development

An essential ingredient in the marketing strategy of practically every industrial marketer is research and development. The reason is the ever-increasing importance of technical know-how in markets which are rapidly becoming more sophisticated. The marketing impact of technology plus the traditional conceptual division between R&D and marketing emphasizes the imperativeness of strategy development in this area.

In recognition of the fact that industrial marketing is largely a battle of technology, the foundation of R&D strategy must be market-oriented. No longer can a firm view marketing solely in terms of the commercialization of R&D output. R&D strategy must be directed toward long-term marketing objectives. More specifically the efforts of the research department should be planned to:

1 Sustain current marketing efforts
2 Provide a steady flow of new technology
3 Create and uphold an image of technical competence

In IBM, for example, R&D strategy sustains current operations by a program which helps to assure a sophisticated level of understanding of present technologies, including the limitations. Another program calls for the demonstration of the feasibility of new-systems applications which in turn helps to provide IBM with greater marketing opportunities. To supply new technology, the R&D at IBM is charged with the responsibility of accumulating scientific and technical knowledge with an eye toward evaluating trends and opportunities. Also involved is the responsibility for the generation of patentable ideas to allow the company's freedom of action in areas of interest. IBM's research gives prestige to the company and maintains an eminent position within the scientific community.[10]

Other factors which should be considered in the development of a R&D strategy include:

1   Coordination of R&D and marketing
2   Organization of the R&D function
3   Measurement of R&D productivity

Traditionally, R&D and marketing have pursued divergent paths. Several reasons account for the wide gap which sunders the two disciplines and thus prevents the necessary close coordination. The primary reason is that the company has not really espoused the marketing management concept. As discussed in the previous chapter, this type of company is product- rather than consumer-oriented. Such an inner-directed attitude is expressed by the question: "Given our technology, what products can we make?"[11] Consequently, products evolve which are makable rather than marketable. Allied with this product orientation is the search by R&D for the "perfect item." Another reason for the conceptual gap between R&D and marketing is the "leave the researchers alone" attitude. This attitude is fostered by top management's failure to comprehend the nature of research and the desire on the part of researchers to operate free of organizational constraints.

Any R&D strategy must close the gap between research and marketing. One approach is to allow researchers greater participation in management. This can be accomplished through a coordinating committee with decision-making powers. Ideally, this committee would be composed of representatives from marketing, research,

[10] By permission of the publisher from E. R. Piore, "Basic Company Policy Regarding Research," in Jerome W. Blood (ed.), *The Management of Scientific Talent,* AMA Management Report No. 76. © 1963 by the American Management Association, Inc.

[11] Reprinted by permission of the publisher from Mark Hanan, *The Market Orientation of R&D,* AMA Management Bulletin No. 72. © 1965 by the American Management Association, Inc.

and possibly production and finance. Another approach is to bring research into the marketing department. To offset the accompanying increase in applied as opposed to pure research, scientific personnel may be released from duties for a specified period of time to pursue projects of personal interest.

How research can be best organized is a question a planner must answer in generating R&D strategy. First, research must be positioned in the overall structure of the firm. One solution, previously stated, is to place research in the marketing department, probably under product development. Such a position acknowledges marketing as the originating source of new-product ideas. Research as a result tends toward applied and corrective as opposed to pure or basic. Firms whose market standing is closely allied to advancements in scientific knowledge brought about by original investigation would tend to shun this organizational solution in favor of one featuring more autonomy.

A recognized position as the fourth organic function along with marketing, production, and finance is a much more common organizational location for research in the corporate structure. The head of research, a vice-president or director, operates from the corporate level. His two primary tasks are the review of all the research work completed in the company and participation in top-level decision making.

Internally, there are five basic structural patterns for the research function—subject, product, process, project, and phase.[12] In a research department structured by subject, each section is staffed with specialists from a particular branch of science or engineering. Among the industrial marketers who make use of the subject approach in R&D are AMF, Lockheed, Raytheon, SKF, and Stanley Tool. A product-type organization combines personnel from various disciplines into permanent teams dealing with specific products or product areas. The research policy of Continental Can Company, for example, is based on the conviction that each product division requires the support of an R&D group which is an intregal part of that product division. A process-type organization closely resembles the product type. The only difference is that the subdivisions are oriented toward functional areas of the firm rather than product areas.

The most flexible structuring of research is the arrangement referred to as a project type. When a problem arises, the head of re-

[12] By permission of the publisher from A. O. Stanley and K. K. White, *Organizing the R & D Function*, AMA Research Study No. 72. © 1965 by the American Management Association, Inc.

search forms a team of scientific personnel chosen on the basis of the applicability of their respective competence to the problem at hand. The tenure of the team continues until solution of the problem. When researchers are not assigned to a team, it might be conceivable to have them pursue their interests in pure research. Occasionally the project-team concept is utilized by a marketer to handle an emergency situation. Under a phase organization, research is segmented according to the particular steps in the creative process. A typical subdivision of a phase-type organization would include basic research, applied research, product development, and product engineering. A phase-structured arrangement can be found in the R&D organizations of Bell Telephone Laboratories, Corning Glass, Du Pont, and Owens-Illinois.

Finally, in planning R&D strategy, consideration should be given to measuring the productivity of research. Measurement can be either qualitative or quantitative. Strict quantitative evaluation is preferable but hardly possible in practice. Qualitative or subjective evaluation based on the judgment of top management will be part of nearly every analysis. The reliability of qualitative evaluation can be enhanced by the addition of objectivity. This may be in the form of budgeting and/or periodic reviews.

Quantitative evaluation is essentially a comparison of input, in this case investment with output or expected benefits. The problem, of course, is to translate benefits into dollars and cents. This usually necessitates an estimate of the effect of a particular research project on the market position of the company. If R&D is to create a new product, the estimated return should be figured at several price levels. It is also important to measure as nearly as possible the effect of the new product, either positive or negative, on the rest of the product line. When R&D is conducted to correct problems in the current product line, past experience can supply some indication of the value of such market maintenance. In oversimplified terms, the value of corrective research might be the gross profits which would have been lost through a decline in sales plus the costs of disposing of present inventory had the action not taken place.

Quite often marketers rely on mathematical models to determine the relative worth of specific R&D projects. These, in turn, permit more effective allocation of available funds. One marketer computes what is called an index of the relative worth of a R&D project.[13] Of

[13] Raymond Villers, *Research and Development: Planning and Control,* New York: Financial Executives Research Foundation, Inc., 1964, pp. 43-44.

practical significance for any technically oriented firm, the index is found by using the following formula:

$$I = \frac{P_1 P_2 P_3 (fE - C)}{R}$$

where I = index of relative worth

P_1 = probability of technical success

P_2 = probability of commercial acceptance from the technical point of view

P_3 = probability of commercial acceptance from the marketing point of view

f = present worth factor based on discounting money at some percentage figure

E = estimated net earnings for project before depreciation, interest, and federal taxation

C = capital requirements for commercialization

R = estimated cost of future R&D necessary to reach commercialization

Simulation of various R&D projects, drawn from past experience and theoretical potentialities, and based on a formula such as the one given above, would provide management with a useful yardstick of absolute worth. The derived indexes could be scaled to indicate the degree of desirability for a R&D project. For example, projects with indexes below a minimum figure on the scale would be subject to more intensive scrutiny and possible discontinuance. Above the minimum index, it might be feasible to divide the scale into marginal, adequate, and highly promising ranges.

SUMMARY

Planning can be conceived of as the managerial task of projecting a course of action into the future to bring about a desired state in the business organization or a portion thereof. Objectives or the desired state provides direction to the planner. A hierarchy of objectives closely paralleling the organizational structure should be developed to add meaning to the vast complex of objectives for a single firm.

Strategies and tactics emerge as planning concepts when the dimension of time is considered. Strategies are courses of action planned to accomplish long-run objectives. As a consequence, strategies will bring about major changes in the relationship between the firm and its competitive environment. The two general categories of strategies are product and market.

Tactics are courses of action directed toward short-run objectives. Management will be involved in tactical planning on almost a continuous basis dealing with either the implementation of strategies or problem situations.

The principle benefit from planning is preparation for the future. Other benefits include the establishment of standards, greater coordination, more effective allocation of resources, and a feeling of readiness for the future.

The fundamental steps in planning can be listed as follows:

1 Statement of objectives
2 Definition of premises or assumptions
3 Setting up alternative courses of action
4 Evaluating alternative courses of action
5 Selecting a course of action
6 Activation of plans

Other planning considerations include the characteristics of a sound plan, future commitment of planning, and organizational relationships. A sound plan is characterized by unity, continuity, flexibility, precision, relevance, measurability, and compulsoriness. The two basic determinants of the commitment period are the nature of the marketer's business and the type of plan. In the sense that a plan commits a marketer to certain obligations, the logical length of time for a plan is directly related to the discharge of those obligations.

Relating organizational structure to planning involves two questions. The first is who will do the strategic planning. The second is what the organizational position of planners will be. At one extreme are those marketers who maintain that planners must be separated from doers. At the other extreme are the marketers who adhere to the principle that planning is a pervasive management activity. A compromise between the two viewpoints is the integration of all concerned portions of the firm into a committee, team, or task force headed up by someone with the fixed responsibility for planning.

At least two strategies defy classification as either product or market. One is diversification, the other R&D. To overcome the formidable obstacles in diversification, the marketer would do well to take a look at the leaders in this field. He would see that the leading firms agree in recognizing the need for (1) personal involvement by the chief executive, (2) the prevailing view that acquisitions are not ends but means to ends, and (3) utilization of a critical financial audit prior to negotiations.

The impact of technology on the industrial market plus the conceptual gap between science and marketing demonstrates the importance of R&D strategy. Specifically such a strategy will:

1 Direct R&D efforts toward the market
2 Coordinate R&D and marketing efforts
3 Organize the R&D function
4 Measure the productivity of R&D

DISCUSSION QUESTIONS

1 What reasons can be given to support the contention that objectives constitute the core of managerial action?
2 Distinguish clearly between product and market strategies.
3 In addition to the element of time, what other differences are there between strategies and tactics?
4 A planner has adopted a philosophy of change. Explain.
5 Trace the planning process.
6 When two alternative courses of action are equally advantageous, why should the planner select the one offering the better basis for future action?
7 The advantages of a hierarchy of objectives are several. Give at least three.
8 What is the value of planning premises in management development?
9 Why is it dangerous for a marketer to rely too heavily on past experience in making planning decisions?
10 What limits are there to a planner's being rational?
11 Define the feature of a plan which clearly differentiates a business from a venture.
12 A longer period of time would be required for adherence to the obligations' principle than for amortization of investment. Explain.
13 What characteristics are desirable in a planner?
14 What are the differences between offensive and defensive diversifications?
15 What aspects other than financial should be considered in a possible acquisition?
16 What are the basic points which should be covered in a R&D strategy?

SUPPLEMENTARY READING

Barnard, Chester, *Functions of the Executive,* Cambridge, Mass.: Harvard University Press, 1938.

Blood, Jerome W. (ed.), *The Management of Scientific Talent,* New York: American Management Association, Inc., 1963.

Bowman, Donald M., *Management—Organization and Planning,* New York: McGraw-Hill Book Company, 1963, secs. 5-8.

Conrad, Gordon R., "Unexplored Assets for Diversification," *Harvard Business Review.* September-October, 1963, pp. 67-73.

Cooper, Arnold C., "R&D Is More Efficient in Small Companies," *Harvard Business Review,* May-June, 1964, pp. 75-83.

Gaber, Norman H., and Edgar S. Cheaney, "Taking Some Guesswork out of R&D," *Business Horizons,* Winter, 1964, pp. 61-72.

Granger, Charles H., "The Hierarchy of Objectives," *Harvard Business Review,* May-June, 1964, pp. 63-74.

Hanan, Mack, *The Market Orientation of R&D,* Management Bulletin No. 72, New York: American Management Association, Inc. 1965.

Smith, Philip T., "A Philosophy of Research for Industry," *Business Horizons,* Winter, 1965, pp. 53-64.

Stanley, Alexander O., and K. K. White, *Organizing the R&D Function,* Research Study No. 72, New York: American Management Association, Inc., 1965.

Villers, Raymond, *Research and Development: Planning and Control,* New York: Financial Executives Research Foundation, Inc., 1964.

managerial action— control

The function of control is to keep the actual operation going according to plan. One aspect of control has to do with the close interrelationship between control and planning. Planners have to deal with the uncertainty of the future, and thus it is only logical to assume that revisions will have to be made in the managerial spectrum to include plans, organization, and possibly objectives. Control, in performing this job, can be viewed as keeping planners informed or closing the "loop" between planned action and actuality.

Another aspect of control is concerned with mistakes—their identification, correction, and prevention. Preoccupation with this aspect is not without its disadvantages. In the first place, by thinking in these terms, management tends to disassociate control from the other functions, particularly planning. This in turn can lead to a sacrifice of effectiveness for efficiency. The mere following of a procedure can become more important than the accomplishment of progress toward an objective. Secondly, emphasis on mistakes may cause management to look upon control solely as a means of fixing the blame for failure. This not only deters initiative, it promotes buck-passing and excuse making, two deteriorating activities.

The dynamic nature of the marketplace and the irredeemable nature of marketing mistakes make control vital in marketing. Despite this, marketing organizations have experienced difficulties in incorporating the control function. There are several explanations for this. The primary one and perhaps the most obvious is the reluctance of marketing management to intrude into an area traditionally bounded by the precepts of intuition. A second explanation is the difficulty of equating profit responsiveness with marketing effort. Yet another reason is the inappropriateness of traditional cost accounting concepts. Finally, marketing efforts rarely coincide with normal accounting periods of a month, quarter, or year. The last explanation is particulary applicable to the industrial market where the selling process is apt to be lengthy.

MEANING OF CONTROL

The control function of management can be broken down into three or possibly four steps. The first step is to set up standards or yardsticks against which actual performance is measured. Objectives expressed in terms of key result areas furnish the basic standards. Once standards are selected, the next step is to create the tools for recording performance. These tools supply the information management needs to make comparisons between actual performance and predetermined standards. The type of information will vary in relation to the management echelon. A field sales manager, for example, may require only a call report and a summary of sales for each salesman. His superiors, on the other hand, will want to know how the firm stands in regard to market penetration, sales growth, and profitability contribution. The variance of content in information by-need-to-know is called the control spectrum.

If control is considered a four-step process, the third step is comparison. Typically, comparison is combined with measurement when only three steps are considered in control. Comparison alerts management to action by monitoring the differences between actual and planned happenings. Action, the fourth step, may be corrective, so that performance is adjusted to standards, or it may be what is called revisionary. The latter type of action involves shifting some portion or all of the managerial spectrum so that it represents current actuality more accurately.

OBJECTIVES OF CONTROL

The function of control must be objective-oriented to keep the marketing organization moving in the desired direction. This is accomplished by correlating standards with the overall marketing objectives as expressed in key result areas. Failing to achieve this, control becomes an end in itself rather than a means to an end.

What should be considered in formulating control objectives can be summarized as follows:

1 Internal balance between authority and responsibility
2 Prevention as opposed to after-the-fact punitive activity
3 Effectiveness and efficiency
4 Promotion of creativity
5 Shielding against the consequences of costly mistakes
6 Facilitation of information flow
7 Greater opportunities for delegation of authority

STANDARDS OF MARKETING PERFORMANCE

Setting up marketing performance standards or measures of adequacy is a most difficult task. The most troublesome problem is finding a standard which is not affected appreciably by factors beyond the control of those being measured. Windfall gains or losses can disrupt the confidence of the organization in standards, thus rendering them virtually useless. Another problem is that of comparability. Ideally all of marketing should be directed toward the same standard or set of standards. Practically, however, this is not possible. Therefore, all standards should have certain essential characteristics in common. These same characteristics in turn will be related to the major objectives of the firm.

Permanency of the selected standards is another perplexing problem confronting the marketer. To be effective, standards must stand the test of time. The job of control will not get done, and in its stead only confusion will reign if standards are changed periodically. This is not to intimate that standards are not to be changed; rather it is to say that the concept of tenure should be considered in selecting a standard. Standards used as yardsticks in measuring marketing performance can be categorized under the following general headings: past performance, market potential, productivity, profit contribution, marketing plans, marketing costs, and job activities.

Past Performance

By far the most common basis for a marketing standard is past performance. The concreteness of past performance is perhaps its biggest advantage. Management can more readily grasp the significance of deviations if they are compared with something within their realm of experience. Past sales are used as a control standard by a chemical company selling a wide range of products to many different types of consumers. Using two-digit SIC numbers to designate each market segment, field sales management receives a monthly report on each salesman showing last month's sales, last month's sales a year ago, and cumulative totals for the current and previous years. Noting that sales in a particular market segment are lower this year than last, the field sales manager can quickly call this variance to the attention of the salesman concerned. The absence of abstractness in past performance facilitates retrospection.

Still another advantage of past performance is self-comparison. This adds to the credibility of the standard and enhances the possibility of using the standard as a motivation tool. Also favoring the use of past-performance standards is their inherent simplicity. Finally, data on past performance are readily available from internal records.

The major obstacle in using past performance is that as a standard it measures only the marketer's efforts, the assumption being that all the other factors remain constant from year to year. There-fore, strict use of past performance does not indicate the actual posi-tion of the marketer. It is because of this limitation that past perform-ance is usually combined with another basis such as market potential or profit contribution.

Market Potential

Market potential represents the total amount of a product which could be sold during a given period of time, probably a year. Since an ideal figure is impractical as a standard, the concept of market potential is narrowed to actual industry sales or an estimate of industry sales. How well a firm or portion thereof is doing in relation to the compe-tition is measured in terms of market share or penetration. Market share as a standard is more appropriately applied to units than it is to individuals. A marketer might want to employ market share as a performance standard for each of its geographic sales divisions.

The obvious advantage of market potential is the continuing re-alignment of the standard to reflect current market conditions. The difficulty of obtaining industry sales data can be overcome by sophis-ticated marketing-research techniques which relate company sales data to some indication of market receptivity outside the company.

Use of a market-potential standard need not be complicated, as the following hypothetical example shows. Suppose a marketer finds a close correlation existing between his total sales and value added by manufacturing for industries comprised in his market. That is, when value added increases, sales increase, and conversely a drop in value added indicates a fall in sales volume. Dividing total sales by value added provides the marketer with a market index. Suppose further that the market index is found to be 0.032 and the value added for a particular salesman's territory is $2 million. Con-verting this into a performance standard, the salesman should derive sales of $64,000 from the designated territory during the next twelve months.

Productivity

Productivity is concerned with the ratio of outputs to inputs. Gen-erally, outputs refer to marketing revenues defined as either sales or gross margins, whereas inputs are the costs of marketing effort. Several combinations of factors are used in computing marketing productivity.

OUTPUTS	INPUTS
Sales	Sales hours worked
Sales	Sales calls
Ad inquiries	Media costs
Sales-invoice lines	Warehouse hours worked
Gross margins of new products	Product-development expenditures

The value of productivity standards is that they emphasize the relationship of return to effort. Productivity measures the ability of the marketer to achieve the best balance. This becomes self-evident when the various ways of improving productivity are reviewed:

1   An increase in outputs with the same level of inputs
2   An increase in outputs with a decrease in inputs
3   An increase in outputs proportionately greater than the increase in inputs
4   No change in outputs with a decrease in inputs
5   A decrease in outputs proportionately less than the decrease in inputs

There are four restrictions to the use of productivity as a standard. The first pertains to the nature of outputs. Many of the marketing outputs for the industrial-good firm are intangible and therefore almost impossible to quantify. Good examples are the enhancement of the technical-competency image by R&D and the education of customers through clinics by salesmen. A second restriction is the difficulty of fitting inputs and outputs into the same time period, a situation common to much of the industrial market.

Third, inability to measure all inputs can restrict the usefulness of a productivity standard. The input base should be broad enough to encompass all elements of effort, particularly investment. It would be inaccurate to say, for example, that a salesman's outputs are the result of his efforts alone. Sales training, marketing research, and possibly even advertising affect his output, and thus they should be included as inputs in terms of amortized dollars.

Finally, a fourth restriction is placed on productivity by the influence of factors outside the marketer's control. Improvements by customers such as more efficient purchasing procedures should be separated from the marketer's operations. Conversely, invasion of market segments where consumers are less efficient or a deterioration of efficiency among present customers should not be reflected in any measurement of productivity.

Profit Contribution

Ideally, the best performance standard is profit, a key result area for the overall operations of the firm. Before looking at the advantages and disadvantages of profit standards, it is necessary to review the various interpretations placed on the term "profit." Gross profit, defined as net sales less cost of goods sold, has wide application in marketing operations where the intent is to direct marketing efforts toward profitable products. The most extensive use of gross profit is in setting up standards for individual salesmen and sales managers. Another possible use of gross profit is measuring the output of product development.

Subtracting marketing expenses from gross profit, one arrives at net marketing profit. Net marketing profit is a useful standard for measuring organizational subdivisions where the desire is to consider both revenues and expenses. A modification of net marketing profit is obtained by substituting standardized for actual marketing expenses in making a deduction from gross profits.

Because profit is a relative rather than an absolute concept, it should be stated in terms of some recognizable basis. The two major bases are sales and investment. Profit as a percentage of sales is used when the purpose of the yardstick is to direct performance toward profitable activities, customers, and products. It is also extremely valuable in making internal comparisons of profit contribution.

The second of the major bases is investment. Profit as related to investment or return on investment, as it is usually termed, is the key concept in appraising the effectiveness of a firm in a free enterprise economy. T. G. Mackensen stated it in these words:

> *True growth comes from the ability of management to employ successfully additional capital at a satisfactory rate of return. This is the final criterion of the soundness and strength of a company's growth, for in a free competitive economy capital gravitates toward the more profitable enterprises. The company that is merely expanding at declining rates of return on investment will eventually be brought to a stop for lack of expansion capital.*[1]

To obtain maximum usefulness from return on investment, many firms have extended this yardstick to the measurement of performance at the lowest echelon practical. Their reasoning is that the establishment of profit control centers at strategic points throughout

[1] Reprinted by permission of the publisher from T. G. Mackensen, "How H. T. Heinz Manages Its Financial Planning and Controls," AMA Financial Management Series, no. 106. © 1953 by the American Management Association, Inc.

the organization helps to pinpoint the dissipation of capital. These strategic points could be a department, section, division, or product.

The principal advantage of profit standards is the focusing of organization attention on what must be described as the critical element in any business. However, the use of profit is not without its disadvantages. In the first place, use of profit standards requires that profit data be disseminated on a rather wide scale. This type of data is considered extremely confidential by many marketers. Subterfuges such as points do little to lessen the basic problem of disclosure. Another disadvantage is the problem of allocation. It is frequently difficult to allocate profits to the various decision elements of the firm. If return on investment is used, the problem is further complicated by the necessity of having to calculate the cost of capital.

An objection to profit standards when expressed as relative to sales or investment, and one which would apply equally to productivity, is the weakening of emphasis on total dollar profits. Some top managements such as General Electric's feel that such weakening reduces appreciably the growth incentive. Further, in a decentralized structure where management operates more or less autonomously, this motivating factor is of vital necessity.

Marketing Plans

As previously defined, plans represent a projection of action over a future period of time. It will be remembered that one of the features of a good plan is the quality of measurability. Thus, it is only logical that the essential elements of a plan be utilized as a source of control standards. Objectives expressed in terms of key result areas are a good example. Another example is the stages of progress toward an objective.

Elements of a plan are particularly applicable in situations where results are difficult to put in the traditional terms of sales or profits. Normally such situations occur in functional areas other than sales. Some of the elements used in measuring performance are:

Advertising
1   An indicated penetration level in a stage of market acceptance
2   An indicated quantity of ad inquiries
3   An indicated quantity of ad inquiries from a designated market segment or purchasing influence

Finance

4   An improvement in customer relations

5   A speedup in credit processing

Logistics

6   A reduction in delivery and/or order-processing time

7   An indicated level of on-time deliveries

8   An indicated level of filled invoice lines

9   A specific reduction in damage claims

Product Development

10   A major improvement in the quality of a designated product

11   The development of a marketable product

12   An improvement in the procedures of product development

13   An expansion in the number of new-product ideas

Customer Services

14   A reduction in call-backs on service calls

15   A reduction in time consumed per service call

16   An upgrading of the technical proficiency of service calls

Using the essential elements of marketing plans helps to strengthen the link between control and planning. It also forces management to couple planning and control together in their thinking. This averts the tendency to think of plans as intentions.

The major disadvantage of marketing plans is the problem of weighting. Which essential element is the most important, the next most important, etc., are questions many managements find almost impossible to answer. Without answers, the resulting array of standards will bring not only confusion but diffusion of effort. It should be noted that as far as objectives are concerned, a properly structured hierarchy can do much to alleviate the problem of assigning relative weights. Another possible drawback to the use of marketing plans as standards is the necessity of having to rely on the ability of the planner. There is no assurance that his plans are the best possible under the given conditions. However, with control acting as a built-in adjuster of plans to reality, it would stand to reason that through a period of trial and error the proficiency of the planner would increase to a point where the accuracy of plans is no longer questionable.

Marketing Costs

Standard costs for units of activity have limited application as yardsticks of marketing performance. Several reasons may be advanced for this. In the first place, standard costs are not normally used where there is variance in the content of the task. Industrial marketing activities, for the most part, are highly divergent. Only in scattered instances is it possible to develop standard cost data. In the case of field sales, for example, the characteristics of the industrial market such as the dispersion of purchasing influence prevent the calculation of a meaningful standard cost per call. Also working against a standard cost per call are the length of the selling period and the use of group-selling techniques.

Secondly, the marketer finds oftentimes he has neither data nor the expertise to develop a standard-cost system. A third reason is that development of standard costs lags behind rapidly changing marketing conditions. Finally, marketers shy away from standard costs because of their negative and restrictive connotations.

Where marketing activities are routinized, standard costs can be applied with a great deal of success. Standard costs are particularly useful in controlling selling expenses. Another use is in setting up budgets for aggregate marketing effort. A marketer may, for example, develop standard costs for distributing, advertising, and logistical support. Frequently this is done according to product or product lines.

List of Activities

Up to now the discussion of control standards has concentrated on the results of performance. A list of activities, normally an outgrowth of a job specification, serves as a yardstick, to measure how successfully results are obtained. A list of activities is particularly helpful in controlling those vital tasks, the results of which are not readily apparent to the individual concerned. Sales auxiliary services such as before- and after-sales service, technical counseling, and inside sales offer excellent possibilities for control through a list of activities.

A list of activities may be used as a standard for a group or an individual as the following example illustrates. One of the jobs of an inside salesman may be to make unsolicited phone calls to assigned customers, inquiring as to the state of relations with each and initiating action as needed. As a group inside salesmen may be expected to improve the coordination between the buyer and seller so that less of their time is spent in dealing with problems in such areas as deliveries, filling of orders, packaging, and billing.

Success in using a list of activities is directly related to the job specification, which in turn is hinged to the job analysis. The overriding considerations are, of course, the objectives and policies of the marketer. Refinement of both objectives and policies will facilitate the development of all three—activities, specification, and analysis.

In looking at the various standards, it is obvious that no one standard is complete in itself or applicable to all businesses. It is also apparent that planning is the key to the development of control standards. The marketer would do well to consider what is required in an adequate control system. As a minimum, a control system should:

1   Reflect the nature and needs of the particular business activity
2   Reflect deviations expeditiously
3   Be flexible
4   Reflect organizational patterns
5   Be understandable
6   Assure corrective action[2]

MEASUREMENT OF MARKETING PERFORMANCE

Once standards are established, the next task in control is to measure actual performance. The task of measurement is accomplished by means of a network which systematically collects relevant information. Two major questions must be answered in developing an information network: (1) What are the requisites of a desirable information network? and (2) What is involved in the installation of an information network?

Requisites of an Information Network

The complexity and decentralization which characterize today's marketing organization necessitate the most sensitive of mechanisms possible to provide the information required in controlling. In designing a network to collect and distribute informative data, the marketer should keep in mind that the purpose of information is to guide managerial action in controlling.

Because management is interested in what is happening rather than what has happened, promptness is an overriding consideration in the furnishing of control information. Promptness in a network requires not only timeliness in the submission of reports, but the selection of appropriate reporting intervals. Another requisite of an information network is the linking up of management with the vital

[2] Harold Koontz and Cyril O'Donnell, *Principles of Management*, 2d ed., New York: McGraw-Hill Book Company, 1959, pp. 588-591.

areas of the marketing operation. Coverage of vital areas should be concentrated on out-of-line performance, definite trends in performance, and the need-to-know for the particular manager concerned.

Recognition and exploration of all sources of control information are still another requisite of a good information network. Perhaps the greatest weakness in many information networks is the exclusive reliance on accounting systems to supply the necessary data. Reported information from accounting systems is normally restricted to dollar-and-cents items which ultimately appear in budgeting and financial statements. The typical approach to improving the coverage of reports has three basic weaknesses.

1   It considers only existing reports and reporting structure.
2   It provides no basis for determining information needs. Personal whim plays a major role in eliminating or keeping existing reports.
3   It fails to recognize the profit potentialities of management information.

Simplicity in both reports and reporting structure or network is a fourth requisite. Usability of reports is directly related to management understanding. Jumbled, complicated reports do nothing but lie around on desks and in drawers. Management, generally, has neither the time nor the inclination to decipher reports. A simplified network facilitates corrective action so that management has no trouble in pinpointing responsibility. Simplicity also enables the preparee to identify the receiver of the report. This can greatly reduce the confusion attendant upon reporting.

Organization of an Information Network

The task of structuring an information network involves assembling all the items of information from every available source into one coherent system. One of the primary considerations is the particular firm's organizational structure. Organization is the principal means of conveying information. Hence, the most effective network is one tailored to the organizational requirements of the firm.

A second consideration in organizing an information network is the relationship of adequacy to management echelon. As successively higher levels are attained, the content of reported information will be altered by condensations, additions, and deletions. Varying content according to echelon frees each manager from the many details of current operations and allows him to apply himself more fully to important tasks such as planning.

Automation of the information network is a third consideration.

There are three distinct stages in the development of an automated information system. These are:[3]

1 Systems specification or the design of all the aspects of the system which are important to the users of information. Frequently included is the defining of the formats for output and input, as well as the report interval.
2 Data processing implementation. The job at this stage is to design a data processing system which will be the most efficient for the implementation of the first stage's specifications.
3 Programming. This stage starts with the systems flow charts and ends when the program is in the computer.

From the foregoing, it is obvious that the efficacy of an automated network is almost wholly dependent upon the information generated. This is the responsibility of the users of the information. It is also the responsibility of the users to bring unity to the network. Not realizing this, management can only become befuddled and confused by the bewildering volume which pours with alarming speed from data processing equipment. Specialists in data processing are charged with maximizing the utilization of equipment in line with its capabilities. Accordingly, the automation of information networks should be looked upon as nothing more than gaining the singular advantage of speed in linking up action areas with decision points.

COMPARISON OF MARKETING PERFORMANCE

The third step in control is comparing actual performance with the applicable standard and analyzing the noted deviation. Devices applicable to the marketing operation include the Du Pont chart system, budgets, and break-even analysis.

Du Pont Chart System

This system is a graphic presentation of performance data on each operating investment.[4] The Executive Committee reviews charts every

---

[3] John Dearden, "How to Organize Information Systems," *Harvard Business Review*, March-April, 1965, pp. 66-67.

[4] Condensed by permission of the publisher from T. C. Davis, "How the Du Pont Organization Appraises Its Performance," AMA Financial Management Series, no. 94. © 1949 by the American Management Association, Inc.

FIGURE 5.1 Outline of DuPont Chart.

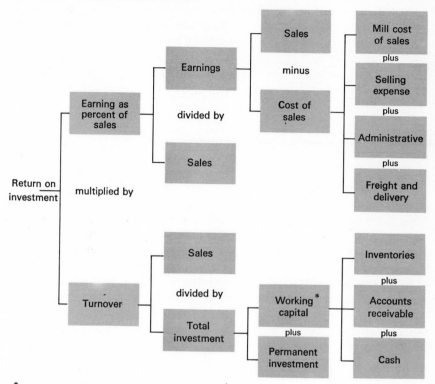

* Includes small amounts of deferred charges

month, the schedule being so arranged that no department is reviewed more than once every three months. The central theme of the chart system is return on investment. The formula using the basic factors of earnings as a percentage of sales and turnover is outlined on a chart (Figure 5.1). The format of the chart never varies, and so comparisons can be made between current and past performance, and internally between operating investments during the current period.

Specific advantages claimed for the chart system include:

1 No chance for narrative to obscure evaluation
2 Relative ease in directing attention toward one point
3 Maximum possible uniformity in the presentation of data
4 Complete rather than haphazard piecemeal changes
5 Presentation rules made by the users—the Executive Committee

In Figure 5.1 it will be noted that investment is defined as the gross value of plant and working capital rather than stockholder-invested capital. To use stockholder-invested capital would necessitate the deduction of liabilities and reserves from the cost of plant and working capital. Du Pont's reasoning is that the firm as represented by the Executive Committee seeks a clear profitability picture of the employment of aggregate property and working capital. Deductions for liabilities and reserves would distort this picture by introducing variables beyond the control of responsible management.

Budgets

A budget is a plan expressed in terms of revenue and costs. Typically, a marketer will draw up an overall budget which in turn is subdivided into other budgets which can parallel either organizational structure or function. The process of budgeting pervades planning and control. To begin with, a budget is a plan which is normally included in the package defined as a program. The role of budgets is to project financial requirements. A budget prepared for a new product is valuable in assessing the commercial possibilities at each stage of development. A flexible sales budget might show, for example, that far more sales than originally forecasted must be obtained to offset the costs of marketing and production. In view of this the evaluation committee might decide to cancel the product or at least postpone its further development.

The control aspect of budgeting is concerned primarily with costs. An operations budget covers those costs which have been standardized. A comparison of actual costs with standard costs provides an indication of efficiency. A difficulty in this type of budget, and one which seriously limits its use in marketing operations, is the necessity for routinized action.

Another general type is called a project budget. With this type of budget, management exercises cost control by deciding the magnitude of the tasks to be undertaken. The emphasis in a project budget is on effectiveness rather than efficiency. Comparisons between actual and budgeted costs are made to ensure that commitments are not exceeded without the knowledge of management. In using an operations budget, however, the pressure is on cost reductions. Another difference between project and operating budgets is that the former is almost always fixed, but the latter may be as flexible as the circumstances dictate.

The following is an outline of a project budget for a staff department:[5]

1   Costs of all activites which must be undertaken and which necessitate no management decision
2   Marginal costs and purposes of all other activities of the department
3   Activities which would have to be pared or canceled with various levels of reduction in the budget
4   Activities which could be increased or started with various levels of increase in the budget

The recommended procedure for budget preparation is to start with the lowest level of responsibility. The budget is then reviewed and consolidated with other budgets at each successive management level as it is forwarded up through the chain of command to top management. The role of the accounting department should be strictly to facilitate providing technical advice and cost data as requested by management.

In preparing the budget itself there is considerable disagreement over the question of a proper starting point. On one side of the argument are those who hold that the person preparing the budget should start with sales as the source of profits and move backwards toward the various cost factors. By putting emphasis on the profit objective, this approach relegates costs to a position depending on what must be done to attain a particular level of profits. The other side looks upon budgets primarily as a defensive tool for the systematic reduction of costs. They would build a budget up from the cost factors. A possible danger in the latter approach is the stressing of cost reduction as the only method for increasing returns. One other shortcoming is that it is less dynamic than the profit approach. However, cost-oriented preparation of a budget is popular in many firms, particularly those whose sales are fairly stable from one period to the next.

Break-even Analysis

Break-even analysis shows the output-value relationships of cost to sales revenue. It can be used along or in conjunction with a bud-

---

[5]John Dearden, *Cost and Budget Analysis,* Englewood Cliffs, N.J.: Prentice-Hall, Inc., 1962, p. 113.

get. Undoubtedly the single major advantage of the break-even concept is flexibility in cost control, a flexibility which is lacking in conventional accounting reports.

Control through the use of break-even analysis is based on an understanding of the effects of specific management decisions on the fixed and variable components of total cost. The break-even point is the point of balance between sales revenue and fixed plus variable costs. It shows management the volume of sales where profits begin and losses stop or vice versa. Movement of the break-even point is a result of changing conditions brought about by managerial decision making. Such a change might be a price change or an increase (decrease) in one of the cost components.

A chart similar to the one in Figure 5.2 is frequently constructed in undertaking a break-even analysis. The basic information needed to construct a chart is a division of total costs into their fixed and variable elements. Fixed costs are shown as a constant amount of dollars which does not vary throughout the year or period of time with the level of sales activity. In a field sales operation, this might include fixed salaries, fringe benefits paid by the firm, office rental and upkeep, utilities, and administrative overhead. Variable costs are entered in direct relation to prescribed units of sales activity. To continue the illustration, suppose each salesman receives a commission based on generated sales volume. Other variable costs would

FIGURE 5.2 Break-even Chart.

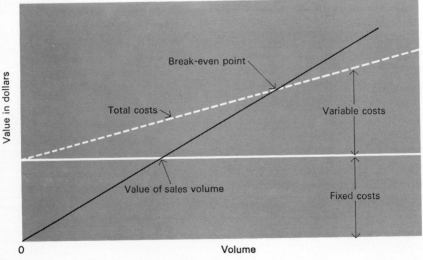

include delivery, warranty servicing, and billing. The last item of information to be added is sales revenue at each of the levels of volume.

To control an operation, management will need to know not only the break-even point but several other relationships shown in break-even analysis. These include:

1   The relationship of the break-even point to the projected sales forecast for the operation
2   The rate at which profits increase past the break-even point
3   The relationship of fixed to variable costs at break-even and forecasted volumes
4   The break-even volume as a percentage of forecasted volume—margin of safety

Break-even analysis can be used in combination with budgeting. The usual procedure is to compare break-even performance with budget requests at the point of forecasted sales volume. Individual differences between the two sets of figures can be obtained by dividing break-even performance by its budgeted counterpart. The lower the percentage thus calculated, the wider the discrepancy between break-even performance and budget request. The following is an example of a comparison for selected variable costs:

VARIABLE COST	BREAK-EVEN PERFORMANCE	BUDGETED COST	CONTROL FACTOR
Selling commissions	$40,000	$40,000	100
Delivery	10,000	11,000	91
Installation	15,000	18,000	83
Warranty servicing	4,000	4,200	95

In taking corrective action, management would start with the widest discrepancy or lowest control factor.

The biggest drawback to break-even analysis is the problem of dividing up total costs into their fixed and variable components. Especially difficult to classify are the so-called semivariable costs such as sales supervision and some of the traveling expenses. With an increasing sales volume these costs will keep repeating a stair-step movement whereby they will vary with sales, then plateau. A decided deterrent to the meaningfulness of break-even analysis is an extensive product offering. It is not possible or practical to analyze each product separately, and grouping products may obscure the control features of the technique.

CORRECTION AND REVISION OF MARKETING PERFORMANCE

The last step in control is now looked upon as taking place before as well as after the fact. It also closes the loop between actuality and planned action. By this it is meant that adjustment or revision of plans to fit reality is part of the last step in control. In actual practice, however, the negative circumstance of finding mistakes and applying penalties persists.

The most basic and at the same time the most troublesome task is remedial action. The obstacle is that management has to work with and through people in bringing about a remedy for a noted deviation from planned performance. Resentment is built up because the person concerned knows he has failed and more importantly he knows his superiors know about it. Remedial action, therefore, should not dwell on the obvious mistake but on how the subordinate as well as the superior can prevent its recurrence. Participation by the subordinate in setting his own standards takes away some of the accompanying tensions and helps turn standards into strong positive incentives.

Closely allied to remedial action is prevention. Preventive action concentrates on anticipating deviations. Its purpose is to keep from making costly mistakes, which usually have a lasting effect on market position. Suppose a monthly report signals an excessive buildup of inventory among distributors in the southeastern part of the United States. On pursuing the matter further, it is found that a new competitor has entered the market and is selling at a very low price. Knowing that any more buildup in inventory could have a disruptive effect on distributor relations, management embarks upon a preventive program. This could include a cutback in deliveries to this area, a special promotional campaign, or an increase in missionary selling efforts by factory men.

Another and very important part of the last step is revising plans to fit actuality or closing the loop, so to speak, between plans and events. To understand this, management must realize that plans are based on estimates of the future. No one can predict the future accurately, so flexibility is incorporated in plans. In the preceding example, the lower competitive price might be deemed permanent, in which case some readjustment would have to be made in the marketing program for that area and possibly other areas of the United States. Unlike the corrective tasks, revision nearly always involves top management.

Many of today's marketers are turning their attention toward the concept of management by exception as it relates to the entire management process and in particular the action step in control. This concept results in a system which signals to a manager only those problems which require his direct action, leaving the other problems for his subordinates. Thus, management need not concern itself with every kind of problem. They can concentrate their efforts because there are fewer problems to tackle. For example, in taking remedial action a general sales manager would consider only such major problems as market share and return on investment, leaving other problems like the failure to obtain the standardized sales-call ratio to the field sales manager. It is also obvious that management by exception emphasizes selectivity in the reporting of information.

Bittel visualizes a threefold problem in adopting management by exception. In the first place, management must discard their instinctive, unconscious approach and replace it with a positive, systematic way of handling every kind of problem encountered. Secondly, management must guard against conformity and a false sense of security. Thirdly, released from the restrictions of routine, management should devote their energies to more creative endeavors.[6]

SUMMARY

Control is the means of keeping an actual operation going according to plan. This is accomplished by (1) keeping planners informed of actual conditions or closing the loop between planned action and actuality and (2) the identification, correction, and prevention of mistakes.

Control is thought of as a three- or four-step process. The first step is to set up standards or yardsticks by which actual performance can be measured. Once this has been done, the next step is to create the tools for recording actual performance. The third step of a four-step process is comparison. When only three steps are considered, comparison is combined with the second step, measurement. Action, the final step, can be corrective or revisionary.

A marketer is confronted with three problems in establishing standards. The most troublesome is finding a standard which is not affected appreciably by factors beyond the control of the individuals being

[6] Lester R. Bittel, *Management by Exception,* New York: McGraw-Hill Book Company, 1964, p. 13.

measured. The other problems are comparability and permanency. General types of standards used in controlling a marketing operation include (1) past performance, (2) market potential, (3) productivity, (4) profit contribution, (5) marketing plans, (6) marketing costs, and (7) job activities. Normally no one standard is complete in itself or appropriate for all businesses. Consequently, planning is the obvious key to the development of control standards.

Collectively the tools for measuring actual performance are called an information network. In developing an information network, two major questions need to be answered: (1) What are the requisites of a good information network? and (2) What is involved in the installation of an information network? The third step in control is comparing actual performance with the applicable standard and analyzing the noted deviation. The Du Pont chart system, budgets, and break-even analysis are illustrative of devices used to accomplish this task.

The last step in control involves corrective and revisionary action. Although the negative image persists, corrective action is now looked upon as taking place before as well as after the fact. Action which takes place after the fact can be called remedial; that which takes place before the fact is preventive. Another and very important part of the last step is revising plans to fit actuality. Revision is usually restricted to the top echelons of management. In taking remedial action, numerous marketers are seriously considering the concept of management by exception. This is the concept whereby only the obviously more important problems are handled by the particular manager. The other problems are handled by subordinates.

DISCUSSION QUESTIONS

1   Explain why control must be concerned with closing the loop between planned action and actuality.
2   Why is control more significant in marketing than in production or finance?
3   Explain how control emphasizes effectiveness rather than efficiency.
4   What are the limitations of using past performance as a standard?
5   Market potential automatically adjusts for competition. What does this statement mean?

6   Criticize the use of a productivity standard.
7   How would you defend the statement that profit is a relative rather than an absolute term?
8   Contrast return on investment with profits as a percentage of sales in their respective roles in control.
9   How does the use of marketing plans help to strengthen the link between control and planning?
10   What evidence can you give that no one standard is complete in itself?
11   What should coverage of vital areas focus on?
12   Explain need-to-know and relate it to the concept of management by exception.
13   Defend Du Pont's concept of investment.
14   Distinguish between an operations budget and a project budget.
15   What difficulties might one experience in using break-even analysis?

SUPPLEMENTARY READING

Alexander, Ralph S., and Thomas L. Berg, *Dynamic Management in Marketing,* Homewood, Ill.: Richard D. Irwin, Inc., 1965, chap. 22.

Bittel, Lester R., *Management by Exception,* New York: McGraw-Hill Book Company, 1964, chaps. 1 and 2.

Dearden, John, *Cost and Budget Analysis,* Englewood Cliffs, N.J.: Prentice-Hall, Inc., 1962.

Emch, Arnold F., "Control Means Action," *Harvard Business Review,* July-August, 1954, pp. 92-98.

Feder, Richard A., "How to Measure Marketing Performance," *Harvard Business Review,* May-June, 1965, 132-142.

Gardner, Fred V., "Breakeven Point Control for Higher Profits," *Harvard Business Review,* September-October, 1954, pp. 123-130.

Gustafson, Philip, "Business Reports: How to Get Facts You Need," *Nation's Business,* August, 1956, pp. 78-82.

How the Du Pont Organization Appraises Its Performance, Financial Management Series, no. 94, New York: American Management Association, 1950.

Perice, James L., "The Budget Comes of Age," *Harvard Business Review,* May-June, 1954, pp. 58-66.

Sevin, Charles H., *Marketing Productivity Analysis,* New York: McGraw-Hill Book Company, 1965.

Sherwin, Douglas S., "The Meaning of Control," *Dun's Review and Modern Industry,* January, 1956, pp. 45+.

Winer, Leon, "A Profit-Oriented Decision System," *Journal of Marketing,* April, 1966, pp. 38-44.

marketing
research

All marketing decisions should be based on information that is pertinent, accurate, and timely. The task of marketing research is to supply this information on a continuing basis so as to enhance the profitability of marketing decisions.

RESEARCH OR FACT GATHERING

Marketing research plays an important and often essential role in managerial decision making. Fact gathering, on the other hand, stands apart from the decision-making process and the problems confronting management. The differences can be identified as definitive and conceptual.

Definitive Differentiation

The most acceptable definition of research is that it is the systematic process of collecting, tabulating, and analyzing data on problems relating to the marketing of goods and services.[1] Fact gathering fits this definition narrowly, but reasearch includes problem definition, interpretation, and presentation.

The first of the additional activities, problem definition, is the process of clearly identifying the actual question or questions that can and should be solved through research. No activity is quite as important as problem definition because it both directs and controls the project. It is hard to imagine a greater waste of effort than finding an answer, even though correct in itself, to a wrong or nebulous question. The initial step in defining the problem is to recognize the casual factors as distinquished from the more obvious symptoms such as a downward trend in sales. Frequently, to accomplish a satisfactory diagnosis, it is necessary to conduct an exploratory study. Such a study might include interviews with members of the marketing organization as well as reviews of internal records and published information. A good rule followed by many researchers in this type of investigation is to assume that someone, somewhere, has studied a situation similar to the one at hand and has published the results.

After diagnosis, the next step is to develop precise terminology. The purpose of this is to prevent confusion in ascertaining the final results of the formalized investigation. Take, for example, the term

[1] Ralph S. Alexander and the Committee on Definitions, *Marketing Definitions,* Chicago: American Marketing Association, 1961, pp. 16-17.

"profit." Quite different perspectives will be obtained of a product, customer, or channel, depending upon how profit is defined. Suppose consideration is focused on the differences between gross profit and net marketing profit. A product or product line which has a high gross profit, or the difference between the value of sales and the cost of goods sold, may have a substantially lower net marketing profit, the latter being defined as gross profit less applicable marketing costs. The third and final step in defining the problem is to list all the possible approaches which might be practical in solving the problem. With the one limitation that all approaches must coincide with company objectives and policies, this step offers an excellent opportunity to break with tradition and make a creative contribution.

Research and fact gathering differ still further in that the tasks of interpretation and presentation are clearly expressed in the former but only implied in the latter. The significance of focusing attention on interpretation and presentation can best be seen if analysis is viewed literally as the culmination of research. Analysis can be defined as the separation of a whole into as many parts as necessary to determine their nature, relative importance, function, and interrelationship. Analysis results in a collection of facts largely incomprehensible to management. Interpretation takes the outflow from analysis and translates it into a form that gives it meaning in relation to a particular problem. Interpretation will also suggest other questions that management may deem important enough for further investigation. In other words, analysis describes in detail what happens, interpretation explains it to management .

The ultimate objective of presentation is complete understanding of the study findings by management. To maximize understanding in presentation, a number of rules should be kept in mind.

1   Keep the reader in mind at all times. A serious mistake for the report writer is to assume that his potential reader's technical background and interests will be the same as his.
2   Be selective in the findings to be included in the main body of the report. Irrelevant facts may be presented in an appendix.
3   Arrange the major findings in a logical manner. The question-by-question analysis should be avoided.
4   Keep the main body of the report as simple as possible. Appendices are an ideal location for the details of research methodology and statistical analytics.
5   Make extensive use of visual techniques, notably tables and charts, to dramatize the more important points of the presentation.

6   Present each research report orally to members of management. Besides encouraging greater understanding, oral presentations help to develop rapport with management.

Conceptual Differentiation

Another basic distinction which can be made between fact gathering and research is the functional role each plays in managerial decision making. Fact gathering is generally conceived of as a staff speciality quite separate from decision making. What role fact gathering has, if any, is usually restricted to an informal one such as directed fact finding. A good example of this is a medical supply company that organized a marketing-research department for the sole purpose of reporting to sales management the field activities of its salesmen.

Research, on the other hand, is a staff activity which has been fully integrated into the decision-making process. It involves the establishment of effective working relationships with line management so that the full potential of research findings can be realized. Seldom, however, is this realized in actual practice.

INTEGRATION OF RESEARCH INTO MARKETING DECISIONS

Industrial marketers experience countless difficulties in integrating research into management decision making. Some progress has been made, but a closer look shows there has been more talk than action. The basic problem is that neither management nor research knows enough about the other to understand how the two are interrelated in the decision-making process.

Roadblocks to Acceptance

Intimacy with their particular market is the principal reason industrial marketers rely upon their own judgment rather than research findings in arriving at decisions. Factors favoring this intimacy are the limited scope of the typical market and the close contacts with customers brought about by direct selling. It is not uncommon to find a vice-president who is on a first-name basis with a sizable proportion of his firm's customers. An obvious weakness of relying solely on personal contacts is that in such a situation the firm can only react to the inevitable changes in the market, not anticipate them. In the parlance of the sports world, the firm is forced into the unenviable position of having to play "the other team's game."

Another deterrent to integration is the lack of communication between line management and research. Even though managers have a very high regard for research, they are hesitant to make greater use of it for fear that it will undermine their position in the company. For example, an advertising manager might think twice before subjecting his "good" ideas to effectiveness testing. Likewise, a sales manager who has always been known for producing sales volume would hesitate to approve a sales analysis. Besides this, a good many line managers lack the ability to delegate, a skill so necessary in utilizing staff specialists such as the market researcher. Researchers, for the most part, have not taken it upon themselves to improve communications. Obsessed with the mechanics of their specialty, researchers have tended to develop a sense of detachment from the realities of everyday marketing. The obvious result is the gathering of facts for their own sake, the suppression of need by technique as well as methodology, and presentations that are at best bewildering to management.

Finally, some industrial marketers, notably small firms, have a decidedly negative attitude toward marketing research. This is fostered not so much by what they have experienced as it is by what they have heard from other businessmen. Research, regardless of its nature, will have practically no chance with managements of small firms who have formed such an attitude until the benefits of fully integrated programs in large firms are patently obvious.

Approaches to Integration
In the past few years several methods have been suggested for gradually removing the aforementioned roadblocks. Working as a catalytic agent in meeting these problems is the ever-increasing adoption of the marketing management concept. The three major approaches which appear to be the most useful are (1) development of a fully coordinated research program, (2) placement of the research department in a proper organizational position, and (3) redefinition of the research director's role. Although each of these approaches may be used separately, it seems only logical to initiate action with all three.

The purpose of a research program is to provide guidelines for the design of studies so that the greatest possible contribution can be made to the marketing knowledge of management. Research programs are based on the product and market strategies formulated to meet the firm's marketing objectives. However, strategies cannot be determined in detail without certain research information. Such a situation dictates the priority of research projects. Another important step that should not be forgotten in the preliminary stages of program development is the initiation of a continuing study of how marketing decisions are made in the particular firm. Some work has been done in this general area by social scientists, but a great deal more needs to be done before the full potential can be obtained from research findings.

Figure 6.1 shows in graphic form the major steps in the evolution of a marketing-research program. Clearly, if the program is to succeed, it must have the wholehearted support of both line and staff managements.

Another help to greater integration of research findings into decision making is proper organizational placement of the research department. There are three important points to consider in choosing a location:

1   Marketing research should be free from the influence of those whom its work affects.

FIGURE 6.1   Evolution of Marketing-research Program.

2 Marketing research should have a location which is conducive to maximum operational efficiency.

3 Marketing research should have the wholehearted support of the executive to whom it reports.[2]

To this list a fourth point might be added: the location of research should be on a high enough organizational level to command the respect of everyone in marketing as well as those in other parts of the company.

These considerations strongly suggest that marketing research report directly to the head of marketing rather than an operating executive, such as the general sales manager. Reporting to the head of marketing permits more direct contact with policy makers and more effective coordination with all the functional areas of marketing. It also emphasizes the vital role marketing research is to play under the marketing management concept. However, resistance from the informal organization can be expected in formally locating marketing research in such a position. To combat this, major consideration should be given to developing vigorous support not only from the executive to whom the department reports, but among each and every member of marketing.

Currently, the most popular approach to integrating research into decision making is redefining the research director's job. This is necessary chiefly because too many directors are research-oriented and not marketing-oriented. Such orientation manifests itself in the research director's inability to talk management's language.

One solution to this problem is to head up the department with a person Newman refers to as a "research generalist."[3] The responsibilities of such a job include:

1 Establishing a mutually satisfactory working relationship with the top marketing executive

2 Acquiring a thorough understanding of marketing problems and the philosophy of the top marketing executive in regard to these problems

3 Suggesting and planning a research program

4 Making sure that the most appropriate technical specialists are called into action at the right time

[2] *Marketing, Business and Commercial Research in Industry,* Studies in Business Policy, no. 72, New York: National Industrial Conference Board, Inc., 1955, p. 7.

[3] Joseph W. Newman, "Put Research into Marketing Decisions," *Harvard Business Review,* March-April, 1962, pp. 105-112.

5   Serving as a middleman between technicans and marketing throughout the research project
6   Helping the marketing manager understand research's contributions to the decision-making process

The implications of such a job description are that the research director becomes a member of the top-management team or at least finds himself in an excellent position to move into top management. There is some disagreement over whether this is the proper role for a director. On one side are those who contend that researchers are more valuable to their companies if they are able to sell themselves and their research. In an article advocating this point of view, a consultant feels that when the marketing-research director takes advantage of his outstanding opportunities, there is no question that he will become a real member of management with broader responsibilities.[4] Opposing this is the contention that having different characteristics and values, researchers should strive for professional excellence, not promotion to other positions, notably those in line management.[5]

Regardless of which side of the controversy is taken, it is obvious that the director must take a more active part in decision making if marketing research is to achieve its full potential. To do this he should:

1   Insist on excellence in all research efforts
2   Direct efforts toward the concept of research
3   Prepare a written research design for every investigation undertaken
4   Constantly sell research throughout the marketing organization
5   Assume full responsibility for research findings
6   Follow up on a continuous basis to see that research expenditures are not being wasted

STATUS OF INDUSTRIAL MARKETING RESEARCH

The surveys undertaken by the American Marketing Association in 1957 and 1963 are particularly helpful in describing the general

[4] Jack O. Vance, "Why Not Promote the Marketing-Research Manager?" *Journal of Marketing,* January, 1959, pp. 253-256.

[5] This stance is ably presented in Stanley L. Payne, "Should the Marketing-Research Manger Be Promoted?" *Journal of Marketing,* July, 1959, pp. 59-61.

status of marketing research in the organizations of industrial-good manufacturers. Status is measured in terms of organization, size, and scope of activities.

Organization of the Marketing-research Function

Three out of every four industrial marketing-research departments in existence at the beginning of 1963 were set up within the preceding ten years. This rate of growth is greater than that experienced by consumer-good manufacturers, particularly in the five-year period 1958 through 1962.

The probability of finding a formal marketing-research department increases with the manufacturer's size in terms of sales volume. For example, 13 percent of the respondent manufacturers with sales of less than $5 million have a formal department as compared with 94

FIGURE 6.2 Formalization of the Marketing-research Function.

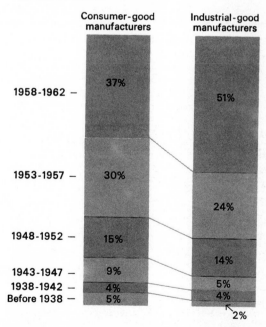

Source: Dik Warren Twedt, ed., *A Survey of Marketing Research* (Chicago: American Marketing Association, 1963) p. 23.

percent of manufacturers having sales in excess of $500 million. A summary of reporting firms by size is as follows:[6]

SIZE OF FIRM (IN MILLIONS OF DOLLARS)	PERCENTAGE OF FIRMS WITH FORMAL DEPARTMENTS
Under 5	13
5 - 25	43
25 - 50	61
50 - 100	80
100 - 200	91
200 - 500	95
Over 500	94

In the majority of firms the person who heads up marketing research reports directly to the principal sales or marketing executive. A comparison between 1957 and 1963 shows a significant drop in the number of research-department heads reporting to top- or corporate-level management. Much of this drop has been absorbed by the growth in

TABLE 6.1   Management Level to Whom the Head of Marketing Research Reports, Industrial-good Manufacturers, 1957 and 1963

HEAD OF MARKETING RESEARCH REPORTS TO	PERCENTAGE OF COMPANIES	
	1957	1963
Top management:		
President and executive vice-president	14 ⎱	9 ⎱
Other corporate or general management:	⎰ 25	⎰ 12
Vice-president, assistant to president, division vice-president, etc.	11 ⎰	3 ⎰
Sales or marketing management:		
Vice-president sales, marketing manager, director of sales, general sales manager, sales manager	59	67
Engineering and development:		
Vice-president, R&D, manager of research and product planning, director new-product development, research director, director, advance planning	14	15
Other	2	6
Total	100	100

Source: Dik Warren Twedt (ed.), *A Survey of Marketing Research,* Chicago: American Marketing Association, 1963, p. 25.

---

[6] Dik Warren Twedt (ed.), *A Survey of Marketing Research,* Chicago: American Marketing Association, 1963, p. 15.

the number responsible to marketing or sales (Table 6.1). The grouping of marketing research with other staff elements in a market-services department is an organizational innovation which has been adopted by several industrial marketers. The organizational arrangement of the marketing-development department of the Monsanto Chemical Company is shown in Figure 6.3.

Size of the Marketing-research Function

Some idea of size can be obtained by looking at budgets and number of persons employed. Larger industrial-good manufacturers spend more money for market research but less as a percentage of sales (Table 6.2). The decided drop in the research budget expressed as a percentage of sales as sales volume increases suggests an absolute rather than a relative basis for the allocation of funds. Irrespective of sales-volume classification, industrial-good manufacturers spend considerably less than their consumer-good counterparts. In fact, the expenditure differential increases as the size of the firm grows larger. As an example, industrial-good manufacturers selling less than $5 million yearly have a median budget which is $1,000 less than that of consumer-good manufacturers of like size. For manufacturers selling between $50 and $100 million yearly the differential is $50,000 with industrial-good manufacturers having a median budget of $50,000 and consumer-good manufacturers, $100,000. Among the largest firms, manufacturers with over $500 million in annual sales, industrial-good manufacturers are outspent by nearly $370,000.[7]

The size of the research function in terms of personnel increases as the industrial-good manufacturer does more business (Table 6.3).

TABLE 6.2 Marketing-research Budgets by Size of Company, 1962

SIZE OF MANUFACTURER (IN MILLIONS OF SALES DOLLARS)	MEDIAN	
	THOUSANDS OF DOLLARS	PERCENTAGE OF SALES
Under 5	11	0.30
5 - 25	25	0.20
25 - 50	30	0.10
50 - 100	50	0.10
100 - 200	70	0.08
200 - 500	130	0.05
Over 500	232	0.03

Source: Dik Warren Twedt (ed.), *A Survey of Marketing Research*, Chicago: American Marketing Association, 1963, pp. 30 and 32.

[7] *Ibid.*, pp. 30 and 32.

FIGURE 6.3   Monsanto Company Advertising and Market-development Department

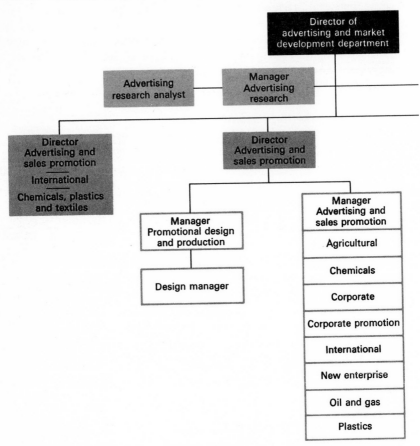

The rate of increase, however, is not as great as that noted earlier for monetary funds. It is also interesting to find that while there is wide disparity between industrial-good and consumer-good manufacturers in the matter of budgeting for research, the sizes of departments in terms of full-time employees closely parallel each other.

Range of Research Activities

A wide variety of activities are performed by marketing-research departments of industrial-good manufacturers. Some idea of the extent of these activities can be gained from the thirty-four topic headings

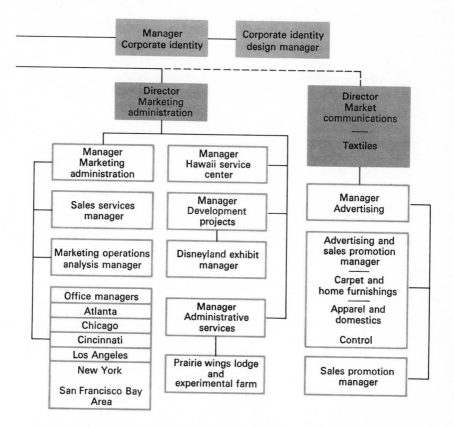

used by the American Marketing Association in reporting this information. Those activities which a majority of firms with research departments reported as being engaged in are listed in Table 6.4. Also shown in the table are the relative degrees of reliance placed on internal research capabilities and on outside agencies. Although industrial-good manufacturers engage in a sizable number of different research activities, there is a strong tendency to involve departments other than research in the project. Then, too, industrial-good manufacturers seldom resort to outside research assistance. As for the monetary appropriation, industrial-good manufacturers in aggregate reported spending about one out of every ten research dollars for outside work in 1962. This is much less than the 37 percent budgeted for outside agencies by consumer-good manufacturers during that year.[8]

MAJOR TYPES OF RESEARCH ACTIVITIES

The research activities undertaken or commissioned out by industrial marketers can be grouped under six major headings: sales, product, consumer or market, competition, advertising, and corporate or economic.

Sales Research

The purpose of sales research is twofold. In the first place, it attempts through analysis to determine the who, what, where, when, and how of existing sales volume. Secondly, through forecasting, sales research attempts to measure future sales volume, principally in terms of magnitude.

The most fundamental and at the same time rewarding sales research activity is *analysis.* Defined as the systematic study and comparison of sales data,[9] analysis has as its primary purpose the organization of sales results along lines that may be useful in pointing out strengths and weaknesses to attain a proper perspective. The bulk of data used in analysis is obtained from the sales invoice. Other possible internal sources include sales-call reports and salesman-expense records.

TABLE 6.3   Full-time Employees in Formalized Departments, 1962

SIZE OF MANUFACTURER (IN MILLIONS OF SALES DOLLARS)	MEDIAN NUMBER	
	INDUSTRIAL-GOOD MANUFACTURERS	CONSUMER-GOOD MANUFACTURERS
5-25	2	2
25-50	2	3
50-100	3	4
100-200	4	7
200-500	7	7
Over 500	10	12

Source: Dik Warren Twedt (ed.), *A Survey of Marketing Research,* Chicago: American Marketing Association, 1963, p. 18.

[8] *Ibid.,* p. 38.

[9] Ralph S. Alexander and the Committee on Definitions, *op. cit.,* p. 20.

Two major questions have to be answered before effective analysis can begin. The first concerns the measurement of sales volume: is it to be in terms of dollars or physical units? For many industrial marketers physical units are preferable to dollars. One reason is that sales data expressed in physical units readily correspond to measurements of productive capacity, a very crucial operating consideration in such industries as chemicals, cement, and steel. Another reason is that comparisons using dollars are relatively meaningless when prices fluctuate widely, as so often happens, over short periods of time and among various sales areas.

The second question is what basis or bases shall be employed in analyzing the data. Because the primary purpose of any sales analysis is to foster awareness throughout the marketing organization, the two bases, product and customer, are used extensively in the

TABLE 6.4   Marketing-research Activities Performed by a Majority of Manufacturers with Formal Departments, 1962

TYPE OF RESEARCH ACTIVITY	PERCENTAGE OF COMPANIES		
		DONE BY	
	DOING	MARKETING RESEARCH	OUTSIDE FIRM
Sales analysis	94	74	
Market-share analysis	94	89	1
Market-potential development	94	92	1
Economic forecasting (up to one year)	92	72	1
New-product acceptance	92	83	3
Competitive-product study	92	78	3
Market characteristics	92	89	2
Economic forecasting (over one year)	91	77	1
Business-trend study	90	78	2
Sales quotas, territories	90	57	
Diversification study	84	62	2
Profit and/or value analysis	83	32	1
Product testing	81	31	2
Purchases of companies, sales of divisions	81	41	2
Distribution-channel and cost studies	80	55	8
Plant and warehouse location	76	40	2
Sales-compensation study	73	32	3
Export and international study	72	41	2
Packaging research design or physical characteristics	59	16	6
Ad-effectiveness study	57	16	26
Media	53	11	26

Source: Dik Warren Twedt (ed.), *A Survey of Marketing Research*, Chicago: American Marketing Association, 1963, p. 44.

initial stages. Usually the results of product and customer analysis disclose that a relatively small proportion of the product line and the actual market account for almost all the sales volume. For example, it is not uncommon to find that 20 percent or less of a firm's customers are responsible for 80 percent or more of the sales volume. After being identified, these major product types and customers are frequently labeled "key" products and "key" accounts.

As management's desire for more facts becomes greater, the analysis program progresses by the use of other bases or combinations of bases. Among the many bases available are geographical territory, salesman, time period, and marketing channel. Probably the most sophisticated approaches are those that combine two or more bases. A good example is an analysis of product sales by type to different classes of customers located in each of the particular sales territories.

Sales analysis reaches its most advanced form when the findings are refined through the application of distribution costs. Distribution or marketing-cost analysis is a study of the relative profitability or costs of performing specific marketing functions using such bases as customer, product, salesman, and order size. Its principal purpose is to aid marketing management in evaluating the efficiency of the individual segments of the marketing organization. Reference to Table 6.4 shows that while eight out of every ten respondent firms are engaged in distribution-cost studies, most of the work is done outside the marketing-research department, undoubtedly by accounting. The reasons for accounting having the responsibility are rather obvious. For one thing, marketing-cost analysis is predicated on the information from cost accounting. Also, the techniques of marketing-cost analysis are primarily variations of those used originally with production costs.

Forecasting is the estimating of future sales for a given period of time, usually a year. The resulting projection serves as the point of departure for all planning in the business organization. In addition to allocating marketing effort, sales forecasts form the basis for such important operations as plant output scheduling and cash-flow budgeting. With no acceptable alternative, almost every industrial marketer is compelled to forecast sales in one way or the other.

Formal approaches to sales forecasting can be broadly classified as discretionary and statistical. Discretionary forecasts assume that the variables affecting sales can best be interpreted by individual or collective judgments. Much of the popularity of discretionary methods stems from the fact that qualitative as well as quantitative variables are considered.

EXECUTIVE OPINION   This type of forecast is prepared from executive judgments of probable changes in variables deemed to be important to future sales. The standard approach is to review and weigh after due consideration all the variable factors which might bring about a change. A distinction is usually made between internal and external factors. Some of the more important variables are:

Internal Factors
1   New products or modifications in existing line
2   Patent qualifications
3   Pricing policies
4   Advertising and sales-promotion programs
5   Field sales personnel
6   Utilization of marketing channels
7   Service programs

External Factors
1   General economic conditions
2   Government relationships
3   Actions of competitors
4   Purchasing policies of customers
5   Growth or decline patterns of customer-industry groupings

If more than one executive is assigned the task, some way must be developed for reconciling differences. Strict averaging is to be avoided because it implies that the overestimates will equal the underestimates. This is hardly likely to happen in actual situations. One way adopted by many firms is to have the designated executives reach agreement through committee action. Another way is for the chief executive to use the forecasts as planning guides in arriving at a final decision.

Besides being very simple, executive opinion is advantageous because it constantly directs the attention of the executive to the marketplace. In the vernacular of the trade this is often referred to as acquiring a "feel" of the market. The major disadvantage is the exclusive reliance upon individual opinion which is subject to all forms of bias.

SALES FORCE COMPOSITE   There is a great deal of similarity between this type of forecast and executive opinion. The only difference is that salesmen rather than executives prepare the initial sales estimates. Field sales managers are charged with the task of cumulating the estimates and making whatever revisions they feel are necessary. The aggregated estimates are then forwarded to the home office, where they are combined into an overall company prediction.

Some firms have each management level go over the forecast with the subordinate responsible for developing it. A comparison with the previous year is the usual basis for the discussion. The advantage of such a review is that it emphasizes the responsibility of the subordinate for preparing the forecast.

Having the salesman prepare the estimate alerts him to thinking of his customers in terms of potential rather than actual sales. With this attitude, the salesman should develop greater accuracy in pinpointing prospects in his territory. More important, however, is that this technique allows the salesman the opportunity to participate in setting goals for his own performance. He will undoubtedly feel such goals are far more equitable than those established without his counsel.

There are several limitations to the sales force composite forecast. Probably the most serious is that salesmen, generally, are not in a position to know all the variables affecting future sales. Their experiences with a customer are often only a small part of the total picture. Also, being optimistic by nature, salesmen will tend to overstate their conclusions. A second limitation exists when salesmen are paid on the basis of quotas derived from their own estimates. In such situations, salesmen will undoubtedly play it safe by estimating on the low side. Finally, the estimate's value may be negligible because the salesman with an antipathy to all paper work does not give it sufficient attention.

CUSTOMER-INTENTION SURVEY   This discretionary approach enumerates the requirements of customers for a coming period of time. Salesmen are relied upon by most firms to obtain the desired information by canvassing every account. Reports of salesmen are then cross-checked with previous surveys and past sales records before being compiled as a company forecast.

This approach has been found to be very useful to industrial marketers especially those supplying capital goods, because the typical customer tends to plan his needs fairly well in advance. Also the relatively small number of customers served by many industrial marketers makes this type of survey more economically feasible for them than it would be for their consumer-good counterparts.

Of course the accuracy of a customer-intention survey is wholly dependent upon the customer's ability to forecast his own sales. To offset this inherent disadvantage, several industrial marketers by-pass the immediate customer and devote major attention to his market. A study of a customer's market, however, can prove to be very costly.

MARKET CANVASS   A variation of the customer-intention survey, this type of forecast depends upon each salesman's collecting information on total past-year purchases of a given product or products from every customer, actual or prospective, within his particular territory. The use of the market canvass tends to be restricted, however, to industrial marketers who have a limited market which is fairly well defined.

One large steel firm feels that a complete enumeration of all consumers every year is an essential part of their forecasting program. The marketing-research department prepares for each mill-lot consumer of steel products a report form showing the figures from the previous year's survey and total annual shipments made by this firm. The form is then forwarded to the salesman with instructions to determine to the best of his ability total purchases of individual consumers from all sources of supply during the past year. The salesman is considered the key to recording steel-industry shipments in terms of geographical areas.

OPINION SURVEY   Some industrial marketers survey those who they feel are most highly qualified to give an expert opinion on future business conditions: either generally or for a specific market segment. Among those frequently polled are economists, bankers, and business leaders. Typically this type of survey is used to supplement other forcasting techniques. For example, a manufacturer of building-construction materials will probably find it desirable to compare his forecast with the annual economic report published by the F. W. Dodge Corporation.

Statistical forecasts are predictions resulting from the application of statistical techniques to historical data and market-potentiality studies, used separately or in conjunction with each other. The growing popularity of statistical forecasts is directly attributable to (1) the desire of managers everywhere to quantify the decision-making process as much as it is practical and (2) the growing availability of electronic data processing equipment which has both speeded up and increased the flow of information.

Two statistical techniques, time-series analysis and correlation, rely extensively upon historical data. The underlying assumption in the use of historical data is that the conditions which determined past sales will continue on into the future without significant alteration.

TIME-SERIES ANALYSIS   One of the most commonly used forecasting techniques, time-series analysis relates sales to time in an effort to establish for future projection the patterns of variable factors causing observable fluctuation. These variable factors can be separated into four general movements: long-term trend, cyclical, seasonal, and irregular or erratic.

A sales forecast based on a projection of the past trend is often used by firms that have experienced a constant sales growth. Identification of cyclical movements is an important help to firms whose sales are significantly influenced by replacement and inventory policy changes. Adjustments for recurrent seasonal variations allow many firms to make forecasts for periods of less than a year. The usual procedure is to use monthly indexes to adjust the yearly sales forecast.

CORRELATION   A forecast can be developed by correlating or measuring the degree of association between sales and other independent variables in the industry or the economy. Simple correlation uses only one independent variable; in multiple correlation two or more are used. Partial correlation analyzes the association of one variable with the other being considered.

Correlation is a much more sophisticated approach than time-series analysis and requires a high degree of technical competence in the forecaster. Often such a person is not available to the small-size firm.

Owing to the derived nature of industrial demand, many marketers seek out independent variables which will lead or precede the sale of their products. The most logical leading indicators are the sales of end products. To illustrate, manufacturers of heating and air-conditioning systems may find that their sales lag behind the letting of building-construction permits. However, the change relationships involved in lead-lag analysis, at best, predict only general shifts in the market.

When the change relationships between sales and other variables are fairly close, econometric models are often constructed. Such models are useful devices for converting estimates of independent variables into sales forecasts. The use of models, however, does not preclude the necessity for continuous study of independent variables, their nature and extent of influence. A good rule of thumb to follow is that any relationship will rarely remain fixed over an extended period of time.

Forecasting techniques applied to market-potentiality studies are essentially projective. Market potentials are derived by projecting study returns using a single or multiple series of published statistical data. The function of the statistical series is to measure the relative purchasing power of each market segment.

The following census data are used frequently as series to project industrial-market activity:

1   Number of plants
2   Value added by manufacturing
3   Value of shipments
4   Number of production workers
5   Value of materials consumed
6   Value of fuels and electrical energy consumed
7   Expenditures for new plant and equipment

There are two sources of possible error in projecting studies of market potential by means of statistical series. The first is the assumption of a fixed relationship between the selected series and the potential for a given product throughout the entire market. It is hardly likely that such a situation will ever exist, and so some inherent error will be present in the best of circumstances. A second source of error is the tendency of a statistical series to magnify the inherent sampling errors contained in the basic market study. It cannot be assumed that all of these errors will cancel each other out.

In addition to analysis and forecasting, which are principally continuous, marketing research will be called upon to undertake certain intermittent sales-related activities. These include sales-compensation studies, analysis of sales-contest results, difficulty analyses, and evaluation of sales training programs.

Product Research
Product research performed by the marketing-research organization can be divided into three major project areas: technical use, product use, and new-product acceptance. Technical-use research strives to determine the performance characteristics of a given product. At the present time most of this type of work is being done by engineers and other technical personnel located outside the marketing-research department. Often research undertaken in such an organizational environment does not visualize performance characteristics in terms

of consumer needs. Too much stress is placed on testing those characteristics which may be of little or no value to the consumer. The following hypothetical example may help to illustrate the necessity for focusing attention on consumer needs.

Suppose the technical research conducted by an industrial valve manufacturer has been devoted exclusively to pressure and temperature ratings. However, a survey of the principal market, the paper and pulp industry, disclosed that neither pressure nor temperature represents a problem to the individual mill. Furthermore, there is very little difference in pressure and temperature requirements among mills. What does concern these consumers in terms of technical performance is the corrosion-erosion of valve materials and the side effects.

Surprisingly, many manufacturers of industrial goods are unaware of the various customer adaptations which have been made in their products. Probably the most unusual illustration of this was the use of baby diapers by a firm that processed optics. Diaper cloth, it seems, has certain absorbent qualities which are highly desirable in polishing operations. The purpose of product-use research is to determine, primarily from the customer, the existing and possible uses of a given item. Also revealed by this type of product research are the changes, if any, which are necessary in order to develop a more acceptable product. When packaging is an important marketing consideration, it too is included in what might be called product-use research.

What is the best type of research design for studying product use? The answer depends upon how much is known already about the uses of a particular product. When knowledge is at a minimum, descriptions of the various uses in their particular operating environments are all that is desired at this time. The case method is the most advantageous here because it studies every aspect of a real situation. The following example may help to illustrate this more clearly.

A new type of adjustable shelving had been on the market for a number of years with limited success. It was originally designed to serve as inexpensive and flexible storage for light manufacturing, but no attempt had been made to keep up with the market. Sales were handled exclusively by industrial distributors. In an effort to determine how the product was being used, the manufacturer conducted case studies of selected customers whose names were submitted to him by industrial distributors. The studies revealed a wide range of applications, not all of which were related to the storage function. For example, a speciality box assembler had even used the shelving to construct his assembly line. One very interesting point brought out by the study was that low-cost considerations completely over-shadowed performance. In one instance, shelving was being used to store heavy objects; in another, it was placed outside as yard storage.

When the uses of the product are known, either through study or experience, more accurate generalizations, such as the extent of usage and the usage by type of customer, are indicated. Statistical studies, in which only a few variable factors are studied in a large number of cases, permit this. Using probability sampling methods, it is even possible to measure mathematically the reliability of estimates made from statistical studies. Therefore, in the preceding example, the changes in shelving to comply with uses could be weighted by the results of a statistical study. Many of the changes might not be advisable because the extent of use would not be sufficient to justify the added cost.

A study by the American Marketing Association found that new-product-acceptance research is performed by almost all the industrial-good manufacturers with formal research departments and a majority of those without (Table 6.4). There are two phases to this type of product research, based upon when it is done in the product development sequence. The first is concerned with determining market reactions to the proposed product prior to commercialization. The purpose is to provide marketing management with more accurate appraisals of product potential during the intermediate stages of development. Such information is almost indispensable when the product idea is not directly comparable to the firm's present offerings or to other established products on the market.

One way to test product acceptance before commercialization is to survey customers who are representative of the various potential market segments to determine their reactions to a model or prototype of the product. About the only danger is the risk of revealing a new-product idea to the competition before being ready for an aggressive marketing effort. Another way to pretest acceptability is to place the new product with a select group of customers. In using this approach, the experiences of the Speer Carbon Company have been that it is advisable to limit the test customers to one convenient geographical area. Having test customers near at hand permits the ironing out of the inevitable bugs at a reduced service cost and with a minimum loss in goodwill.

The second phase of product-acceptance research analyzes new-product sales, usually by customer type and area, in an effort to measure market acceptance during introduction. The evidence accumulated will help marketing management define the degrees of progress the new product is making during the crucial introduction period. A major limitation is the difficulty of interpreting the results of introduction tests. The many extraneous factors which can affect the results must be weeded out to arrive at a proper interpretation. Another limitation is the unreasonable length of time the test may have to run, thus adding to research costs and prolonging the decision on the given product.

Market Research

Normally, market research or analysis is said to involve the continual identification and characterization of the demand function for a given product or line of products. Identification and measurement of the total market to arrive at potential aid the industrial marketer in achieving greater effectiveness and efficiency in allocating marketing resources. It would be almost impossible, for example, to follow a policy of market segmentation without extensive information regarding market potential. Other uses of market-potential information include:

1 The determination of sales territories
2 The development of quotas and other techniques for control of sales force performance
3 The selection of marketing channels to reach the various segments of the market
4 The measurement of market share or penetration
5 The targeting of prospective customers

In analyzing industrial markets, researchers rely extensively on published statistics. The basic source of information is the Census of Manufactures. Other prominent sources include specific documents prepared periodically by the Department of Commerce, trade association reports, and studies by various publications such as the *American Machinist Inventory of Metalworking Equipment.* Because almost all these data are categorized by Standard Industrial Classification Code, industrial market segments are usually identified by the same numbering system.

Extremely helpful in pinpointing customers and prospects in a given market or segment are the so-called plant lists sold by business-magazine publishers. The lists available from the McGraw-Hill Research Department contain the names and addresses, number of employees, and the primary and secondary products made by manufacturing plants with twenty or more employees (see Figure 6.4 for an example). Lists can be obtained in the form of listing sheets, cards,

FIGURE 6.4 Plant Lists of McGraw-Hill Research Department.

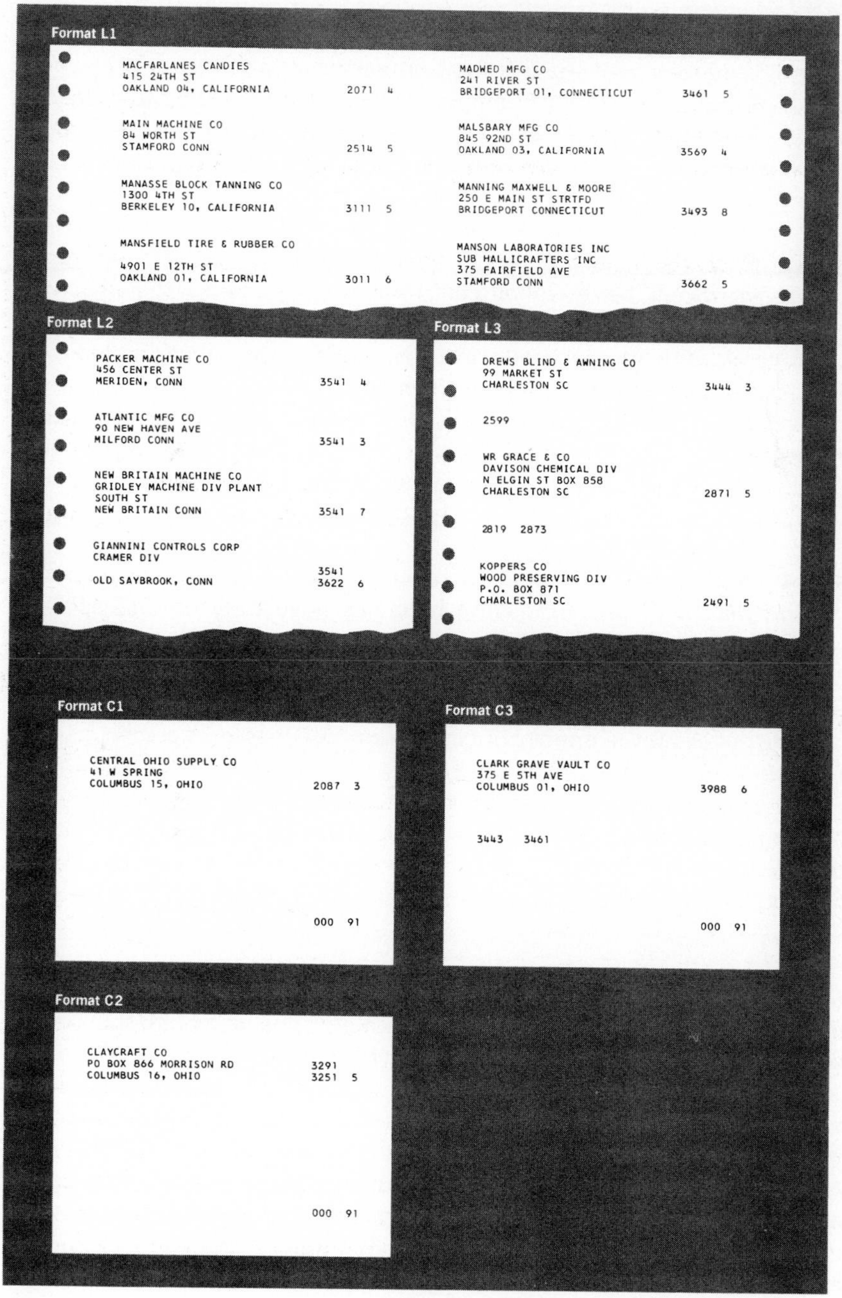

Format L1

```
MACFARLANES CANDIES              MADWED MFG CO
415 24TH ST                      241 RIVER ST
OAKLAND 04, CALIFORNIA   2071  4 BRIDGEPORT 01, CONNECTICUT   3461  5


MAIN MACHINE CO                  MALSBARY MFG CO
84 WORTH ST                      845 92ND ST
STAMFORD CONN            2514  5 OAKLAND 03, CALIFORNIA      3569  4


MANASSE BLOCK TANNING CO         MANNING MAXWELL & MOORE
1300 4TH ST                      250 E MAIN ST STRTFD
BERKELEY 10, CALIFORNIA  3111  5 BRIDGEPORT CONNECTICUT      3493  8


MANSFIELD TIRE & RUBBER CO       MANSON LABORATORIES INC
                                 SUB HALLICRAFTERS INC
4901 E 12TH ST                   375 FAIRFIELD AVE
OAKLAND 01, CALIFORNIA   3011  6 STAMFORD CONN               3662  5
```

Format L2

```
PACKER MACHINE CO
456 CENTER ST
MERIDEN, CONN           3541  4


ATLANTIC MFG CO
90 NEW HAVEN AVE
MILFORD CONN            3541  3


NEW BRITAIN MACHINE CO
GRIDLEY MACHINE DIV PLANT
SOUTH ST
NEW BRITAIN CONN        3541  7


GIANNINI CONTROLS CORP
CRAMER DIV
                        3541
OLD SAYBROOK, CONN      3622  6
```

Format L3

```
DREWS BLIND & AWNING CO
99 MARKET ST
CHARLESTON SC           3444  3


2599


WR GRACE & CO
DAVISON CHEMICAL DIV
N ELGIN ST BOX 858
CHARLESTON SC           2871  5


2819  2873


KOPPERS CO
WOOD PRESERVING DIV
P.O. BOX 871
CHARLESTON SC           2491  5
```

Format C1

```
CENTRAL OHIO SUPPLY CO
41 W SPRING
COLUMBUS 15, OHIO       2087  3




000  91
```

Format C3

```
CLARK GRAVE VAULT CO
375 E 5TH AVE
COLUMBUS 01, OHIO       3988  6


3443   3461




000  91
```

Format C2

```
CLAYCRAFT CO
PO BOX 866 MORRISON RD  3291
COLUMBUS 16, OHIO       3251  5




000  91
```

punched cards, or magnetic tape. Similar lists are sold by *Iron Age* and *Sales Management.*

Field surveys by personal interview, telephone, or mail questionnaire provide most of the information on market characteristics. The objective is to secure more insight into (1) the product requirements of the consumer and (2) the buying practices and needs of the consumer. If the firm has a marketing-research department, it is usually here that such work is done (Table 6.4).

A study of market characteristics offers a wealth of information to the firm which is adopting the marketing management concept or has no direct buyer-seller communication because the products are distributed through middlemen. A pumping-equipment manufacturer, in allocating the efforts of his sales force, was inclined toward growers with large irrigation systems until a market-characteristics study showed that the service demands for this type of customer were greater than his organization would ever be able to provide. As the result of another study, a manufacturer of aircraft components found that his organization was the only supplier that would do precision machining at no extra cost.

The techniques of motivation research which are aimed at determining the "why" of purchasing behavior have only limited application for the industrial marketer. In an isolated situation a consultant was hired by a firm to study purchasing behavior through group discussions with customer panels. Although scarcely anything new was discovered, the sponsoring firm did feel that group discussions provide customers with an opportunity to get what is bothering them "off their chests." Such therapeutic values, however, do not outweigh the practical obstacles to the use of motivation research techniques in industrial marketing. Perhaps the most formidable of these obstacles is the small role emotional motives play in the buying process.

Competitor Research

Whereas no military commander or athletic coach would think seriously of entering into an engagement without a good idea of the opposing forces, industrial marketers make decisions occasionally without any information whatsoever on competitors. At no time are the consequences of ignoring competitors more evident than when a marketing organization develops almost semiparalysis upon learning of a drastic change in the marketing program of a major competitor.

The view that any attempt to obtain information about competitors is unethical has been the biggest deterrent to research of this type. To be sure, there have been and will continue to be scattered instances of unethical conduct in investigating competitors but this should not keep a marketer from installing such a research program. Cognizance of competitor actions is an absolute must for the marketer who hopes to adopt tactics which are both effective and efficient.

What any industrial marketer will want to know about his competitors is briefly summarized by the following questions:

1   Who are the competitors? The names, locations, manpower, organizational structure, markets, sales, and profits are among the items of identifying information which should be collected for every competitor, particularly the major ones.
2   What are the marketing and technical characteristics of competitors' products? As many products as possible should be subjected to the same tests as the firm's own products so that comparative evaluations can be made. A marketer may even go so far as to study the uses customers make of competitors' products. Realization of the need for studies of this type is borne out by the high proportion of respondent firms in the American Marketing Association survey who indicated they regularly engage in such research (Table 6.4).
3   How do competitors market their products? Comprehensive studies should be made of competitors' marketing programs. Factors to consider are marketing channels, type of salesman, sales training, use of sales contests, methods of compensating salesmen, advertising, and pricing policies.

Although the principal source of information on competitors is the salesman, most companies rely too heavily on him for collecting data. As a result they do not exploit other sources which may be quite valuable in certain circumstances. The purchasing department is an excellent internal source which is frequently ignored. The purchasing agent can learn a lot about competitors through suppliers, particularly in regard to the new products and processes which are in the planning stages. Many companies feel that supplier information relayed through the purchasing agent is the best source in the industrial field, much better than the salesman because there is less chance that it will be biased. Outside consultants as a third party are extremely valuable in acquiring data which are not otherwise available.

To get the most out of competitor research, the following points should be kept in mind in designing a program:

1   Be selective, collect only essential data.
2   Exploit every possible source, at least in the introductory stages, until a full appraisal can be made.

3   Set up processing and communication operations which will supply on a routine basis accurate and timely information to all interested members of the organization.
4   Educate all concerned as to the role they are to play in the program. In particular stress that sufficient data are available without resorting to unethical means.

Advertising Research

Research of this type counsels the industrial marketer in two major advertising decisions—selection of media and selection of ad messages. Information on the other major advertising decision, selection of appeals, is best obtained from product and market-research activities. Because most industrial marketers do not attach much importance to advertising as a tool, it is less likely that they will undertake studies of this kind. The data contained in Table 6.4 show that only a little more than 50 percent of the respondent firms with research departments engage in either media research or studies of ad effectiveness. Of firms without a research department, the relative number doing advertising research in these two areas is appreciably smaller.

Media research includes all the different types of studies used to evaluate the exposures of the various media under consideration. The sources for most of these data are outside the marketing-research department (Table 6.4). Advertising is probably the other department in the firm most actively engaged in the media research. Among the outside firms, the most prominent is the Audit Bureau of Circulation, more commonly referred to as the ABC. This impartial agency verifies the circulation claims of member newspapers and magazines. Magazine publishers are another type of outside firm which supplies media information, more notably reader profiles. To aid in the analysis of media-supplied information, the Association of Industrial Advertisers has developed a standard Media Data Form for the use of publishers in reporting media information (Figure 14.1).

Tests for effectiveness of messages are made after an ad has run to determine what changes should be made in planning future campaigns. As in the case of media research, most of these studies are undertaken outside the marketing-research department (Table 6.4).

There are four basic designs used in testing ad effectiveness. Two of them, recall and recognition, attempt to measure the impression made by the advertising message. If a relationship can be said to exist between advertising remembrance and sales, these tests have a great deal of validity. The best-known recognition tests are the readership studies conducted by Daniel Starch and Staff. The Starch procedure measures readership in terms of noted, seen and associated, and read most.

Although sales results are the only true measure of advertising effectiveness, measurement is all but impossible. The problem is even greater in the industrial market, principally because of the manifold purchasing influences and the extended time lag between impression and purchase. Because the sole objective of many industrial ads is to provoke direct response, the worth of separate ads can be judged by inquiry tests. This type of test can be designed to measure quantitatively different ads in the same medium, the same ad in different media, and different offers with any combination of the preceding. The readers' service listings supplied to advertisers by publishers are helpful in rating the inquiries in regard to originator.

Corporate Research

The purpose of corporate research is to provide a factual basis for planning the overall operations of the firm. In many large organizations, this type of research is a separate department attached to general management at the home office. Among the activities commonly grouped under the heading of corporate research are:

1 Economic forecasting, both short- and long-range
2 Location studies for plants and warehouses
3 Diversification studies
4 Situational audits of firms which might someday be purchased
5 Studies of the export and international markets
6 Applicability studies of linear programming and operations-research techniques

According to the American Marketing Association survey, value analysis, PERT, and employee morale studies are other projects which are assigned to corporate research by industrial-good manufacturers. It is also quite likely that corporate research would handle (at least in the initial stages) special projects such as linking up field salesmen with computers.

MARKETING RESEARCH FOR SMALLER FIRMS

A substantial number of smaller firms do not engage in marketing research although their managements freely admit that survival may depend upon its use. Perpetuating this ambivalence is the feeling, often justified, that any undertaking in this field would be too great a financial burden.

Often overlooked by the small marketer are several approaches which are possible on a modest budget. One is to build a library of marketing facts. The U.S. Department of Commerce is the biggest single source of marketing information. A majority of its publications are available at little or no cost. A visit to one of the field offices in a major city would be a good starting point. *The Marketing Information Guide* provides on a monthly basis an up-to-date listing of current marketing publications, governmental as well as private. Other fairly economical sources of marketing information include trade associations, vertical and horizontal business media, industrial buyers' guides such as *Thomas' Register,* and industrial directories.

Another approach is to retain a consultant on a project basis. This is advisable when specific information is needed for a crucial decision. To keep from wasting research dollars, it is imperative that the selected consultant has a good understanding of the problems and full agreement is reached on the essentials of the research design. A further reduction in costs will be possible if an arrangement can be made with the consultant to handle within the firm all the clerical and tabulation work on the project.

Yet another approach is what consultants have come to call do-it-almost-by-yourself marketing research.[10] What happens is that the consultant sets up a program whereby a client's employee is indoctrinated, supervised, and assisted in conducting a study. The advantages of this approach to the firm are twofold. In the first place, the firm obtains the desired research for much less than would be possible under other circumstances. Secondly, the firm now has a valuable asset in the employee or employees who took part in the study.

SUMMARY

In providing pertinent, accurate, and timely information, marketing research helps to enhance the profitability of marketing decisions. Distinct differences can be noted between marketing research and fact gathering. Definitively, the term research is more comprehensive in that it includes a broader range of activities, which includes problem definition, interpretation, and presentation. From a concep-

---

[10] For a more detailed explanation see H. Jay Bullen, "Do-It-Almost-By-Yourself Research for the Smaller Company," *Industrial Marketing,* December, 1963, pp. 77-81.

tual standpoint, the differences between research and fact gathering are based on the role of each in the decision-making process. Research is fully integrated into decision making, but fact gathering is generally conceived of as a separate staff speciality concerned with directed fact finding.

Several roadblocks deter the integration of research into decision making. The most basic is that neither management nor research knows enough about the other to understand how their roles are interrelated. Another formidable roadblock is the industrial marketer's intimacy with his own particular market. Other noticeable roadblocks are the lack of communication between management and research, and the negative attitude of some industrial marketers toward research.

To circumvent these roadblocks, three approaches can be suggested. First a fully coordinated research program should be developed. Second, the research department should be placed in an appropriate organizational position. Third, the job of the research director should be redefined. The third approach appears to be the most popular of the three at the present time.

The status of marketing research in the organizations of industrial-good manufacturers can be summarized as follows:

1 The formalization of the marketing-research function as departments has taken place primarily in recent years.
2 The probability of having a research department increases with the manufacturer's size in terms of sales volume.
3 The person in charge of the marketing-research department will report to top marketing or sales management among a substantial majority of manufacturers.
4 The larger industrial-good manufacturer spends more money on research but less as a proportion of sales.
5 The industrial-good manufacturer, regardless of size, spends less on research than his counterparts manufacturing consumer goods.
6 The marketing-research department of an industrial-good manufacturer performs a wide variety of activities.

Research activities undertaken or commissioned out by industrial marketers can be grouped under sales, product, market, competitor, and corporate. Sales research involves both analysis and forecasting. Analysis provides a proper perspective toward sales; forecasts are the cornerstone of business planning. Product research can be divided into three major project areas: technical use, product use, and new-product acceptance. New-product acceptance will be phased in during the intermediate stages of product development as well as during introduction.

Market research is the identification and characterization of the demand function for a given product or line of products. Its most vital contribution is the determination of market potential. Another important part of market research is the study of consumer characteristics. Such studies provide more insight into (1) the product requirements of the consumer and (2) the buying practices and needs of the consumer.

Research on competitor actions, although restricted by ethical considerations, is a must for the marketer who hopes to develop effective and efficient tactics. Proper design of competitor-research programs will help to lessen much of the concern over ethics. Advertising research counsels the industrial marketer on the questions of media selection and ad effectiveness. The purpose of corporate research is to provide a factual basis for planning the overall operations of the firm. With such a goal corporate research will often exist as a separate department attached to corporate headquarters.

Many smaller firms do not engage in marketing research because of the large financial burden, but they overlook several approaches which are possible on a modest budget. One of these is to build a library of marketing facts. Another is to retain a consultant to set up what is called a do-it-almost-by-yourself marketing-research study.

DISCUSSION QUESTIONS

1   Explain the differences between research and fact gathering.
2   Why is problem definition perhaps the most important research activity?
3   Discuss how a fully coordinated research program can strengthen communications between management and research.
4   What qualifications does a research generalist have that are not found in the typical research director?
5   How does sales analysis develop a proper perspective?
6   What advantages accrue from having salesmen collect the data for sales forecasting?
7   In product-acceptance testing during introduction, why does interpretation present a significant problem?
8   In what ways will a knowledge of market potential help in market segmentation?

9 Discuss the ethical considerations involved in competitor research.

10 What types of information should be collected about competitors?

11 Explain the advantages of do-it-almost-by-yourself market research.

SUPPLEMENTARY READING

Adler, Lee, "Phasing Research into the Marketing Plan," *Harvard Business Review,* May - June, 1960, pp. 113 - 122.

McLaughlin, F. L., *Time Series Forecasting,* Marketing Research Technique Series, no. 6, Chicago: American Marketing Association, 1962.

Newman, Joseph W., "Put Research into Marketing Decisions," *Harvard Business Review,* March - April, 1962, pp. 105 - 112.

Rosenzweig, James E., *The Demand for Aluminum: A Case Study in Forecasting,* Urbana: Bureau of Economic and Business Administration, University of Illinois, April, 1957.

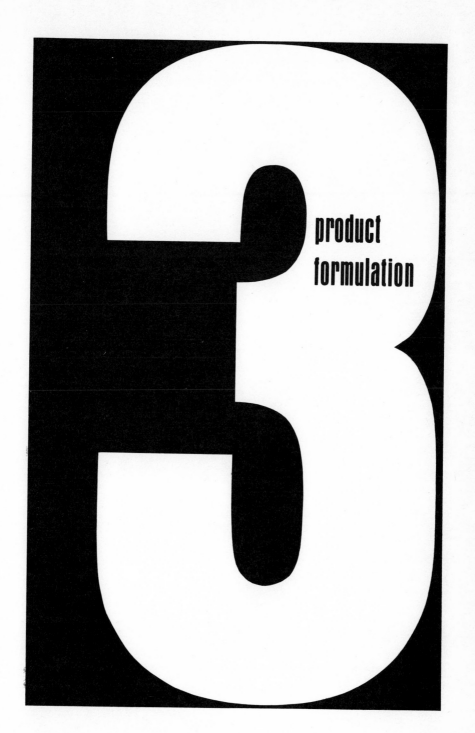

3

product
formulation

product development— general considerations

Products serve as the link between manufacturer and consumer. Assuming they have such a vital role, it is not surprising to find numerous firms, both large and small, instituting the changes necessary to improve their product offerings. Changes in product mix may take the form of additions to the product line, deletions from the product line, functional modifications in existing products, or major revisions in pricing policies. Product development, or product planning as it is sometimes called, is charged with the task of establishing continuity in bringing about these changes.

Current sentiment favors the creation of a product-development department, traditionally the exclusive province of manufacturing, near or under marketing. Except for large and complex operations like those found in the paper and metals industries, a completely separate existence is seldom feasible. Committees, although not as much in evidence as departments, are considered by many firms to be the best organizational arrangement for eliciting the utmost cooperation from both marketing and manufacturing.

CONTRIBUTIONS OF NEW PRODUCTS

The growth of an individual firm, possibly even its survival, is keyed to new products. Their important contributions can be grouped under three major headings: (1) acclimation to change, (2) influence on sales, and (3) influence on profits.

Acclimation to Change

Firms must recognize that the market environment in which they function is constantly changing. Trying to preserve present conditions will only lead to stagnancy, perhaps even ruin.

New products help a firm adapt to change by aiding its entry into high-growth markets. The outlook for continued prosperity in the aircraft industry even with a slackening off of defense business is a good example of this. Every approach possible is being taken or being seriously contemplated to supply the accelerated buildup in jetliner demand which is expected to continue on into the 1980s. The Boeing 707 and the Douglas DC-8 are being enlarged to enhance their appeal to both old and new customers. Aircraft makers are also hopeful that they can tap two new markets estimated to be worth more than $3 billion in sales by 1975. In one market, short-range sixty- to ninety-passenger jets, Douglas has already introduced its DC-9, and Boeing is countering with a 737 model. In the other market, no firm has announced any definite plans as yet for very small jetliners to be used principally by local service carriers.

To a limited extent giants such as Du Pont, IBM, and AT&T can manipulate their markets and thus create rather than react to change. However, most manufacturers of industrial goods lack the financial resources necessary to undertake extensive R&D programs. Table 7.1 clearly illustrates the R&D imbalance that exists between and within selected industries.

Influence on Sales Volume

Probably the most obvious impact of new products is on a firm's sales volume. To illustrate, Black & Decker, a maker of power tools, estimated that as much as 12.5 percent of its United States sales during a recent twelve-month span were from new products introduced during the same time period. Although tangible results such as sales volume are seldom as immediate as in the foregoing example, the last five years have seen a gradual reduction in the time lapse between introduction and contribution.

There appear to be several reasons for this. One is the attempt to

TABLE 7.1   Distribution of Industrial R&D Budget, Selected Industries, 1960

INDUSTRY	TOTAL R&D BUDGET (IN MILLIONS)	PERCENTAGE OF INDUSTRY BUDGET			
		FIRST 4 FIRMS	NEXT 4 FIRMS	NEXT 12 FIRMS	ALL OTHER FIRMS
Aircraft and missiles	$3,621	50	20	25	5
Communication equipment and electronic components	1,249	62	16	12	10
Other electrical equipment	1,184	82	5	5	8
Machinery	949	50	11	10	29
Industrial chemicals	664	60	14	16	10
Scientific and mechanical measuring instruments	215	78	7	9	6
Other chemicals	165	52	11	16	21
Fabricated metal products	112	51	15	10	24
Primary ferrous products	93	60	21	14	5
Nonferrous and other metal products	69	59	17	19	5
Textiles	32	53	11	13	23

Source: Funds for Research and Industry, Washington: National Science Foundation, 1958 and 1960, p. 16 and pp. 73, 62.

keep up with the ever-accelerating pace of technological change. This is particularly true of industries which have a high level of research spending relative to sales. Another reason is that after refraining from or paying only scant attention to new-product development, many firms have instituted "crash programs" to catch up with changes in their particular marketing environments. Finally, a considerable number of new products currently emerge from either small or young firms that can ill afford lengthy investment without payoff. This usually means low-risk innovations such as the redesigning of existing products. For example, one young business-machine company has prospered by building its new products so that they can be used in conjunction with those of the industry leader.

Influence on Profits

The main result of new products is their contribution to a firm's long-run profit position. To accept this, it is necessary to consider the concept of the product life cycle. This concept is based on two assumptions: (1) all products move through a cycle at a speed which varies in relation to their respective institutional and marketing environments and (2) all the phases of the cycle are clearly discernible in terms of sales and profit shifts. Figure 7.1 shows a general out-

FIGURE 7.1 The Product Life Cycle

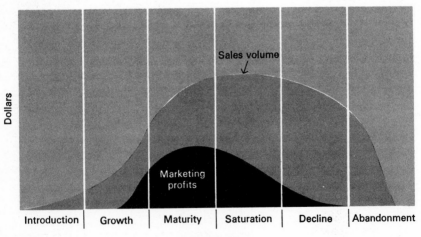

line of the sales and profit curves as they pass through each phase of the product life cycle.

Both curves follow essentially the same pattern, but they are almost completely out-of-step with each other. Emerging profits climb quite rapidly in the growth period and then under competitive pressures diminish in the maturity phase while sales continue to rise. The shifts in the profit-sales relationship can best be observed by comparing the changes in the marketing environment as the product moves through various phases of its life.

In the introductory phase, sales volume is nearly sufficient to sustain engineering and marketing developmental costs. How long this period lasts is determined primarily by how well product development has done its job. As sales volume picks up momentum, the product moves into its second or growth phase. It is during this period that the product first becomes profitable, or in other words a commercial success. Exactly when this will happen depends upon the magnitude of developmental costs and individual company policies regarding their amortization. The major problem in this phase is to match demand. Pressures are placed on both manufacturing and logistics to get adequate quantities of the product in the right place at the right time. Actual carelessness such as the continued failure to meet promised delivery dates, while not disastrous at this time, should be avoided because of the possibility of image carry-over into the more competitive phases which follow.

The maturity phase is characterized by slowly rising sales in the face of mounting competition. More intensive marketing efforts and the surrendering of some of the gross margin eventually cause profits to slip. The decline in profits can be offset somewhat by the discovery of new market segments for the product or a slightly altered version of the product.

The need to control costs is more apparent as the market becomes saturated. During saturation and even more in the decline phase, emphasis is on optimizing returns from each succeeding dollar of cost. When this becomes impossible, abandonment of the product is called for. However, structural inertia prevents most companies from taking this action until well past the point where marginal costs exceed marginal revenues.

The foregoing analysis demonstrates quite clearly that successful growth is planned around profits rather than sales. Product strategy, therefore, should call for a continuing flow of new products so timed as to perpetuate profits.

REASONS FOR NEW-PRODUCT COMMERCIALIZATION FAILURE

Chances are only about fifty-fifty that a new product placed on the market will be a commercial success. The waste in new-product expense dollars is a problem that plagues every industrial-good manufacturer, although the success rate will undoubtedly vary widely from firm to firm in relation to the obvious differences in management effectiveness. The probability of success for selected industry groupings, as compiled by the consulting firm of Booz-Allen & Hamilton, is shown in Table 7.2.

According to a survey by the National Industrial Conference Board, the principal reasons for disappointing results from new products are almost wholly within the control of the individual firm's management. Of the eight reasons cited for failure, external competitive forces ranked well down the list in frequency of mention.[1]

Accordingly, one must look within the firm itself to ascertain the reasons for lack of success with new products. These reasons can be broadly categorized in terms of (1) insufficient knowledge of the target market, (2) inadequate planning of the product introduction process, and (3) insensitivity to organizational limitations.

Insufficient Knowledge

Insufficient or faulty market study appears to be the principal cause for disappointment with new products. Management does not seem capable of gauging accurately the nature or the size of the market. In part, this difficulty lies in the unwillingness of line management

TABLE 7.2 Commercial Success Experience in New-product Introductions

SELECTED INDUSTRY GROUPING	PERCENTAGE SUCCESSFUL
Raw-material processors	60
Electrical machinery	57
Nonelectrical machinery	52
Chemical	47
Metal fabricators	38

Source: *Management of New Products*, 3d ed., Chicago: Booz-Allen & Hamilton, Inc., 1963, p. 14.

[1] "Why New Products Fail, Survey of Business Opinion and Experience," *The Conference Board Record*, October, 1964, pp. 11-18.

to finance painstaking research and testing. This is accentuated by a fairly widespread disaffection toward the whole area of marketing research. One executive commented that "Marketing research is often a dangerous tool because it is only human to want to agree with preconceptions of superiors so long as it doesn't cost anything at that particular moment."

Another difficulty is that a good number of manufacturers are reluctant to expose new products to testing because they want to keep their ideas from competitors. This is a very pertinent consideration when proprietary rights cannot be legally protected and/or the originating firm is small compared with competition. Explaining his decision not to engage in preintroduction market study, a small manufacturer declared: "It's too big a risk to expose a nonpatentable product—no doubt about it, our competition has more production and marketing know-how."

Inadequate Planning

The consequences of inadequate planning are far from subtle, as demonstrated by the disaster that attends the discovery that a new product is out of date before it reaches the market. Without planning, the period between conception and introduction can drag out over a long period of time, increasing the chances of technical obsolescence. One of the delays Bethlehem Steel encountered in development was getting into regular operating mills to test their new products. Consequently, in plans for their new research laboratories, a steelmaking facility was included.

In addition to poor timing, the lack of planning is evident in a number of developmental problems. One of these is the discovery that the costs of producing a new product exceed planned expectations. Usually this will lead to higher prices and a smaller share of the market. Highly technical industries that are used to selling to the federal government find this problem quite troublesome. Occasionally newproduct failure can be attributed to the design of a top-quality product whose excessive quality itself increased cost to an extent that would not meet competition.

Other developmental problems are related to launching the new product. They include improper allocation of marketing effort, illprepared and uninformed salesmen, and ill-advised selection and utilization of distribution channels. According to the vice-president of marketing for a chemical company, their most serious new-product failure in recent times was due to the lack of specific marketing plans relating to the distribution required.

Insensitivity to Limitations

Failure of a firm to recognize its own limitations has led to a considerable number of problems in the development of new products. The most critical appear as product defects. Engineering may not be able to design the product so that it is acceptable to the market in terms of performance and durability. For example, a components manufacturer lost a major OEM account when it failed after two years to create an acceptable product from its own idea.

Difficulties in maintaining quality control can also result in an unsalable new product. This is often the case with new fabricated materials. One problem may be the failure of the regular plant output to match the quality of pilot plant materials. This discrepancy may be increased if samples of the pilot runs have been extensively distributed to potential customers during market-testing operations.

ESTABLISHING A PROGRAM FOR PRODUCT DEVELOPMENT

From the preceding, it is plainly evident that while the burden of corporate profit growth rests with the new products, their development is fraught with peril. Thus it would seem appropriate to draw upon the practices of the more successful firms in this area, whether industrial or consumer. Although no hard-and-fast rules on how to do it are apparent, careful review of the information available suggests that a sound product-development program is founded on:

1 Wholehearted acceptance of the role of innovator
2 Full realization of the inherent risks involved
3 Critical self-appraisal (situational analysis or audit)
4 Ever-increasing reliance on the use of quantitative tools in making decisions
5 Formalizing the new-product evolution process

Role of Innovator

The innovator is the company that has boldly committed itself to create an environment that is responsive to market change. What technical research effort there is, is guided by the potential desires of the market rather than the concept of invention. Even in the segments of the industrial market dominated by "pure research," some evidence of a change in thinking is apparent. The electronics industry, for instance, came up with microminiaturization in answer to the demands of the space program for desired capabilities.

In addition to emphasizing marketing throughout product development, the firm that is an innovator will invest in applied research in any area where there is a possibility that its own technological competence may become obsolete.[2] The innovator, in other words, defines markets in terms of satisfactions rather than products. One example is the Clark Equipment Company, a manufacturer of lift trucks, that has developed a materials-handling system without lift trucks; it has push-button control of loads that move via special compressed-air pallets and floor sections. Another innovator is a large West Coast gas utility that is doing extensive pioneer research on the energy fuel cell.

Finally, the innovator conceives of product development as a company-wide activity under the direction of marketing. The question of whether to take a chance on a new product involves financial and production considerations as well as marketing. The marketing man must know enough about both of the other functional areas to request the necessary information to screen the product from all standpoints. When all the relevant data have been assembled, the marketing man submits his report to top management for their deliberation.

Inherent Risks.
Although the notoriously high failure rate for new products has undoubtedly been exaggerated, there are risks in new-product development.[3] The firms with the best batting averages recognize these risks and attempt to reduce their degree while maximizing payoffs.

The grid diagram in Figure 7.2 will help to explain the risks inherent in marketing and manufacturing a new product. With respect

[2] Marshall C. Lewis, "The Still-Reluctant Entrepreneurs," *Printers' Ink - New Products Marketing,* May 29, 1964, p. 39.

[3] It seems reasonable to assume that the oft-quoted failure rates of 80 and 90 percent are overstatements or at least not applicable to the industrial market. In regard to the latter, a study in 1954 of some 82 New England industrial-good manufacturers revealed that about 71 percent (357 out of 515) of the new products introduced during a five-year period were successful. William B. Martz, *A Survey of Reasons behind the Introduction of New Industrial Products,* Cambridge, Mass.: School of Industrial Management, Massachusetts Institute of Technology, unpublished thesis, 1954, p. 37.

to marketing it can be noted that the degree of risk increases as the market becomes more alien. Low-risk situations involve selling new products to market segments that are already customers of the firm. No change is necessary in the basic marketing strategy. New products that fit such a marketing situation are modifications of existing products and those expressly designed to mesh with the current product-line offering.

About the only evidences of risk are the presence of different purchasing influence patterns and intra-line competition. The case of the new materials-handling system developed by the Clark Equipment Company affords a good example of such a situation. The marketing targets will be essentially the same as for forklift trucks, but the significant ramifications of the special system will cause purchasing influence to shift to the upper echelons of management. There will also be some evidence of competition between the new system and forklift trucks for the materials-handling purchasing dollar. This intra-line competition will not have nearly the intensity experienced in the chemical industry. Here, for example, many of the firms pro-

FIGURE 7.2   Inherent Risks with New Products.

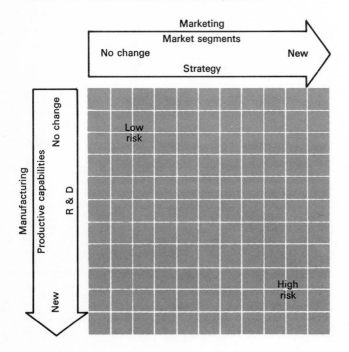

ducing plastic foams also make vinyl plastics, both of which are used in making water sports gear. End uses of plastic foam, the new product, are cutting into the market for inflatable goods made primarily from vinyl plastics. Another example from the chemical industry is the introduction of a new chemical solvent, chlorothene, by the Dow Chemical Company in 1954. The new product competed directly with two other solvents, trichloroethylene and carbon tetrachloride, in the industrial-cleaning market. At the time of introduction Dow Chemical was a major supplier of carbon tetrachloride.

At the other extreme, a high-risk situation exists for a firm when it introduces a new product to a market it is totally unfamiliar with and in which it has no established reputation. To adjust, a marketing strategy that specifically focuses on this alien market will have to be developed. Often this entails the creation of separate selling and advertising programs for the new product. This approach met with success for the E. L. Bruce Company, known as the world's largest manufacturer of hardwood flooring, when it invaded the truck-flooring market.

From a production standpoint, the degree of risk is related to the question of whether the new product can be made with existing know-how and facilities. If it can, the risk is lower than it would be if additional capital expenditures must be made and/or additional engineering skills are needed. However, the attraction of being able to use existing production facilities, particularly when there is idle capacity, should not mislead firms into developing new products they cannot market successfully.

Looking again at Figure 7.2, one sees clearly that when new products are sorted graphically in relation to the risk framework, those providing the greatest risk cluster around the lower right-hand corner of the diagram. Here all new manufacturing facilities are needed to make a product that is to be sold to a completely alien market. A few years ago, Allis-Chalmers Manufacturing Company faced just such a high-risk situation with a new product, powdered boron silicide. Joining Allis-Chalmers' product line, boron silicide represented a radical departure from the firm's traditional manufacturing and marketing operations. Up to this time, Allis-Chalmers had restricted itself to machinery and equipment. Boron silicide, a high-temperature-resistent fabricated material, is produced and sold through an independent New Products Department.

The risks inherent in developing new products can be offset to some extent by (1) transferring portions of the task to others and (2) decreasing their probability of incidence through the application of sound management practices. Frequently the job of introducing a new product can be shifted to functional middlemen. The manufacturers' agent is often called upon for this purpose, especially when he has entrée to the potential market for the new product. The use of functional middlemen does not eliminate the risk of new-product failure, but it does reduce the possible losses, both financial and prestigious, that would have been encountered had the firm's own sales force been involved.

The risks in employing capital and manpower to produce a new product can be shifted almost entirely by subcontracting; the only problem is finding a competent and reliable subcontractor who will perform the work at a reasonable cost. Then, too, if more than one subcontractor is necessary, there is the problem of coordinating their activities. Research and development investment risks can be substantially reduced by the utilization of outside research organizations such as Arthur D. Little, Inc., of Cambridge, Massachusetts, and the Battelle Memorial Institute of Columbus, Ohio. In this regard, a firm's R&D capacities can be as expansive as necessary in a new-product area without the need for an extensive long-term commitment in what may be a short-term venture if the product is not successful or a decision is made not to explore the particular area any further.

The application of sound management practices is basic to the alleviation of the risks attending the development of new products. In fact, the other general method of minimizing risk through transfer implies good management. The ways management can improve its handling of risks include:[4]

1   Deciding beforehand how much is to be risked on the new product
2   Maintaining the momentum of the developmental process once it is started
3   Deciding what is to be done if things go wrong

The first consideration is the amount and timing of company effort. The new product and not the present mood of the company should be the determining factor. As important as the decision on the amount of effort is how it is to be committed. Can it be commited a little at a time or must it all be at once?

Regardless of what developmental stage they are in, new products should not be allowed to languish. Neither should they require crash programs in which every decision is made in an atmosphere of crisis. Rather, new products should move steadily in a series of related steps

[4] © 1964, *Nation's Business,* the Chamber of Commerce of the United States. Reprinted from the July issue.

from conception to practicality. The individualistic nature of each new product prevents strict scheduling, but progress reviews can be undertaken by top management periodically.

Finally, effective management of risk means preparing alternative courses of action in the event that something goes astray. Never should management have to face a situation where the only two choices are going ahead grudgingly with what appears to be an ill-fated project and writing it off entirely. Because adjustments are exceedingly difficult to make as the new product moves ahead inexorably through the developmental process, trouble should be anticipated and planned for accordingly.

Critical Self-appraisal

Before tackling the task of formulating a new-product program, a firm should audit its own resources objectively. The self-appraisal or situational audit, as it is sometimes called, will help a firm take advantage of its strengths while at the same time avoiding its weaknesses. A new-product program should never be expected to overcome a weakness. It is more likely that a weakness will hamper a program, perhaps even submerge it.

The resources of the firm which can affect the development of new products include:

1   Product mix
2   Technological capabilities
3   Production facilities (both plant and personnel)
4   Marketing facilities
5   Location (if this is a factor)
6   Management
7   Finances

A brief review of each will help to point out what the firm should be looking for in its audit. The yardsticks for comparison are competition and the average for the industry.

Sales analysis and possibly distribution-cost analysis are the methods used in auditing the product mix. Usually it is advisable to establish a historical pattern for each product in order to obtain some idea of its stage in the life cycle. To supplement these analyses, a study of customer use might be made.

Technological capabilities are probably the most difficult resource to evaluate objectively. However, this should not act as a deterrent for the results are worthwhile, even essential to the manufacturer of industrial goods. A record of accomplishments, new products, and R&D contracts is one way to size up capabilities. Another is to make an assessment of the engineering and research people in terms of creativity and proficiency in the various technical areas. Still another is to evaluate research output in relation to what one author calls key factors.[5]

1   Economic value of technology as opposed to the cost of the research that proposed it
2   Amount of technological output per unit of scientific effort extended
3   The degree to which the technological program supports company goals. Scientific publication is extremely useful for comparing the firm's research activities with those of competitors.[6]

Appraisal of production facilities entails determining the types of products that can be made (plant flexibility), production rates, plant capacity, and the ability to maintain quality standards. An analysis of production costs for a period of time, say five years, will reveal the proficiencies experienced in making various products. From a practical standpoint, competitive comparisons of production facilities will be most difficult to make.

Measurement of marketing strengths and weaknesses is accomplished by what is usually referred to as a marketing organization audit or appraisal. Some of the questions this type of investigation would attempt to answer are:

1   In what markets and market segments does the firm function?
2   What is the competence (i.e. market and product knowledge, servicing facilities) of the sales force and/or the middleman organization in each designated market and market segment?
3   What is the stature of the firm in each designated market and market segment?
4   What is the productivity and the capacity of the sales force and/or middleman organization?
5   How much flexibility is there in the sales force and/or middleman organization?
6   What are the capabilities of advertising and marketing research in terms of manpower?

[5] James Brian Quinn, "How to Evaluate Research Output," *Harvard Business Review*, March-April, 1960, p. 70. See also his *Yardsticks for Industrial Research*, New York: The Ronald Press Company, 1959.

[6] For a more complete discussion of scientific publication and its advantages as a basis for evaluation, see Melville H. Hodge, Jr., "Rate Your Company's Research Productivity," *Harvard Business Review*, November-December, 1963, pp. 109-122.

Nowhere is comparison with competitors as important as it is in appraising marketing capabilities. Increasingly, firms are calling upon their own marketing-research departments to provide much of the data for these comparisons.

Often a firm will overlook the advantages and disadvantages associated with its geographical location. In certain industries the time-distance between buyer and seller can often mean the difference between gaining and losing a sale.

The most important resource a firm has is its management team. Their capabilities are reflected in every aspect of company activity. The major problem in appraising this resource is ascertaining just what role circumstantial luck has played. While even an incompetent and overextended management can keep some businesses going, new-product development is quite another matter. Product development presents a real challenge in that management must have the time and the skills to perform a lot of unfamiliar jobs.

Objective bases should be used as much as possible in evaluating management as a group. One of the best yardsticks is the firm's accomplishment of stated objectives, the underlying assumption being that objectives are fundamental to the efficient practice of management. Another yardstick is management's work level in relation to capacity. If management is already overextended, it is hardly likely that they could take on a task as involved as product development. Also suggested as yardsticks are several personnel factors. These include the individual experience of managers, the number of years the managers have worked together as a team, the ages of the managers, and provisions for executive replenishment.

Financial capabilities act as a control on the funds available for new-product development. While knowing how much can be spent is vitally important, some idea of management's willingness to spend it should also be obtained. The latter consideration is of special concern in small, closely knit firms whose managers are likely to be owners. Comparisons with competitors are directed toward determining their financial abilities to counteract new-product development.

Quantitative Tools for Decision Making

Successful developers are coming to rely more and more on quantitative tools in making new-product decisions. Accelerating this trend is the ready availability of electronic computers to solve the complex mathematical problems involved. The quantitative tools used in new-product development are essentially projective in character, assisting management to forecast the consequences of alternative courses of action.

Bayesian Theory is one of the most talked-about analytical approaches to decision making under conditions of uncertainty. The distinguishing feature of Bayesian Theory is the assigning of subjective probability assessments to events that determine the profitability of alternative courses of action open to a decision maker.[7] By using the probability assessments as weights, a weighted average of the possible profits for each alternative can be computed. The following oversimplified example will help to illustrate the Bayesian approach.

A manufacturer has found from preintroduction marketing tests that several minor modifications are necessary for his new product to be commercially successful. The modifications can be grouped under two major headings: (1) changes in materials and (2) changes in components. In considering this situation, the head of the product-development department is faced with three alternative courses of action:

1   Change materials
2   Change components
3   Do both

To construct the decision matrix (Table 7.3), the product-development manager requests sales forecast probabilities from marketing research and payoff estimates for the varying sales forecasts from cost accounting. As a decision rule,[8] the manager decides to select that alternative which would give the best overall chance of payoff. This

TABLE 7.3   New-product Payoff Expectation Decision Matrix (in thousands of dollars)

ALTERNATIVES	UNIT SALES FORECASTS				AGGREGATE PAYOFF EXPECTATIONS
	0 - 25,000	25,001 - 50,000	50,001 - 75,000	75,001 - 100,000	
Probabilities	0.10	0.25	0.40	0.25	
Change materials	− 1,500	− 1,000	800	1,500	
	(− 150)	(− 250)	(320)	(375)	(295)
Change components	− 1,000	− 200	700	1,000	
	(− 100)	(− 50)	(280)	(250)	(380)
Do both	− 2,200	− 1,500	400	2,000	
	(− 220)	(− 375)	(160)	(500)	(65)

[7] Harry V. Roberts, "Bayesian Statistics in Marketing," *Journal of Marketing*, January, 1963, p. 1.

[8] A decision rule is defined as the means by which the most attractive alternative can be identified. The most common rule is profit maximization.

is found by multiplying the payoff in each cell by its sales forecast probability and summing the results for each alternative.

Under the given conditions, the product-development manager finds that his best course of action is to change the components. It is also possible for him to determine the limit that he can spend for more accurate predictions. This is calculated by subtracting the aggregate payoff expectation of the best course of action from the summation of the expected payoffs as a consequence of taking the best course of action for each given sales forecast. This is computed as follows:

$$EVPI = [.10\,(-\$1,000,000) + .25\,(-\$200,000)$$
$$+\ .40\,(\$800,000) + .25\,(\$2,000,000) - \$380,000]$$
$$= \$670,000 - \$380,000 = \$290,000$$

The illustration would be more realistic if the manager were given the option of delaying his decision for successive periods of time. To do this, three additional assumptions have to be made. They are:

1 The reduction in payoffs as a result of the delay
2 The effect on market penetration caused by the delay
3 The cost of acquiring additional marketing information

Critical Path Analysis and three variations of this basic technique— Critical Path Method, Program Evaluation and Review Technique, and Resource Summary and Leveling—are all applicable to product development, particularly in scheduling the new-product evolution cycle. Critical Path Analysis can be defined as the development of realistic schedules by the logical sequencing of related activities. In that the resulting schedule gives an overall view of a particular job, the use of Critical Path Analysis promotes the concept of management by exception. What is involved can best be explained by using the testing phase of the evolution cycle as an example.

There are essentially two project areas in the testing phase: technical or engineering testing and market testing. First, a network is constructed by arranging in sequential order the related activities in each of the two projects into paths. This is shown in Figure 7.3. The sequential flow of the network is usually measured in terms of time, although it would be possible to use volume or specifications. Once the duration of each activity is determined, the times are summed for each path. The longest path is called the critical path. Critical activities make up a critical path, and those on a noncritical path are referred to as float because their start and finish times are flexible. All activities begin and end with events or nodes. These indi-

FIGURE 7.3 Network for Testing Phase of New-product Evolution.

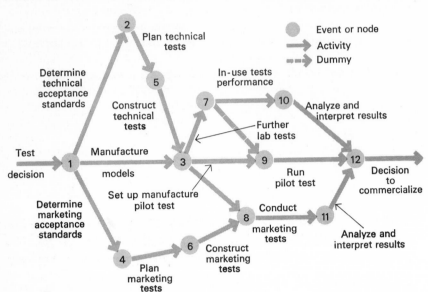

cate the completion of one activity and the start of the dependent succeeding activities.

No attempt has been made to scale the arrows to convey the time duration of each activity. Rather, the network in Figure 7.3 illustrates in simplified form the sequential flow of activities that are to be completed in the testing phase. For example, activities 3/8 and 6/8 must be completed before activity 8/11 can commence.

The Critical Path Method answers the question: Should additional expenditures be employed to reduce the duration of a project? Time and cost data, of course, must be available. With such information a time-cost relationship can be calculated for each activity and the overall project, making it possible to know the higher cost increments entailed in expediting as well as the maximum reduction that can be made in time.

Program Evaluation and Review Technique, more commonly known as PERT, is ideally suited for developmental systems that depend much upon the effectiveness of people. The reason for this is that PERT tends to minimize the traits and characteristics of human behavior which influence the adequacy of any system.[9] Since lower

[9] Richard A. Johnson, Fremont E. Kast, James E. Rosenzweig, *The Theory and Management of Systems,*. New York: McGraw-Hill Book Company, 1963, p. 254.

and middle management must make both optimistic and pessimistic time estimates for their own activities, their most likely estimate is liable to be more precise. It is even possible to apply an "experience" factor after a particular manager has made a number of estimates.

Under PERT the formula for computing the expected time for each activity is:

$$TE = \frac{a + 4m + b}{6}$$

where $a =$ the optimistic estimate
$m =$ the most likely estimate
$b =$ the pessimistic estimate

Once a project is scheduled, the next problem management faces is assigning the available resources of manpower, equipment, and materials. Ideally management will want to acquaint itself as early as possible with the demands on resources. One way to accomplish this is by a resource summary.

First, a major project or job is divided up into time intervals. Then the summation of resource requirements for each interval is compared with availabilities. Although additional resources can eliminate deficits, this is not always practical from a cost standpoint.

Another approach, leveling, shifts resources around to eliminate deficits.[10] This may be done by transferring resources from noncritical to critical activities or deferring some activities. Since leveling usually extends the duration of a project, it seems advisable to weigh the costs of delay against those of employing additional resources. Certainly the current emphasis on accelerating the evolutionary cycle of new products would work against the technique of leveling.

Finally, quantitative tools can be used profitably in the selection of new products. A decision framework involving a systemized four-step profit evaluation is applicable to new industrial products.[11]

The first step is to construct a decision matrix for evaluating all new products. To do this, it is necessary to define both the marketing factors and the rating scale that are to be used. Usually several major factors are subdivided, and mutually exclusive descriptions of each subfactor are developed for the various designated rating

[10] Yung Wong, "Critical Path Analysis for New Product Planning," *Journal of Marketing*, October, 1964, p. 58.

[11] For a more comprehensive discussion see John T. O'Meara, Jr., "Selecting Profitable Products," in Edward C. Bursk and John F. Chapman (eds.), *New Decision-Making Tools for Managers*, Cambridge, Mass.: Harvard University Press, 1963, pp. 334-348.

levels. The number of levels or degrees in the rating scale depends upon how finite the evaluation is to be. However, it probably would not be worthwhile to have a range of more than five degrees.

After the ratings for all the subfactors have been delineated, the next step is the application of weights to indicate relative importance. As far as factors are concerned, the best procedure is to weigh the major factors in relation to the objectives and policies of the new-product-development program before going ahead with the subfactors.

The third step is to estimate the likelihood of a particular new product having a rating for a subfactor. Suppose an evaluator, in looking over the decision matrix, decides that a new product has good possibilities of being accepted by 60 percent of the firm's franchised distributors. Among the remaining 40 percent the chances of securing acceptance are about fifty-fifty. With a rating scale of good, average, and poor, he assigns the probabilities of 0.6 for good, 0.2 for average, and 0.2 for poor. These probabilities are then multiplied by their respective rating weights, and the results are summed for each subfactor.

After this has been done, the next and final step is to arrive at a weighted aggregate probability for the new product. This is accomplished by applying each major factor's weight to the total of its component subfactors, and then summing these to arrive at an aggregate total.

Development of probabilities, such as described, facilitates comparisons between new products. This is extremely important when management must decide which product should be commercialized or in what order the new products should be commercialized. Another use of probabilities is the construction of what can be called long- and short-run profit indexes. [12]

New-product Evolutionary Cycle
Although no statistics can be cited, it seems reasonable to assume that successful product innovators have formalized the evolution process. A formalized evolutionary cycle serves five main functions:

1 It directs the activities of product development toward the single goal of successful new products. This is especially important since product development requires a wide range of company talents—engineering, marketing, production, and finance.

[12] *Ibid.,* pp. 344-347.

2   It breaks down the complex job of product development into manageable tasks.
3   It helps to ensure the proper assignment of resources.
4   It serves as a check on the progress of the product as it moves through the cycle. This will improve the timing and speed of the new-product flow, two vital factors in today's industrial market.
5   It clarifies authority and responsibility in product development.

Booz-Allen & Hamilton, in their investigation of several hundred companies' new-product activities, found that regardless of type of company, industry, or product there are six fairly clear phases or stages in the evolutionary cycle.[13] These phases are labeled exploration, screening, business analysis, development, testing, and commercialization. It was also discovered that in each phase about one-half of the new-product ideas entering the phase are either eliminated or deferred for future consideration.[14] The cost experiences of eighty companies in developing new-product ideas are summarized in Figure 7.4. In the following discussion of the individual phases, extensive re-

FIGURE 7.4   Comparison of New-product Expenses.

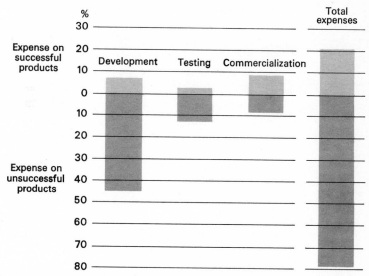

Source: Management of New Products, 3rd ed. (Chicago: Booz-Allen & Hamilton Inc., 1963) p. 14.

[13] *Management of New Products,* 3d ed., Chicago: Booz-Allen & Hamilton, Inc., 1963, pp. 10-11.

[14] *Ibid.,* p. 11

liance is placed on the points brought out by the Booz-Allen & Hamilton study.

Product development can be visualized as a funnel with ideas pouring into the top and successful products coming out of the bottom. As an idea or product moves through the developmental process, a decision on whether to retain or reject must be made at the culmination of each phase including the final one, commercialization.

The first phase, solicitation, is the organized search for new-product ideas. Several important points are to be considered:

FIGURE 7.5   New-product Evolutionary Cycle.

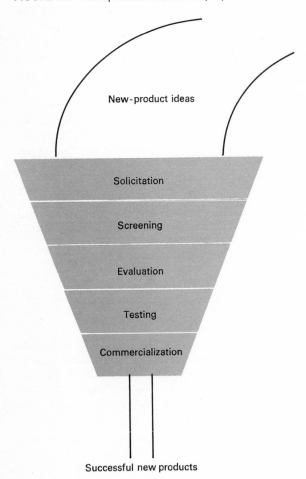

New-product ideas

Solicitation

Screening

Evaluation

Testing

Commercialization

Successful new products

1   Identify the product areas of interest to the company. Contrary to what might be supposed, the problem is not a scarcity of new ideas, but rather finding those that will match up with company capabilities while at the same time offering long-term growth potential. The smaller the firm, the more imperative it is to match up new-product ideas with capabilities.
2   Select the sources that are to be relied upon for the generation of new ideas. Undoubtedly top management will have set the guidelines for the use of external and internal sources.[15]
3   Set up a collection network. Besides providing comprehensive coverage of sources, a definite systemized approach helps prevent the legal and other dangers inherent in idea collection.

In the specification phase new-product ideas are translated into reality. From an engineering standpoint, blueprints are drawn up, mock-ups and then prototypes are built, and preliminary laboratory tests are undertaken to ascertain functional characteristics. Once blueprints and prototypes are made available, production people analyze the new product's manufacturing requisites.

From a marketing standpoint, each functional area reviews and makes a report on the demands placed on it by the new product. For example, advertising develops tentative campaigns for the introductory period and the subsequent six or twelve months. In the later campaign special note is made wherever additional expenditures will be necessary.

As soon as the specifications are formulated by engineering, production, and marketing, they are forwarded to accounting for the preparation of cost estimates. These cost estimates together with the specifications are reduced to a specific business proposition. The decision to enter the next phase of the evolution cycle is based upon this proposition.

Up to this point the emphasis has been on determining the suitability of the new product for the given company. In the evaluation phase the emphasis is shifted to the marketability of the new product. The rational nature of the industrial market necessitates that functional features be appraised and revised accordingly before proceeding with the marketing features. First the major functional features of the new product which must prove out are clearly identified. Then each feature is appraised in terms of ideal performance and competition. The performance appraisal seeks to determine how and for how long the new product will work under varying operational

---

[15] The major questions concerning R&D strategy are discussed in Chap. 4.

conditions. If bugs or deficiencies are observed, design changes are promptly initiated wherever practical. The principle of diminishing returns is used to assess the practicality of both functional and marketing changes. Patent work started when the new-product idea passed the solicitation phase is begun in earnest once the design is set.

Direct comparison of the new product's functions with those of competitive products revises many of the marketing features that will differentiate and sell the product. These plus the other major marketing features such as price,[16] company reputation, and distribution organization are competitively analyzed in making the marketing evaluation. Another important part of marketing evaluation is the determination of the size of the market for the new product.

Perhaps greater understanding will evolve if two major features of a new torque control device, one functional and the other marketing, are traced through the evaluation phase. Deflection, the functional feature, is defined as the degree of output motion in going from a moving to a stationary condition. Ideally, deflection should equal zero, but engineering reports that within dimension limits, maximum efficiency is 10 minutes for 50 inch-pounds, 16 minutes for 100 inch-pounds, and so forth. Comparison with devices already on the market shows that minimum deflection averages about 10 percent above that reported by competition. This deviation, however, is almost nonexistent for the lower-load range.

With a normal markup for this type of product, it is found that the control's price will be considerably below that of competing products. Deflection error and lower price together with the other distinguishing features are then submitted to marketing intelligence for definition of both the existing and potential markets.

The decision facing top management in the evaluation phase is whether the new product's tangible and intangible returns will justify the investment. Although returns on investment have been traditionally measured in profit dollars, more and more weight is being given to the intangible returns that can be obtained from a new product. These include strengthening the product line, gaining for the whole product line access to new markets, increasing the significance of the firm to the distributor organization, and establishing a reputation for technical competence. Once it has been decided that returns are sufficient to warrant proceeding with the development of

---

[16] Only estimates of price based upon costs are available at this point. The final pricing decision is arrived at during the early part of the commercialization phase.

the new product, the timetable which was originally drawn up for the product as it emerged from the solicitation phase is closely reviewed to achieve the best possible timing of introduction.

The next phase, as outlined in Figure 7.3, measures market acceptability through technical and market testing. The emphasis on market acceptability means that even the technical tests in the laboratory and the field are geared toward functional features which will help sell the new product. No experiments should be undertaken by engineering simply to satisfy intellectual curiosity.

For a valid response from market testing it is necessary to observe several precautions:

1 Test markets should represent the various market segments.
2 Test markets should be self-contained in terms of distribution factors and media coverage.
3 All influencing factors in each test market should be measured.
4 Ample time should be allowed for market reaction.
5 Promotional expenditures in each test market should be on a par with what would be normally spent by the company.

The decision to proceed to the next phase is a crucial one because from here on developmental costs rise sharply. It is here too that a distinction can be noted between industrial- and consumer-product development. For consumer products a cost increment usually appears at the beginning of the preceding phase because of the more elaborate market tests that are employed.

In the final phase, called commercialization, the new product is introduced to the market. This involves five major tasks:

1 Determining the final pricing schedule
2 Setting up production pilot runs
3 Orienting the distribution organization to the new product
4 Planning the implementation of the promotional campaign
5 Establishing a feedback mechanism

Coordination is important in every phase of the evolutionary cycle, but it is absolutely essential in commercialization. For this reason and because management must keep on top of the project at all times, many firms find it expedient to organize product teams. Their exact makeup as a matter of course will vary from firm to firm, but ideally a product team is composed of representatives from field sales, advertising, production, logistics, and marketing research. If the firm has a product-development department, the team will probably be headed up by a product-development manager.

Liaison with field sales may be handled by an administrative staff assistant to the vice-president or possibly the product manager who will be assigned the new product. His biggest job will be to see to it that all the salesmen are properly informed about the new product. The advertising representative is usually the person who was in charge of preparing the campaign for the new product. The engineer from production should be adept at solving quickly the minor technical problems that always seem to arise and gauging the desirability of design changes at this point of product development. The primary reason for including someone from logistics on the product team is to avoid snags in matching demand. The representative from marketing research reports almost daily on market acceptability in terms of volume and specific type of consumer.

Commercialization is concluded when the new product has been deemed a "going" commercial success and absorbed into the product line or when it has been decided to withdraw the new product from the market. The latter decision does not necessarily imply abandonment; it could be merely postponement till a more opportune time. Regardless of how carefully development is planned, unforeseen events over which the firm has no control can impair commercialization seriously.

PRODUCT DECISIONS

In developing a product policy, marketing management has to make several significant decisions. These can be summarized under four major headings:

1   Market segmentation versus product differentiation
2   Product-line simplification
3   Product-line diversification
4   Planned obsolescence

Market Segmentation versus Product Differentiation

Fundamentally there are two strategy alternatives upon which to base product policy. One of these, market segmentation, has already been discussed in some detail as the logical extension of the marketing management concept. It recognizes the disaggregative qualities of the market and thus orients the firm's products and marketing efforts to this operating concept. Under such a system of action market depth is achieved by subdividing and redefining individual segments as they are penetrated. An added advantage of segmentation to the industrial marketer is that it helps reduce the confusion generated by alternate-product completion.

Product differentiation is the policy of emphasizing differences between a product and those that compete directly with it. Substantial selling and promotional efforts are made by the seller to secure control over demand. This usually results in nonprice competitive conditions.

It has been argued that successful marketing requires the utilization of both market segmentation and product differentiation,[17] but it would appear that the latter strategy is more suited to consumer markets than it is to industrial. To support this contention, one needs only to remember the rational nature of selective motives in industrial purchasing. Then, too, product differentiation tends to place the industrial marketer on the perpetual merry-go-round of having to lower production costs to avoid the occurrence of untenable price levels pushed up by higher marketing costs.

The most advantageous use of product differentiation appears to be in the maturity and saturation stages of the product life cycle. Conditions prevalent in these stages and favorable to such a strategy include intense competition, a high degree of homogeneity in competitive offerings, and the impracticality of further segmentation.

Product-line Simplification

When a firm produces more than one product, it is faced with the possibility of a cost burden it can ill afford unless relief is sought through product-line simplfication. The failure of numerous industrial marketers to recognize this can be attributed to the hidden nature of many of the costs associated with weak products. According to one author, these hidden costs result from:[18]

1   The disproportiate amount of time management has to spend on weak products
2   The requirement for frequent price and inventory adjustments
3   The generally short production runs in spite of expensive setup times

[17] See Wendell R. Smith, "Product Differentiation and Market Segmentation as Alternative Marketing Strategies," *Journal of Marketing,* July, 1956, pp. 3-8.

[18] Philip Kotler, "Phasing Out Weak Products," *Harvard Business Review,* March-April, 1965, p. 109.

4   The attention of advertising and sales that might be better applied to more profitable products

5   The reflection on the company's image

6   The deterring effect on the company's future—delay of the aggressive search for replacement products, creation of a lopsided product mix, and depressed present profitability weakening the foothold on the future

The basic ingredient in a simplification program is the list of criteria for appraising the product line. Traditionally, firms undertaking a simplification program have relied upon a hodgepodge of quantitative and qualitative factors. Which factors have the greatest relative importance depends upon the firm's informal organizational structure and the particular areas of sensitivity at the current time. From a quantitative viewpoint, reliance has been placed on the accountant's measurement of items in terms of dollars and cents. Distribution-cost analysis, besides providing the basis for many programs, has helped to overcome much of the inertia coupled with product simplification.

Most of the qualitative factors that are used have a distinct retention bias. This is not surprising since management is frequently repelled by the thought of having to drop a product that has been in the line for years. Then, too, the job of deletion, so aptly phrased by R. S. Alexander, "is a drab business, and often engenders much of the sadness of a final parting with old and tried friends."[19]

Management intuition, especially that of the sales manager, usually plays an important qualitative role in product-line simplification. Other qualitative factors are the possible disruptive effect on customer relations, the entrée a product provides to certain markets, the responsibilities the firm has to its employees and suppliers, and the attitude the government might take toward deletion.

Recent literature suggests that decisions on whether to retain or delete a product be focused on the following five critical factors: sales, profits, marketing considerations, production considerations, and competition. To formalize the decision-making process, each criterion should be assigned a weight according to its relative importance to the particular firm at the time simplification is undertaken. A brief description of each criterion is as follows:

1   Analysis of sales over a period of time will help place the product

---

[19] R. S. Alexander, "The Death and Burial of 'Sick' Products," *Journal of Marketing*, April, 1964, p. 1.

in its life cycle. It might also be advantageous to make an analysis by customer to learn who is buying the product and what patterns of consumption are evident over a period of the last few years.

2   More and more, profit as related to investment is being relied upon as a major or even sole consideration in evaluating a product's worth to a company. While there are about as many ways to compute return on investment as there are companies using this criterion, it would seem desirable that investment be valuated in terms of direct costs and direct costs plus overhead. Regardless of how return on investment is figured, it should be compared with alternative opportunities. Another profit measure is gross margin. What the trend has been and how sufficient its coverage is are two questions that need to be asked about gross margins.

3   Among the more prominent marketing factors are multiproduct sales, full-line forcing, patent and trademark position, type of customer, and influence on company image. Obviously factors such as these are all but impossible to quantify. The best approach seems to be a rating scale for each marketing criterion.

4   Grouped under production considerations are joint-cost interrelationships, equipment tied up in making a product, the degree of discretion in manufacturing costs, supplier relations particularly where reciprocity is involved, and the flexibility of the labor force. In rare instances the firm will have to consider its responsibilities to the community and the attitude the government might take toward product deletion.

5   No product-line simplification program is complete without an analysis of competition. In this analysis a product's penetration or share of the market, especially the trend, is especially important. It is also helpful to know the tactics utilized by competitors in selling and pricing specific products.

Concomitant with product simplification are the problems associated with the retention or discontinuance of a dubious product. For a dubious product to be retained, there must be some indication that a change from either a marketing or functional standpoint will reverse the present decline. Implied in this is the assumption that the returns from the change will exceed by an adequate margin the costs of the change. If the dubious product is to be discontinued, the problem is timing the action. The firm can pull the product out of its line immediately or run it out. The latter course of action is fostered by the view that there is a segment of the market which will continue to buy the product and by cutting back on all discretionary costs a profit can be made that would not be obtainable otherwise.[20] The use of computers to simulate future market behavior can help management in deciding on whether to retain, drop, or phase out a dubious product.

Product-line Diversification

Through a strategy of diversification a firm strives to attain one or more of the following major objectives:

1   A greater rate of growth in sales and profits
2   An exploitation of markets evolving from general economic trends
3   A stabilization of sales and profits
4   A spreading of risks

But diversification is not without its perils. To be successful, diversification must be viewed as a blending of a company's resources with the market situation as well as with the change.[21] The limit to diversification is the amount of funds available for expansion of investment in production and marketing.

A firm that is attracted to diversification should ask itself two questions. The first is what the firm hopes to gain from a diversified product line. If the answer is not related to one or more of the previously stated diversification objectives, it is very unlikely that the firm should be interested in such a policy. Most assuredly, diversification is not a business of perpetuating existing weaknesses.

The second question is what the yardsticks for evaluating diversified products are to be. The most important yardstick is market potential. How big is the market? What will be the effect of future technological changes on the size and composition of the market? Another yardstick is the situational audit. This should be compared with the product's production and marketing requirements to find the additional financial commitments entailed in the diversification action. Finally, the firm will probably want to set up a schedule of amounts it is willing to spend in diversification.

---

[20] For an excellent discussion of product run-out and the choices within run-out, see Walter J. Talley, Jr., "Profiting from the Declining Product," *Business Horizons*, Spring, 1964, pp. 77-84.

[21] Charles M. Sanders, "Blending Company and Market Requirements into a Planned Diversification," in Robert S. Hancock (ed.), *Dynamic Marketing for a Changing World*, Chicago: American Marketing Association, 1960, p. 515.

Planned Obsolescence

Two points are uppermost in any consideration of a planned-obsolescence policy. First, planned obsolescence as it pertains to the industrial market must be carefully defined. Probably the best definition is that planned obsolescence is the policy of determining during development how and when a product's usefulness will be terminated. This definition does not include the yearly styling changes one encounters so frequently in consumer goods or purposeful underengineering to speed up replacement.

Second, the factors which reduce a product's usefulness must be determined and correlated to some form of schedule, either in time or extensiveness of use. These factors can be grouped under two major headings—performance exhaustion and changing technology. Performance exhaustion pertains to those factors which fix product durability under normal operating conditions. During development, usually the specification phase, the innovator must face a decision on the life span of the new product. In many an engineering-oriented firm the tendency is to strive for longevity and "build a product that lasts." A New England manufacturer likes to cite the fact that their components were still functioning accurately even after the textile machinery to which they were attached had to be torn down because of physical deterioration. While long product life is all well and good, it makes no more sense from a marketing standpoint than the other extreme—intentional shortening of product life to speed up replacement. Both can fail in the job of satisfying consumer needs. The use of value analysis by industrial purchasers has clearly demonstrated the long-run significance of gauging product life to consumer needs.

In most situations the innovator, without market knowledge, has only two options. One is to make a highly durable item which he will undoubtedly have to price at a premium. There is also a good chance that he will have to advertise extensively to familiarize the market with his product's durability. The other option is to make a low-durability product with full knowledge that in doing so there is the risk of consumer disaffection over frequent replacement. Where there is a high degree of conformity among competitive products, there is also the risk of brand switching by purchasers who enter and reenter the market.

Obsolescence comes about through changing technology as well as performance exhaustion. It seems prudent for the innovator to determine the rate at which changes are accepted by his particular market. If possible, the rate of acceptance should be found for each market segment. This information will form the basis for planning and controlling the degree of change and the timing of change.

There is another problem in technological change. This is the staggering of introduction so that at any one time only a part of the change is made available.[22] The purpose of such a policy is to hasten the obsolescence of the product. Various industries have been seriously criticized on this point, but it is highly unlikely that any firm would seriously consider such a hazardous short-run policy. It is a common occurrence, however, for the design of a new product to be frozen despite full knowledge that further improvements now in the embryonic phases will be available at some later date. This course of action is taken not to hasten obsolescence by rationing change, but to keep pace with the market rate of technological change and to avoid as much as possible the risks of poor timing. Doubtless this decision has to be made time and time again in those industries such as the pharmaceutical, where the primary basis of competition is technological change.

ORGANIZATIONAL DECISIONS

In organizing the product-development function several critical questions need to be answered by top management.

1   What are the limitations on product development in terms of time and budget?
2   How is product development to be organized?
3   Where is product development to be positioned in the firm's overall structure?
4   Who will be comprised in the staff of product development?

Time and Budget Consideration

There are at least two primary requisites for success in product development. The first and perhaps the more important of the two, is for top management to think in terms of permanency in regard to the product-development function. This requires clearly specified objectives and policies to direct and limit both the short- and long-run programs. All too often, product development is viewed as a panacea for all sorts of problems to be used as needed on a temporary basis. A good example of this is firms that look at new products only as a way of avoiding idle plant capacity.

[22] Gerald B. Tallman, "Planned Obsolescence: The Setting—The Issues Involved," in Lynn H. Stockman (ed.), *Advancing Marketing Efficiency*, Chicago: American Marketing Association, 1959, p. 36.

The second requisite for success is to make a substantial invest-ment in highly skilled manpower, facilities, and budget, all allocated specifically to product development. This requisite, obviously, pro-motes an imbalance between large and small companies. Small com-panies can compensate to some degree for their lack of financial ca-pacity by putting all their available funds into development rather than spreading them out over both development and technical re-search. Carrying this one step further, a company may find that by con-centrating its limited resources on just the marketing aspects of devel-opment, it can sustain a continued flow of successful new products. Of course, in industries which are heavily oriented toward scientif-ic research, such as the electronic and pharmaceutical, this approach is not as applicable.

Type of Organizational Structure

From studies of product-development organizations it can be con-cluded that there is no one best way for all companies; each must structure the function of product development to meet its own par-ticular needs. There appear to be four basic types of organization: (1) sponsor group, (2) product-development team, (3) product-de-velopment committee, and (4) product-development department.[23]

Sponsor groups are an arrangement whereby the originator of a new-product idea is given the responsibility of heading up a devel-opment group. The assignment of other personnel is made on the basis of need for a particular developmental talent. The advantages of this arrangement are that the creator has the opportunity of pushing his idea through to reality and his infectious enthusiasm invigorates what might otherwise be a rather perfunctory task for developmental personnel. While the preceding are desirable from a human-relations standpoint, it is questionable whether enthusiasm is an adequate replacement for managerial know-how or a formalized system of development. It is also doubtful whether a creator could be called upon to make a completely unbiased decision on his own product idea.

The product-team type of organization is an attempt to formalize the developmental process without losing the close working rela-tionships possible in a small group. The usual procedure is to assign a new-product idea to a team at the onset of the specification phase. The team assumes responsibility for guiding the product through

[23] Ferdinand F. Mauser, "Which System Works Best?" *New Products Marketing,* New York: *Printers' Ink,* May 29, 1964, p. 88.

the evolutionary cycle. Each team is composed of representatives from the various functional areas appointed on a more or less permanent basis. Heading up the team is an administrator who reports directly to a coordinator or a member of top management. When the teams are situated in a product-development department, the administrator assumes more line authority over his team. Black & Decker Manufacturing Company credits quick decisions by a decentralized product team for bringing about an eight-month reduction in development time for a new circular saw. A variation of the team concept has been put into operation by the Elkton Division of Thiokol Chemical. Seven five-man research teams, all volunteers, have been created to conduct product research after working hours and on weekends.

The committee approach has met with varying success in product development. Generally its adoption rate is highest among firms whose top management has a favorable attitude toward committees. The one major disadvantage of the committee seems to be that it is frequently used as a substitute for individual responsibility, so vital if product development is to be successful.[24] Some firms have employed product committees to good advantage in breaking down the traditional barriers between functional areas. At Robertshaw Controls, for example, a committee has been established to improve communications between research and production.

Departmentalization, growing rapidly in popularity, is the most common form of organizational structure for product development.[25] The principal reason for this seems to be the recognition of the need to accord product development a distinct status in the firm's organization. Prior to adopting the departmental concept, many firms will have experimented with one or more of the other types of organization and found them wanting. The size of the typical department is relatively small in terms of staff. Although there are instances of one-man departments, it appears that at least three men are needed, one from each of the functional areas—marketing, manufacturing, and engineering.

Organization Position of Product Development
The importance of new products to a firm makes it imperative that product development report to top management. In small companies this is probably the chief executive. If the president has been the in-

24 *Management of New Products* 3d ed., Chicago: Booz-Allen & Hamilton, Inc., 1963, p. 28.

25 *Ibid.*, pp. 26 - 27.

ventor of most of the firm's product line, he may turn over the day-to-day operations of the business to a subordinate executive and spend all of his time on new products. In this situation, the president solic-its the advice of various specialists as the need arises. The president of a small manufacturing concern, instead of relying upon members of his own firm and disrupting their work schedules, can retain out-side consultants on an annual basis.

The larger the firm is, the more unlikely it is that product devel-opment will report directly to the president. For those firms that have adopted the marketing management concept, the logical location of product development is in marketing on a reporting level paral-lel with the other marketing functions such as sales.

The newest trend seems to be the creation of R&D divisions hav-ing the same organizational status as the traditional organic busi-ness functions. Technical research and product development are combined under a vice-president or an executive vice-president. A R&D division should promote the ever-important coordination that is needed for new products, but its application appears to be limit-ed to those firms that maintain extensive technical research facili-ties.

Staffing Product Development

On the subject of staffing the product-development department, the best approach is to look at what is required from representatives of each of the various functions.

1 Manufacturing
   a Evaluation of the new product's producibility
   b Determination of manufacturing requirements in terms of man-power, materials, and equipment
   c Production of models and prototypes
   d Liaison between product development and manufacturing
2 Marketing
   a Evaluation of the new product's marketability
   b Determination of marketing requirements in terms of man-power, advertising, and sales-promotional materials
   c Determination of the effect the new product will have on the firm's marketing position—other products in the line, com-petition, reputation, etc.
   d Establishment of marketing tests and feedback informational systems
   e Liaison between product development and marketing

3 Engineering
    a Evaluation of the new product's functional capabilities
    b Arrangement of the series of technical tests in the lab and the field
    c Exploration on a continuing basis of current happenings in pure research for new-product ideas
    d Liaison between product development and engineering

As the new product nears the final developmental phases, specialists from the functional areas are called upon in increasing numbers. These might include representatives from quality control, advertising, service, sales promotion, logistics, and packaging. The necessity of a close working relationship with marketing research will eventually lead to the permanent assignment of a researcher to the product-development staff.

The head of product development has the job of coordinating the functional areas. This is made difficult by the vested viewpoints of each function and subfunction. Exercising extraordinary skills in the area of human relations, a product-development head should remain strictly neutral except in regard to the viewpoints of the potential consumer. This situation often forces a firm to go outside when hiring a man to head up product development. Robert Anderson, vice-president of product planning for Chrysler, described the qualifications of persons heading up product development as follows: "They need to know the product, be creative, be broad gauge and articulate people. The best qualification is a strong product background, with above-average interest in the market."[26]

SUMMARY

The growth, perhaps even the survival, of a firm is keyed to new-product offerings. These may be defined to include additions to or deletions from the product line, functional modifications in existing products, and major pricing revisions. The task of formalized product development or product planning is to establish continuity in bringing about these changes.

Although new products help the firm acclimate to change and have an obvious impact on sales, their most vital contribution is improving a firm's long-run profit position. To accept this, it is necessary

[26] Ferdinand F. Mauser, *op. cit.*, p. 90.

to give credence to the concept of the product life cycle, which indictes the desirability of a continuing flow of new products so timed as to perpetuate profits. This cycle is based on two assumptions: (1) all products move through a cycle at a rate directly proportional to that of their institutional and marketing environments; and (2) each and every phase of the cycle is clearly discernible in terms of sales and profit shifts.

The development of new products is fraught with peril. Chances are only about fifty-fifty that a new product placed on the market will result in commercial success. The lack of success with new products can be traced to three internal reasons: (1) insufficient knowledge of the target market, (2) inadequate planning of the product-introduction process, and (3) insensitivity to organizational limitations.

To help overcome these problems, a firm should institute a sound developmental program founded on the practices of the more successful firms in this area, whether they are industrial or consumer. Such practices include (1) wholehearted acceptance of the role of innovator, (2) full realization of the inherent risks involved, (3) critical self-appraisal, (4) ever-increasing reliance on the use of quantitative tools in making decisions, and (5) formalization of the new-product evolution process.

Marketing management must make several crucial decisions in regard to product policy. These decisions involve the fundamental approach—whether it should be based on market segmentation, product differentiation, or a combination of both; product-line simplication; diversification of the product line; and the planning of the obsolescence factor.

In organizing the product-development function, top management needs to ask several pertinent questions. The first concerns the time and budget limitations. In answering, top management should keep in mind that the requisites to success are permanency and substantial investment. The second and third questions concern the organizational structure of product development from an internal as well as external standpoint. The fourth and final question is what personnel types are required in staffing product development.

DISCUSSION QUESTIONS

1 As head of product development, how would you justify next year's departmental budget in terms of the contributions of new products?

2   What are the obstacles to market manipulation?
3   Trace sales and profit through each of the phases of a product's life.
4   How does an innovator view product development?
5   In what ways can the risks of product development be transferred?
6   Outline a new product's evolutionary process.
7   Contrast market segmentation with product differentiation.
8   How can one defend the statement that there are several costs associated with weak products?
9   What are the bases for retention of a product?
10 On what grounds can planned obsolescence be defended?
11 What are the perils in product diversification?
12 In staffing product development, why should one set up a listing of desirable qualities before looking at what is actually available in the personnel market?

SUPPLEMENTARY READING

Berg, Thomas L., and Abe Shuchman (eds.), *Product Strategy and Management,* New York: Holt, Rinehart and Winston, Inc., 1963.

Hodge, Melville H., Jr., "Rate Your Company's Research Productivity," *Harvard Business Review,* November-December, 1963, pp. 109-122.

Kotler, Philip, "Phasing Out Weak Products," *Harvard Business Review,* March-April, 1965, pp. 108-118.

Management of New Products, 3d ed., Chicago: Booz-Allen & Hamilton, Inc., 1963.

New Products Marketing, New York: *Printers' Ink,* May 29, 1964.

O'Meara, John T. Jr., "Selecting Profitable Products," in Edward C. Bursk and John F. Chapman (eds.), *New Decision-Making Tools for Managers,* Cambridge, Mass.: Harvard University Press, 1963, pp. 334-348.

Talley, Walter J. Jr., "Profiting from the Declining Product," *Business Horizons,* Spring, 1964, pp. 77-84.

Tallman, Gerald B., "Planned Obsolescence: The Setting—The Issues Involved," in Lynn H. Stockman (ed.), *Advancing Marketing Efficiency,* Chicago: American Marketing Association, 1959, pp. 27-39.

**product
development—
pricing
decisions**

The price affixed to an industrial good or service would seem to be a most critical strategy in a market characterized as rational. This does not appear to be the case in actual practice, however. A study of sixty-eight industrial-good producers, the results of which are summarized in Table 8.1, indicates that the nonprice aspects of both product development and sales efforts were selected more often than pricing in contributing to market success. This finding is further substantiated when industrial-good manufacturers are grouped by industry. For example, all of the twelve capital-goods manufacturers surveyed selected product research and development and product service.[1] Illustrative of the emphasis on nonprice competitive strategy is the following statement by a Pratt & Whitney Aircraft executive: "Our two most valuable assets saleswise are the technical excellence of our products and our policy of rendering the best possible product service to our customers both before and after the sale."[2]

One possible explanation for the subordination of pricing is that the industrial-marketing executive, realizing the enormous amount

TABLE 8.1 Competitive Strategies Which Contribute to Market Success as Selected by Industrial-good Manufacturers

STRATEGY	PERCENTAGE OF FIRMS SELECTING STRATEGY
Product:	
Product research and development	79
Product service	79
Average product-selection ratio	79
Sales efforts:	
Sales research and sales planning	63
Management of sales personnel	49
Advertising and sales promotion	37
Average sales-effort-selection ratio	50
Pricing	47
Other areas:	
Distribution channels and control	50
Organizational structure	34
Marketing cost budgeting and control	18
Financing and credit	12
Transportation and storage	9
Public relations	7

Source: Jon G. Udell, "How Important Is Pricing in Competitive Strategy?" *Journal of Marketing*, January, 1964, table 2, p. 46.

[1] Jon G. Udell, "How Important Is Pricing in Competitive Strategy?" *Journal of Marketing*, January, 1964, p. 46.

[2] *Ibid.*, p. 45.

of market know-how possessed by himself and his competitors, has shelved the idea of using price differentials as part of his strategy. Instead every attempt is made to incorporate flexibility into the pricing structure so as to facilitate the immediacy of reaction to competitive price changes. Such defensiveness in pricing is extremely hazardous, however, for it promotes an atmosphere of "management by crisis."

Another explanation may be that intense competition allows little freedom in pricing. Thus, management has tended to rely more heavily on product and selling differentiations.

Yet another possible explanation is that market-oriented firms have recognized the growing interest of buyers in more than just price and have adjusted their strategy accordingly. Evidence of consumer interest in factors besides price are the supplier-performance evaluation programs sponsored by the National Association of Purchasing Agents. Here both product quality and delivery record are considered along with price in evaluating suppliers.

Finally, pricing other than in response to the dictates of the market may be deliberately shunned to avoid any legal entanglements with the federal government. This would seem particularly true of firms that have a dominant market position or are in markets that are characterized by a fewness of sellers.

TYPES OF PRICING DECISIONS

Pricing is not just one decision but a series of decisions. First, it must be determined whether prices are to be based on costs, competition, or some combination of the two. A rule of thumb that is often applied is the greater the differentiation in product and/or marketing effort, the greater can be the reliance on cost as a basis in pricing.

Second, it has to be decided whether to price products separately or in conjunction with other products in the line. Excellent reasons for interdependent pricing are the existence of joint demand or the desirability of pricing one product to promote the rest of the line. As an example of the latter situation, a manufacturer of stapling equipment and supplies would probably wish to price staple guns low enough to maximize the potential market for staples.

Third, a decision must be made on whether a product is to be priced in one market to gain entry to another. Traditionally, manufacturers of automotive components have priced original equipment with a view toward the replacement market.

Fourth, a decision has to be reached on how consumers are to be classified in relation to quantity and functional discounts. Fifth, it has to be decided what consideration if any is to be given the geographical location of consumers. Sixth is the question of whether prices are to be administered systematically. This might involve scheduling price reductions to coincide with the stages in the product-line cycle or seasonal business variations such as a summer slump. Administered pricing systems are also installed to implement an adequate return on products regardless of the state of demand.

In the firm that utilizes middlemen a decision must be reached on whether resale prices are to be maintained and, if so, what enforcement means are to be employed. Whenever a firm decentralizes profit responsibility to its divisions, this necessitates a decision on the systemization of interdivisional pricing.

A decision all firms should make, but do not, is what effect social and ethical considerations are to have on pricing. Questions that may arise from social and ethical issues include such subject areas as (1) profit maximization, (2) illegal pricing tactics of competitors, (3) persuasive pricing such as inflated list prices, and (4) inflation.

MAJOR DETERMINANTS OF PRICES

In attempting to arrive at what is the best price for a given product, the marketer must carefully study the major factors influencing price. These are (1) costs, (2) market conditions, (3) marketing objectives of the firm, (4) geographical location of consumers, and (5) legal implications.

Costs

Without knowledge of costs, an industrial marketer can only hope he has made the best pricing decision. Nowhere is this more obvious than where the price of a product is set below cost. Just how disastrous this can be is vividly illustrated by the predicament Convair found itself in when the startling finding was made that outlays for vendor-supplied components would total more than the price for the 880.[3] Mounting pressure for a greater knowledge of costs also

---

[3] Richard Austin Smith, "How a Great Corporation Got out of Control," *Fortune,* February, 1962, pp. 120-121.

comes from the industrial consumer who is using value analysis increasingly to determine what he is willing to pay.

The acquisition of knowledge in the area of costs can be divided into two tasks. The primary task is to define the types of costs that enter into the pricing decision. Once these have been determined, the next task is to set up a system for collecting cost data accurately and promptly.

In regard to the types of costs the marketer will be concerned with in pricing, a basic distinction is usually made between the general categories of fixed and variable. Fixed costs, also referred to as constant or horizontal costs, do not vary to any significant degree with the volume of output over a stated period of time. They are costs which require a management decision to commit funds for a period of time, usually a year. Examples are salaries, rent, insurance, taxes, maintenance, and interest.

Variable costs increase or decrease, often proportionately to variations in output volume. The two best examples of variable costs are materials utilized directly in the manufacture of products and the labor costs attributed to manufacturing products. At any given output level total costs equal fixed costs plus variable costs. As variable costs constitute the only changing portion of total costs, variable and not fixed costs are an important consideration in making pricing decisions. One limitation to the concept of variable costs as a continuous function of output is that in actual circumstances such costs frequently remain fixed over a range of production and then increase abruptly. This is particularly true of many marketing costs.

Another useful classification of costs is one based on their relationship to the calendar—past, present, and future. Although the distinctions between these costs are self-evident, the implication of using future rather than past costs in pricing is often ignored. As in other decisions, management must look to the future in pricing. Therefore, the only relevancy past costs have is as a guide to what might be expected in the future. The concreteness of past costs should not mislead the decision maker into relying too heavily on past costs in making forecasts because in doing so there is the implicit assumption that the future will be an exact replica of the past. For new products, the forecasting of future costs is especially important in that the cost structure will undoubtedly change as the firm gains experience. The application of the learning-curve principle to the labor costs of aircraft assembly is an excellent example of the changes reflected by future costs.

Other cost concepts which are relevant to pricing decisions are sunk costs, incremental costs, and common costs. A cost resulting from a decision which is now irrevocable is referred to as a sunk cost. Because sunk costs cannot be altered by any current action, they should be ignored in pricing decisions. The most common sunk cost for the industrial-goods manufacturer is research and development. When an attempt is made to amortize sunk costs through pricing, the price is excessive to most of the market. A far better approach is to view sunk costs as an operating condition for a particular industry.

Incremental or differential costs represent the added costs resulting from a change in business activity. Incremental costs will arise in pricing decisions when it is necessary to consider a new activity. This might be a new product, a foreseen shift in marketing channels once a specific stage in the product life cycle has been reached, or an improvement in an existing product.

Costs that are not traceable to individual products are called common costs. One type of common cost arises from so-called joint products. Two or more products are said to be joint when increasing the output of one (e.g. butter) means an increase in the other (e.g. nonfat dry milk). Common costs also arise with alternative products. This type of product is found where an increase in the output of one (e.g. fluid milk) brings about a decrease in the others (e.g. cheeses). Common costs can come about from accounting practices. Cost classification for financial reporting often makes it necessary to allocate "general costs" that cannot be directly traced to a specific product.

The second task, efficient systemizing of cost data collection, usually requires setting up a research unit reporting directly to the product-development or marketing-research manager. There are two very good reasons for not assigning the task to accounting. The most obvious is that it is not the traditional accounting point of view toward costs which is desired. The second reason is that it is much more sound from an organizational standpoint to group interrelated tasks together.

Market Conditions

An understanding of the various types of market structures is an invaluable tool in analyzing the problems attendant upon pricing decisions. What with diversification and the rapid changes that are likely to occur in any market, it is not enough nowadays for a marketer to know just the market in which he is presently operating.

Figure 8.1 presents schematically the different sets of market con-

FIGURE 8.1   Schematic Presentation of Possible Industrial Market Structures.

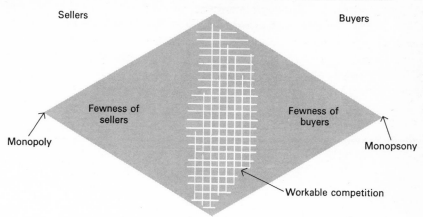

ditions. At one end of the diagram are found market situations close-ly paralleling the concept of a monopoly or one seller. Pure monop-olies do not exist in fact, principally because of alternate-product competition. However, there are scattered instances where a mar-ket or market segment tends to be monopolistic in nature. One of these occurs during the early stages of new-product introduction. Other instances of monopoly may result from a highly differentiated product and/or marketing effort.

With pricing under his complete control, the monopolist's objective is to keep from dissipating the existing barriers to market entry. Usu-ally this implies setting the price low enough to discourage poten-tial competition by the lack of profit opportunity. It is also possible that low prices acting as an indication of not wishing to exploit the buyer tend to preserve the so-called institutional barriers such as control of strategic patents.

Oligopolies, or market situations characterized by a fewness of sellers, are not unlike monopolies in that entry to the market is blocked. The most significant of the barriers is the great size the indi-vidual firm must have to reach an optimum scale of production. The steel, aluminum, agricultural machinery, and heavy electrical machin-ery industries are typical oligopolies. In a discussion of pricing tactics, oligopolies are classified into two general categories according to the degree of product uniformity in a given industry. These can be labeled standardized product output and nonstandardized product out-put.

What is unique about pricing in an oligopoly is that the marketer must take into account the effect of his policy on the other members of the industry. The primary objective is to select the price that will stimulate the interrelated market reactions in such a way as to give promise of the maximum return on investment. In the absence of nonprice competition a price change by one firm is likely to result in a new price level for the entire industry with a standardized product output. This in effect rules out a price reduction unless an anticipated enlargement of the market can compensate for the loss of revenue. When product output is not standardized, a price change under the preceding circumstances will undoubtedly alter each oligopolist's market share, at least in the short run. The presence of formidable nonprice competition serves only to complicate the assessment of moves and countermoves by oligopolists with standardized and non-standardized products. The theory of games has been applied with some success in the development of criteria for choosing price strategies under oligopolistic conditions.[4]

In many oligopolistic markets with standardized product output sellers follow some scheme of price leadership. For this to happen there must be industry dominance by one or possibly two member firms. Economic dominance arises when one firm has a major share of the market and the financial strength to sustain extensive R&D as well as withstand price wars. When the largest firm takes upon itself to evaluate the market and determine what price is best for the whole industry, there exists what might be called barometric leadership. This usually follows a period of destructive price competition. Such a role, regardless of its altruistic intent, may have been discarded by many price leaders after the steel price controversy in 1961. Local or regional markets may see a type of dominance that is occasioned by one firm's aggressive pricing policy. The continuous precipitation of price wars typifies this form of price leadership.

Price leadership offers advantages to all constituents of an industry. The foremost is that each firm knows its market share is safe from a price invasion by competitors. This is ensured by each of the followers operating within informal limits set by tacit industry agreement. Followers are also aware that price leadership relieves them of having to make major pricing decisions. Follower firms can also benefit from the implied responsibility of the leader to foster expansion of the total market through R&D.

---

[4] A pioneer treatise on the theory of games is John von Neumann and Oskar Morgenstern, *Theory of Games and Economic Behavior,* 3d ed., New York: John Wiley & Sons, 1946.

At the other end of the diagram are found market situations characterized as monopsonies, or single-buyer markets. If there are only a few buyers, the market is called an oligopsony. The most obvious examples of a monopsonist are the Department of Defense and the National Aeronautical and Space Administration. A comparative fewness of buyers is encountered quite frequently in industrial markets. Basically, this is caused by a vertical market involving an oligopolistic industry in the industrial- or consumer-goods field. In the automotive original-equipment market, a manufacturer of component parts has only four potential buyers. This could be further diminished to a monopsony if selling to one alienated the rest. A reduction in buyers can also develop from the awarding of a concession to one or a limited group of firms. A situation such as this occurs when a syndicate of petroleum companies is granted the drilling rights for a specific land or offshore area. These monopsonies, however, tend to be localized and temporary.

Much as in a monopoly, entry to a monopsonistic market is barred. Like monopolists and oligopolists, buyers in analogous positions dare not exercise their full powers lest they be subjected to a poor public image and government scrutiny. Also, it is to the monopsonist's advantage to maintain good supplier relations.

The requisites for effective pricing in a market with a limited number of buyers are (1) knowledge of the demand function for the buyer's product, (2) knowledge of the buyer's cost structure, and (3) flexibility in pricing policy. Perhaps nowhere is the industrial seller as dependent upon the demand for his customer's products as under monopsonistic market conditions. An understanding of direct demand will provide the seller with the answers to when and how much, around which he can plan his pricing tactics. What is more, such information will point up the opportunities there are for joint promotional and product-development projects with the buyer to enlarge his market. Knowing the cost structure enables the seller to predict when and to what extent pressures will be brought by the buyer. This combined with a flexible pricing policy will help the seller achieve responsiveness which can often be the difference between success and failure in such a market.

The market situation the majority of industrial sellers find themselves in can best be described as workable competition. Workable competition is distinguished by:

1 Surmountable barriers to market entry
2 Differentiated products in terms of physical characteristics and nonprice competitive tools

3   Differentiated conditions under which goods and services are bought and sold
4   Sufficient buyers and sellers to ensure that no one functioning independently can dominant the market for any extended period of time

Under workable competition, the marketer attempts to maintain a certain relationship between selling price and cost. This relationship is characterized by the degree of product differentiation, the role of pricing in the firm's marketing mix, the stage of the product in its life cycle, and the state of general business conditions. By the use of product differentiation and other nonprice competitive tools it is very possible for a marketer under workable competition to control demand at least in the short run. Where there is very little opportunity to differentiate products or use nonprice competitive tools, marketers turn their attention toward gaining greater efficiency in operation.

Marketing Objectives
The marketing objectives of a firm determine the marketing mix, which in turn establishes what emphasis is to be placed upon the different components of the marketing and product strategies. Thus, by specifying the strategic role price is to play, marketing objectives exert a tremendous influence on pricing decisions.

As previously discussed, makers of industrial goods tend to rely more heavily on the nonprice aspects of product and sales than on price. Perhaps never is price more in the background than it is when a firm adopts a policy that all changes in basic costs are to be automatically passed along to its customers. While most firms are not willing to go this far, there are countless examples even in standardized product industries where the stress is on nonprice tools as the basis of competition. The chemical industry is a good example of a competitive situation where the nonprice aspects of product innovation overshadow price.

Other prominent constituents of the marketing mix tantamount to price include credit, before-and-after technical services, and sales promotion. All of these stand out more clearly as the firm expands its market. This can be most vividly shown in the case of credit. Suppose a farm-machinery manufacturer wishes to expand its market. Two of its primary targets are small, almost marginal farmers for their first or overdue replacement tractor and medium-size farmers for an additional tractor. Price to both of these consumers is not nearly as decisive in the purchasing decision as are credit terms, which in this case would have to be more liberal than usual.

The objective of achieving or maintaining a market share has an unequivocal effect on pricing. If the goal is to gain greater market penetration, pricing will vary with the marketing position of the firm, market conditions, and the marketing target. A price leader in an oligopoly would probably want to keep prices steady and use non-price marketing tools to elicit new customers for his type of product. This often takes the form of establishing new distributive outlets in geographical areas heretofore considered below minimum profitability.

When a firm is attempting to maintain its market share, it is much more difficult to predict the effect this will have on price. It is quite likely, however, that price stability varies inversely with consumer exposure to the market. Prices will remain fairly stable when consumers make only infrequent entries into the market. Conversely, repeated market exposure is liable to result in unstable prices. To illustrate, it is extremely doubtful whether a meat packer could hope to maintain its share of the restaurant market without accepting the possibility of almost weekly price changes.

Geographical Location of Consumers

When the location of consumers is such that transportation charges have a significant effect on the price of a product or product line, geographical differentials must be considered an integral part of any pricing system. Geographical pricing is based on either the point of origin or the point of destination.

Under point-of-origin or f.o.b. pricing the buyer pays the mill price for the product plus the actual freight costs. He may or may not have the option of selecting the means of transportation. A uniform return on each sale and the avoidance of any illegal discrimination are the chief advantages of f.o.b. pricing. When competitors are widely scattered, the use of this basis tends to create exclusive trading areas, for f.o.b. pricing puts the seller at a disadvantage in that he is excluded spatially from extending his market except through overall price reductions.

When the basis is the point of destination, the so-called delivered price includes the cost of transporting the products to the buyer's location. There are three types of delivered pricing—postage stamp, basing point, and zone. Postage-stamp pricing involves charging a uniform delivered price to all buyers regardless of location. Quotations are usually arrived at by adding the average freight expenditures to the mill price. The purpose of this type of delivered pricing is to give the seller access to all geographical markets. Even though postage-stamp pricing economically discriminates against nearby buyers by having them pay more for freight than those located farther away, the Supreme Court has held it to be legal. Occasionally a variation is used to reduce some of the more ostensible economic discrimination. One of these is for each buyer to pay a uniform mill price less the actual freight charges incurred.

The earliest attempts by industrial marketers at delivered pricing were those involving basing points. With a single basing point the delivered price consists of the quoted mill price at the basing point plus transportation charges from the basing point regardless of the shipping point. The best-known example of the single basing point system was "Pittsburgh Plus," employed by the steel industry until set aside in 1924 as a result of a case against the United States Steel Corporation.

The same principle applies in the case of multiple basing point systems except that two or more producing centers are designated as basing points. A buyer will pay the mill price at the nearest basing point plus the transportation charges from that point. Prices quoted at the various basing points may be uniform or varied. Both phantom freight and freight absorption are involved in basing point pricing systems. Phantom freight is incurred when the freight charges paid by the buyer exceed actual freight charges. It usually comes about when there are fewer basing points than mills and the buyer is nearer to the mill than to a basing point. Whereas phantom freight is a profit to the seller, freight absorption represents an expense. Originally under a basing point system, freight costs were absorbed when the buyer was closer to a basing point than to a mill. The seller might have a mill at the particular basing point in question, but it might not produce the desired product.

Today a seller will absorb freight costs primarily when it is necessary to meet a competitor's lower delivered price. Stated another way, freight absorption is a tactic a firm with a delivered pricing system uses to expand its geographical market below the spatial limits set by freight rates. In announcing this philosophy in the 1953 annual report, the United States Steel Corporation said it was consistent with the stand long taken by the Corporation—"that it has the right to compete in good faith in any market for the business of any consumer."[5] Freight absorption is also used fairly extensively by

[5] *Annual Report, 1953*. Pittsburgh: United States Steel Corporation, 1953, p. 12.

the Du Pont Company. A good example is the following excerpt from a summary of their pricing systems.[6]

Graselli Chemicals Department
Most acids and heavy chemicals, such as technical sulfuric acid and sodium nitrite, are priced f.o.b. mill, freight equalized with nearest competitor's producing point. Some are delivered free within certain metropolitan areas and others are f.o.b. mill. With a few exceptions, industrial speciality products are f.o.b. mill. Slab zinc for all grades but the Intermediate is an exception, selling f.o.b. at a base point which is not the shipping point.

Most agricultural chemicals are f.o.b. mill or nearest warehouse, minimum freight allowed or prepaid to common carrier destination on 96 pounds or over. Others are f.o.b. mill, freight equalized with nearest competitor. Sales to retailers are at a delivered price.

In zone pricing the nation is divided up into specified areas or zones, each with a different delivered price. To arrive at the delivered price, the average transportation charge experienced in serving buyers in the zone is added to the f.o.b. mill price. A firm should experience no legal hazards when pricing zones closely approximate freight-rate zones for the transportation medium generally used to ship the product. As a rule a high ratio of transportation costs to the value of a product will indicate a great number of small pricing zones.

Impact of the Government

The two areas where the federal government exerts an undeniable influence are price fixing and price discrimination. In spite of the fact that price fixing has been construed to be illegal per se since the turn of the century, it still may exist at various times in many sectors of the industrial market. The reason is that many marketers think that given the economic conditions under which they must operate, profits will suffer without some degree of price fixing.

Among the more significant economic conditions inducing price fixing are:

1 So few sellers that the pricing actions of one are fully felt by the others
2 Fairly inelastic demand resulting from the existence of either effective nonprice competition or market saturation

---

[6] A. D. H. Kaplan, Joel B. Dirlam, and Robert F. Lanzillotti, *Pricing in Big Business*, Washington: The Brookings Institution, 1958, p. 301.

3   Effective price leadership by a firm that has a substantial share
    of the market
4   No substantial cost advantage enjoyed by any industry member
5   No excess plant capacity for any industry member

Although the quotation of identical prices by competing sellers
may be a tip off to collusion as it was in the cement and electrical-
equipment cases, any misconduct must still be proved. Evidence
of conspiracy usually hinges on the agreement of witnesses to testify about their associates under the cloak of immunity. The threat
of jail sentences probably had a lot to do with overcoming the reluctance of many electrical-equipment industry executives to testify.

The legality of delivered pricing systems has always been over-
clouded by the collusive behavior of sellers, often under the guise
of a trade association. A case in point involves the Cement Institute.
An identical bid of $3.286854 per barrel was received from eleven
different cement producers. If this was not ample evidence of conspiracy, it was revealed at the trial that all members of the Institute
were supplied railroad freight-rate books which in many instances
were at variance with actual rates.[7]

It is not necessary that prices be identical for price fixing to exist
between sellers. Members of the electrical-equipment industry had
an agreement whereby each would take its turn as the low bidder
on a contract. Oftentimes formal or informal agreements are in effect on who is to have a particular segment of the market. The only
price competition a seller will experience in his allotted segment or
segments will be in the form of "courtesy" bids.[8] These are bids at
a higher price submitted by competitors to ensure a sufficient number.

The impact of the government on price discrimination is through
the Robinson-Patman Act. This federal law, enacted in 1936, amended
Section 2 of the Clayton Act of 1914. The provision of this act that
industrial marketers are most concerned with is Section 2(a), which
declares that price discrimination is unlawful where its effect may
be substantially to lessen competition or tend to create a monopoly
in any line of commerce, or to injure, destroy, or prevent competition with any person who either grants or knowingly receives the
benefit from such discrimination, or with customers of either of them.

---

[7] *Federal Trade Commission v. Cement Institute*, 333 U.S. 683 (1948).

[8] Marshall C. Howard, *Legal Aspects of Marketing*, New York: McGraw-Hill Book Company,
1964, p. 36.

Thus, for price discrimination to be unlawful, it must substantially lessen competition.

There are three levels of competition where unlawful price discrimination can be found under the terms of the Robinson-Patman Act. The first is what is generally called the primary seller level. In an effort to force Seller B out of a particular geographical market, Seller A cuts his prices in this market while maintaining them elsewhere. The purpose of such action is to reduce competition in a particular market. This could even be construed as an attempt to monopolize a market. It would make no difference whether Seller B, the injured party, sold only in this geographical market or on a nationwide scale.

The second or buyer level of competition involves price discrimination that occurs when a seller charges different prices to like buyers of like quantity and quality. The effect on competition is that the buyer who pays the higher price is at a disadvantage in competing with the buyer who receives the lower price. How great a disadvantage the buyer will have depends upon what part of his cost structure is represented by the goods in question. A good example of price discrimination at the secondary competitive level is found in the Corn Products cases.[9] Candy manufacturers outside Chicago were paying a higher price for corn syrup than were Chicago-based manufacturers. This was effected by the employment of a single basing point pricing system. Delivered prices quoted by the Corn Products Refining Company often included phantom freight because the corn syrup was actually shipped from Kansas City, Missouri. The obvious price discrimination was sufficient for the courts to hold that it lessened competition between candy manufacturers.

The third competitive level involves customers of the customer. While the adverse competitive effect of price discrimination at this level is most difficult to trace, it is liable to be a problem of increasing concern for industrial marketers in the years to come. The reason is that through an ever-growing use of segmentation industrial marketers have had to distinquish in pricing between classes of customers in different marketing channels. Suppose a manufacturer of auto parts markets through just two channels. One is automobile manufacturers for original equipment and dealer replacement. The other is auto-parts wholesalers who sell in turn to garages, gasoline stations, and the like. A lower price to automobile manufacturers would not be unlawful price discrimination at the buyer or sec-

---

[9] *Corn Products Refining Co. v. Federal Trade Commission,* 324 U.S. 726 (1945) and *A. E. Staley Mfg. Co. v. Federal Trade Commission,* 324 U.S. 746 (1945).

ondary level primarily because the buyers are not in competition with each other. However, if the price differential is passed along to automobile dealers, this will injure competition by placing the customers of wholesalers at a disadvantage.

The Robinson-Patman Act specifies two defenses the seller can avail himself of in an attempt to justify price discrimination. One defense is to show that price discrimination is a reflection of cost differentiations. These differentiations can result from cost savings in the manufacture, sale, or delivery of a product to a specific customer or general group of customers. An obvious limitation to cost justification is proving that savings are directly attributable to differing methods or quantities of sale or delivery.

The other defense under the Robinson-Patman Act is that the seller acting in good faith has lowered his price to meet competition. As with cost justification, the defense of meeting competition is hampered in that it can be employed only after the fact, i.e. illegal price discrimination. The position of the Federal Trade Commission on this line of defense has not been very favorable nor is it expected to improve in the future. There are several restrictions to a good-faith defense.

1 This defense is limited to the primary or seller level and cannot be passed along the channel of distribution. Therefore a seller cannot help his customers meet the lower prices of a price cutter.
2 This defense states that the seller may meet but not undercut the lower price of a competitor.
3 This defense allows the seller to meet only those prices that are lawful.
4 This defense disallows any price cuts the seller knows are changes in the permanent price schedule. In other words the discriminatory price must be a temporary price.
5 This defense is available only when a lower price is granted to retain an old customer. Lower prices that are utilized as part of a program to gain new customers cannot be defended on the basis of good faith as legal price discrimination.
6 This defense is applicable only when the seller is quoting a lower price on the same quantity as that in the competitor's quotation.
7 This defense is limited to meeting a specific price of a competitor to a specific customer or group of customers.

In two major segments of the industrial market, sellers are exempted from the provisions of Section 2(a). Exempted are sales to governmental units at the local, state, and federal level and sales of supplies to nonprofit institutions such as churches and schools. Other exemptions not quite so important to the industrial marketer are transactions in which price is lowered in response to changing market or product conditions affecting the salability of the goods concerned. This might happen when physical deterioration and ensuing loss is imminent if the goods in question are not disposed of immediately.

PRICING GOALS

What the industrial marketer hopes to realize through pricing is maximum long-term profitability. Any other aim would be inconsistent with the overall objective of any business—namely, to establish a continuity of existence. The exact pricing goals adopted by an individual firm depend entirely upon the nature of its market or markets. When a firm serves more than one market, it is quite likely that different pricing goals will be in effect for each one.

The Brookings Institution, in its well-known 1958 study of pricing in big business, found the most common pricing goals to be:[10]

1   Pricing to achieve a target return on investment
2   Pricing to stabilize price and margin
3   Pricing to maintain or improve market share
4   Pricing to meet or follow competition

To this list might be added one or possibly two more goals. First, the overriding consideration in pricing may be to discourage entry of potential competition. Second, pricing that permits maximization of product adoption permits flexibility in pricing to match the stages of the product life cycle.

Target Return on Investment
With this objective the selling price is determined by adding to an estimate of standard costs a margin that will yield a desired average return on capital employed. Implied in the use of this highly popular basis for pricing are several vital considerations. One is the allocation of costs on a product-by-product basis. Another considera-

---

[10] A. D. H. Kaplan, Joel B. Dirlam, and Robert F. Lanzillotti, *op. cit.*, p. 128.

tion is what long-term plant capacity factor is to be brought to bear in calculating standard costs. Usually a particular product mix is assumed as normal. To avoid having to charge higher prices when output is less than anticipated, Alcoa applies fixed costs on the basis of current capacity. The remaining fixed-cost burden is treated as a period expense.[11]

Undoubtedly the most important consideration, and one which the firm may be called upon to justify, is the size of the target return. It probably will range anywhere from 7 to 20 percent after taxes. The industry to which the firm belongs, intuitive judgment on what the market will bear, and the historical rate of return attained by the firm, all play a prominent role in selecting a target return. Instead of a specific target, some firms, to be on the safe side, may wish to set up a range with both a minimum and a maximum rate of return.

Stabilization of Prices and Margins
By stabilization of price and margin, firms can limit the variation of two very important ingredients in forward planning. Typically this pricing objective is adopted by firms which have a large share of markets characterized by fluctuating prices. As an example, the Kennecott Copper Corporation has long sought greater price stability for refined copper.[12]

Like target returns on investment, stabilization goals rely on a cost-plus method of pricing. Initially a price is set which will yield a "fair or reasonable" return during periods of normal market activity. When a sellers' market develops, instead of charging what the traffic will bear, the firm will lag below the market as long as it is possible. Conversely, in a buyers' market the firm may withdraw from the market until a higher price level is restored.

From the foregoing it is apparent that only firms having market dominance can hope to achieve the goal of price stability. The firm which does attain some measure of success in stabilizing prices must contend with two interrelated problems. The first is that prices resulting from a stabilization objective are liable to be defined as administrative because they do not fluctuate with supply and demand. Just use of the term "administrative pricing" is enough to stir a controversy. Among those prominently aligned against this type of pric-

[11] T. W. Kerry, Aluminum Company of America, in a speech delivered before the South Florida National Association of Cost Accountants, March, 1956.

[12] A. D. H. Kaplan, Joel B. Dirlam, and Robert F. Lanzillotti, *op. cit.*, p. 176.

ing are influential members of the federal government and economists. It is their contention that in using this technique big businesses
are pricing in excess of a reasonable return, thus augmenting the
economic peril of inflation.[13]

Akin to the problem of administrative pricing is that of justifying
the "fairness" or "reasonableness" of a return. The problem of answering the question of what is fair or reasonable has been a source of
irritation to businessmen for many years. Implied in justification is
the assumption that the rate is too high because the firm has neglected
so-called public interests. Business spokesmen usually counter this
by explaining the disposition of the return. An oft-repeated defense
is the statement made by Benjamin Fairless when he headed up U.S.
Steel:[14]

> *A price is reasonable if it nets a reasonable return to our company;
> if it permits us to pay good wages to our employees to keep our
> facilities in excellent condition, to keep our equipment abreast
> of the developments within this industry, also if possible to pay
> a fair return to the owners of the business.*

Maintaining or Improving Market Share

Maintenance or improvement of market share is an agressive pricing objective adopted by firms in highly competitive markets. It is
rarely employed by firms that enjoy a distinct competitive advantage
such as through patent protection.

Market-share objectives are frequently used when products have
reached the maturity stage of their life cycle. If there is any evidence
of demand being elastic, the marketer will undoubtedly want to concentrate on maximizing his total profit by gaining a greater market
share through lower prices.

A market-share objective for a fabricated-materials producer will
probably entail expanding into heretofore untapped end-use segments.
Prices will have to be adjusted to match or undercut those of competing alternate products for each end-use segment it is necessary
to exploit in attaining the desired market share. Assuming homogeneous buyer behavior in each segment, a decision matrix such as

---

[13] For a synopsis of the pros and cons regarding administrative pricing see William H. Peterson, "Divergent Views on Pricing Policy," *Harvard Business Review*, March-April, 1963,
p. 20.

[14] *Investigation of Concentration of Economic Power*, Hearings before the Temporary National Economic Committee, 76th Cong., 2d Sess. (1949), pt. 19, p. 10526.

TABLE 8.2 Pricing Payoff Decision Matrix

PRICE LEVELS	END-USE MARKET SEGMENTS						AGGREGATE EXPECTED DEMAND
	S_1	S_2	S_3	S_4	S_5	S_6	
P_1	a_{11}	a_{12}	a_{13}	a_{14}	a_{15}	a_{16}	P_1D_1
P_2	a_{21}	a_{22}	a_{23}	a_{24}	a_{25}	a_{26}	P_2D_2
P_3	a_{31}	a_{32}	a_{33}	a_{34}	a_{35}	a_{36}	P_3D_3
P_4	a_{41}	a_{42}	a_{43}	a_{44}	a_{45}	a_{46}	P_4D_4
P_5	a_{51}	a_{52}	a_{53}	a_{54}	a_{55}	a_{56}	P_5D_5
AGGREGATE EXPECTED DEMAND	S_1D_1	S_2D_2	S_3D_3	S_4D_4	S_5D_5	S_6D_6	TD

a_{11}, a_{12}, etc. = estimated units of P_1D_1

$$SD_J = \sum_{I=1}^{m} a_{IJ}\, PD_I \qquad PD_I = \sum_{J=1}^{n} a_{IJ}\, UD_J \qquad TD = \sum_{J=1}^{n} \sum_{I=1}^{m} a_{IJ}\, UD_J$$

the one depicted in Table 8.2 might be constructed to aid in selecting the best price for a given product.

On a somewhat smaller scale, an industrial distributor may want to specify a minimum market share in order to break even on a service installation required by the franchise. A franchise for many equipment dealers may mean providing twenty-four hour service for customers. If sufficient repair volume is not generated through sales, the dealer's profit margin will be reduced by his having to shift the unabsorbed costs. An industrial distributor may also wish to secure a certain market share to write off the promotional work involved in holding a franchise.

Competitive Parity

When prices are believed to be determined by market forces beyond the control of the seller, a goal of meeting or following competition is frequently adopted. It also seems to be the type of pricing goal managements resort to when they are overwhelmed by the fear of losing competitive status in markets characterized by a fewness of sellers or buyers.

The decision to follow or meet competition necessitates defining both competition and the position the seller wishes to maintain in relation to competition. Competition may mean the industry price leader, a major competitor, or all competitors. When a price leader is defined as the competition, it is usually because the seller respects the retaliatory power of the much larger firm. Whether one or all rivals are designated as competition depends primarily upon the structure of the market. If each rival has about the same size of market share and there has been very little change in the overall pattern during the last five years, all rivals, or in other words the market, will undoubtedly be labeled the competition. If, on the other hand, one rival firm stands out from the rest as an aggressive marketer, it will be specified as the competition. In the latter situation the major competitor need not be any larger than the seller. A good example is a rival firm that strives for differentiation through product development.

There are three positions the seller can occupy in respect to competition. The most obvious is to match competition by citing an identical price. While many feel that this position simplifies pricing decisions, there are the implicit assumptions that the seller is as efficient as the competition and can compete equally well using nonprice tools. Too, any firm holding such a position must organize an informational system to keep on top of changes the competition may make. Salesmen, properly instructed, can be very helpful in obtaining competitive price information from common customers.

Taking a position above the competition's price implies that the seller has some advantage which can be made readily discernible to the consumer through marketing efforts. This affords a good example of the coordination that needs to be effected between product and marketing strategies. Suppose R&D wants to add a feature that will prolong product life but will necessarily mean an increase in price over that of the competition. Marketing research should be consulted as to whether the improvement is important to the consumer; if it is, the information on the new feature should be passed along to marketing strategists for inclusion in plans for selling and advertising efforts. A mistake many industrial marketers make is assuming rational purchasers will ferret out new developments without being told or shown.

The safest position in a market characterized by frequent and abrupt price changes is below the competition. Exactly how far below depends upon the range of variation in competitive prices. Usually a price will be set at or slightly below the lower limit of the range. Holding such a position, the seller can all but ignore the multiplicity of price changes made by the competition. Even if there is a desire to follow the price movements, this position affords the advantage of not having to take immediate action. In fact, by lagging behind price increases, the seller may find that the wider price differential attracts certain segments of the market. Another advantage of quoting below the competition is that it tends to ensure against losing present customers temporarily through price cuts by other firms.

Dissuading Potential Competition

If the market entry of potential competitors is directly related to current profitability, a seller might wish to give careful consideration to this threat in his pricing. Smaller firms rather than larger ones are inclined to adopt this type of objective to protect their market, say in a particular geographical region. The optimum price under these conditions is determined by scaling in terms of gross profit the probability of competitive market entry, the implication being that the seller will price lower than he would if it were not for potential competition.

When financial barriers exist, the seller will probably want to refrain from full-cost pricing. By treating many of the fixed costs as sunk costs, potential competition will be thwarted in that it will not be able to meet the market price and still recover its investment as rapidly as it would like. In an attempt to diversify into the gear market, a defense contractor discovered much to his chagrin that full-cost pricing resulted in a figure which was about twice the market level.

There are situations, however, where potential competition is not as interested in profitability as in the possible volume of business. About the only defense is to divide up the total market into segments, none of which has a volume which would tempt entry. The seller might then solicit business from only a limited number of the segments, charging what the traffic will bear. The sales volume will be less, but profits can be maintained through higher unit prices. High unit prices coupled with small expected sales volume are usually enough to discourage most potential competitors.

Maximization of Product Status

Typically, sellers' interests in the product life cycle are limited to pricing new and declining products. With both, however, consideration tends to be in terms of particular situations rather than cyclical stages. The pricing goal of maximizing product status is based on the theory that products pass through a life cycle and in doing so cannot be expected always to make the same contribution to profits. The advantage in adopting this goal is that it frees pricing decisions from the rigidities imposed by cost-plus and margin uniformity. In addition it emphasizes the dominant role played by demand and the need of making independent pricing decisions for each product in the line.

PARTICULAR PROBLEMS IN PRODUCT-LINE PRICING

There are several problems a seller will have to face in pricing a product line. Among the more significant are (1) quantity differentials, (2) status of purchaser differentials, (3) new products, (4) declining products, (5) repair parts, and (6) interdivisional pricing.

Quantity Differentials

Based on the amount of purchase, quantity discounts can be either cumulative or noncumulative. Cumulative discounts are given on total purchases over a period of time. This may be a month, a quarter, or possibly a year. The discounts are treated either as deductions on subsequent purchases or as rebates. The former is by far the most effective way to ensure continued patronage.

The primary purpose of cumulative discounts is to foster the patronage of large buyers, particularly when sizable single orders do not represent any savings to the buyer or the seller. In the sale of heavy industrial equipment, for example, it is highly doubtful whether there would be any advantage to the buyer or seller in ordering more than one at a time as needed. In fact, it is doubtful whether any savings could accrue in transportation charges with a large single order since one item of equipment would probably take up an entire railroad car.

The legality of cumulative discounts has been seriously challenged. The difficulty lies in trying to justify price differences between buyers when they all are ordering identical quantities. This can be substantially avoided with no loss in advantages by what is called a negotiated annual contract. This is a contract whereby the seller agrees to purchase a given quantity during the year but retains the right to specify throughout the year the amount of each individual shipment.

Noncumulative discounts are based on the quantity purchased at one given time. Their purpose is to overcome the problem of high-cost small orders. The scale of discounts will vary directly with the economies of scale. Here again cost savings must be demonstrated for each increment. The Federal Trade Commission has the authority to fix quantity limits if it finds the possible number of purchasers in greater quantities is so small as to be discriminatory or promotive of monopoly.[15] Since this authority was unsuccessfully exercised in 1952, there have been no guides as to what constitutes a small number of purchasers.

[15] Federal Trade Commission Quantity Limit Rule 203-1, Jan. 4, 1952.

Physical quantities are the preferable unit of measurement for order size. They make it easier to trace cost savings and there is no distortion from changes in price. However, the product lines of many firms are too diversified to permit adding up physical units. In such cases orders are measured in dollar values.

Status of Purchaser Differentials

Discounts given on the basis of the purchaser's status in the marketing channel are known as functional or distributor discounts. The purpose of functional discounts is to compensate middlemen for the performance of the marketing functions at their particular level in the distribution system. In the sense that a seller must compete for middleman support or assist the middleman in his own competitive environment, functional discounts can be conceived of as buying distribution.[16]

The basis of a functional-discount structure should be the results of a distribution-cost analysis. The exact functional discount will vary in accordance with marketing objectives and the necessity to buy distribution. When extensive market coverage is the overriding objective, the discount will have to be set so as to allow for the marginal middleman. This might be the case for a manufacturer of metal fasteners. If, on the other hand, the coverage objective calls for intensive distribution, the discount is probably set in terms of the average middleman.

The usual practice is to quote functional discounts from a list price. While this permits flexibility in dealing with diverse marketing channels, it does not have the simplicity of net prices. Many manufacturers are also under the impression that discounts from list price offer greater resale control. Usually, effective control is possible only through franchise agreements.

The legality of functional discounts is not clear-cut. The reason for this is that the Robinson-Patman Act makes no mention of functional discounts as such. This places two major encumbrances upon the seller. The first is that middlemen must be classified as strictly as possible according to their particular functions. Chances of price discrimination are materially reduced if each middleman classification is matched with a mutually exclusive market segment. A component producer might use manufacturers' reps to sell to the origin-

[16] Martin R. Warshaw, "Pricing to Gain Wholesalers' Selling Support," *Journal of Marketing*, July, 1962, p. 53.

al-equipment market and industrial distributors to handle replacement sales.

Secondly, the functional discounts granted must not exceed cost savings. This requires maintaining adequate cost records on each middleman channel. One significant complication in gathering relevant cost data is that savings from selling to a particular class of purchaser must be kept separate from savings by selling in quantity.

Pricing New Products

Pricing new products is a complex problem. In the first place the marketer may find himself working in the dark in regard to market reaction and costs. Intuitive judgment is of some help, but for all intents and purposes it is an unreliable predictor of market behavior. The existence of alternate-product competition as a market indicator puts the industrial marketer at less of a disadvantage than his consumer counterpart. Yet even this affords the industrial marketer only a generalized picture, and as such it is of limited value in pricing a distinctly new and different product. One fairly large industrial marketer feels so unsure of the market for a new product that he delays making a sales forecast until there has been commercial exposure for at least a year. As far as costs are concerned, the industrial marketer has to work with data that are necessarily incomplete and frequently incorrect. More than one firm has successfully introduced a new product only to find that actual costs far exceed the original estimate used in pricing.

Secondly, the industrial marketer approaches the problem of pricing a new product with no planned method of attack. Under these circumstances the overriding consideration is very likely to be short-run expediency rather than long-run market acceptance.

Joel Dean breaks down the job of pricing new products into two essential tasks: (1) selecting a basic pricing strategy and (2) factor analysis.[17] There are really only two positions a marketer can take in pricing a new product. A high-price or skimming position attempts to maximize the recovery rate of new-product investment. The increasing costs of R&D plus the current speed of competitive emulation make this strategy almost a competitive necessity for all but the very large firm. Some experts feel that the payoff period may be stretched to three or four times its previous length. Among the other advan-

---

[17] The discussion on new-product pricing is based in part on Joel Dean, "Pricing Policies for New Products," *Harvard Business Review,* November - December, 1950, pp. 28-36.

tages of a skimming price policy are that it reduces the risk inherent in gauging the potential market and simplifies price adjustments by making it much easier to decrease than increase prices.

At the other extreme is the position of low or penetration pricing. Such a policy is designed to saturate as much of the potential market as possible within a relatively short time after introduction. Conditions favoring this type of pricing include a high degree of price elasticity, substantial economies of scale in manufacturing, and a complete absence of patent barriers.

After deciding upon a basic pricing position, a marketer must analyze the marketing and production factors of the new product. The most important is arriving at an estimate of the new product's potential market at several possible price levels. To be on the safe side, a range of estimates rather than one estimate should be utilized. Once this has been determined, a marketing target can be tentatively selected and strategies developed accordingly. Finally, an analysis must be made of the cost factors pertaining to producing and marketing the new product. Ideally a cost structure should be evolved for each proposed price level.

Pricing Declining Products

When a marketer discovers that a product's downward trend in sales is either unprofitable or irreversible through greater promotional outlays, the typical reaction is to resort to large discounts in an effort to "clean house" as quickly as possible. This may be unwise for at least two reasons.

1 It disrupts ties with the hard core of loyal customers who would otherwise keep on buying the product. In fact, if products are dropped repeatedly, the firm's image can seriously suffer.
2 It ignores the profit possibilities in running out a product.

Pricing policies must be decided upon for each practical alternative within a run-out program. The availability of sales and cost records plus the experience gained in marketing the product in question for a substantial period of time provides a sound basis for making these pricing decisions. In addition there are several important influences which must be appraised and weighed for price to fulfill its prescribed role with each alternative. These influences are the nature of demand, competitive reaction, and, where applicable, middleman reaction.

Suppose, for example, a machinery manufacturer has decided to run out a particular model of drill press that has been losing sales for the past few years. Suppose further that one alternative is to concentrate on selling the drill press to small, possibly marginal machine shops. At first glance this would appear to be a market segment that is very sensitive to price. However, sales records show that when price reductions were effected, there was no accompanying increase in sales to this particular market segment. Moreover, salesmen report that members of this segment frequently equate quality with price. From past history it can be expected that competitors will interpret any price reduction as a sign of weakness and start on an intensive campaign to win over the machinery manufacturer's customers. Finally, analysis of the cost structure of the drill press reveals that only at the present price level would it be possible to provide enough margin to compensate industrial distributors for cultivating intensely this particular market segment. Accordingly, it is decided to retain the present price level with this alternative.

Pricing Repair Parts

Competition, actual or potential, is so important in the pricing of repair parts that costs are virtually ignored. Competition will take several forms:

1 Consumers of machinery and equipment may add to the original purchase price the costs of those repair parts which, according to their maintenance records, will most likely need replacing over a certain operating span. In such a situation repair parts are important in the initial sale.
2 Consumers of machinery and equipment may take it upon themselves to produce or rebuild their own repair parts. When they do so, their costs provide a rough measure of the price level above which potential competition can be expected.
3 Manufacturers may do nothing but make repair parts. Often called "parts bandits," these firms make it a practice to price below machinery and equipment manufacturers.
4 Manufacturers may specialize in rebuilding repair parts. The savings offered by rebuilt parts are often substantial enough to interest industrial consumers.

Before making a pricing decision, it is necessary to classify repair parts in line with the degree of competition faced. Two broad classifications are (1) parts readily available from many sources and (2) parts available only from the manufacturer of the original machinery or equipment. Parts that are available from many sources should be priced to equate the buyer's lowest comparable alternative. The key is determining without bias what the comparable alternatives are.

When the original machinery or equipment manufacturer enjoys a monopoly status in making parts, his best approach is to exploit this opportunity by charging what the traffic will bear. About the only limitation is the potential competition from the consumer himself in making his own repair parts.

Interdivisional Pricing.
Because of the wide diversification of many industrial-good manufacturers, one division or subsidiary may buy from another. This has led to problems in establishing an internal pricing system. In seeking an answer to these problems, it must be remembered that the primary purpose of an internal price system is to decentralize the profit incentive to make it consistent with the profit goals of the firm from an overall standpoint.

One approach that can be suggested is to simplify pricing by classifying the products bought and sold within the firm into three groups:

1 Products which have a low probability of ever being produced by an outside supplier. There may be no known outside source, or the company may wish to exercise control over production for security reasons. Typically the prices of these products are set so as to earn the seller a minimal profit. Let us say that if the average markup on outside sales is 30 percent, the margin on sales within the firm might be as low as 8 or 10 percent.

2 Products which are available from a limited number of outside sources. The oligopolistic nature of this market will probably inflate the price level of these products. Thus, direct comparison is unrealistic as a basis for pricing. Sellers of products in this category should be allowed more than a minimal profit margin. The price of outside sources will set the upper limit on price.

3 Products which are readily available from outside sources. Such products should be priced at the outside level unless this happens to be below cost plus minimal markup. In the event that it is and the lower outside price is not a short-term depression, the pricing decision will have to be referred to top management for arbitration.

SUMMARY

Contrary to what might be supposed, the price affixed to a good or service is not the most critical element in the formulation of product and market strategies. There are several reasons for this. First, because of the extent of market know-how, the marketer may have shelved pricing as a formidable competitive weapon. Second, intense competition may permit little freedom in pricing. Third, the marketer may have recognized the fact that his customers are interested in more than just the price of the product. Finally, pricing policy may be geared to market reaction in order to avoid governmental interference.

The decisions which must be made in pricing are as follows:

1   The basis or bases for pricing
2   The degree of interdependence in the pricing of product lines
3   The use of pricing to gain entry to other markets
4   The classification of consumers in relation to quantity and quality discounts
5   The consideration to be given the consumer's geographical location
6   The question of whether prices are to be administered systematically
7   The emphasis or absence of emphasis placed on the social and ethical considerations involved

The major factors which should be analyzed in arriving at the best price for a given product are (1) costs, (2) market conditions, (3) market objectives, (4) geographical location of consumers, and (5) legal implications.

Maximum long-term profitability is what the industrial marketer hopes to realize through pricing. More specifically, the Brookings Institution found the most common pricing goals to be:

1   Pricing to achieve a target return on investment
2   Pricing to stabilize both price and margin
3   Pricing to maintain or improve market share
4   Pricing to meet or follow competition

To this list might be added the goals of discouraging the entry of potential competition and maximizing product status.

Among the more significant problems which may exist in pricing a product line are (1) quantity differentials, (2) purchaser status differentials, (3) new products, (4) declining products, (5) repair parts, and (6) interdivisional pricing.

DISCUSSION QUESTIONS

1 Explain the subordination of pricing in the formulation of product and marketing strategies.
2 What are the reasons for interdependent pricing?
3 Define the various cost classifications which may be important to the industrial marketer.
4 What is unique about pricing under oligopolistic conditions?
5 What are the advantages of being a follower under conditions of price leadership?
6 What are the requisites for effective pricing in a market characterized by a limited number of buyers?
7 Contrast zone pricing with basing point pricing.
8 What is the basic purpose of freight absorption?
9 Describe the three levels of competition where unlawful price discrimination can be found.
10 What considerations play an important role in setting the goal of a target return on investment?
11 Describe the three positions a seller may take in respect to competition.
12 Why might it be a mistake to eliminate too quickly a product which has shown an irreversible downward trend in sales?
13 What is a workable classification for products which are bought and sold within a business organization?

SUPPLEMENTARY READING

Dean, Joel, *Managerial Economics,* New York: Prentice-Hall, Inc., 1951.

———, "Pricing Policies for New Products," *Harvard Business Review,* November - December, 1950, pp. 28 - 36.

Kaplan, A. D. H., Joel B. Dirlam, and Robert F. Lanzillotti, *Pricing in Big Business,* Washington: The Brookings Institution, 1958.

Oxenfeldt, Alfred R., *Pricing for Marketing Executives,* San Francisco: Wadsworth Publishing Company, Inc., 1961.

Peterson, William H., "Divergent Views on Pricing Policy," *Harvard Business Review,* March - April, 1963, p. 20.

**product
development—
customer
financing**

The third and final aspect of product development is customer financing. Customer in this case is defined to include middlemen as well as consumers of the product. Customer financing can be defined as the facilitative means by which both middlemen and consumers can obtain goods and services in exchange for promises to pay. The basic purpose of customer financing is to speed up the flow of goods and services from the manufacturer to the consumer.

Customer financing is not synonymous with credit; rather it is based on credit. One noted authority has made the point that, contrary to popular belief, it is the buyer rather than the seller who extends credit. He added by way of explanation that the buyer offers his credit or promise for future repayment in return for desired products.[1] Credit offered by one business to another is labeled mercantile credit.

THE MARKETING ROLE OF CUSTOMER FINANCING

In accepting the mercantile credit offered by a middleman and/or an industrial consumer, a manufacturer assumes less risk than those who accept consumer credit. The reason is the productive character of mercantile credit. By definition industrial goods and services liquidate through utilization the debt incurred by their purchase. For example, the operation of a machine by the buyer creates the income to discharge the debt incurred by its purchase.

With respect to marketing, the vital role of customer financing can be explained in four ways. First and foremost is the necessity of customer financing in every phase of industrial selling, a necessity which is steadily increasing as industrial marketers expand their markets and competition intensifies. In the business-equipment industry, for example, expansion of the market will mean selling to small, less well-financed, possibly marginal customers. Some form of customer financing is an absolute necessity in selling to this type of customer. At the same time, the buildup in competition found in selling additional and/or replacement equipment can be partially offset through the development of unique customer-financing plans.

A second reason, and one which is closely allied to the preceding one, is the concern of sales executives for customer financing. A vice-president of sales for a statewide industrial distributor of earth-

---

[1] Theodore N. Beckman, *Credits and Collections,* 7th ed., New York: McGraw-Hill Book Company, 1962 p. 4.

moving equipment contends that nearly 90 percent of his time is spent on credit planning. Obviously, he is neglecting the other aspects of his job to concentrate on what he feels is the most critical sales ingredient. The fact that planning might save some of this executive's time in no way dilutes the emphasis that seemingly must be placed on customer financing in industrial marketing.

The apparent regard for potential profits in credit is yet another reason. One industrial marketer cited two motives for the decision to acquire a commercial finance and factoring firm. One was that the firm would be of help in financing the paper involved in the leasing of its equipment. The other was that the new subsidiary would be of immense help in the contributions it could make to the parent company's profit position. The latter eventuality is undoubtedly of major importance in the development or retention of a credit subsidiary or division.

Finally, customer-financing plans are important in promoting the sale of goods through middlemen, principally industrial distributors. The task of customer-financing plans is twofold. In the first place, customer-financing plans must create an inventory, an inventory of sufficient size to allow for demonstration, sale, and rental. Secondly, customer-financing plans must facilitate the extension of credit or a rental arrangement by the distributor. This is necessary because only the very large distributor can finance his own paper.

The head of a trade association is of the opinion that most manufacturers in his capital-goods industry are twenty years behind in the utilization of customer financing to promote the sale of their products through distributors. New yardsticks, he feels, are necessary. For example, instead of a ratio such as debt to equity, he suggests an evaluation of distributor management capabilities.

METHODS OF CUSTOMER FINANCING

There are four principal methods of customer financing—accounts receivable, installment purchase contracts, leasing, and consignment.

Accounts Receivable

Accounts receivable as a method of customer financing are utilized by practically every industrial marketer. Accounts receivable are entries on the marketer's books representing the amounts owed by various customers—hence the term "open book accounts." Documents supporting these entries are the signed sales slip and/or the signed delivery receipt. Normally, customers are billed by means of an invoice once a month.

The conditions set forth by the invoice are referred to as the terms of sale. The net period is the length of time extended to the customer. Normally, the net period for a regular account is thirty days. However, differences can be noted. These may be based on (1) the type of customer, particularly in respect to the credit risk involved; (2) the location of customers in respect to delivery and regional credit characteristics; (3) the type of goods or services involved; and (4) competition.

The starting date for the net period is determined by customer needs. A customer some distance from the shipping point may be accorded a starting date which coincides with his receipt of the goods. This might be estimated by the seller on the basis of shipping date, or, if a cash discount period is involved, through the utilization of r.o.g. (receipt of goods) or a.o.g. (arrival of goods) terms. The latter terms, however, affect only the starting date for the cash discount period and not the net credit period.

To allow sufficient time to inspect the goods or to make sure the purchased product is functioning as intended, the seller may indicate a date other than the shipping date as the start of the net credit period. Often, too, such a date will facilitate payment by the purchaser. Special dating terms include:

E.o.m. (end of month): The starting date for both the net credit period and the cash discount period is the end of the month in which shipment is made. This permits a single payment for the invoices accumulated over a month's time and allows the buyer varying amounts of time to appraise his purchases. The calendar date considered as the end of the month will vary with the line of trade.

M.o.m. (middle of the month): The same as e.o.m. except that the starting date is the middle of the month.

Proximo: A term used in conjunction with a date to indicate the end of the net credit period or when payment is due. It may also be used to indicate the end of cash discount period.

Extra: Additional or extra days are interjected between invoice date and the starting date of the cash discount and net credit periods. The purpose of "extra" terms is to add flexibility to credit so that adjustment can be made for competitive or seasonal variations.

For example, a marketer might extend the net credit period for industrial distributors who stock up during the off-season.

Cash discounts are given to induce payment before the due date. For the marketer there are several good reasons for the use of cash discounts. Perhaps the most significant reason is that if taken by the purchaser they speed up the marketer's cash flow. In accomplishing this task, cash discounts are looked upon as internal financing. Another reason is that advance payments tend to reduce bad debts and the inherent credit risk, as well as the attendant collection expenses. Still another reason is the promotive effect of offering another discount to the customer.

The marketer encounters two serious problems in using cash discounts. First is the problem of what should be done about the buyers who take unearned discounts. Marketers will find that buyers may take the cash discount even though the discount period has expired. Unwarranted yet fairly common, this action destroys the whole concept of cash discounts. Many marketers hope to avoid corrective action for fear of losing a customer, but they waver between leniency and strictness even while their one desire is to halt the spread of this abuse among customers. A moderate approach is to accept payment but notify the customer through the assigned salesmen that this is not a usual practice.

Second, the marketer must decide upon the size of the cash discount. If it is too small, it will not achieve its intended purpose. That is, the volume of receivables attracted is less than sufficient. Too high a discount will result in an unnecessary loss of revenue. Competition is a major determinant of discount size. In the absence of the competition, the best approach is to start low, raising the rate as conditions indicate.

There are two sources of cost in accounts receivable. The more obvious is the establishment of the credit function within the structure of the firm. This will include the costs of credit investigation, billing, collection, and bad debts. Not as apparent is the cost of financing accounts receivable. Suppose a marketer sells $3,000 a day on credit. Customers take thirty-eight days on the average to settle their accounts. Therefore, the marketer has a permanent investment of $114,000 in accounts receivable. The cost of this investment is equal to the opportunity loss from not being able to use the funds to otherwise expand the profits of the firm, plus the interest charges on possible borrowing to maintain adequate working capital.

By employing the services of a factor, the marketer is able to shift the credit function and sell his receivables, thus eliminating in large part the related costs. About the best way to understand factoring is to look at its functional nature. Generally, factors working under a continuous agreement perform the following six functions for their clients.

1   Assumption of the credit function to include credit investigation, accepting and declining of accounts and of invoices arising thereon, accounts receivable bookkeeping, billing, collection, and assumption of bad-debt losses. With regard to invoices arising thereon, for example, the factor sets a credit limit for each customer of his client. If the client sends in invoices which mount up to a figure exceeding the credit limit prescribed for a particular customer, the factor may revise the credit limit upward, or he may decline to purchase without recourse invoices exceeding the limit. In the latter case, those sales made in excess of the approved credit limit are referred to as "client's risk sales." Accounts receivable bookkeeping involves a great amount of detailed work. For example, as to billing, the factor may send each customer of his client just one bill each month. But during the month every invoice, along with its maturity date, and every credit (for returned goods, canceled orders, allowances, etc.) affecting the account must be posted.

2   Purchase of accounts receivable with no recourse to the seller in the event of credit losses.

3   Advancement of cash for accounts receivable factored when so desired by the seller. A marketer may not sell all of his accounts to the factor. He may keep a few to handle himself, sometimes because their excessive credit requirements may not be accepted by the factor.

4   Loans on inventory. The client may need more funds than are available through the sale of receivables. To satisfy such a demand, the factor will make a loan using the client's inventory as collateral.

5   Loans on fixed assets, other forms of security, and on open credit. In making such loans, the factor, because of his close working relationship, is often in a better position to serve the client.

6   Advisory service in regard to financial matters and the broad aspects of the client's industry. The industry experience of a factor provides him with a broader perspective than is normally found within the client's firm.[2]

[2] Clyde William Phelps, *The Role of Factoring in Modern Business Finance,* Studies in Commercial Financing, no. 1, Baltimore: Commercial Credit Company, Educational Division, 1962, pp. 14-16.

There are two costs in factoring. The first is referred to as a commission. Expressed as percentage of net receivables sold, this compensates the factor for performing the various aspects of the credit function. The exact rate is a result of negotiation. Among the cost elements considered are (1) the client's industry, (2) the client's annual sales volume, (3) the average order size, (4) the average volume of sales per customer, (5) the customer's level and type of business, (6) the credit character of the client's customers, (7) the credit terms offered by the client, and (8) the extra services to be performed by the factoring firm.[3]

The second cost is the interest on money advanced to the client prior to the average due date. The rate of interest will reflect current monetary conditions and the degree of competition present. It should be pointed out that the interest rate is not considered a discount or flat charge.

When a marketer is considering the possibility of factoring, the two costs involved must be evaluated separately and compared with different alternatives. Two reasons are obvious:

1   The commission paid to a factor, like the commission paid to a salesman, is simply a payment for work performed—not a payment for the use of money. The money cost of the commission must be compared to the money cost of the apparent alternative— namely, the cost to the marketer for handling the credit function, including bad-debt losses, himself.

2   The fact that the commission is paid for work and not money advanced or loaned by the factor is made clear by the use of "maturity factoring" by many marketers. In using maturity factoring, the marketer sells accounts receivable and invoices thereon to the factor. As the invoices mature, the marketer receives payments from the factor. The marketer pays only a commission because no cash advance or loans were made to him prior to the maturity date of the invoices.

Some marketers adhere to a policy of maturity factoring throughout the year. Others use maturity factoring in all but peak periods when their need for cash working capital necessitates advances from the factor.

The charge for the factor's cash advances is at a true rate of simple interest per year. This charge should be compared with the rates for funds from other sources after conversion has been made to a true yearly rate of simple interest.

[3] *Ibid.*, pp. 52-63.

If the marketer is not interested in shifting the credit function, he may assign his accounts receivable or pledge them as collateral for a loan. Assignment is generally thought of as the sale of accounts receivable with recourse. In either case, the marketer is interested in transferring his investment from accounts' receivable to working capital, and not in credit protection. It is difficult for the marketer to compare the charges for accounts receivable financing because of the related practices of banks and other financial institutions. For example, service charges may be added or a bank may require borrowers to carry compensating balances.

Installment Purchase Contracts

Installment purchase contracts spread the payments for a product over a period of time. Some form of installment purchase plan is an absolute must for industrial marketers of "big-ticket" items. The only alternative is to limit the market to those few who are both willing and able to provide their own financing, either internally or from third-party sources. Whereas accounts receivable are offered as a convenience to the customer, installment contracts are a necessity.

Installment credit may be based on a conditional sales contract or a chattel mortgage. Under a conditional sales contract the title remains with the seller until the final payment has been made. Repossession is easier if the customer defaults on this payment. Thus there is no practical difference between a conditional sales contract and a lease-purchase plan. Under a chattel mortgage, title passes to the customer. Either the title is transferred back to the seller or a lien is placed on the goods involved. The decision to use one form or the other rests primarily on the applicable state laws in the marketer's territory and secondarily on the character of the credit risk.

In managing installment purchase contracts, Bartels offers some helpful suggestions:

1   Installment purchase contracts should be extended on the basis of the customer's ability to pay, notwithstanding the value of the purchase.
2   Installment interest charges should reflect not only the interest rate value of the money involved, but the costs of account acquisition, maintenance, and collection.
3   Installment contract provisions should be fully disclosed to customers.

4   Payments should be matched with income generation.
5   When credit approval is based to a large extent upon the re-
possesion value of the goods in question, the balance outstanding at any time should be less than the value of the goods. This
condition can be achieved by equating the down payment with
initial depreciation or the gross margin of the goods in question.[4]

Several large industrial marketers have organized sales-financing
subsidiaries to handle installment purchases of their goods. One
credit subsidiary has developed a unique installment contract which
relates the amount of monthly payment to the Sum-of-the-Digits method of depreciation permitted by the Internal Revenue Act of 1954.
Repayment follows the same decelerating pattern as the write-off
of depreciation. Payments become smaller as equipment becomes
older and maintenance is on the upswing.

Using a financing charge of 4.25 percent per annum, the monthly payments over a period of three years for a $20,000 item would
be calculated as follows:

Purchase price	$20,000
Down payment (10% minimum)	2,000
Unpaid balance	18,000
Financing charges	2,295
Total deferred balance	$20,295

Under a three-year contract, the rates to be applied to the total deferred balance to determine the amount of monthly payment are 4.2
percent the first year; 2.8 percent the second year; and 1.33 percent
the third and final year.

	MONTHLY TOTAL	YEARLY TOTAL
First-year payments	$852.39	$10,228.68
Second-year payments	568.26	6,819.12
Third-year payments	270.60*	3,247.20

*Adjusted to pay off balance.

Many installment plans charge varying rates of interest depending upon the size of the unpaid balance. For example, one industrial marketer of business equipment ranging in price from about $500
to a little less than $3,000 charges 8 percent per annum on unpaid

[4] Robert Bartels, *Credit Management,* New York: The Ronald Press Company 1967, p. 164.

balances of less than $1,000 and 6.5 percent for unpaid balances exceeding $1,000.

For all intents and purposes, a lease with an option to buy is the same as an installment contract. To reduce customer confusion, many industrial marketers make no real distinction between the two, selling the concept of installment purchasing as a leasing variation.

Revolving accounts combine the concepts of an installment purchase contract with those of an account receivable or open account. What results is a customer-financing plan which has two basic features:

1   Purchases on a continuous basis up to a predetermined dollar limit. The limit is based primarily on the credit character of the customer.
2   Payments of a predetermined amount monthly plus a service charge based on the unpaid balance. The amount of partial payment is arrived at through conferring with the customer.

Used extensively for many years in the retail trade, revolving accounts have only recently been introduced into the industrial market. In selling such farm supplies as feed and fertilizer, several marketers have experimented with revolving accounts and have been highly pleased with the results. The principal advantage of revolving accounts, compared with installment purchase contracts, is exemption from state regulation of installment sales. This type of plan would seem advantageous where purchasing tends to be repetitive. Such might be the case with operating supplies, and possibly component parts and fabricated materials. As in retailing, revolving accounts are useful in selling to customers with marginal credit who fail to qualify for a regular account receivable, and where an installment contract is not applicable.

Leasing

Leasing has attracted a great deal of attention in the last few years. From the standpoint of the customer, there are three strong arguments favoring leasing as a form of customer financing. The first is based on the concept known as the "bundle of services." To understand this concept, suppose a machine costs $2,000. Its usable life is estimated as six years, after which the salvage value will be $200. Therefore, at the time of purchase the machine can be considered a bundle of six services, each valued at $300.

With this information, a comparison can be made between the cost of leasing and the cost of owning for the first year of operation:

COST OF LEASING		COST OF OWNING	
Cost of first year's service	$360	Cost of first year's service	$300
		Opportunity lost on funds invested in the other five years of service	300
Total cost	$360	Total cost	$600

Assuming a 20 percent return on investment, it becomes obvious that ownership of the machine ties up five years of services yet to be used, and in doing so brings the cost of owning up to $600, or $240 more than the cost of the lease on the same machine. Making the same analysis for the remaining five years, it is found that owning costs more during the second through the fourth years, is equal to the leasing cost in the fifth year, and is $60 less in the sixth and final year, when there is no opportunity loss. The net gain from leasing instead of owning is $540.

Therefore, the "bundle of services" concept stresses the services rendered by an item of machinery or equipment or, in other words, its productive character. In opposition to this is the deep-seated idea of ownership. The desire to own is based on a combination of several factors, the most predominant of which are the fear of losing the item in question sometime in the future and the pride or prestige derived from acknowledgment of ownership. A good illustration of the latter feeling was displayed by the owner of a medium-size plant doing precision machining for major aerospace contractors. During the course of a plant tour, he told the author that "everything you have seen and will see I own." He went on to add that not a dollar of credit was used in acquiring the machinery and equipment. It is hardly likely that pride of ownership in this owner or for that matter any business can be defended as a decision based on rational grounds.

The question mark in applying the "bundle of services" concept is the return on the funds released by leasing. The applicability of the concept is thus based on the rates of return from investment opportunities actually available to the customer. The minimum acceptable rate is one which will amortize over the period of the lease the premium of leasing as opposed to service costs. In the previous example, the premium was equal to $360.

A second argument favoring leasing rather than ownership is the risk of continued need. In owning a machine or piece of equipment, the owner in essence assumes the risk of continued need for the services offered or the products made by the machine or equipment. This risk might be more than some customers want to assume, particularly in the earlier stages of development.

The tax advantage claimed for leasing is that it permits a faster write-off than normal depreciation. The faster write-off does not reduce taxes; rather it postpones their payment. The argument that in leasing there is a tax advantage is then based on the fact that this method of customer financing postpones payment of taxes, thus allowing use of these funds for a longer period of time. The accelerating of depreciation allowed by the tax code of 1954 and the revision in 1958 diminished to a considerable extent the tax advantage of leasing.

Marketing characteristics conducive to leasing include:

1   Highly complex machines which require extensive and perhaps continuous servicing
2   Machines and equipment which are subject to rapid technological obsolescence
3   The marketer's enjoyment of a strong competitive position because of patents and/or product superiority
4   The marketer's wish to widen his market
5   The marketer's wish to sell related supplies and equipment

The practice of leasing, common for a number of industrial-good manufacturers, extends to:

1   Shoe-manufacturing machinery
2   Electronic computers
3   Office and duplicating equipment
4   Transportation equipment
5   Machine tools of a specialized nature
6   Container machinery
7   Heavy construction equipment
8   Textile machinery
9   Tobacco machinery
10 Refrigeration equipment

Basically there are just two types of leases. One type is called a straight lease. Under a straight lease the rental payments will amount to the purchase price of the item plus service charges. The term of the lease will normally cover a period less than the useful life of the item in question. If the rental term is considerably shorter than the useful life of the item, renewal will be at a much-reduced rate; however, purchase rather than renewal is much the wiser course at the conclusion of the leasing period. In leasing business equipment for a three-year period, one firm sets up a monthly charge ranging from 3.0 to 3.4 percent of the original purchase price. The exact rate will depend upon competition and/or the amount of goods under lease. At the conclusion of the lease, the lessee can buy the rental property for about 10 percent of the original purchase price.

Lessors of electronic computers, duplication equipment, and other specialized products include service as part of the leasing arrangement. However, this is the exception rather than the rule. Normally, the lessee is responsible for insurance, taxes, maintenance, and related expenses. A lease can be noncancelable or have a purchase option that the lessee can exercise at any time. If the lessor rejects the option, the lease is automatically voided. In the event that the lessee has a poor credit rating or one that is lower than desired by the lessor, a down payment may be required. The amount of the down payment is less than required under an installment purchase contract.

The other basic type of lease is a lease purchase. Under such a lease, the item of machinery or equipment is rented until the lessee has sufficient funds from a percentage of the rentals to make the necessary down payment. After the down payment, the lease is converted to an installment purchase contract. If the marketer wishes to sell to firms with less than adequate financial capacity, it may be necessary to make available an alternative such as lease purchase.

As attractive as leasing is to the marketer, a number of problems exist in its utilization as a sales tool. These include:

1   A heavy financial burden placed on the marketer. The investment in finished products increases with each transaction.
2   A risk of loss attributable to the obsolescence of leased equipment.
3   A troublesome task in educating salesmen to use leasing as a sales tool. Salesmen do not want to be bothered with the red tape and paper work involved in leases.
4   A risk of legal difficulties. A manufacturer that leases his products extensively may be suspected of withholding technological improvements because of his strong market position. This, in turn, may make the manufacturer vulnerable to prosecution for monopoly or restraint of trade.
5   A possibility that a contract giving the lessee an option to pur-

chase will be treated as a sale. This may cause poor customer relations or even outright ill will.[5]

In the leasing of electronic computers, independent leasing specialists have emerged to take a dominant marketing role. These firms owe their existence in large part to the 1956 consent decree under which IBM agreed to sell its products at prices in line with its rental charges, and to provide maintenance and incidental programming services to any user of its products.

Lower rental charges are the advantage in dealing with an independent leasing specialist rather than a manufacturer. On brand-new— so-called third-generation— equipment, specialists will be from 10 to 15 percent lower than the manufacturer of the equipment. On second-generation computers and systems the discount may go as high as 35 percent off the manufacturer's original charge. Some observers feel that manufacturers welcome the competition as a way of easing the strain on cash flow. IBM, for example, lowered the purchase price and raised the rental charges on the "360 system." This, in effect, widened the gap between the specialist and the manufacturer.

The basis of the lower rate structure for the specialist is a longer payoff period, hopefully estimated as twice the time span used by manufacturers. Typically, manufacturers try to amortize original cost over a three- to five-year period. An overnight technological breakthrough is the only danger to the specialist in going beyond the manufacturer's payoff period.

Two other points favor leasing from a specialist. One is that in exercising the option to upgrade his equipment, the lessee will receive credit for as much as 90 percent of rentals paid, whereas the maximum allowance from a manufacturer seldom exceeds 50 percent. The other is that in upgrading equipment, the specialist may offer the lessee the opportunity to switch to another manufacturer's product without losing his 90 percent rental credit.

Consignment

Consignment may be a valuable customer-financing plan to the marketer of components, fabricated materials, and operating supplies. It may also prove highly useful to manufacturers who market indirect-

[5] *Leasing in Industry,* Studies in Business Policy, no. 127, New York: National Industrial Conference Board, Inc., 1968, p. 5.

ly through merchant middlemen such as the industrial distributor. Consignment offers a financing service to the customer by allowing him to adjust his partial payments to the utilization of the product and still qualify for the quantity discount. For example, to get a significant quantity discount, a customer might have to order enough fabricated materials to last his operation a period of several months. Sale under consignment would eliminate the need to pay for the materials before they become part of the customer's product.

Under consignment title to the goods would pass at certain predetermined intervals, there being no sale to activate the process as in retailing. Partial payments might be made weekly, semimonthly, or monthly. From the standpoint of the marketer the advantages of consignment are that he not only can make sales which would otherwise be unobtainable but can make them in desirable quantities. The obvious disadvantage is the risk involved. To the customer, consignment narrows the time span between payment and the generation of revenue through the sale of their finished product. This will have a decided positive effect on cash flow.

INTEGRATION INTO THE MARKETING PROGRAM

For a customer-financing plan to be effective, it must be fully integrated into the marketing program. To do this, it is necessary first of all to develop a proper philosophy in regard to customer financing. Based on an appreciation of the vital marketing role played by customer financing, this philosophy should be an operating one for all marketing personnel. When credit personnel are part of accounting, it is essential that they realize the purpose of all customer financing plans.

The next task is to design the composite of customer-financing plans which will reflect the needs of the individual marketer. This will involve selection of the major method as well as the planning of financing specifics such as credit terms, down payments, and service charges. Once this task has been completed, or in conjunction with it, the marketer must take on the job of locating and evaluating sources of capital for his customer-financing program. Every attempt should be made to interject flexibility into the customer-financing program to include the type and specifications of the plans offered and capital sources.

A fourth job is the creation of sales-promotional materials dealing with the available customer-financing plans. In making his presentation, the salesman will need flip charts to illustrate the plan and a computer wheel to figure payments. Brochures explaining the details of the various customer-financing plans along with an outline of each plan's particular advantages to the customer would be helpful to the customer.

Finally, sales personnel have to be trained to sell the customer-financing plans. The salesman must be trained to classify customers so that each can be matched up with the right plan. Training of salesmen should be continuous to keep them alerted to new financing plans and changes in the money market. At all times it should be emphasized to the salesman that he alone is responsible for the success in serving the customer through financing plans.

SUMMARY

Customer financing has as its purpose the speeding up of the flow of goods and services from the manufacturer to the consumer. Based on the credit of the customer, financing plans play a vital marketing role. This contention is founded on the necessity of financing plans in practically every industrial transaction, the attention of sales executives to this aspect of the sale, the apparent regard for financing profits, and the financing demands placed on manufacturers by merchant middlemen.

There are four major methods of customer financing—accounts receivable or open accounts, installment purchase contracts, leasing, and consignment. Accounts receivable, used by almost every industrial marketer, are offered as a convenience to the customer. Both installment purchase contracts and leasing are methods of spreading out the original purchase cost over a period of time. Which plan is best for a customer depends upon a complex array of factors. Both installment purchase contracts and leasing act as stimulants to the expansion of the market. Leasing is often preferable to the installment purchase contract because of the absence of legal complications. Consignment, the fourth major method, is adaptable to the sale of products which are consumed over a period of time. Examples include components, fabricated materials, and operating supplies. Consignment may also be used in marketing through merchant middlemen.

If customer-financing plans are to be successful, they must be completely integrated into the marketing program. Essentially integration is made up of five primary tasks. These are (1) development and adherence to a proper philosophy in regard to customer financing, (2) custom design of a customer-financing program, (3) location and evaluation of capital sources for the customer-financing program, (4) development of sales-promotional materials for use by the salesman and distribution to the customer, and (5) training of all sales personnel on a continuous basis.

DISCUSSION QUESTIONS

1   Explain the concept of credit. Why may the accompanying risk be less for the industrial marketer?
2   Discuss the reasons for the vital marketing role of customer financing.
3   In setting up credit terms, what are the important considerations?
4   From the standpoint of the customer, what are the differences between a conditional sales contract and a chattel mortgage?
5   From the standpoint of the marketer, why would a leasing plan be better than either of the two forms of installment purchase contract?
6   What factors have contributed to the growth of the independent leasing specialist?
7   What, if any, are the tax advantages associated with leasing?
8   Explain the "bundle of services" concept.
9   What would be the major problem in consignment for the marketer?
10   What suggestions would you make to firms regarding the integration of customer-financing plans into their marketing program?

SUPPLEMENTARY READINGS

Bartels, Robert, *Credit Management,* New York: The Ronald Press Company, 1967.
Beckman, Theodore N., and Ronald S. Foster, *Credits and Collections,* 8th ed., New York: McGraw-Hill Book Company, in press.

Eiteman, Wilford John, and Davisson, Charles N., *The Lease,* Ann Arbor: School of Business Administration, University of Michigan, 1951.

Phelps, Clyde William, *The Role of Factoring in Modern Business Finance,* Studies in Commercial Financing, no.1, Baltimore: Commercial Credit Company, Educational Division, 1962.

———, *Accounts Receivable Financing as a Method of Securing Business Loans,* Studies in Commercial Financing, no. 2, 2d ed., Baltimore: Commercial Credit Company, 1962.

———, *Commercial Credit Insurance as a Management Tool,* Studies in Commercial Financing, no. 3, Baltimore: Commercial Credit Company, 1961.

product distribution

4

**product
distribution**

marketing channels— management

The cornerstone of market strategy is the method or system by which goods and services are distributed. This method or system, hereafter called a marketing channel, can be likened to a pipeline from the producer to the consumer.

A marketing channel can be visualized also as a set of marketing units which perform certain tasks in bridging the gap between the manufacturer and the consumer; or each of the marketing units in a channel can be considered a link. A direct channel, in which the manufacturer assumes all the marketing responsibilities, has only one link. Indirect channels have two or more links, depending upon the number of middlemen and/or facilitating agencies interposed between the manufacturer and the consumer.

Some marketing units in a channel may have a more dominant role than others. This may occur when the channel includes both middlemen and facilitating agencies. Occasionally it may happen that one middleman dominates another middleman. In the marketing of certain agricultural products, for example, the role of assemblers is subordinate to that of terminal market middlemen. As a channel functions, its marketing units or links operate in such a way as to maintain the competitive status of their channel. Some actions that resist the challenge of competitive channels include franchise agreements, full-line forcing, resale controls, collective activity by trade associations, and establishment of strong buyer-seller relationships.

Structuring the marketing channel involves matching up the tasks that are essential in moving the goods into the marketplace with the available marketing units. While the emphasis is on effectiveness, the manufacturer should keep in mind the possible implications of his action. For example, a channel with several links may be considered excessive and therefore inefficient. On the other hand, a single-link channel may appear monopolistic in nature.

Management of marketing channels encompasses four major activities: (1) selection, (2) assistance, (3) coordination, and (4) control. When considering which activity is the most important, an industrial-good manufacturer should not delude himself into believing that the whole job is over and done with as soon as channels and their respective constituents are selected and organized. Granted, selection of channels is a most important decision, but it is only the beginning of a series of decisions that must be made by the manufacturer on a continuing basis if distribution is to be both effective and efficient.

SELECTION OF CHANNELS AND OUTLETS

The overriding consideration in selecting both channels and outlets is the extent of market coverage desired. Once this has been determined, the marketer can proceed with selecting the channels and then the specific outlets. This is a departure from the traditional approach which has determination of coverage following channel selection, but it places needed emphasis on long-term market-penetration goals.

Lack of consideration for the long-term aspects of market penetration can bring about significant problems, as witnessed by the following two situations. The first one has to do with the electronics industry, in which sales volume has outgrown the marketing channel that built it.[1] Initially the manufacturers' reps were retained for a very good reason. They normally have the engineering know-how so necessary in selling products of this kind. With the passage of time, however, many of the items have become standardized through greater consumer familiarity. Moreover, the market for electronic gear has expanded and is still expanding. Thus, today manufacturers of electronic products and their reps are seeking solutions to such problems as the stocking of inventory which probably could have been averted by careful planning of market coverage.

The second situation involves the Dresser Manufacturing Division of Dresser Industries, Inc.[2] This manufacturer of pipe-joining and repair parts for oil, gas, waterworks, sewage disposal, and sundry other industries had completely oversaturated the market by selling to practically every distributor with a good credit rating. As a result, it was common for distributors to find themselves competing with each other for the same sale. To correct this situation without damaging desired market coverage, Dresser undertook an extensive distributor evaluation program which reduced the number of distributors from the unwieldy total of 2,500 to only 200.

Extent of Market Coverage

There are three general plans of market coverage—limited, selective, and mass. Limited coverage implies one or a limited number of outlets per designated trading area. The size of the trading area

---

[1] "Easing the Squeeze on the Sales Rep," *Business Week,* July 15, 1963, p. 130.

[2] Reprinted by permission from *Sales Management, The Marketing Magazine.*   Copyright 1960 Sales Management, Inc.

depends upon the sales and servicing requirements of the product or product line, and the density of the market measured in terms of potential consumers. This can be put in the form of an equation as follows:

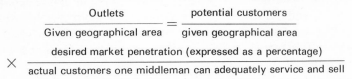

$$\frac{\text{Outlets}}{\text{Given geographical area}} = \frac{\text{potential customers}}{\text{given geographical area}}$$
$$\times \frac{\text{desired market penetration (expressed as a percentage)}}{\text{actual customers one middleman can adequately service and sell}}$$

If the manufacturer stipulates in the contract that no sales will be made in the area other than through an authorized middleman, the resulting distribution arrangement is referred to as exclusive.

The manufacturer who adopts a plan of selective coverage wishes to restrict the number of outlets to those who can serve him profitably. This type of coverage plan is used when it is not conceivable from a marketing standpoint to use limited distribution or it is not economical to sell to everyone. The basis for selective distribution is a distribution-cost analysis by customer. The object is to determine the minimum sales volume necessary for an outlet to be regarded as profitable. Other criteria that might be relied upon in selecting outlets include (1) willingness to stock what is deemed a representative inventory, (2) quality and adequacy of service facilities, (3) competence of the sales force, (4) financial condition, and (5) trading area served.

The third type of general plan, mass distribution, is adopted by a manufacturer on the premise that an adequate level of sales can be engendered only through blanket coverage of the market. Mass distribution is frequently used for standardized products such as supplies that are sold to a horizontal market. Under this plan the manufacturer wants to minimize the possibility of losing a customer because the product is not conveniently available. Another advantage is that mass distribution tends to stabilize sales volume.

The widening use of distribution-cost analysis has keyed a decided shift from mass to selective distribution. Even where mass distribution is retained, there is a tendency to classify outlets for allocation of marketing efforts. The usual reason is that such an analysis will show blanket coverage to be neither economical nor necessary.

After carefully reviewing the characteristics of each of the general coverage plans, the next step is to analyze the factors which determine the extent of market coverage. These are:

1   Consumer buying practices. What is the frequency and average

size of a purchase? Is the product purchased separately or in conjunction with other products? Does each purchase necessitate recurrent selling effort? In answering these questions, attention should be directed toward potential as well as actual customers.

2 Costs. What are the cost-coverage ratios for each alternative marketing channel? Do there appear to be any trends which would significantly affect future costs? Are there any geographical differences in coverage costs?

3 Competition. What coverage plans are used by competitors? Do competitors have any peculiar advantages or disadvantages in market coverage?

4 Marketing mix. What is the mix at various degrees of market coverage? By way of explanation, a certain degree of market coverage even though desirable from the standpoint of the other three factors may place too great a burden on one of the components of the marketing mix.

Types of Major Marketing Channels

Selecting channels and outlets is necessarily a never-ending job. Review of existing channels should be made at least once a year. This will facilitate gradual rather than abrupt adjustments to meet the dynamics of the market.

Greater insight into the selection process can be gained by conceiving of it as a series of decisions. The first is to determine whether to sell directly, indirectly through middlemen, or by some combination of both. Selling directly is favored by industrial-good manufacturers for several important reasons.

1 The manufacturer is able to control the sale of his products and thus has a definite advantage in servicing and installing. Traditionally considered essential for machinery and equipment, these two functions are also taking on added significance in the sale of components and fabricated materials. An Eastern components manufacturer, for example, finds it imperative to maintain a sales branch in southern California for the express purpose of installing and servicing a fairly standardized product which is sold to the electronic and aerospace industries.

2 The manufacturer's salesman tends to have a greater knowledge of the product and consumer requirements than his middleman counterpart. What is more important, the manufacturer's salesman has a well-established image in these two knowledge areas. A survey of purchasing agents and design engineers in the elec-

tronics industry indicated that both types of buyers believe quite strongly that manufacturers' salesmen have more technical product knowledge and know more about customer requirements than middlemen. Summarized below are the responses to the two questions regarding product knowledge and customer requirements.[3]

Do you find that manufacturers' salesmen have better technical knowledge?

PURCHASING AGENTS		DESIGN ENGINEERS	
Yes	84 percent	Yes	75 percent
No	7	No	5
No difference	9	No difference	20

Do you feel that manufacturers' salesmen have a better knowledge of your company's requirements?

PURCHASING AGENTS		DESIGN ENGINEERS	
Yes	49 percent	Yes	54 percent
No	27	No	11
No difference	24	No difference	35

3 The manufacturer is able to retain close contact with the market. This places him in a position where the needs of the consumer can be studied at first hand. The rapid pace of technological change makes this almost imperative to many industrial-good manufacturers.

4 The manufacturer can cater to the desires of consumers who wish to buy directly. In addition to superior knowledge and service, consumers may have the impression that they can obtain lower prices without the middleman's margin. An indication of this partiality in the electronics industry is that if anyone is to be given more time by both purchasing agents and design engineers, it is the manufacturer's salesman.[4]

5 The manufacturer may be able to reduce his marketing costs. Occasionally circumstances will dictate that direct selling is the most economical channel alternative. Such circumstances would include an advanced stage of market development, a market that is concentrated in a limited geographical area, and infrequent purchase orders of high unit value.

6 The manufacturer gains a certain degree of prestige and recogni-

3 Adapted from Table 1, Norman J. Gallop, "Manufacturers' Representative or Company Salesman?" *Journal of Marketing*, April, 1964, p. 63.

4 *Ibid.*

tion among not only consumers but the general public as well. This is often important in overcoming the handicap of not being "big enough" to handle an order.

Direct selling is not without its disadvantages. Foremost among these are time and money. The buildup of a field sales and service organization is a lengthy process made even more so when the manufacturer seeks entry into overseas markets. Manpower must be recruited and trained, sales branches located, and related policies formulated. Consequently, to expand market coverage or to invade new markets will require significant investment long before any profits are forthcoming. In the case of Pratt and Whitney's switch from their own sales engineers to industrial distributors in an effort to gain a more satisfactory rate of sales growth, two of the major considerations working against direct selling were the delay in market entry and the necessity for a long-term commitment of funds.[5]

Undoubtedly one of the biggest obstacles for many manufacturers is that they lack the financial capacity to support direct selling. This is especially true when the market is extensive or when it is necessary to remain in close and frequent contact with customers. In addition to the obvious costs incurred in developing and maintaining a field organization, the manufacturer who sells directly must bear the financial burden arising from the multiplication of inventory requirements and selling on possibly more lengthy credit terms.

Despite the formidable advantages of direct selling, many industrial-good manufacturers make use of the indirect or middleman channel. As a matter of fact the middleman channel is dominant in the distribution of several types of industrial goods, notably operating supplies and accessory equipment. Several of the more significant reasons for utilizing middleman channels are:

1   The manufacturer need not make a large financial commitment on a long-term basis. National as well as international markets can be tapped by even the smallest of manufacturers utilizing middlemen.
2   The manufacturer can avail himself of the middleman's knowledge of and experience with a given market area or group of consumers.
3   The manufacturer can sell through middlemen whose prestige in their individual areas is far greater than his own. Selling through

[5] Reprinted by permission from *Sales Management, The Marketing Magazine.* Copyright 1960 Sales Management, Inc.

reputable middlemen is a very effective method of securing favorable consumer recognition throughout the market.

4   The manufacturer can gain access to market segments otherwise barred to him. Consumers may prefer a particular middleman because of an established relationship or because of a desire to buy numerous lines from a single local source.

5   The manufacturer can utilize middlemen where direct sales are unprofitable. Certain geographical areas may not constitute enough immediate potential to justify a branch operation. Good examples of such areas in the industrial market are the Pacific Northwest, the Mountain states, and the South.

6   The manufacturer can utilize middlemen where direct sales are impractical for the time being. A manufacturer may wish to introduce a new product or enter a new market without too much of a financial or image commitment.

A frequent complaint manufacturers make about the indirect or middleman channel is about the loss of control over the sale of the product. The following statements are suggestive of manufacturers' criticism.

1   Middlemen do not try to sell, they just take orders.

2   Middlemen lose a lot of sales because they lack the flexibility of a manufacturer's own salesman.

3   Middlemen cannot be expected to devote sufficient time to one manufacturer's products or customers.

4   Middlemen are reluctant to seek out new customers. Middleman-customer relationships are fairly static within a given locale.

5   Middlemen place the burden of product knowledge on the consumer.

Other major complaints are that middlemen fail to stock an adequate inventory at all times and that manufacturer-sponsored programs are repeatedly ignored by middlemen. These complaints are serious handicaps, however, only if the manufacturer allows them to be.

Undoubtedly a manufacturer's financial resources are a major determinant in deciding the major type of channel to be used. When there is recourse to ample funds, the tendency is to sell directly to as much of his market as possible. If mass coverage is planned, the manufacturer absorbs the geographical segment with greatest immediate potential, then the one with the next greatest immediate potential, and so on until allocated funds have been exhausted or the market coverage objective has been attained. The philosophy of this procedure is that a major share of current business should be approached via the channel the manufacturer believes is his most effective alternative. Depending upon the collective size, what remains of the market is handled in one of two ways. When the collective size is significant, middlemen are retained to cover specific geographical or consumer segments. In the event that no suitable middleman is available for a geographical segment, the manufacturer may be able to make arrangements with a middleman in a neighboring territory. Usually this will entail a guarantee to reimburse the middleman for the extra expenses incurred in developing the market areas. A case in point was the agreement between an aircraft-supplies company and a large manufacturers' rep based on the East Coast. In return for covering the Midwest market a promise was made to underwrite all losses during the first three years related to expansion of the rep's sales force.

When funds are limited, a manufacturer may still find it possible to sell directly if he is located near the market. When the market is highly concentrated, so much the better. The aerospace complex in southern California and the auto suppliers clustered around Detroit are excellent examples of plant location to facilitate direct sale. Manufacturers that are not tied to their present location by overwhelming supply considerations tend to move their plants to adjust to changes in their particular markets. In addition to facilitating direct sale, the manufacturer is able, by orienting his plant facilities to the market, to develop a certain degree of both spatial and temporal leverage from just being convenient.

When coverage is to be selective or exclusive, the availability of financial resources is not nearly as critical. The worst that can happen is a slowdown in program implementation. Under a plan of selective coverage, limited funds will probably mean an absolute increase in the profitability level necessary to qualify as an acceptable outlet. In the case of exclusive distribution, a lack of finances usually results in larger territories for each outlet.

Major Types of Outlets

The task of selecting marketing outlets involves two decisions. The first is a determination of the major type of outlet to be utilized. Once this is accomplished, specific outlets have to be selected or located. In selecting a major type of outlet, the manufacturer has to match up marketing outlets with the purchasing demands of consumers. To do this effectively, he must know not only everything there is to know about the purchasing of the product or product line in question, but the general capabilities of all the various types of marketing outlet. Other considerations which take on added significance in the short run are industry distribution patterns, anticipated competitor reactions, and the restrictions imposed by financial resources.

For the manufacturer who wishes to sell directly, there are four possible alternatives: (1) the home office, (2) sales branches without stock, (3) sales branches with stock, or (4) some combination of the previously listed alternatives. Ordinarily, use of the home office is restricted to situations where substantially all of the market is concentrated in an adjoining geographical area or where there is no need for continuous customer contact. The latter situation is encountered in the marketing of installations and certain items of single-purpose equipment. If the distribution system is to be developed gradually over a period of years, selling from the home office is usually the first step.

Whether or not a sales branch stocks an inventory depends upon consumer purchasing requirements and the financial resources of the manufacturer. The greater the tendency for consumers to buy often and/or in small quantities, the more necessary it is that sales branches be stocked. Inventories are also likely to be maintained when customer service is normally performed at the branch level.

The data in Table 10.1 seem to bear out the reasoning of the preceding paragraph. For those product lines for which consumer buying practices or service commitments would seem to indicate a convenient inventory location, manufacturers' sales branches with stock are used almost exclusively. Conversely, for those product lines for which a convenient supply source is not required by consumers; manufacturers' sales branches without stock are almost always used. This may seem contradictory in the case of paper and allied products. However, direct sale as a supplementary marketing channel is used pri-

TABLE 10.1 Economic Importance of Manufacturers' Sales Branches with and without Stock on the Basis of Number of Establishments and Sales Volume, Selected Product Lines, 1958.

PRODUCT LINE	PERCENTAGE OF ESTABLISHMENTS		PERCENTAGE OF SALES	
	WITH	WITHOUT	WITH	WITHOUT
Instruments and related products	85.5	14.5	84.3	15.7
Office and store machines and devices	86.4	13.6	76.4	23.6
Paper and allied products	21.5	78.5	18.0	82.0
Primary metal products	18.5	81.5	12.3	87.7

Source: *U.S. Census of Business 1958 — Wholesale Trade,* volume III, Washington: Department of Commerce, 1961, table 1C, pp. 1 - 14 and 1 - 15.

marily to solicit business from consumers who purchase in large quantities and/or have special technical problems.

The drawback in having each sales branch stock an inventory is the added financial burden it places on the manufacturer. He has to build or lease warehouse facilities in areas where land costs more often than not are exceptionally high. In addition there are the costs associated with the added investment in inventory.[6]

To alleviate this situation somewhat, many manufacturers have gone to a regional warehousing plan. Under such a scheme practically all the inventories for sales branches in a particular region are centralized in one warehouse. The warehouse will be located to provide one-day or at the most two-day, delivery service to all of its branches. For example, a regional warehouse might be set up in Fort Smith, Arkansas, to serve sales branches in the cities of Dallas, Little Rock, Memphis, Oklahoma City, Tulsa, Shreveport, Kansas City, and Wichita.

One of the biggest problems facing the manufacturer who sells indirectly is gaining a comprehensive picture of each of the major types of middleman. In making a decision on the major type of middleman to be utilized, the manufacturer cannot allow himself to be influenced unduly by:

1 Good or bad past experiences with several middlemen of a particular type.
2 One operating or service characteristic to the exclusion of all others. Neither the carrying of an inventory nor the technical qualifications of sales personnel should be the only factor in selecting one type of middleman rather than another.
3 Industry tradition especially when there is evidence that the market is undergoing change. A lot of sales can be lost waiting for the eventual adjustment of middlemen.

After studying the various types of middleman, the manufacturer is faced with the task of comparing the resulting descriptions with the purchasing requirements of his market, considered as a whole or by segments. In making this comparison, the most important question he must answer is which type of middleman can best serve this market or segment at the present time and five years from now. Corollary questions might include:

1 Will this type of middleman cover the entire market or segment?
2 What experience has this type of middleman had in selling our product line?

[6] Detailed explanation of the costs incurred by regionalizing inventory is presented in Chap. 15.

3   What experience has this type of middleman had in selling to the designated market or segment?
4   What evidences are there that this type of middleman will streamline his operations?
5   What assistance must be provided this type of middleman?
6   How amenable is this type of middleman to envisioned control techniques?

Specific Types of Outlet
The final selection task is locating specific outlets. Manufacturers' sales branches are invariably located in large metropolitan areas within major wholesale trading areas. The exact site in an urban area depends upon the availability of facilities in the particular locale, the limitations imposed by the product line, and the image the manufacturer wishes to convey to consumers as well as the general public. Currently there is a decided tendency for manufacturers' sales branches with stock to cluster in the suburbs, usually along a major traffic artery.

The selection of individual middlemen poses a crucial problem for the manufacturer. Mistakes are quite costly in terms of time and money. Then, too, desirable middlemen will shy away from manufacturers that have a reputation for making frequent changes. To reduce much of the risk inherent in this decision, progressive manufacturers have initiated selection programs or refined those already in existence.

Basic to all selection programs is the systematic collection of information about the type of middleman in question. Primary sources of this information include (1) consumers in the respective areas, (2) trade associations, (3) trade publications, (4) professional location firms, (5) manufacturers of noncompeting product lines sold through the same type of middleman, and (6) the middleman himself. The field sales force is the normal collection agency for much of the desired data.

Usually consumers are very willing to give their recommendations since it is to their advantage to be serviced by the most competent and compatible middleman in the immediate area. It is also extremely helpful to check consumer reactions by having a salesman accompany a middleman's salesman on his calls. On the value of making joint sales calls to survey consumer attitudes; Robert A. Fergusson, president of Rust-Oleum Corp., had this to say:

The reaction on reception, acquaintance, etc., on sales calls is noted very carefully by our representatives to determine whether the salesman knows his way or whether the calls are "cold turkey." Substantially and in this measure, if he does not adequately stock to give service and he does not know his customers well, it is obvious that a great deal of time and effort will be required to gain attention and develop the interest of his accounts. On the other hand, if our man is well received because of the acquaintanceship and confidence of the distributor's customer, we often can come out with an order, even though it may be small. This situation is one which enables us to predict a successful distributor.[7]

Trade associations are usually willing to give information on their members. Seemingly, more pertinent information will be obtainable from a trade association, if one exists, whose members are a major type of middleman in the same industry as the particular manufacturer. The preference for a specialized trade association rather than one whose membership is more broadly based is borne out by the findings in a study of electronic manufacturers. Of the thirty-six reporting, fifteen or a little less than one-half used the Electronic Representatives Association as a source, whereas only five manufacturers used the Manufacturers' Agents National Association.[8]

Several publishers of trade publications offer their assistance in selecting middlemen of a major type in one industry or trade grouping. Such a publisher is the Instruments Publishing Company of Pittsburgh, Pennsylvania. Their rep service includes an opportunity to discuss representation needs with a staff member and access to a file of over 3,000 manufacturers' representatives handling industrial instruments, valves, electronic and electrical test instruments, mechanical and electronic components, dimensional gages, precision tools, and machinery. Each file on a particular rep will contain the following data:

1   Name of rep organization
2   Name of person to contact
3   Address of organization
4   Branch offices
5   Number of salesmen

[7] Reprinted by permission from *Sales Management, the Marketing Magazine.* Copyright 1951 Sales Management, Inc.

[8] Jack E. Bryer, "Finding and Hiring Good Manufacturers Reps," *Industrial Marketing,* January, 1964, table 1, p. 93.

6   Territory covered
7   Service facilities
8   List of manufacturers and products already represented

There is no charge for this service. The only restriction imposed by the publisher is that the consultation be face-to-face.

Firms that undertake to locate middlemen on a fee basis constitute another primary source for the manufacturer. Using the qualifications set forth by the manufacturer, these organizations seek out interested middlemen. To further assist the manufacturer in closing the agreement, detailed operating information is supplied on each prospective middleman. L. H. Simmond & Co., a firm specializing in locating manufacturers' reps, receives the biggest portion of its revenue from sharing commissions with reps appointed through them. Manufacturers pay a one-time administrative charge of $100 plus $100 per rep retained more than sixty days.

Manufacturers of noncompeting product lines are likely to be a rather profuse source of information because they can see the benefit in giving their outlets the opportunity for additional profits. However, extreme caution should be exercised in deciding whom to ask and in interpreting recommendations. As a general rule, only progressive manufacturers with similar distribution objectives should be requested to give an opinion. Because a particular middleman may be good for one line and not another, and very proficient middlemen are frequently weak in certain lines, the safest policy is to rely upon recommendations only if they are affirmed by other findings.

The best source of information is the middleman himself. Manufacturers depend upon the personal interview to gather this information.[9] The Link-Belt Co. has its own salesmen fill out a questionnaire on each prospective industrial distributor. The following areas are covered in the questionnaire:

1   *Compatibility.* What principal manufacturers are now represented by this distributor? Does the distributor understand our OEM, engineering, and nonexclusive sales policies? Is the distributor willing to carry an adequate inventory of all Link-Belt products?
2   *Relationships with market target.* Does this distributor sell competitive products? Who are the principal consumers of Link-Belt products now served by this distributor? How many of the distributor's salesmen are experienced in the sale of our types of

---

[9] A survey of thirty-six electronic manufacturers revealed that thirty-three gather information on prospective reps by personal interview. *Ibid.,* p. 95.

product? How many application engineers are employed by the distributor?

3 *Competition.* Who are the area competitors and what is the nature of their respective inventories? Will this distributor give us the best representation in the area? Will there be any territorial overlap with other Link-Belt distributors?

4 *Capabilities.* How many outside and inside salesmen are employed? What is the status of the physical facilities possessed by the distributor? What is the condition of the distributor's inventory? Who are the officers? How efficiently has the distributor been operating? What is the financial standing of the distributor?

Several manufacturers involve their officers in the interviewing of prospective middlemen. It is their opinion that active participation by management helps to impress upon the individual middleman the importance attached to the selection decision. It may also serve as the basis for establishing rapport with the selected middlemen. Mr. Gilbert Richards, president of Jordan Valve Division, Richard Industries, Inc., feels that involvement of management, although adding to the costs of operation, is a must for the small to medium-size manufacturer. "We have learned that the greater resources of larger firms usually mean there are reps begging to secure these lines. While we are growing, we still are in the position of having to sell good, prospective reps on working for us."[10]

The second part of the selection program is a concerted campaign to induce desirable middlemen to represent the manufacturer. To do this effectively, it is necessary to comprehend what middlemen want to know about their principals. There are a number of studies available to assist the manufacturer in this task. Two studies, one of the manufacturers' reps and another of industrial distributors, can be cited to show what is considered by the different types of middleman in evaluating prospective principals. Table 10.2 summarizes the findings on the relative importance of factors considered by manufacturing reps. It is immediately apparent that reps are more interested in the product—its compatibility, quality, and salability—than in the company which produces it. Surprisingly, reps attach very little importance to the principal's management and their policies, particularly those pertaining to advertising and technical assistance.

The obvious unimportance of price as compared with quality was brought out in yet another study of manufacturing reps. A survey

TABLE 10.2   Factors Manufacturers' Reps Use in Evaluating New Principals

EVALUATION FACTOR	PERCENTAGE OF IMPORTANCE
Compatibility with current lines	65.0
Product quality	38.3
Good sales potential	36.7
Principal's reputation	35.0
Rate of commission	11.7
Principal's financial standing	11.7
Existing volume	10.0
General company policy	8.3
Product price	6.7
Availability of field technical help	6.7
Advertising	3.3
Principal's management	3.3

Source: J. M. Pierce, "A Comparison of Manufacturers' Representatives with Company Salesmen," unpublished M.B.A. thesis, New York Graduate School of Business, 1962.

of reps handling electronic components indicated that quality can often overcome the lower-price advantage of competitors.[11]

In a study of industrial distributors, the question was what rules of thumb or methods are followed in considering new principals.[12] Among the most frequently considered were the following twenty factors:

1   Is the line established in terms of local user acceptance?
2   Does the manufacturer have the factory capacity and materials to supply merchandise under today's conditions?
3   What is the sales potential?
4   What is the profit margin?
5   How much inventory is required?
6   How many other distributors are there in the same trading area?
7   What is the manufacturer's financial rating?
8   Does the line fit into our operation?
9   How are other distributors doing in regard to sales with the product?
10   Does the manufacturer have a printed policy?
11   What is the product's value per pound?
12   How many competitive products are sold locally?
13   How much sales cooperation will the manufacturer give?
14   Does the manufacturer conduct training schools?

[11] Survey conducted by Mohr & Co., New York, and reported in "Marketing Milestones," *Industrial Marketing*, October, 1963, pp. 75-76.
[12] Reprinted by permission from *Sales Management, The Marketing Magazine.* Copyright 1951 Sales Management, Inc.

15 What about slow-moving stock?
16 Is the product used up and repurchased, thus making way for repeat business?
17 Is packaging convenient and attractive?
18 What are the advertising and sales-promotion policies?
19 Is the product guaranteed?
20 What is the principal's future?

These studies illustrate two vital points that should be observed in formulating a promotional campaign to solicit desirable middlemen. First, in taking on a new product, middlemen feel they should not have to fly blind. They want to know all the facts which might have some bearing on the proposed relationship with a given manufacturer. As evidence of this, manufacturers' reps mentioned twelve factors and industrial distributors twenty factors in the two studies.

Second, campaigns should be individualized not only by type of middleman but by specific outlet. The basis of this individualization is a thorough market analysis of each prospective middleman's trading area. With the resulting data, the manufacturer will be in a position to anticipate all the middleman's questions on sales potential, classification of consumers, and competition.

The third and final part of the selection program is concerned with writing up the formal agreement between the manufacturer and the middleman. The basic purpose of such a contract is to spell out the particular obligations agreed to in good faith by each party. The language of the contract should be clear and concise.

A contract with either a manufacturers' rep or an industrial distributor will usually cover the following broad areas:

1 Definition of territory and how much, if any, protection is to be afforded. A territory can be defined in terms of a geographical area or a particular grouping of consumers. Of utmost concern to most middlemen is the manufacturer's policy toward house accounts. One firm has classified the selling rights of its distributors in this regard by making this statement: "All direct inquiries and orders from industrial users and prospects shall be referred to Stocking Distributors."
2 Responsibilities of the middleman. These might include reports required from the field, procedures for placing orders, protection of manufacturer's interests, and product-education requirements.
3 Field sales assistance. Manufacturers should clearly define the types of assistance—technical, missionary sales, promotional,

etc.—they are in a position to offer as well as the conditions under which they are to be offered. This sort of positive declaration helps assure the middleman that he has the support of the manufacturer.

4   Methods for terminating contract. Contracts should contain provisions detailing the reasons for cancellation and the steps in the termination procedure. The life of the agreement may be a fixed period of time with option to renew or continuous until canceled. For manufacturers' reps it is not unusual for the contract to read that either party can cancel with thirty to sixty days' notice. Cessation of financial obligations is an important clause in the termination procedure. A sliding-commission scale may be used to determine payment to manufacturers' reps. Arrangements with industrial distributors will probably include a release from obligations relating to deliveries in transit as well as the procedures for evaluating and disposing of existing inventories.

If the manufacturer utilizes reps, he will want to indicate in the contract the exact terms of commission payment such as the bases for determining the amount of compensation, and when and how payment is to be made. Contracts with industrial distributors generally cover inventory requirements, resale prices, return-goods policies, and guarantees.

ASSISTANCE

Acknowledging that selection is only part of the job, progressive manufacturers have initiated or stepped up assistance to their marketing outlets. Even manufacturers who sell directly through their own branches have come to realize the necessity of aiding their marketing units in the field. Probably the most compelling reason is the ever-increasing pressure from the marketplace to do away with inefficiencies and reduce the cost of distribution.

In offering assistance to marketing outlets as a home office, principal, or supplier, there are several essential points that should be recognized by manufacturers. The first and possibly the most important is that coordination is likely to be greater if the outlet is regarded as a full partner rather than a customer. There is considerable sentiment in favor of selling middlemen, especially when they take title to the goods, but this tends to disrupt the cooperation so vital if assistance projects are to attain long-term developmental objectives.

Second, a manufacturer should base assistance projects on the problems of his outlets. A survey will help delineate the problems and their significance. Third, as long as it is practical, actual assistance should be individualized. This serves to emphasize the close working relationship that is desired. It also helps to overcome the reluctance of middlemen to seek outside aid.

The types of assistance provided marketing outlets cover a wide range from minor adjustments such as in billing to extensive training programs. With some overlap, the more common types of assistance can be broadly classified as follows: (1) credit, billing, and pricing, (2) technical field assistance, (3) training, (4) inventory backup, (5) management consultation, (6) promotion, and (7) advertising.

Credit, Billing, and Pricing

Frequently a slight alteration in credit, billing, or pricing can be very helpful to the outlet. Credit terms might be more closely correlated to the turnover of each distributor. The home office can render speedy price quotations. A simplified price structure will save a lot of time and reduce the chances for miscalculation. For example, an industrial distributor was quoted as saying he spent a good part of his life working arithmetic.[13] To illustrate his point, he referred to an item with a list price of $1,193.87, to which he had to apply discounts of 20 percent and 8 percent.

Technical Field Assistance

The complexities and rapidly changing environment of the industrial market make it imperative that the salesman in the field be technically supported. Field salesmen are finding it more and more difficult to keep abreast of applications for their present line, much less the numerous new products. To span this "information gap," manufacturers rely on so-called factory men.

One factory man described his role in the following way: "My philosophy is that I should work for, not with, distributor salesmen. I work alone about 90 percent of the time, mostly on problem calls

---

[13] John W. De Wolf, "How to Prepare to Sell More through Industrial Distributors," in Robert S. Hancock (ed.), *Dynamic Marketing for a Changing World,* Chicago: American Marketing Association, 1960, p. 246.

or missionary calls. On problem calls, I like to have a distributor salesman tell me what the problem is, and then go out and try to solve it."[14]
Besides providing information, the factory man does missionary selling, trains new salesmen, helps the salesman gain entry to certain
consumers, and through joint calls enhances the prestige of the salesman.

Training

Manufacturers rely on three principal methods to train field salesmen. These are factory schools, sales meetings, and joint calls made
by factory men. Factory schooling is usually worthwhile because
product-engineering specialists and top management are readily available. For manufacturers who market indirectly, the side benefit is
the opportunity for management to resell the middleman on the product line.

The major complaint middlemen have about factory schools is that
collectively they take the salesman away from his territory far too
much. This can be illustrated by the following hypothetical example.
Suppose an industrial distributor handles about twenty major lines.
If schools last about a week and are scheduled every other year, a
salesman would be out of his territory over two months a year. Added
to this are the costs of sending each salesman to ten schools every
year. Usually these costs are shared fifty-fifty with the manufacturer.

Formal training is brought to the field primarily through regional sales meetings. Time and expenses are drastically reduced and
increased exposure is possible because of a greater willingness on
the part of the middleman to allow a large number of men to attend.
To conduct these meetings, manufacturers rely heavily upon factory men assigned to the area. If factory men have no aptitude for holding meetings, this can be a serious drawback.

A noticeable change in both factory schools and sales meetings
has been the expansion of training to include selling skills. Long considered outside the manufacturer's province, salesmanship is being
stressed more and more, particularly by those whose products are
fairly standardized. Although most of the sales training offered is
directed toward the salesman, a few companies, such as the Dayco
Corp., have instituted programs to assist the middleman's sales manager in teaching selling.

[14] "Which Role for the Factory Salesman?" *Industrial Distribution*, December, 1965, p. 55.

Inventory Backup

The most significant tactical advantage of the marketing outlet, particularly if inventories are carried, is time. The reason is that delay to the industrial consumer is almost always quite costly. For example, downtime losses on an assembly line can amount to thousands of dollars a minute.

The manufacturer can maximize the advantage that his outlets have by virtue of their position, by backing them up with inventory reserves. The value of helping an outlet fill an order can be most dramatically shown in two unusual circumstances—disaster and emergency.

Management Consultation

Efficient distribution hinges on the management of the marketing outlet, whether it is a marketer's own sales branch or a middleman. The basis of any such management development program should be a survey of the outlets involved. A typical training program would probably cover the major management functions with special emphasis on their application to noted areas of weakness.

Management consultation can be provided on an individual or group basis. Which is used depends primarily on the nature of the counsel being offered. Although individual counseling is preferable because it creates the close relationship so essential for the free exchange of confidences, economy induces the manufacturer to resort to group methods such as a seminar. Besides providing a sounding board for middleman opinion, advisory councils present an excellent opportunity for the dissemination of management know-how.

Regardless of which basis is used, the success of a management consultation program depends upon how the advisee employs his new-found knowledge. This is keyed to the manufacturer's presentation. It must inspire confidence and enthusiasm. When a large number of outlets are involved, the manufacturer faces a more difficult problem in selling his program. One manufacturer with a large group of middlemen has shown a sound film which explains their management development program to over 5,000 dealers throughout the country.[15]

Promotion

Promotional tools include flip charts, films, demonstration models, catalogs, specification sheets, brochures, sales kits, and mission-

[15] James W. Redfield, "A Program for Dealership Management," *Business Horizons*, Fall, 1964, p. 59.

ary selling. One recent innovation has been the consumer-education clinic. The manufacturer supplies a demonstrator, possibly in a mobile van, and several factory personnel for an application training session at the marketing outlet.

The key to success with promotional aids is tying them in with the operations of the marketing outlet at the local level. The best way to enlist the support of the outlet, particularly if it is a middleman organization, is to solicit suggestions from the sales personnel involved and then follow through with as many as are practical. As an example, a middleman might want a consumer-education clinic only if the manufacturer avoids making any concerted "sales pitch."

Advertising

The manufacturer assists the local outlet by tying in or merchandising his advertising. He can accomplish this in four basic ways. One way is to mention the local outlets, preferably by name, in advertisements. When it is not conceivable to mention each and every outlet, the phrase "buy from your local industrial distributor" might be inserted. Another way to bring the local outlet into the ad is to feature a different regional grouping in each insertion.

A second way to enlist the support of the outlet is to supply tear sheets of future ads. These will serve to alert the management of the outlet so that they can keep in step and obtain the maximum value from the manufacturer's advertising efforts. Reprints of ads, a third way, serve a dual merchandising role. They keep the outlets apprised of the manufacturer's advertising and are useful as "leave-behinds" and direct-mail pieces.

The fourth and final way is to supply periodically the names of consumers in the outlet's geographical territory being reached by the manufacturer's advertising efforts. Separate lists should be maintained by medium. This practice tends to be expensive, but it is well worth the effort because it explains what each medium is doing for each outlet. It also facilitates the follow-up of particular ads by field salesmen.

CONTROL OF DISTRIBUTION SYSTEM

Control of his distribution system is vital to the manufacturer for two very important reasons. In the first place, the ever-changing nature of the industrial market needs constant reappraisal. Such changes as those previously noted for the electronics industry are a good example. Secondly, the market will no longer tolerate waste in distribution. Industrial consumers have come to realize that significant cost savings can be forthcoming only if duplications and other inefficiencies are eliminated from the distribution system, and every opportunity to help the individual customer save money is fully exploited.

Past performance and more recently distribution costs, market potentials, and marketing objectives are used as standards. Ensuring feedback, especially from middlemen, is the essential feature of channel control. Waiting for comments or complaints to filter through does not permit the manufacturer to keep on top of what is happening in the marketplace. Clear-cut lines for periodic communication must be established. To foster the goodwill of each outlet, the manufacturer should avoid unnecessary or time-consuming demands. Control reports, therefore, should be kept to a minimum in both size and number.

There are certain legal aspects to controlling distribution when marketing indirectly. The first question concerns the legality of entering into exclusive agreements with middlemen. The answer is that exclusive dealing is not illegal per se. Each case will be determined on the basis of (1) the type of goods involved, (2) the geographic area of effective competition, and (3) the degree of competition foreclosed.[16] Frequently exclusive agency contracts require a franchised middleman to purchase all or a substantial portion of his product needs from the manufacturer. Such contracts have been held to be illegal when the result is to reduce competition substantially.[17]

The second question is whether the manufacturer has the right to set up a middleman in a designated geographical territory. From the decision in the Philco case it can be inferred that the manufacturer has the right to designate sales territories as a middleman's primary responsibility, but he cannot enter into any other restrictive or limiting practices.[18]

Can a manufacturer refuse to sell to a prospective middleman who wishes to operate in the same territory as an established representative? The answer to this third question is a qualified yes, the qualification being that the right of a manufacturer to use his own dis-

[16] *Tampa Electric Co. v. Nashville Coal Co.,* U.S. 365 320, 327-329 (1961).

[17] *Standard Oil Co. of California et al. v. United States,* U.S. 337 293, 314 (1949).

[18] *United States v. Philco Corporation,* U.S. District Court, Eastern District of Pennsylvania, Civil Action No. 18216, filed July 13, 1956.

cretion in choosing whom he wishes to deal with cannot be used to create illegal or monopolistic situations. Moreover, this right applies to discontinuing dealings. The ruling of the court in one case was that a manufacturer has the right to stop dealing with a distributor who is acting unfairly toward his products.[19] When a contract exists, it must be legal and terminable.[20]

SUMMARY

A marketing channel can be likened to a pipeline through which goods and services flow from the manufacturer to the consumer. Selection, often regarded as the only job, is actually one of four major decision areas which a manufacturer must involve himself in on a constant basis. The other major areas are assistance, coordination, and control.

Four steps are distinguishable in the selection process. The first is to determine whether market coverage is to be limited, selective, or mass. Making this decision before selecting a major channel is more logical from the standpoint of long-run market penetration, but represents a departure from tradition. The decision on major marketing channels revolves around the question of marketing directly or indirectly. The general tendency is to market directly whenever permitted by financial resources. The next step calls for the manufacturer to decide on the major type of outlet. If marketing is to be direct, the alternatives will include the home office, a manufacturers' sales branch without stock, and a manufacturers' branch with stock. The choice in indirect marketing is primarily between the industrial distributor, a merchant middleman, and a functional middleman called a manufacturers' rep or agent. The fourth and final step is the selection or location of the various outlets. Successful selection of specific outlets is based on a carefully formulated program which is oriented to the outlets' interests.

The purpose of assistance is to help the selected outlet fulfill its assigned role in the marketing channel. This assistance may be in the form of (1) credit, billing, and pricing, (2) technical field assistance, (3) training, (4) inventory backup, (5) management consulta-

[19] *Technical Tape Corp. v. Minnesota Mining and Mfg. Co.*, 143 Supp. 429 (1956), CA-2 (1957); Certiorari denied (U.S. Sup. Ct., 1958).

[20] *Leo J. Meyerberg Co. v. Eureka Williams Corp.*, 215 F. 2d 100, CA-9 (1954); Certiorari denied (U.S. Sup. Ct., 1954), 348 U.S. 875.

tion, (6) promotion, or (7) advertising. The experiences of the more progressive manufacturers indicate several guidelines in providing this assistance. These are (1) to recognize the outlet as a full partner, (2) to gear assistance to actual problems, and (3) to individualize assistance as much as possible.

Control of marketing channels is an absolute necessity for two very good reasons. First, the market is ever-changing at an accelerated pace. Second, the market will no longer tolerate waste in distribution. Successful control is predicated on the principle of reports which obtain the desired information without unnecessarily burdening the outlet.

DISCUSSION QUESTIONS

1　Differentiate clearly between selective and limited coverage.
2　Under what circumstances is limited coverage titled exclusive?
3　What would a manufacturer need to know in order to determine the number of outlets in a given geographical area?
4　What is the basic premise of mass coverage?
5　Why is there a general tendency to market directly?
6　List the two major reasons for marketing indirectly.
7　What would cause a manufacturer to make use of a sales branch without stock rather than one with stock?
8　List the three factors the manufacturer should not consider in selecting the major type of outlet to be used.
9　Name at least three sources of information about specific outlets.
10　What are the normal provisions contained in a contract between a manufacturer and a middleman?
11　What is the major problem with factory schools from the standpoint of the outlet?
12　How can a manufacturer achieve the greatest possible success with the sales aids he provides the outlet?

SUPPLEMENTARY READING

Alexander, Ralph S., and Thomas L. Berg, *Dynamic Management in Marketing*, Homewood, Ill.: Richard D. Irwin, Inc., 1965, chap. 10.

Clewett, Richard M., *Marketing Channels*, Homewood, Ill.: Richard D. Irwin, Inc., 1954, chaps. 10-20.

Davidson, William R., "Channels of Distribution—One Aspect of Marketing Strategy," *Business Horizons,* Special Issue, February, 1961, pp. 84-90.

Oxenfeldt, Alfred R., *Executive Action in Marketing,* Belmont, Calif.: Wadsworth Publishing Company, Inc., 1966, chaps. 13-14.

marketing channels— united states

An understanding of the structure of present-day marketing channels is essential to the industrial-good manufacturer in all four phases of channel management. Nowhere is this knowledge of the types of establishment and the marketing environments in which they operate more obviously necessary than in the selection phase.

DIRECT MARKETING CHANNELS

In marketing directly to the consumer, the manufacturer of industrial goods will make use of branch establishments separate from either general or plant offices. These separate establishments can be labeled manufacturers' sales branches with stock and manufacturers' sales branches without stock. The latter type of branch is termed a manufacturers' sales office by the Bureau of the Census.

Manufacturers' Sales Branches with Stock

Sales branches maintain an inventory to meet a substantial portion of the market demand from the assigned geographical territory. Very likely the branch will also house the service installation when before- and/or after-sales service is part of the marketing program. With a warehouse and possibly a service installation, it is not surprising to find that branches may have more employees and higher operating-cost ratios than offices. In fact, a comparison of branches with offices shows that the average branch has from 1/3 to 21 times as many employees per establishment and from 1/2 to 7 times greater operating expenses expressed as a percentage of sales.

Sales branches, generally used by large, well-financed manufacturers, offer the possibility of comparatively lower marketing costs than industrial distributors. The savings could in turn be passed on to customers to gain a competitive advantage. That the sales branch does tend to have a lower operating cost is clearly reflected by the data in Table 11.1. In eight of the nine selected lines of industrial goods, sales branches incurred lower operating costs than industrial distributors. However, this might not be a valid comparison. One reason is that the general offices may perform and not allocate the costs to branches of several functions such as credit, billing, and inventory control. Another possible reason is that branches have a larger proportion of customers who tend to buy in sizable, more economical quantities. This is certainly true for some of the lines, such as electronic parts and equipment, but not all the other industrial lines listed in Table 11.1.

Whether a branch is larger than an office depends upon the line of goods handled. Surprisingly, several of the selected lines show very little sales-size difference between branches and offices. Average sales per establishment are shown in Table 11.2.

Manufacturers' Sales Branches without Stock

Manufacturers' sales branches without stock or sales offices serve as the focal point of sales activity in a given geographical territory. Typically, orders obtained by salesmen are shipped from a plant or public warehouse. The latter is gaining favor because it allows for quicker delivery and hence possible competitive advantage without the fixed investment of a branch.

The number of employees in a sales office will depend primarily upon the sales size of the assigned market area. In relatively undeveloped and limited potential markets, a sales office may be operated with as few as three people. A field sales manager who doubles as a salesman, a salesman, and a secretary-receptionist. In a market with larger actual and potential sales the same company may have a sales office with as many as twenty outside salesmen, several technical counsels, and countless inside sales and stenographic personnel. The field sales manager in the larger office may even have staff assistants in such specialized areas as training. Occasionally an industrial-good manufacturer will follow a policy of an ideal number of outside salesmen per office. When the number of salesmen exceeds

TABLE 11.1 Operating Expenses as a Percentage of Sales, Selected Lines of Industrial Goods, 1963

LINE OF GOODS	SALES BRANCHES WITH STOCK (PERCENT)	INDUSTRIAL DISTRIBUTORS (PERCENT)
Commercial machines, equipment	27.3	24.9
Professional equipment, supplies	22.8	23.8
Service-establishment equipment, supplies	22.5	26.3
Transportation equipment, supplies (excluding auto)	17.0	21.2
Industrial machinery, equipment	14.7	19.5
Industrial supplies	12.1	20.2
Farm supplies	10.9	11.6
Electronic parts, equipment	10.6	21.6
Construction, mining machinery, equipment	9.2	18.2

Source: *1963 Census of Wholesale Trade—United States Summary,* Washington: U.S. Department of Commerce, 1965.

TABLE 11.2   Average Sales per Establishment, Selected Lines of Industrial Goods, 1963 (in thousands of dollars)

LINE OF GOODS	SALES BRANCHES	SALES OFFICES
Transportation equipment, supplies (excluding auto)	5,541	5,392
Industrial machinery, equipment	1,495	1,449
Commercial machines, equipment	1,371	1,316
Service-establishment equipment, supplies	693	799
Electronic parts, equipment	3,238	2,389
Construction, mining machinery, equipment	2,999	4,572
Industrial supplies	1,834	3,051
Farm supplies	1,472	2,927
Professional equipment, supplies	524	1,438

Source: *1963 Census of Wholesale Trade—United States Summary*, Washington: U.S. Department of Commerce, 1965.

this level, the territory is divided up and another sales office is established. Suppose the ideal number is found to be twelve outside salesmen. A sales territory which requires eighteen outside salesmen for adequate coverage will be redefined and a new sales office will be established.

INDIRECT MARKETING CHANNELS

Marketing indirectly, the manufacturer of industrial goods will make use of middlemen. When a middleman takes title to the goods and earns a profit or loss, he is termed a merchant middleman. Functional middlemen do not take title to the goods handled and are compensated by a commission, usually based on the dollar volume of transactions.

Industrial Distributors

Not everyone will define the term "industrial distributor" in the same way. Indeed, the defining of industrial distributor presents somewhat of a problem. Adding to the confusion are the different trade names an industrial distributor may be known by in local areas. The different names include mill supply house; marine, oil-well, or mine supply house; and machinery or equipment dealer. Relying on the nature of the market served and the scope of functions performed, industrial distributors can be broadly conceived of as full-service merchant wholesalers selling primarily to the industrial market.

By full service it is meant that the industrial distributor performs all or most of the marketing functions. For the manufacturer, the industrial distributor provides intensive market coverage of a given geographical area; warehousing convenient to the market; customer-service facilities; customer credit, billing, and collection; and advice on local market requirements. For the industrial consumer the industrial distributor acts as purchasing agent; stores and delivers goods; extends credit; services and makes adjustments in products; and supplies information.

Quantitative measurement of what is meant by selling primarily to the industrial market gives rise to a problem of interpretation. Table 11.3 lists by kind of business the merchant wholesalers who sell 60 percent or more of their total volume to the industrial market. The total industrial sales of merchant wholesalers so classified amounts to almost one-half (47 percent) of the industrial volume for all merchant wholesalers.

It is possible to identify four types of industrial distributors. One is what might be called a general-merchandise distributor. This type of distributor stocks a wide range of industrial lines used in his trading area. In Los Angeles, one of the nation's largest distributors has 60 lines, 12,000 customers, and a 35-pound catalog listing 65,000 items.

General-line distributors, a second type, carry a complete assortment of goods in one line. An industrial line will usually correspond to a vertical market such as mining, marine, or oil drilling. However, there are instances of a line corresponding to the functional roles of the product involved. Probably the best example of a functionalized line is office equipment and machines.

A third type, speciality distributors, confine themselves to a limited range of products in a given line. Specialization implies greater product knowledge on the part of sales personnel. Integration of any of the first three distributor types with a manufacturing facility constitutes the fourth type of industrial distributor. Manufacturing by distributors of metals is frequently encountered, basically because of market demand. Their typical customer desires the metal products in various forms, extensions, and fabrications, but owing to his size lacks the facilities to do the job himself. Rather than draw a third party into the transaction, metal distributors have tended to assume the manufacturing function. Another illustration of integration is the industrial distributor, often a multiunit organization, who owns a plant which produces one of his basic lines. Ownership of a captive plant is usually restricted to industrial distributors who are large enough to absorb all of the output and who have extensive financial resources.

TABLE 11.3 Sales of Merchant Wholesalers Classified as Industrial Distributors on the Basis of Primary Selling Effort, 1963 (in thousands of dollars)

KIND OF BUSINESS	INDUSTRIAL SALES VOLUME	PERCENTAGE OF TOTAL VOLUME
Transportation equipment other than auto, aircraft, and marine	55,489	89.2
Metal service centers	3,474,254	82.1
Industrial machinery, equipment	2,643,789	79.5
Professional equipment, supplies	1,483,068	79.1
Electrical supplies, apparatus	3,044,640	78.9
Industrial supplies	2,622,875	78.8
Office, business furniture	322,098	78.1
Printing and writing paper	1,371,911	77.0
Brick, tile, cement, sand, and gravel	476,611	76.6
Plumbing and heating equipment, supplies	2,315,958	73.4
Miscellaneous farm products	1,082,251	71.1
Waste materials	954,039	70.3
Commercial machines, equipment	830,898	68.8
Trucks, tractors—road type	666,215	67.4
Iron, steel scrap	1,164,417	66.2
Other chemicals, allied products	1,168,830	66.0
Livestock, except horses and mules	333,314	65.0
Raw cotton	1,527,567	62.2
Total	25,538,274	

Source: *1963 Census of Wholesale Trade—Sales by Class of Customer,* Washington: U.S. Department of Commerce, 1965.

The competitive status of industrial distributors can be briefly summarized as follows:

1 Extensive reliance is placed on industrial distributors as the resellers of standardized products which tend to be purchased on a hand-to-mouth basis.

2 More and more, industrial distributors are finding themselves in direct competition with manufacturers. A case in point is abrasives.

3 Competitive pressures have led industrial distributors to expand their marketing program, particularly in regard to service.

4 Expansion and mergers have caused industrial distributors to grow larger.

5 Specialization is a dominant trend among industrial distributors, primarily because it fosters greater product knowledge. Bearings, power transmission and material-handling equipment, cutting tools, fluid-power components, fasteners, mechanical

rubber, pipe and valves, and precision tooling are lines most often handled by specialist organizations.[1]

6   Lack of product knowledge on the part of salesmen persists as a problem for the industrial distributor. In a test of his own salesmen, one large general-line distributor found that over 90 percent did not know the answers to the questions put to them in regard to product knowledge.

7   Utilization of industrial distributors tends to be more common among manufacturers with small sales volume than among manufacturers with larger sales volume.

8   Size of the margin allowed industrial distributors varies inversely with the sales-volume size of the manufacturer. The reasons for this are fairly obvious. First, larger manufacturers absorb a larger proportion of the services normally performed by industrial distributors. Second, smaller manufacturers attempt to offset any disadvantages inherent in size by offering larger margins.[2]

9   Proportion of sales done on a drop-shipment basis has a bearing on the gross-margin ratios realized by industrial distributors. The smaller gross margins earned on drop shipments have a diminishing effect on the distributor's overall gross-margin ratio.[3]

10   There is evidence of a trend toward joint efforts by distributors to provide one-source automated purchasing programs. These joint efforts are in response to market desires to reduce procurement costs and to concentrate purchasing at one source. Normally a cooperating distributor will not carry a major line which is competitive with major lines of other distributors. One distributor complex in Wisconsin is composed of five distributors who draw on stocks of nearly 100,000 items worth almost $3 million located in ten warehouses.

Drop Shippers

A shipment of goods from the producer to the consumer without any storage by the middleman is called a drop shipment. A merchant

[1] *The Industrial Distributor,* Philadelphia: Industrial Distributor News, Ames Publishing Co., 1964, p. 3.

[2] William T. Diamond, *Distribution Channels for Industrial Goods,* Columbus: Bureau of Business Research, College of Commerce and Administration, The Ohio State University, 1963, p. 115.

[3] Robert D. Buzzell, *Value Added by Industrial Distributors and Their Productivity,* Columbus: Bureau of Business Research, College of Commerce and Administration, The Ohio State University, 1959, pp. 63-64.

wholesaler who does all of his business in this manner is called a drop shipper. The operations of a drop shipper are much the same as a full-service wholesaler with the one exception of the storage function. He solicits orders, arranges for transportation, and extends credit. His risks are substantially less than the full-service wholesaler because he does not stock an inventory and orders are not placed with the producer until the sale has been made. The efforts of a drop shipper are directed toward those product lines which are bulky and difficult to store and which consumers are likely to purchase in quantity lots—carload or truckload.

By limiting or not performing various marketing functions, drop shippers incur operational costs which are far below those of industrial distributors in the same line of business. For metals sales offices without warehouses, operating costs in 1963 were 8.0 percent of sales, while for metals service centers with warehouses they were 16.3 percent. Undoubtedly much of this difference in cost burdens can be attributed to the greater number of nonselling personnel necessitated by the presence of a warehouse. Metals sales offices averaging slightly more than seven employees generate about $146,000 in sales per employee. The typical metals service center, on the other hand, has around twenty-six employees and obtains only $76,000 in sales per paid employee. The distinction between centers and offices is further emphasized by the minimal variation of average weekly payroll per employee in the two types of wholesale establishment.

Manufacturers' Agents

Most numerous of all functional middlemen and second in total sales to brokers are the manufacturers' agents or reps. In 1963, 11,189 manufacturers' agents sold almost $11 billion worth of goods, most of which was concentrated in industrial lines.

The typical manufacturers' agent handles several brands of related but noncompetitive goods. Territorial scope, selling price, and terms of sale are all set by the manufacturer. The principal service of manufacturers' agents is technical sales development. Such agents can be expected to have an engineering background. Manufacturers' agents, as a rule, do not provide warehousing facilities. When they do, as is the case currently with electronic parts, it is the result of market pressures. Usually a "stocking agent or rep" will receive a higher commission to reimburse him for this additional service.

Commission rates vary inversely with expected dollar volume. Lower commissions are paid when each manufacturers' agent can be expected to sell a large dollar volume and/or minimal sales effort is involved. Conversely, higher commissions are used to reward agents when a lower dollar volume is expected and/or greater sales efforts are indicated.

Manufacturers' agents operating as either proprietorships or partnerships are normally small business units. In 1963, for example, 6,597 of the 11,189 manufacturers' agents were proprietorships and unincorporated. The average number of paid employees was slightly more than four per establishment. One manufacturers' agent handling aircraft components is organized like a law firm, with senior and junior partners. New salesmen enter the firm as junior partners. After building up their sales volume over a period of several years, they are advanced to senior status and a greater share of the profits. An interesting sidelight is that to be a partner in this firm, a person must not only hold an engineering degree but also have a pilot's license. Company airplanes rather than automobiles are furnished to partners.

Marketing situations favoring the employment of manufacturers' agents include:

1 Insufficient sales potential to warrant direct selling efforts in a given area some distance from the home office.
2 Introduction of a new product. It often happens that the manufacturer is new or relatively unknown in the particular market area.
3 Importance of technical know-how in the middleman's sales force.
4 Necessity of having to gain entrance to a market segment. It may be that purchasing agents in a particular industry place a great deal of confidence in certain manufacturers' agents.
5 Severe seasonal fluctuations in demand.
6 Expansion of marketing efforts without the risks of heavy fixed investment.
7 Representation for a product totally unlike, from a marketing standpoint, the remainder of the manufacturer's output.

Brokers

Brokers, the most important functional middlemen in terms of sales volume, may buy or sell on behalf of their principals. Census figures for 1958 show that the majority of brokers represent sellers rather than buyers. For every six brokers operating in 1958, five acted in behalf of sellers and one represented buyers. Although no such breakdown is available for 1963, when there was an increase from 4,359 to 5,083 in the total number of brokers, it would seem likely that brokers representing sellers have remained predominant.

The basis of operation for a broker is a single transaction or series of related transactions. Since the principal service is price negotiation, brokers tend to be concentrated in those industrial lines which are highly standarized and consequently can be bought and sold by description. Raw materials of an agricultural or nonagricultural nature are good examples.

The average broker will do over twice as much business as the average manufacturers' agent. The noncontinuous relationship brokers have with their principals eliminates much of the necessity for many of the marketing services, thus allowing them to function on a 2.8 percent expense-to-sales ratio as compared with 6.0 percent for all manufacturers' agents. An example of the limited services offered by brokers is that only rarely will they handle any part of the billing procedure.

Circumstances which strongly favor the utilization of a broker are a wide seasonal variation in output, such as might be experienced with agricultural raw materials, and a strong desire to remain anonymous, as in the case of a seller who might wish to dispose of nonbranded merchandise without disrupting his major marketing channels. In providing noncontinuous representation, a broker is seldom associated with one particular seller, and normally he will not reveal the name of the principal until after the sale has been completed.

Brokers receive a commission based on the dollar volume of goods involved in the transaction. Occasionally, a fee per given quantity such as a bale or carload is substituted for a percentage rate of dollar value. The rate of commission is determined by the line of trade. The range is from less than 1 percent to as much as 7 percent.

Selling Agents

Selling agents are functional middlemen who contract to sell the entire output of a principal without specifications as to territory, price, or terms of sale. Representation is continuous and likely to be firmly established through association over a number of years. Functioning much as the sales department of the principal, selling agents render perhaps the widest range of services for any functional middleman. In addition to pricing, assistance may be given in product development, production scheduling, inventory control, and financing.

Firmly entrenched in the marketing of textiles, selling agents can also be found in such industrial lines as coal, metals, chemicals, machinery, and industrial supplies. As the largest of the functional middlemen, selling agents average over $3 million in sales per establishment. The extra services offered push operating expenses up to 3.9 percent of sales, which is higher than brokers but still well below manufacturers' agents. Many of the larger selling agents have branch offices. For example, in the textile trade the home office will probably be in New York with branches in Los Angeles and Dallas.

The marketing significance of selling agents is greatest if manufacturers are fairly small, have limited management capacity in the area of marketing, produce less than a full line, and require continuous representation over an extensive market area. The basic differences between selling agents and manufacturers' agents are the particular roles each assumes in the marketing process and the location of marketing decisions. Selling agents assume the entire selling function and make all the attendant decisions. For manufacturers' agents, on the other hand, the role is frequently supplemental and the marketing decisions remain with the principal.

SUMMARY

A knowledge of the types of establishments and the marketing environments in which they operate is essential in channel management. Nowhere is this more obvious than in the task of selection.

Marketing directly, manufacturers make use of sales branches with stock and offices without stock. Generally limited to large manufacturers, sales branches maintain an inventory to meet a substantial portion of market demand from the assigned geographical territory. It is also likely that the branch will house the service installation if this is part of the marketing program. In addition to the advantages accruing from a conveniently located supply, manufacturers may make use of branches in anticipation of lower marketing costs.

Sales offices function as the focal point of selling activity in a given geographical territory. Deliveries of orders are made from plants or strategically located public warehouses. The number of employees in a sales office will depend primarily upon the sales size of the assigned market area. A few manufacturers follow a policy of an ideal span of control for the head of each sales office. When a sales office has more than the ideal number of salesmen, territories are redefined and a new sales office is created.

Middlemen the manufacturer utilizes in marketing indirectly can be classified into two groups on the basis of whether or not they take title to the goods handled. Merchant middlemen take title and thus the risks of ownership, but functional middlemen do not take title. Foremost of the merchant middlemen is the industrial distributor. Although some disagreement is evident on the exact meaning of the term "industrial distributor," such a middleman can be broadly conceived of as a merchant wholesaler who sells primarily to the industrial market. Four types of industrial distributors can be distinguished: general merchandise, general line, speciality, and integration of either of the preceding types with a manufacturing facility. Industrial distributors can be characterized as primary resellers of standardized products which tend to be purchased on a hand-to-mouth basis. Facing increasing competition, often from manufacturers, industrial distributors have turned toward expanded marketing programs, specialization, and mergers.

Drop shippers are merchant wholsesalers who do not store, but rather have the goods shipped directly from the producer to the consumer. Not performing the inventory function, drop shippers do not have nearly the risks or the operating costs of the full-service industrial distributor. Generally, drop shippers limit their product offerings to bulky, difficult-to-store products which are normally purchased in quantity lots.

Typically, manufacturers' agents or reps handle several brands of related but noncompetitive goods. The principal service of an agent is technical sales development. When warehousing is provided for principals, the "stocking agent or rep" will receive a higher than normal commission rate to reimburse him for this additional service. Commission rates vary inversely with the expected dollar volume of sales. The commission rate will be less for a high dollar volume than for a low one. Invariably manufacturers' agents are small firms, averaging about four paid employees. Conditions favoring employment include a critical need for technical selling know-how and the feasibility of using an agent as a supplement to the regular marketing effort.

Although brokers may buy or sell for their principals, a significant portion specialize in selling. The basis of operation for a broker is a single transaction or series of related transactions. Usual payment is in the form of a commission based on the dollar volume of the transaction. Brokers are frequently utilized when supply is irregular and when the buyer or seller wishes to preserve anonymity.

Firmly established in the marketing of textiles, selling agents contract to sell the entire output of a principal without reservations as to territory, price, or terms of sale. Selling agents operate much as the sales department for a principal. The wide range of services includes pricing, product development, production scheduling, inventory control, and financing. The marketing significance of selling agents is greatest if manufacturers are fairly small, have limited management capacity in the area of marketing, produce less than a full line, and require continuous representation over an extensive market area.

DISCUSSION QUESTIONS

1   From the standpoint of a small manufacturer, what are the advantages of a merchant middleman, a functional middleman?
2   Defend the view that the marketing costs of manufacturers' sales branches are not necessarily lower than those of industrial distributors.
3   Contrast manufacturers' sales branches with manufacturers' sales offices.
4   In the marketing of professional equipment and supplies, what explanation is there for almost three times as many sales offices as sales branches?
5   Give the reasons why an industrial distributor might find it desirable to merge with a manufacturing facility.
6   Is there any correlation between the trends of industrial distributors toward specialization and joint efforts to provide one-source automated purchasing?
7   What competitive advantages, if any, does a drop shipper have?
8   Why would a manufacturer prefer to use the services of a broker?
9   Contrast a manufacturers' agent with a selling agent.
10   How should a manufacturers' agent counteract the trend toward specialization among industrial distributors?
11   What advantages are there in using manufacturers' agents to introduce a new product?

SUPPLEMENTARY READING

Burnon, Richard H., "The 'Stockless Purchasing' Salesman," *Industrial Distribution,* January, 1965, pp. 49-50.

Buzzell, Robert D., *Value Added by Industrial Distributors and Their Productivity,* Columbus: Bureau of Business Research, College of Commerce and Administration, The Ohio State University, 1959.

Diamond, William T., *Distribution Channels for Industrial Goods,* Columbus: Bureau of Business Research, College of Commerce and Administration, The Ohio State University, 1963.

Ketchum, Brad, Jr., "Ordermation Kansas City," *Industrial Distribution,* October, 1965, pp. 60-65.

Philip, Van Ness, "MIP Wisconsin Makes the Grade," *Industrial Distribution,* September, 1965, pp. 66-71.

marketing channels— in other nations

Foreign markets represent an enormous potential to the United States manufacturer. Some estimates place foreign market growth at a rate nearly twice that expected for the domestic market. This becomes all the more alluring when profits are shrinking at home.

Unlike many of their consumer counterparts, manufacturers of industrial goods are not total strangers to foreign markets. Many industrial marketers have had long-standing foreign relationships. Marketers of production machinery, construction equipment, and agricultural implements are but a few examples which come to mind. It is not unusual for a single United States firm to hold unchallenged market leadership.

There are at least three major reasons for the tenure and frequent dominance of foreign markets by United States manufacturers of industrial goods. Perhaps the most obvious reason is the almost insatiable demand registered by overseas markets for United States industrial know-how. This demand has been increased by the destruction of two world wars and the clamor of a seemingly endless number of emerging nations. A second reason, and one which is closely allied to the first, is the acknowledged superiority of United States goods and services. An agricultural expert traveling through the Middle East during the thirties wrote that no one seemed to be able to build as good an irrigation pump as the Americans. He went on to say that the failure to allow American pumping equipment in one country was a major detriment in a depressed agricultural industry. Currently, American-made electronic data processing equipment tends to hold a dominant position in foreign markets.

The universality of industrial goods and services is a third reason. Industrial products need not be adapted to conform to a foreign market nor is a foreign market automatically ruled out as lacking potential. Indeed, the so-called emerging nations which require greatly modified consumer products are among the best customers of industrial marketers. Then, too, political philosophies present less of a barrier to industrial marketers than to marketers of consumer goods. In India, for example, the dire need for fertilizer plants has at least partially overcome the local government's predilection for government ownership of productive capacity.

The decision of an industrial-good manufacturer to make a foreign investment is governed mainly by marketing considerations—the expansion of an existing market or the tapping of a new market. Profitability is the next most important reason. Availability of raw materials seems to be a factor for primary metals and to a much smaller extent for electrical machinery (Table 12.1).

TABLE 12.1   Reasons Given for Overseas Investment, Selected Industries (percentage of respondents)

INDUSTRY	EXPANDING MARKET SHARE	NEW MARKETS	HIGHER PROFITS	AVAILABILITY OF RAW MATERIALS	LOWER LABOR COST	TRADE RESTRICTIONS	COMPETITION	OTHER
Primary metals	..	13	13	53	..	7	..	14
Machinery	46	21	8	..	4	4	13	4
Electrical machinery	50	13	13	6	6	6	..	6
Other transportation equipment	60	20	..	..	20	..	..	..
Instruments and fabricated materials	22	34	33	..	11	..	..	..
Chemicals	27	9	36	..	..	19	9	..

Source: Adapted from *Overseas Operations of U.S. Industrial Companies, 1967-1968*, New York: McGraw-Hill Department of Economics, Aug. 4, 1967, table VIII.

TABLE 12.2   Foreign Activities by Selected Industrial-good Manufacturers, Six-year Period, July 1960-June 1966*

TYPE OF MANUFACTURER	NEW ESTABLISHMENTS			EXPANSIONS			LICENSES†		
	1960-1963	1963-1966	1960-1966	1960-1963	1963-1966	1960-1966	1960-1963	1963-1966	1960-1966
Manufacturing facilities:									
Chemical and allied products	18.1	18.8	18.5	21.1	23.1	22.0	6.6	10.3	8.4
Nonelectrical machinery	13.4	11.6	12.5	12.2	10.3	11.3	14.9	16.7	15.8
Electrical machinery	9.6	8.3	8.9	7.3	8.1	7.7	16.5	11.7	14.2
Fabricated metal products	6.2	6.3	6.2	3.7	3.7	3.7	8.4	7.2	7.8
Primary metal products	6.1	5.5	5.8	4.1	3.9	4.0	4.1	5.5	4.8
Scientific instruments	4.3	4.0	4.1	4.9	4.6	4.8	2.4	4.3	3.3
Total	57.7	54.5	56.0	53.3	53.7	53.5	52.9	55.7	54.3
Nonmanufacturing facilities:									
Chemical and allied products	10.0	8.6	9.1	9.3	7.5	9.0			
Nonelectrical machinery	14.4	8.2	10.8	11.2	5.7	10.1			
Electrical machinery	9.1	4.8	6.6	4.7	5.7	4.9			
Fabricated metal products	3.6	2.7	3.1	0.9	3.8	1.5			
Primary metal products	2.6	2.4	2.5	2.8	3.8	3.0			
Scientific instruments	3.2	3.7	3.5	5.1	..	4.1			
Total	42.9	30.4	35.6	34.0	26.5	32.6			

*Percentage of total activities.   †Licenses classified as neither manufacturing nor nonmanufacturing.

Source: Adapted from *Six Years (1960-1966)* of *New Foreign Business Activity of U.S. Firms*, Chicago: Booz-Allen & Hamilton, Inc., 1966, pp. 22-25.

Whatever the reason for foreign investment, industrial-good manufacturers expect quick payoff of their investment. A McGraw-Hill survey reported that a substantial number of firms expect a payoff in less than ten years:[1]

INDUSTRY	PERCENTAGE OF MANUFACTURERS EXPECTING PAYOFF	
	IN LESS THAN 5 YEARS	IN 5-9 YEARS
Transportation equipment (other than autos or trucks)	50	50
Chemicals	25	75
Electrical machinery	50	38
Instruments and fabricated materials	29	57
Machinery	35	35
Primary metals	10	50

PATTERN OF FOREIGN ACTIVITIES

The factual data compiled in Table 12.2 show that industrial-good manufacturers account for a substantial portion of all types of foreign activity. It is also apparent that these industrial-good manufacturers are more important in setting up manufacturing facilities than in establishing nonmanufacturing facilities. Further investigation reveals a decided tendency for industrial-good manufacturers to favor manufacturing facilities in locating overseas. In the six-year period covered by a Booz Allen & Hamilton study, the decided preference for a manufacturing facility is obvious:

	NEW ESTABLISHMENTS		EXPANSIONS	
	MANU-FACTURING	NON-MANU-FACTURING	MANU-FACTURING	NON-MANU-FACTURING
Chemical and allied products	504	110	213	24
Nonelectrical machinery	341	131	109	27
Electrical machinery	244	80	74	13
Fabricated metal products	170	37	36	4
Primary metal products	158	30	39	8
Scientific instruments	112	42	46	11

Individual firms report extensive use of manufacturing facilities in overseas markets. At the end of 1966, IBM had sixteen overseas

[1] *Overseas Operations of U.S. Industrial Companies, 1967-1969,* New York: McGraw-Hill Department of Economics, Aug. 4, 1967, table XI.

plants and eight new facilities and expansions were completed or under construction during the previous year. Manufacturing subsidiaries are operated by the International Harvester Company in eleven foreign countries. In addition, International Harvester participates in manufacturing joint ventures in six other countries. Alcoa lists eighteen principal manufacturing subsidiaries and affiliates in fourteen different countries. These do not include five bauxite operations.

The emphasis on manufacturing operations plus the overseas plants of consumer-good firms creates a potential for industrial goods and services. In 1960, 21 percent ($276 million) of the total amount invested in overseas manufacturing operations was for industrial equipment exported from the United States. The primary-metals industries buy the largest amount, followed by machinery, transportation equipment, and chemical industries.[2] Surpassing the total for manufacturing, the petroleum industry purchased over $1.1 billion worth of exported industrial goods from the United States.

The next question to be asked is where the industrial-good manufacturer has located his overseas operations. A Booz Allen & Hamilton study provides information on all firms without any breakdown by industrial classification. The location of overseas manufacturing facilities and licenses for the entire six-year period of the study as well as the last twelve months of the period is shown in Figure 12.1.

If industrial-good manufacturers follow the same spatial pattern as all United States firms, it is obvious that in establishing and expanding manufacturing facilities they have concentrated their efforts in the Western European and Western Hemisphere markets. In a comparison of the last twelve months with the entire six-year period, the only noticeable deviation is a lessening of attention in regard to Asia. The degree of market sophistication, particularly in Western Europe, would seem to be a primary reason for the obvious location preference. That is to say, countless industrial products are too advanced to be sold in large quantities outside the more highly industrialized nations.

As for licensing, Western Europe is the location for almost one-half of the agreements. This is very similar to the spatial pattern for the other two types of activities. The major difference is the relative importance of Asiatic locations. It would appear that licensing is the preferred and perhaps necessary form of activity when locating in Asia. During the six-year period from 1960 to 1966, Japan led all countries with 337 licenses. In fact, the number of licenses located

[2] *Ibid.*, table X.

FIGURE 12.1   Regional Location of Foreign Activity, All United States Firms, July 1960–June 1966.

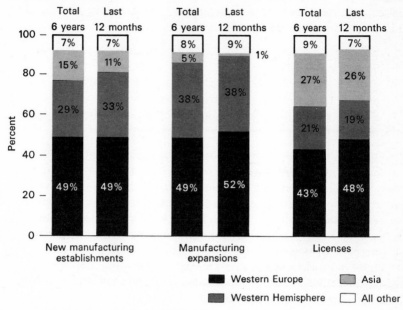

Source: Adapted from *Six Years (1960–1966) of New Foreign Business Activity of U. S. Firms,* Chicago: Booz Allen & Hamilton, Inc., 1966, pp. 18 and 21.

in Japan very nearly approximates the total for the European Common Market.

In one industry, electronics, 170 overseas subsidiaries and affiliates or joint ventures are listed for 86 United States-based firms. They were regionally distributed as follows:[3]

Western Europe	67
Western Hemisphere:	
Canada	42
Latin America	25
Asia:	
Japan	17
Oceania:	
Australia	9
All other	10

This breakdown follows roughly the relative significance of the various regions reported for all firms during the period from 1960 to

[3] *Electronics in the Free World,* Menlo Park, Calif.: Stanford Research Institute, 1963.

1966. Western Europe and the Western Hemisphere received the major share of attention, followed by Asia. Hugh M. Hyde, publisher of *International Electronics,* gives the following reasons for the attention directed toward Western Europe:

1   Europe is second only to Japan in the growth of the electronics industry.
2   Europe and particularly the Common Market countries are experiencing rapid overall industrial expansion.
3   Europe has military programs which have been steadily increasing.

Yet another look at the geographical pattern of foreign activity is supplied by a McGraw-Hill continuing study of overseas investment. Table 12.3 shows the percentage distribution of overseas investment for industrial-good manufacturers in six industries. The overall pattern reported for them closely parallels the breakdown shown in Figure 12.1. For example, Western Europe accounts for 49 percent of new manufacturing establishments and 52 percent of the manufacturing expansion. This area is about as important in terms of relative investment, with 46 percent of capital vested in Common Market countries and the rest of Europe.

Industry differences in capital investment are very evident. Manufacturers of nonelectrical machinery concentrate their overseas investing in Europe; manufacturers of electrical machinery appear more interested in the Western Hemisphere and in particular Canada. It is also obvious that primary-metals manufacturers tend to locate near raw-material sources and that makers of instruments and fabricated metals are investing heavily in Europe, especially those countries outside the Common Market.

DIRECT MARKETING CHANNELS

In foreign markets much as in domestic markets, industrial-good manufacturers prefer to market directly. The principal difference is that both the advantages and the disadvantages for direct channels are magnified in the foreign market. To illustrate, control of the selling function, if possible, is even more vital in foreign operations than it is within the United States. Coupled with this, the cost disadvantage of direct channels becomes much more awesome.

TABLE 12.3 Actual Capital Expenditures by Region, Selected Industries, 1966

INDUSTRY	PERCENTAGE OF INDUSTRY TOTAL						INDUSTRY TOTAL*
	COMMON MARKET	REST OF EUROPE	CANADA	LATIN AMERICA	OCEANIA	OTHER	
Chemicals	30.0	13.0	35.0	10.0	2.0	10.0	1,063
Machinery	46.0	29.0	7.0	10.0	3.0	5.0	751
Primary metals	5.0	1.0	13.0	34.0	39.0	8.0	406
Electrical machinery	10.0	16.0	47.0	10.0	13.0	4.0	258
Instruments and fabricated materials	23.0	43.0	24.0	2.0	4.0	4.0	150
Other transportation equipment	12.2	7.6	27.6	1.0	..	2.6	51
Total	28.3	17.7	24.7	13.0	9.0	7.3	2,679
All manufacturing	30.1	17.8	27.5	11.6	6.9	6.1	4,554

*Millions of dollars

Source: Adapted from *Overseas Operations of U.S. Industrial Companies, 1967 - 1968*, New York: McGraw-Hill Department of Economics, Aug. 4, 1967, table II.

International Company

The truly international company, although rarely found in actual practice, is viewed by many experts as the ideal organizational structure for dealing with worldwide markets. In an internationally oriented firm, top management has worldwide responsibilities. No separate division or subsidiary is set up to handle foreign markets. The vice-president of marketing, for example, is concerned with worldwide marketing conditions and opportunities.

Organizational division by geographical area is accomplished at the middle and lower management levels. Even here, however, every attempt is made to use a regional rather than a country basis. So-called area managers may be appointed for North America, Latin America, Europe, the Middle East, Africa, and the Far East. The exact span of geographical control is determined largely by the stage of market development. Heading up his area, the manager is charged with the task of attaining the objectives spelled out by top management with the marketing as well as the production facilities located within his assigned territory.

An international company is often looked upon as the end result of an organizational evolution. To start out, a United States manufacturer probably exports through middlemen to reach foreign markets. As sales mount and the manufacturer gains greater insight into foreign markets, he may feel licensing or a joint venture is more advantageous. He may also be influenced by the legal barriers in some countries which preclude doing business on a strictly export basis. The next step is consolidation of foreign marketing operations into a separate division or subsidiary. Depending upon the manufacturer's financial capacity, this consolidation often takes place about the same time the decision is made or implemented to develop his own foreign operations. When, if ever, a manufacturer becomes an international company depends largely upon the importance of foreign markets as contrasted with domestic markets. Another factor is the willingness of top management to tackle the job of running an international company.

International Division or Subsidiary

Undoubtedly the most popular type of foreign marketing organization is a self-sufficient division or subsidiary. A large measure of its popularity is due to the fact that a firm can centralize in one organizational unit all the activities relating to foreign markets. This is an advantage to any manufacturer regardless of size. Another reason for this form of organization is that it can be located wherever it is most appropriate. This may be at the home office or in an international trading center such as New York or San Francisco. Internal organization of a division may be based on function, geographical territory, product, or some combination.

There are about as many variations of the division or subsidiary organizational structure as there are firms using it. IBM conducts its international business through the IBM World Trade Corporation. At the end of 1966, World Trade was reported to have over 69,000 employees spread among 331 sales offices, 223 service bureaus and data centers, 6 development laboratories, and 16 manufacturing plants; these facilities are located in 103 countries. Alcoa International, Inc., the overseas marketing arm, handles a wide array of activities including export sales, licensing, partially owned affiliates, and wholly owned subsidiaries operating abroad. In a third company, Crown Zellerbach International, Inc., a wholly owned subsidiary holds equity in all operations outside the United States.

Joint Ventures

A joint venture can be likened to a partnership between a United States manufacturer and a foreign-based enterprise. The foreign enterprise may be an established firm or one which is created at the time of the agreement. To illustrate the latter, the Aluminum Company of Libya, Limited, was formed by Alcoa International, Inc., and Libyan investors. In each of the six years covered by a Booz-Allen & Hamilton study, United States companies showed a decided preference for a majority financial interest. New establishments in which a majority interest is held number almost 36 percent more than those in which a minority interest is held (457 as compared to 337).[4]

Circumstances favoring the use of a joint venture include:

1 The lack of the financial and/or management capabilities necessary for wholly owned facilities
2 The absence of suitable license candidates
3 The presence of legal barriers to wholly owned facilities
4 The presence of nationalism as a strong purchasing influence

The heart of a successful joint venture is selecting who is to be the partner in the other nation. The job of selecting a partner takes

---

[4] *Six Years (1960-1966) of New Foreign Business Activity of U.S. Firms,* Chicago: Booz-Allen & Hamilton, Inc., 1966, p. 17.

on even added importance when the permanence of the association is recognized. Typically, contracts run five years. However, injury to one's image is likely to stretch out over a greater number of years. To obtain the right partner in a given country, many United States manufacturers are sacrificing financial control of the venture. In addition to the successful development of foreign market potential, the right partner offers several significant advantages:

1   He is entirely familiar with the marketing practices of the particular country.
2   He knows his way through the labyrinth of local business laws.
3   He may be able to supply skilled labor in a country plagued by labor shortages.
4   He may furnish protection against local governmental interference.

In Mexico, joint ventures have been advantageous because of the profit opportunities brought about by export credits. The dollar value of the products exported by the joint venture earns a credit which can be used to offset the duties on imports into Mexico from the United States or another country. This export credit can be applied to components and materials used in the products manufactured by the venture or in other products manufactured by the United States firm. Thus, the United States partner can take advantage of the operating conditions in Mexico while at the same time gaining a competitive marketing advantage. To organize such a venture, the United States manufacturer must be willing to let his Mexican partners have a 74 percent majority interest. Another stipulation is that the capital contributed by the United States partner must be tangible.

Licensing

A licensing agreement with a foreign firm to manufacture a particular product is popular with industrial-good manufacturers—especially those with limited resources who wish to enter an overseas market in the shortest possible time. Such a firm is Swartwout Fabricators, a relatively small manufacturer of commercial and industrial ventilation equipment. In just five years, a six-nation network was built through the use of licensing agreements. Rapid market entry is an advantage also to the larger manufacturer, particularly in those areas where direct investment is not justifiable.

Other apparent advantages of licensing are:

1   The avoidance of staffing problems
2   The advantageous use of the licensee's local reputation
3   The shifting of the burden of dealing with local restrictions
4   The possibility of obtaining reciprocal technology and research from foreign partners.
5   The proliferation of income sources
6   The spreading of tooling and development costs
7   Being the only approach acceptable to a local government in an important market

This array of advantages is undoubtedly responsible for the popularity of licenses. In the six years covered by the Booz Allen & Hamilton study, licenses accounted for almost one out of every four overseas activities (24.3 percent) and were second in importance only to manufacturing establishments. [5]

Although licensing has all the appearances of a quick and easy solution to overseas marketing, it has several weaknesses. The severity of these weaknesses is such that many businessmen believe that the use of licensing should be limited to unrelated products of minimal sales potential. The most obvious weakness is the loss of control. It is conceivable that the licensee may not manufacture or market the product as would the United States firm. Lack of marketing control, another and perhaps the biggest problem, may result because few overseas firms practice aggressive and sophisticated marketing tactics in terms of United States standards.

Another weakness is the possibility that the licensee will take advantage of the United States firm without redress in local courts. Retaliatory action will probably mean loss of a manufacturer as well as a market. Another significant weakness of licensing is the creation of a future competitor. There is always the chance that the licensee is using the agreement to entrench himself competitively. Finally, currency regulations of the licensee's country may hinder the flow of royalties. Changes in conversion rates can also have a deterring effect on royalties.

The built-in risks of licensing make careful consideration an utmost necessity. Several questions need to be asked before awarding a license:

1   What is the market potential for the product or products?
2   What is to be gained from the licensing agreement?

[5] *Ibid.*, p. 22.

3 Who is the best licensee prospect?
4 What type of contractural relationship will ensure the best working relationship?
5 What provisions should be included to allow for possible future
   changes in the contract?
6 What shall be the rate, timing, currency, and tax liability of the
   royalty payment?
7 What shall be the respective responsibilities of the licensor and
   licensee?

INDIRECT MARKETING CHANNELS

While the tendency is to market directly, many industrial-good manufacturers still prefer an indirect approach to markets in other nations.
This preference is based mainly on two operating advantages of middleman employment. One of these is the market expertness of middlemen. Middlemen have a knowledge of local marketing practices
which would take infinitely long to duplicate. This is especially true
of those who specialize in one particular country or region.

The second major advantage in using middlemen is the decidedly reduced financial outlay. The minimum requirement would be sales-
promotional materials; the maximum requirement would be the expenses incurred by assigning factory men to work with middlemen.
Other related advantages of an indirect approach are the lessening
of risk, the possibility of rapid sales-volume buildup, and the gearing
of marketing efforts to local conditions.

The most significant hindrance to the utilization of middlemen is
their attitude of independence. Insufficient sales effort and lack of
attention cause many United States manufacturers to categorize middlemen as simply order takers. Nationalistic differences and the distance separating the two parties intensify this feeling. Another disadvantage is that selling costs remain at a fixed percentage of sales
volume and never level out as they might in the manufacturer's own
operation. Finally, product goodwill is transferred to the middleman.
This makes it especially difficult to change representation or set up
a company branch.

Much like domestic middlemen, those functioning in overseas markets can be classified as merchant or functional on the basis of whether or not title has passed. The advantages of either general type are
essentially the same as under domestic marketing conditions.

Merchant Middlemen

The *export merchant* or house operates much as an industrial distributor. He buys and sells on his own account, usually on a nonexclusive basis. Typically, the export merchant is a large, well-established firm located in a major port such as San Francisco, New York, or New Orleans. It is not uncommon for him to have branch offices and warehouses scattered throughout the United States and the foreign markets he serves. Some even have their own docking and shipping facilities. Average sales volume per establishment in 1963 was $3.1 million. This was almost 25 percent more than the average in 1958 with slightly fewer merchants. Other differences between 1963 and 1958 were:

1   Operating expenses as a percentage of sales were considerably lower in 1963. Operating expenses in 1963 were 4.4 percent of sales or nearly one-third lower than the 6.2 percent for 1958.
2   Annual payroll and number of employees per establishment increased from 1958 to 1963.
3   Unincorporated business units were much less a factor in 1963. Between 1958 and 1963, active proprietors of unincorporated businesses declined from 879 to 684 or from about one out of every three export merchants to one out of every four.[6]

The size of the export merchant, which seemingly is ever increasing, is his greatest advantage as well as his major limitation. The advantage in channeling goods through an export merchant is the market dominance exercised by this type of middleman. This implies a sizable volume of business through this outlet. The only problem is establishing a working relationship with the "right" export merchant. Being large, however, the export merchant is in a strong bargaining position. In such a position he is not likely to allow those selling to him much more than a minimal profit. It is also doubtful whether the export merchant will want to handle a product which entails extensive market development.

Outside the United States, export merchants are known as trading companies. Many have been in business for a long time, their past inextricably intertwined with the political history of their own countries. Two well-known Japanese trading companies are Mitsui & Company, Ltd., and Mitsubishi International Corporation.

A variation of the export merchant is the middleman known as an

---

[6]Statistics extracted from *1963 Census of Business Wholesale Trade—U.S. Summary*, Washington: U.S. Department of Commerce, 1965, pp. 1-11 and 1-18.

export drop shipper or desk jobber. He functions much as his domestic counterpart and does not provide storage. Principal products handled are raw materials. Unlike domestic operations, the export drop shipper's operation tends to be more on a transaction basis. The main service he offers the producer is his extensive knowledge of foreign markets. Such knowledge may lead to speculation on the part of the export drop shipper, a practice which is not in line with long-term market development.

Another merchant middleman operating in the export market is the *raw-material merchant.* Specialization is by commodity rather than foreign market area, and the tendency is for imports to be equal to or greater than exports. This is understandable when it is remembered that the United States is a big importer of raw materials.

Functional Middlemen

An *export agent* acts as the exclusive representative of his principal in foreign markets. The actual selling is handled by a network of representatives, distributors, or salesmen. In terms of sales volume, export agents doubled in average size during the five years from 1958 to 1963. Average sales volume in 1958 was $2.1 million. By 1963 this had grown to $4 million. Another notable difference between 1958 and 1963 was the drop in the operating expense-to-sales ratio. For all export agents the drop was from 3.5 percent of sales to 2.8 percent.[7]

Almost identical to the export agent is the functional middleman called a *combination export manager.* However, he has a much closer relationship with his principals, so close in fact that he functions much as an internal export department. This type of middleman does business in his principal's name. He uses his principal's letterhead, and all of his representatives operate in the principal's name rather than their own firm's. Normally the combination export manager will not assume the credit risk although he will furnish credit information on foreign customers. The usual method of payment is a commission basis with a minimum retainer.

Surprisingly, to be successful, a combination export manager will work himself out of a job. By this it is meant that he willingly helps his principals set up their own export department when it is advisable in terms of sales volume. He knows that if he successfully builds

---

[7] *Ibid.*

up one company's overseas sales, other firms will hear of it and seek out his services.

Unlike other middlemen, the combination export manager assumes responsibility for sales development. This plus the fact that he functions in the principal's name rather than his own makes the combination export manager ideal as the initial means of entering foreign markets. About the only problem is ascertaining the rate of commission. Very few combination export managers offer the same array of services. This results in virtually no standardization of fees. The main consideration for the manufacturer is to pay enough to ensure adequate sales development.

An *export commission house* is a buyer of United States goods for foreign companies. Accordingly, commissions are paid by foreign firms. The way an export commission house operates is to scan the United States market for goods desired by their foreign principals. Specifications with invitations to bid may be sent out to qualified United States manufacturers. The amount of business done with this type of middleman is insignificant. One authority estimates that there are only five firms functioning today strictly as export commission houses.[8] Most of the tasks of the export commission house are now performed by other export middlemen such as the export merchant.

Some manufacturers act as functional middlemen in order to fill out the lines they market directly to foreign markets. These firms, which could be called *manufacturing exporters,* feel they can strengthen both their competitive and cost position by adding complementary products. A manufacturing exporter is usually financially able to go it alone in marketing his product directly. However, he is well aware that complementary products will undoubtedly broaden the market for his foreign branches, while at the same time absorbing a portion of the overhead. Another advantage for the manufacturing exporter is that he assumes no risk of ownership with the complementary products.

The firms marketing through this channel have all the advantages of direct marketing, with the possible exception of complete control, without incurring any of the disadvantages. One difficulty is the possible delegating of jobbed items to a second-class status in terms of marketing emphasis. However, it stands to reason that the better

[8] Laurence P. Dowd, *Principles of World Business,* Boston: Allyn and Bacon, Inc., 1965, p. 214.

manufacturing exporters would not consciously take such a course of action. Locating the "right" manufacturing exporter presents a formidable problem. There are only a limited number of middlemen, and their presence is not always readily apparent to would-be principals.

SPECIALIZED ORGANIZATIONS IN EXPORT TRADE

There are a number of export organizations which defy classification as orthodox middlemen or marketing channels. Some are financial in nature, others are an outgrowth of laws, while still others result from the intricacies of international trade. Nevertheless, these specialized organizations play an important, often vital, role in overseas marketing.

Export-Import Bank

Of the eight national and multinational agencies financing foreign trade, two are particularly important in the planning of foreign marketing. One of these is the Export-Import Bank; the other, which functions more indirectly, is the International Monetary Fund.[9] The Export-Import Bank with $7 billion of resources was established for the express purpose of facilitating United States foreign trade through lending assistance. The two objectives are (1) to help the foreign trade of the United States and (2) to encourage and supplement private capital. The bank makes four types of loans. Project loans account for the largest volume. Examples include fertilizer plants, steel mills, and power-generation installations. For a project loan the Export-Import Bank will finance all goods and services purchased from the United States. Other costs must be met through equity financing. The other three types of loans are exporter credits, medium-term comprehensive guarantees or insurance, and short-term comprehensive insurance.

The Export-Import Bank is a hard-money institution; that is, the going market rate is paid for money borrowed on their statutory authority of $6 billion. Repayment of loans is in United States dollars. A list of those eligible to apply includes:

[9] The other six agencies are the Agency for International Development (AID); the International Bank (BRD); International Finance Corporation (IFC); the International Development Association (IDA); the Inter-American Development Bank (IDB); and the Inter-American Social Progress Trust Fund.

1   A United States or foreign firm
2   The government of a friendly country
3   A United States exporter
4   A United States bank or exporter until cover becomes available at Foreign Credit Insurance Association (FCIA)
5   A United States exporter at FCIA

International Monetary Fund (IMF)

The International Monetary Fund, through its concern with the free world's foreign exchange markets, has an indirect rather than a direct effect on foreign trade. The functions of the IMF can be summarized as follows:

1   It administers a code which provides that all member countries should attempt to keep currencies on a fully convertible basis without any restrictive covenants.
2   It has the authority to approve or disapprove changes in par values.
3   It has resources of gold and member country currencies to render short-term assistance on balance-of-payments problems.
4   It has improved the tools and techniques of monetary analysis and provided technical assistance to member countries on budget, taxation, and financial controls.

To the industrial-good manufacturer marketing overseas, the International Monetary Fund can make a valuable contribution. A good example of this is in the so-called developing countries which have a great need for capital goods. To obtain these goods, however, developing countries have had to borrow constantly. This, in turn, has placed an excessive burden on their balance-of-payments positions. The IMF in a few cases has been able to exert a corrective influence as a dispenser of technical assistance and monetary resources.[10]

Confirming Houses

Confirming houses might be described as financial middlemen. They operate where international credit conditions are uncertain and/or credit costs are unusually high. They also act as financial representatives for buyers in overseas countries. Letters of credit are drawn

---

[10] For a more complete discussion of the role of IMF, see Pierre-Paul Schweitzer, "Monetary Aspects of World Trade and Economic Development," *Proceedings Fifty-first National Foreign Trade Convention,* New York: National Foreign Trade Council, Inc., November, 1964, pp. 34-45.

in favor of the confirming house so that they can act as the buyer's agent in all aspects of exporting.

Very few confirming houses are located in the United States, where their financial function is performed by export commission houses. Confirming houses are much more common in England, where many in London handle a large proportion of the trade between India and other nations of the world.

Export Discount Houses

Few in number, export discount houses are factors who operate exclusively in the export market. This type of financial house charges a higher rate of discount than do commercial banks. There are two reasons for the higher fee. First, the export discount house assumes the exporter's credit function and the credit risks up to the level of the advances. Therefore, the exporter need not maintain a credit department. Second, the export discount house supplies expertise on credit matters relating to foreign markets.

Edge Act Organizations

Under the Edge Act of 1919 and subsequent regulations, two types of banking activities can be established outside the United States. The difference between the two is emphasis. One type is devoted chiefly to commercial banking, and the other is mainly concerned with investment banking. It was estimated in 1963 that only ten United States commercial banks had both types as subsidiaries, while four had one type but not the other.

The objectives of one Edge Act subsidiary, Chase International Investment Corporation, are to provide services in other nations for customers of the parent and to realize a profit on any transaction which may materialize.[11] The services supplement those which are otherwise available through the International Department and other divisions of the parent. The subsidiary is also called upon to supply a wide array of information on overseas markets.

Edge Act subsidiaries can fill many different financial roles as seen by the following list of actual transactions:

[11] Adapted by permission of the publisher from Victor E. Rockhill, "The Role of the Edge Act Companies in International Financing," in *Sources and Methods of International Financing*, AMA Management Report No. 59. © 1961 by the American Management Association, Inc.

1   An Edge Act subsidiary and another investment banker agreed to supply buyers for an aggregate of $18.5 million of Class B ten-year debentures, partially on a "best efforts" basis, and partially on a "commitment" basis.

2   An Edge Act subsidiary purchased an entire issue of participating preferred stock.

3   An Edge Act subsidiary took a first mortgage on 90 percent of the debt and purchased a substantial portion of the common shares. The interest rate was lower than normal for the foreign country and common stock was purchased at no discount in price.

4   An Edge Act subsidiary arranged for 100 percent of the financial funds from three private sources and one foreign government development corporation.

5   An Edge Act subsidiary loaned money to an enterprise in a country with currency problems. A potential equity reward was provided the lender by common stock warrants.

Webb-Pomerene Joint Export Operations

The Webb-Pomerene Export Trade Act of 1918 exempts voluntary export agreements or associations from the Sherman Act. The purpose of the act was to strengthen the competitive position of United States manufacturers, particularly chemical, in foreign markets. This exemption holds generally as long as those concerned do not restrain trade or attempt to fix domestic prices. Another possible illegal activity of a joint export operation would be a foreign manufacturing venture.[12]

Three distinct types of joint export operation are recognized. One type handles all the activities related to the exporting of members' commodities. It is usually a closed corporation with all of the stock held by members. Another type of joint export operation handles one or more, but not all, of the export activities for its members. It also does not have an "exclusive" on the overseas distribution of its members' products. An example would be a coal or lumber shipping association. The third type is a marketing association which buys members' products for resale in foreign markets.

Joint export operations organized under provisions of the Webb-Pomerene Act have not been popular with United States manufacturers. The biggest reason is a general aversion to combinations of

---

[12] *United States v. Minnesota Mining and Manufacturing Company*, 92 F. Supp. 947 (D. Mass., 1950).

any type which would mean a loss of indentity. Such an attitude is particularly prevalent among industrial-good manufacturers who have spent a lot of time and effort building up brand identity. It is also possible that the legal complications have dismayed many manufacturers.

Intermerchants

The basic function of an intermerchant is to arrange for the exporting of goods from a hard-currency country to a soft-currency country. The problem is to arrange for payment of the goods. To do this, an intermerchant must have a vast knowledge of foreign marketing and international financing so that he will be able to put together a switch or triangular deal. Generally, such a deal involves organizations in three or more countries. Continual international monetary problems should contribute to an already steadily increasing volume of business for intermerchants.

Development Corporations

These corporations are organized to help an emerging nation industrialize. Their objective is to help, not exploit, an underdeveloped country. One of the most successful is the International Basic Economy Corporation, a nonprofit enterprise. Its primary goal is to help selected countries attain a higher standard of living through economic improvement.

SUMMARY

Markets in other nations represent a potential which has been growing at about twice the rate of the domestic market. Unlike their consumer-good counterparts, manufacturers of industrial goods are not total strangers to foreign markets. Many industrial marketers have experienced long-standing relationships with foreign markets. Today, the decision of an industrial-good manufacturer to make a foreign investment is governed mainly by marketing considerations. Regardless of the reason, all industrial-good manufacturers expect a quick payoff of their foreign investment.

Establishment and expansion of manufacturing facilities are by far the most common approach to foreign markets. Along with the foreign plants of consumer-good manufacturers, they create a potential for industrial goods and services. In 1966, more than one out of every six dollars invested in foreign manufacturing operations was for capital equipment exported from the United States.

The geographical pattern of foreign operations shows a concentration in what could be considered the more sophisticated markets, such as Western Europe. The next most important area is the Western Hemisphere and in particular Canada, followed by Asia or Oceania. An exception to this pattern is the primary-metals manufacturer who tends to locate adjacent to sources of raw materials.

As in domestic markets, industrial-good manufacturers prefer to market directly. In foreign markets, however, the advantages and disadvantages of direct marketing are greatly magnified. Direct marketing channels include an international company, an international division or subsidiary, joint ventures, and licensing.

Still very much a theoretical concept, the truly international company is structured to reflect the worldwide responsibilities of top management. No attempt is made at organizational division by geographical area above the lower management levels. The international division or subsidiary is probably the most common approach to foreign marketing. A large measure of its popularity is due to the fact that firms can centralize in one organizational unit all the activities relating to foreign marketing. Joint ventures are essentially partnerships between United States manufacturers and foreign-based firms. The foreign-based firm may be either already established or created at the time of the agreement. About the fastest way to enter a foreign market is through licensing. This is particularly true for the manufacturer with limited resources.

Preference for marketing indirectly is based on two operating advantages of middlemen:

1 Middlemen have a market expertness which would take infinitely long to duplicate.
2 Middlemen reduce the necessary financial outlay.

Among the merchant middlemen operating in foreign markets are the export merchant, the export drop shipper, and the raw-material merchant. Functional middlemen include the export agent, the combination export manager, the export commission house, and the manufacturing exporter.

Several export organizations defy characterization as orthodox middlemen or marketing channels. Such specialized organizations play an important and often vital role in foreign marketing. Some of a financial nature are the Export-Import Bank, the International

Monetary Fund, confirming houses, and export discount houses. Those which are an outgrowth of laws are Edge Act organizations and joint export operations as prescribed by the Webb-Pomerene Act. Intermerchants and development corporations result from the intricacies of foreign commerce in today's world.

DISCUSSION QUESTIONS

1   What evidence is there to support the contention that industrial-good manufacturers generally have more experience in foreign marketing than their consumer-good counterparts?
2   Why would lower labor costs be a better reason for foreign investment for makers of instruments and fabricated materials than for machinery manufacturers?
3   Explain the longer payout period expected by members of the primary-metals industry.
4   Discuss the type and geographical pattern of foreign activity for all types of firms and industrial-good manufacturers.
5   Describe the differences between an international company and an international subsidiary.
6   What would cause a United States manufacturer to enter into a joint venture?
7   Outside of rapid market entry, what advantages does licensing offer the large, well-financed manufacturer?
8   Discuss the most significant hindrance to the utilization of middlemen in foreign markets.
9   Contrast an export merchant with an industrial distributor.
10 How can a combination export manager attain success by continually working himself out of a job?
11 Confirming houses and intermerchants function in similar circumstances. Explain.
12 What is the test of a true development corporation?

SUPPLEMENTARY READINGS

Coyle, John J., and Mock, Edward J. (eds.), *Readings in International Business,* Scranton, Pa.: International Textbook Company, 1965.

Dowd, Laurence P. (ed.), *International Business: Essential Considerations for Growing Midwest Enterprise,* Ann Arbor: Bureau of Business Research, School of Business Administration, The University of Michigan, 1960.

Fayerweather, John, *Management of International Operations,* New York: McGraw-Hill Book Company, 1960.

Obstacles and Incentives to Private Foreign Investment 1962-1964, Studies in Business Policy, No. 115, New York: National Industrial Conference Board, Inc., 1965.

Proceedings Fifty-first National Foreign Trade Convention, New York: National Foreign Trade Council, Inc., 1964.

Sources and Methods of International Financing, Report No. 59, New York: International Management Division, American Management Association, Inc., 1961.

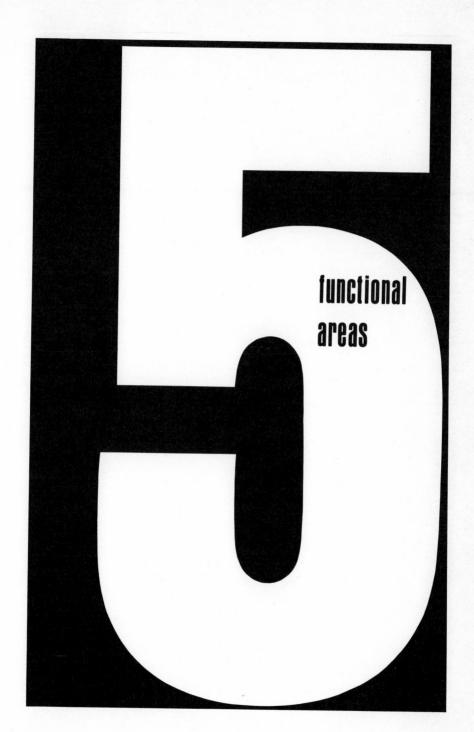

5 functional areas

sales
and service

Regardless of whether the manufacturer markets directly or indirectly he must build some form of organization for sales and service. Much the same can be said for the middleman who operates in the industrial market. The chief concerns of the manufacturer or middleman are the structural form of the organization, the major characteristics of industrial sales operations, and the functions of field sales management.

ORGANIZATIONAL STRUCTURE

Prior to the emergence of emphasis on the marketing management concept, the sales function was headed by a vice-president or general manager who reported directly to top management. Under the marketing management concept, sales become part of marketing. The job of sales remains the same, but the chief sales executive now assumes the direction of other marketing functions as the head of marketing or reports to the vice-president or director of marketing who, in turn, reports to top management. Thus, adoption of the marketing management concept can conceivably alter the relationship of sales to top management.

Another likely change brought about by the marketing management concept is that functions such as advertising, marketing research, and sales service are removed from the sales department and given independent status often on the same organizational level as sales. Frequently the disruptive effects of this alteration on the sales organization are diluted by the circumstances accompanying the change. Probably the most distracting circumstance is that simultaneously with this change the head of sales is frequently promoted to the top marketing job. Hence his stature as well as that of sales is enhanced appreciably. Another alleviating circumstance is the willingness of many sales heads to forgo responsibility for other functions in order to concentrate on what they know best, line sales management.

The bases used in organizing the sales operation include product, consumer, geographical territory, and function. More often than not, two or more of the bases are used in combination.

Product Organization

Organization by product is popular among industrial marketers who have a diverse range of products or product lines. Their rationale in using this structural form is to make the salesman more of a specialist by restricting the product types he is responsible for. If product types have extreme technical complexity, specialized product knowledge can be very important.

The main drawback to a product organization is the duplication of effort. Sometimes two or more salesmen from the same company will operate in the same geographical territory. They may even call upon the same customers, but it is hardly likely the same purchasing influence is contacted by both.

To retain the advantages of product specialization without its disadvantages, many marketers have grouped sales geographically or by consumer and set up product managers in a staff capacity. An example of such a modification is the hypothetical sales organization illustrated in Figure 13.1.

Consumer Organization
Adherence to the marketing management concept has meant for many companies the organization of the sales department by consumer class or market segment. These segments often correspond to SIC categories as shown in Figure 13.1.

The all-important advantage in carrying the concept of consum-

FIGURE 13.1   Hypothetical Sales Organization.

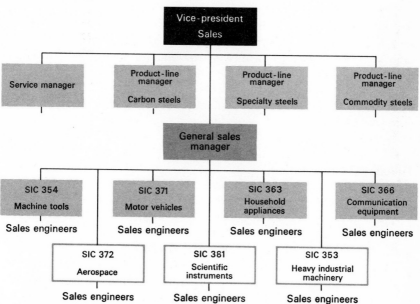

er orientation through to the sales organization is that it enables the individual salesman to become an expert at servicing the needs of a particular group of consumers. Factors relating to each market segment which are conducive to the use of a consumer base include:

1 *Geographical concentration* so that customer segments can be equated with geographical assignments
2 *Substantial sales and profits* from each customer segment to justify the particular assignments of sales personnel
3 *Distinctiveness in needs,* which allows clear differentiation between customer segments

For marketers with diverse product offerings, organizing on the basis of consumers rather than products represents a more practical opportunity for specialization because there is much less overlapping of sales effort.

Geographical Organization

Location or geography is considered in structuring the sales organization. The only exceptions are the firms whose salesmen operate out of the home office, making calls as occasioned by market demands. Such a firm might be one making custom fire-fighting equipment.

The primary reason for using a geographical base is the convenience it affords the marketer in serving his consumers. Geographical autonomy fosters flexibility to local conditions. Business provincialism, while not as significant as, say, thirty years ago, can still be noted in certain areas of the country. However, this very autonomy works against uniformity of action and functional specialization at the local level. To balance the advantages against the disadvantages, many marketers combine the geographical base with one or more of the other bases. Typically, this is either product or consumer.

Functional Organization

Under a functional type of organization, staff executives such as product managers exercise line authority over field sales for a given product or product line. Thus, as shown in Figure 13.2, the number of superiors a salesman has is directly related to the number of products handled. The obvious conflicts of interest that result have seriously limited the adoption of the functional concept of organization.

Functional organizations have also been set up where line direc-

FIGURE 13.2   Functional-type Sales Organization (Hypothetical Firm).

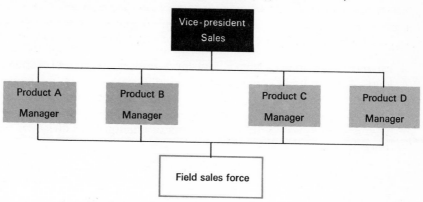

tion over field sales is given staff executives representing advertising, marketing research, sales control, services, sales promotion, and engineering. This type of functional organization has tended to disappear as the role of sales has changed with the marketing management concept. Functional organization of sales into the two broad areas of operations and service is frequently used in combination with other bases.

DISTINGUISHING CHARACTERISTICS OF THE INDUSTRIAL SALES FORCE

An industrial sales force is distinctive in several ways. The most obvious is the presence of inside salesmen and technical counsels who tend to have no counterpart in the sales organizations of consumer-goods organizations. Others not quite so obvious are the different roles of the product manager and customer service.

Product Managers

Broadly conceived of, the product manager has staff responsibility for the development and implementation of marketing programs for a single product or product line. The position of product manager has evolved as marketing has grown more and more complex for the multiproduct company. The primary advantage of a product manager is that through him all the firm's activities are related to the marketing of a given product or product line.

The specific responsibilities assigned a product manager are likely to include all or a sizable portion of the following tasks:[1]

1 Formulate tactics and strategies for each of his products. Most firms require the product manager to submit comprehensive plans for the attainment of short- and long-term marketing objectives. Until the emphasis on marketing, industrial product managers tended to be technically oriented, concerning themselves primarily with such activities as technical counseling, after-sales service, and analysis of the implications of changes in consumer requirements.

2 Assist implementation once plans have been accepted by the respective line and staff executives involved. Interest and support for new plans must be stimulated by the product manager particularly among members of the field sales force.

3 Assemble pertinent data on all the marketing aspects of each assigned product. Besides having technical and manufacturing information, the product manager must familiarize himself with every feature of each product's market.

4 Advise top management on all matters pertaining to the marketing of assigned products.

5 Conduct field investigations to get a firsthand picture of the market. In this regard, top executives from many manufacturers feel that even though the product manager does not make sales directly, he must go into the field from time to time to get the feel of market conditions and the effectiveness of what he puts in the hands of the salesmen. In the event that a product manager is called upon to sell, his efforts are usually limited to a few key accounts.

6 Coordinate the total resources of the company for marketing new products assigned to him.

The position of product manager is a paradox in terms of authority and responsibility because the product manager is a *staff* executive who requires *line* authority to perform his job adequately. The line authority may not be forthcoming for several reasons:[2]

1 Doubt of his capabilities
2 Opposition of entrenched, more senior functional managers

[1] For a more detailed discussion see *The Product Manager System*, Experiences in Marketing Management, no. 8, New York: The National Industrial Conference Board, 1965, pp. 20-32; and David J. Luck and Theodore Nowak, "Product Management—Vision Unfulfilled," *Harvard Business Review*, May-June, 1965, p. 144.

[2] Luck and Nowak, *op. cit.*, p. 148.

3   Lack of comprehension of the basic organizational principle of this managerial system

Despite the possibility of not having any clear-cut line authority, the product manager, nonetheless, is usually held fully or partially accountable for the profits on each of his products. When accountability is shared, it is usually with his superior, e.g. the head of marketing or sales. In actual practice, however, top management is generally hesitant to pinpoint profit responsibility, preferring instead to create the impression that the product manager does have marketing responsibility.

A profile developed from in-depth interviewing shows that the typical product manager for an industrial-goods manufacturer has the following personal characteristics:[3]

1   Is from thirty-five to forty years old
2   Holds an undergraduate degree in a physical science or engineering
3   Will likely spend entire career with one or possibly two firms
4   Has a background of laboratory and technical service work
5   Associates generally with technically oriented personnel both within and outside his firm
6   Earns about $13,000 per year, with exceptions

Inside Salesmen
Inside salesmen can be found working for industrial distributors and for manufacturers in their sales branches. The main job of the inside salesman is customer relations as opposed to selling. He spends about one-half of his day on the telephone: (1) making follow-ups in regard to product performance, quotations, and deliveries, (2) solving service problems, and (3) answering complaints. An in-depth study of inside salesmen employed by industrial distributors revealed that in the average 8 1/2-hour day, 57 percent of the time is spent with customers, 35 percent is taken up with paper work, and the remaining 8 percent, or thirty-nine minutes, is consumed by meetings.[4]

To maximize the usefulness of inside salesmen, their efforts must be closely coordinated with those of outside salesmen. Assigning specific customers to each inside salesman enables him to function much as a regular salesman. He can sell creatively because he knows his customers and can anticipate many of their needs. Working with

[3] *Ibid.*, p. 145.

[4] "Special Report: The Inside Salesman," *Industrial Distribution*, November, 1963, p. 59.

only assigned accounts, the inside man is in an ideal position to pass along to his outside partner helpful suggestions on such matters as the current interests or mood of a particular customer. Thus, greater coordination is possible when specific responsibilities are delegated to the inside salesman and he is made to feel a member of the sales team.

J. R. Fauver, a Detroit distributor, feels coordination has been achieved by the implementation of a plan management has labeled the "sales coordinator." Under this plan inside salesmen, upgraded in title to coordinator, are each made responsible for the customers of two outside salesmen. With two telephones—one to shipping, the other to other coordinators and customers—the coordinator shepherds every order through to delivery. In doing this he will price the entire order, check current inventory to see if the order can be filled from current stocks, and oversee shipping so that the order is delivered as requested.[5]

Besides providing greater coordination, the assignment of specific customers facilitates the installation of a financial incentive system for inside salesmen. By means of definite assignments the accomplishments of an inside salesman can be compared with those of other inside salesmen, past performance, and/or various other standards. Since inside salesmen are basically oriented toward servicing existing customers, the best use of financial incentives seems to be to relate them to how quickly and efficiently this is done. For example, the inside salesman might receive a bonus based on the reductions effected in customer-service time or in the number of customer complaints.

The opportunity to move outside serves as the singular motivation for most inside salesmen. It is not surprising to find that fixed salary is about the only form of compensation. A very good reason for the extensive use of fixed salary is that sales trainees work as inside salesmen. Numerous manufacturers and some large distributors have sales trainees take over as inside salesmen to gain their first practical on-the-job sales experience.

Technical Counsels

Technical counsels or specialists play an important part in industrial selling, particularly when salesmen call upon a wide variety of consumers or sell a bewildering array of products. The main job of the

---

[5] "Fauver Finds a Cure for Chaos," *Industrial Distribution*, January, 1966, pp. 60-61.

technical counsel is to furnish technical information as requested to the consumer. For example, a salesman for a primary-metals manufacturer might seek the services of an architect in selling to a builder, a metallurgist in selling to an aerospace firm, or a production-applications engineer in selling to a food processor. The technical specialist may accompany the salesman in his calls or supply requested data to the salesman for his personal presentation to the client.

While almost every industrial marketer employs what might be called technical counsels in one capacity or another, the true role of the counsel is seldom evaluated. The *first* question that might be asked is why the organization should have a technical counsel. For the industrial distributor this is often simply answered by stating that in order to handle a particular line, it was necessary to hire a specialist. Manufacturers, on the other hand, have employed technical counsels in response to consumer demands for more technical data on product applications, although initially it is quite possible that a few firms used counsels strictly as solvers of field problems. The growing complexity and buyer sophistication in today's industrial market has added still more reasons for hiring technical counsels.

Granted that technical counsels are almost a necessity, the *next* question is how full advantage can be taken of their services. Profit is the dominant consideration in answering this. A technical counsel should be assigned to a position in which he can exert the greatest influence on the attainment of profitable sales. This might be overcoming competitor activity in profitable market segments or increasing the sale of high-margin products. As an example of the former, a manufacturer of electrical kitchen equipment might hire a cooking specialist to build up volume in the restaurant market long dominated by gas-operated equipment. For the distributor, the most profitable assignment of the specialist is often a position in which he relieves the salesman of the responsibility for a line or the problems associated with a line. This will enhance profits if, by being relieved of responsibility, line salesmen can in turn generate more sales from their other lines and there is no appreciable drop in sales for the line assigned on one basis or another to the specialist.

A *third* question is how the technical counsel should be compensated. About the only generalization possible is that there is a significant difference either in form or in basis between the technical counsel's pay plan and the one for salesmen in the same firm. Fixed salary is the usual form of pay for technical counsels. When an extra incentive is included, its basis is related more to overall company performance than to sales volume.

The *fourth* and perhaps most difficult question is where technical counsels should be located in the organization to attain both effectiveness and efficiency. There are four possibilities: (1) field sales,
(2) engineering, (3) product-manager system, and (4) separate department. Locating the technical counsel in sales facilitates coordination at the point of sale. With the emphasis in sales on product applications, counsels are inclined to be more practical-minded. Also
less time is wasted in getting the counsel to the customer. As part
of engineering better use can be made of the counsel's time. He can
be employed on various projects in the engineering department when
not making calls with salesmen. Another advantage is that fewer
counsels need to be hired when their services are centrally controlled.
However, with only infrequent market exposure, counsels tend to
be too theoretical with little or no "sales sense."

Having technical counsels report to product managers or forming them into a separate department, possibly with customer service,
denotes a compromise between sales and engineering. The technical
orientation of the product manager in many firms favors the arrangement whereby counsels are assigned to him. The only possible
disadvantage would be an overlapping of effort due to specialization by product rather than by need. Combining the technical counsel with customer service in a separate department provides all the
advantages of functional specialization. The only problem is where
to place the newly created department in the overall structure of the
firm.

Customer Service

Whereas service is important in the sale of consumer goods, as witness the factory service centers for appliances, it is absolutely essential in industrial marketing. Customer service rendered by the
industrial marketer is performed before as well as after the sale. Before-sales service is aimed at greater product utilization through customer preparation. This may involve one or more of the following
activities: (1) installation, (2) assistance in getting an operation started, (3) on-site field demonstrations, and (4) instruction on operation
and maintenance.

The Grace Service Plan, as outlined below, is a good illustration
of before-sales service combined as it often is with technical counseling.[6]

---

[6] Richard L. Moore, "That Extra Touch of Service-Sells," in Henry Gomez (ed.), *Innovation—
Key to Marketing Progress,* Chicago: American Marketing Association, 1963, pp. 661-
662.

1 Marketing research to determine how much plastic of what types is used
2 Technical information on how to store, pigment, handle, test, and fabricate products with Grace plastics
3 Assistance in selecting the right product for each proposed application
4 Professional, creative help in developing product designs
5 Help in designing molds
6 Advice on the physical distribution of plastic products
7 Technical backup for production runs
8 Assistance in stimulating demand among end users for the new product
9 Advice on credit and other financial problems
10 Support in merchandising the new finished products

Another chemical firm has published, in an effort to educate the customer, a preventive maintenance checklist covering 103 potential trouble spots in manufacturing fertilizer.

After-sales service is corrective in nature and as such has certain negative connotations. This, coupled with the realization that customer satisfaction and continued patronage often depend on after-sales service, means that repair and maintenance programs must be planned with infinite care. Among the major factors that need to be considered are (1) customer requirements, (2) competitive implications, and (3) costs.

The first question the marketer must ask is: "What do my customers want in the way of after-sales services?" In the marketing of road-construction equipment, for example, the market dominance of a particular distributor may depend more on service than on the brands handled. Railroads, on the other hand, maintain their own shops and have no need for any repair or maintenance service from the marketer of rolling stock.

Competition exerts tremendous pressures on the service program, often to the point of profit erosion. A balance must be maintained between what must be accomplished from a service point of view to retain competitive and profitability objectives. To do this, management will need a great deal of data on service costs, customer attitudes, and competitor practices. It might also be helpful to confer with members of the field sales force. Budgets constitute useful tools for controlling the various programs judged to be essential.

A vice-president of marketing for American Potash & Chemical Corporation has suggested the following guidelines for controlling both before- and after-sales customer service:

1   Customer service should be related to the company's primary objective of providing quality products.
2   Customer service should be adequate to permit maximum product satisfaction for any customer.
3   Customer service should be in direct support or related to the use of the product.
4   Customer service of more than mimimal nature must bear a reasonable cost relationship to the value of the account.
5   Customer service must satisfy a real need.
6   Customer service must not violate antitrust regulations.

Finally, every marketer will want to appraise his philosophy of customer service to determine whether or not it is in accord with marketing objectives. As often as not, the marketer will discover he has more than one philosophy, each operating in conflict with the other, with marketing objectives, and with the marketing management concept. Some of the predominant philosophies can be described briefly as follows:[7]

NEGATIVISM   This philosophy conceives of customer service in terms of after-sales "fire-fighting" operations to correct product mistakes. Under this philosophy management is concerned with driving costs down rather than enhancing the values of service. Paradoxically, service costs have a tendency to mount steadily notwithstanding this pressure.

QUALITY CONTROL   The inescapability of a certain number of product errors on the basis of chance alone is another service philosophy. The difficulties in this philosophy are mainly those of orientation. Service personnel become fact gatherers rather than counselors or repairmen. Emphasis shifts from the consumer to the products currently in production. Although highly applicable to the service programs of manufacturers of component parts and fabricated materials, this philosophy may be perilous in that before-sales assistance tends to be neglected in favor of product-improvement work. This takes on added significance when market conditions reflect a high degree of competition and/or relatively small consumers.

[7] Adapted in part from E. A. Anthony, "Product Service, The Fourth Dimension of Marketing," in Stewart H. Rewoldt (ed.), *Conference on Sales Management,* Michigan Business Papers, no. 34, Ann Arbor: Bureau of Business Research, University of Michigan, 1957, pp. 11-26.

PAY-AS-YOU-GO   Highly popular is the philosophy of treating service as a separate business which must earn a return or at least pay its own way. Such a view is vulnerable in two respects. First, it is all but impossible to measure in dollars and cents many of the activities included in customer service—for example, the difficult question of what portion of a particular product's profit should be allocated to before-sales service. Second, the responsibilities for customer satisfaction impose too much of a cost burden on the service function to consider it a business unit. Middlemen are strong adherents of the pay-as-you-go philosophy because they have not nearly the manufacturer's product responsibility.

FACTORY ONLY   The exact opposite of the "closest-seller" philosophy is the view that only manufacturer personnel are competent to perform customer service. Practically speaking, the major limitation to this view is the investment necessary to provide field facilities. The exact amount of investment will be directly related to the degree of geographical dispersion in the total market.

COMPETITIVE TOOL   When customer service is conceived of as a marketing tool, the basic rationale is that service exerts a tremendous impact on sales. Manufacturer and distributor alike, regardless of size, design customer-service programs to attain such sales goals as greater market penetration, retention of present market share, or invasion of new market segments.

WARRANTY LIMITED   This philosophy is held by marketers who regard the product warranty as a protective device. The benefit to the customer, they argue, is that holding to strict interpretation of the warrantly will permit long-run cost reductions. What marketers fail to realize is that liberal administration of warranty provisions is by far the most persuasive factor in countless market situations.

INHERENT PROBLEM   Invariably customer service is considered a troublesome area of business with scarcely any foreseeable change. Problems are bound to occur, if not of one kind, then another. The principal danger in this resignation is that it obscures the marketing possibilities of well-planned service programs. In the short run it may cause the marketer to disregard entirely the relative severity of specific service problems.

MANAGEMENT OF THE FIELD SALES FORCE

In terms of functions performed and his role in the field sales organization, a sales manager for an industrial-goods manufacturer does not differ markedly from one employed by a manufacturer of consumer goods. Generally, a field sales manager will be wholly or partially responsible for (1) recruiting and selection of salesmen, (2) training salesmen, (3) supervision of salesmen, (4) motivating salesmen, (5) personal sales, (6) administration of the field office, and (7) local representation.

What is different is the interpretation of each of the seven functions by the dictates of the particular market. To illustrate, the field sales manager in an industrial-goods firm is in a position to individualize his supervisory efforts simply because he tends to have a smaller span of control than his consumer-goods counterpart. Probably the most apparent difference is to be found in the development and motivation of salesmen.

Recruitment and Selection of Salesmen

A most difficult responsibility of a field sales manager is the recruitment and selection of salesmen. Making it a task of even more formidable proportions is the awareness of the costs, explicit as well as implicit, which result from ineffectiveness.

Currently it takes in excess of $10,000 to develop an outside salesman, the price tag rising proportionately to the technical complexity of the particular market. Efficiency in training, supervision, and motivation may all go for naught; actual performance depends entirely upon whether the persons making up the field sales force have the necessary characteristics to succeed. To ascertain this prior to employment is the basic task of recruiting and selection.

The most obvious costs are those related to high turnover. Measurable are the direct expenditures for hiring, training, and supervising. Added to these, but impossible to quantify accurately, is the loss of goodwill among prospective applicants, other members of the sales force, and customers. The loss a firm can least afford is among customers. Customers as a whole resent frequent changes in representation, and therefore it is only logical to assume that sales will never attain their full potential.

A well-designed program which has not only the full but also the enthusiastic support of field sales management is a must if the firm hopes to improve the capabilities of its field sales force. Although the responsibility of the field sales manager will vary, usually in relation to the size of the firm, he is rarely denied the final employment decision on a candidate. His support, therefore, is absolutely essential to the success of the program. About the best way to enlist the support of field sales management is to involve them in the preparation of the program.

The major considerations in evolving a recruiting-selection program are:

1 Defining the sales job
2 Determining the man specification, or the list of characteristics desired in the man who is to hold the job
3 Defining the recruiting sources
4 Determining the respective roles for the tools of selection—application blank, personal interview, and tests

It is obvious that the foundation of any program is knowing what is entailed in the salesman's job. This can be accomplished by analyzing the job, the results of which will be comprised in what is termed a job description. Typically, a formal job description lists the responsibilities and duties of a salesman. In Figure 13.3, for example, an outside salesman for Screw Machine Supply Co. of Chicago has a responsibility for knowing his products and customers and a specific duty of keeping records of customers' personnel and purchases.

The *advantages* of a job description go beyond hiring. Here are a few:

1 It provides the objectives for the tools used in selection.
2 It serves as a guide to what is expected of the individual upon employment.
3 It determines the basic content of training programs.
4 It is a standard against which actual performance can be measured, evaluated, and rewarded accordingly.

The question of what kind of individual would make the best salesman is answered generally by the personality traits associated with success in industrial selling and specifically by the man description which together with the job description results from a job analysis.

A consensus of writers on the subject of the sales personality are agreed on the following traits.

1 *Empathy* or sensitivity to the feelings of those he comes in contact with. This enables the salesman to establish effective sales relationships with a wide variety of people and to develop effective interaction between himself and a particular prospect or customer.

FIGURE 13.3

JOB DESCRIPTION FOR AN OUTSIDE SALESMAN: SCREW MACHINE SUPPLY, CHICAGO

I Territory Management

A. Know the territory.
B. Evaluate individual customers and prospects.
C. Keep records of customers' personnel and purchases.
D. Allocate sales time according to customer's present and future potential.
E. Plan itineraries to minimize lost time. Determine call frequencies according to customer importance. Make regular calls.
F. Submit all routine reports to management plus special reports on competitive activities, economic trends, etc., as requested.
G. Allow time for calls on new prospects.
H. Participate in community and trade activities.

II Selling

A. Know 1) your products and applications 2) customers' needs and characteristics.
B. In selling 1) make effective sales presentations on product *benefits*. 2) Sell yourself and your company. 3) Put extra effort behind profitable key lines. 4) Keep buyers aware of all lines handled. 5) Establish contacts with all personnel who influence buying decisions. 6) Follow up pending orders. 7) Use entertainment judiciously.
C. Sales Equipment 1) Use demonstrators and samples when appropriate. 2) Keep your own catalogs and literature up to date. 3) Keep customers supplied with them as necessary.

III Customer Services

A. Make regular calls.
B. Follow up orders and deliveries.
C. Follow up products in use.
D. Handle complaints and adjustments promptly.
E. Notify customers of price changes.
F. Arrange for technical assistance by factory representatives as required.
G. Keep customers informed of new products and developments.
H. Educate customers on efficient purchasing—i.e. frequency, quantities.

IV Responsibilities To The House

A. Provide credit information on new accounts or credit status changes.
B. Assist when requested in credit handling and collection.
C. Handle reports and correspondence.
D. Explain to customers changes in company policies, delivery schedules, lines, etc.
E. Avoid orders the house isn't equipped to handle.
F. Keep price information up to date.
G. Keep house informed on markets, reasons for lost orders, new competitive products, etc.
H. When handling complaints, explaining policies, etc., be loyal to the house.

V Miscellaneous

A. Maintain neat, businesslike personal appearance.
B. Keep automobile and literature in good condition.
C. Take advantage of opportunities to increase your knowledge and abilities.
D. Maintain a positive, enthusiastic attitude.

Source: Screw Machine Supply Co., Chicago, Ill.

2 *Personal drive,* which may be termed ambition, ego involvement, the will to succeed, self-starting ability, or the need to win. The relationship between personal drive and successful selling has been aptly described as follows:

Because of the nature of all selling, the salesman will fail to sell more often than he will succeed. Thus, since failure tends to diminish his self-picture, his ego cannot be so weak that the poor self-picture continues for too long a time. Rather, the failure must act as a trigger—as a motivation toward greater efforts—which with success will bring the ego enhancement he seeks. A subtle balance must be found between (a) an ego partially weakened in precisely the right way to need a great deal of enhancement (the sale) and (b) an ego sufficiently strong to be motivated by failure but not shattered by it.[8]

3 *Communicative skills* especially from an oral standpoint are an absolute necessity for the industrial salesman. He must be able to present concepts, draw out consumer thinking, and quell resistance. The degree of empathy possessed by a salesman will determine to a large extent his ability to perfect this trait. Skills in written communication, although generally subordinated, are coming to the forefront particularly among those firms in which written proposals are commonplace or sales candidates are hired primarily on the basis of management potential.

4 *Analytical skill* is important for two important reasons. First, the salesman must be able to diagnose consumer problems so that product applications can be related to needs in the most beneficial manner. Second, the salesman must be able to relay or feed back to engineering and production meaningful descriptions of problems encountered in the field.

5 *Self-discipline* is the ability to work diligently regardless of whether the job is procedural or new and different. It also involves the ability to see a project through to completion. This trait is paramount in acquiring knowledgableness and utilizing time.

The specific qualities needed by an individual firm are set forth in the man description or specification. This profile will enumerate requirements in regard to age, education, experience, speaking fluency, and absence of physical handicaps. Its value in pinpointing sources, developing the application blank, interviewing, and setting up test-

[8] David Mayer and Herbert M. Greenberg, "What Makes a Good Salesman," *Harvard Business Review,* July-August, 1964, pp. 120-121.

ing programs is readily apparent. In using the profile it is a good rule to expect neither too much nor too little of the sales candidate.

In recruiting it seems safe to conclude that for a given firm there is no one best source, but rather a combination of sources. Which sources are resorted to depends upon the man description and practically upon the firm's experiences with a source as well as the circumstances under which the recruiting is accomplished. In regard to the latter, the imperativeness of finding a man quickly rules out all but professional employment agencies and newspaper advertising. "The Sales Employment Procedures Manual" for Friden, Inc., lists three recruiting sources: (1) personal contact, (2) professional employment or personnel agencies, and (3) advertising in newspapers or magazines. A clear picture of the various sources available can be obtained from the results of a survey conducted among members of the Sales Executives Club of New York, many of whom are employed by industrial marketers.

The basic purpose of the selection tools—application blanks, personal interview, and testing—is to screen out candidates. An application blank provides the means for making a quick assessment of qualifications to determine whether or not a candidate meets mimimum employment standards. Gaining popularity is a system whereby the various personal factors are individually weighted and a total critical score is developed. The problem of validity is the major obstacle in weighting an application blank.

The role of the personal interview in selection is twofold. In the first place, it reveals personal traits which are not disclosed by the utilization of the other two selection tools. These traits include speak-

TABLE 13.1 Recruiting Sources for New Salesmen, Both Trainee and Experienced, Sales Executives Club of New York

SOURCE	PERCENTAGE OF RESPONDENTS MENTIONING	
	FOR TRAINEE	FOR EXPERIENCED
Schools and colleges	57.9	21.1
Employment agencies	50.0	61.9
Present employees	45.8	46.3
Newspaper advertising	36.4	50.7
Present customers	32.2	43.1
Business associates	32.2	56.3
Sales executives clubs	22.4	19.6
Trade publication ads	20.1	28.7
Other	6.5	10.3

Source: Sales Executives Club of New York.

ing voice, bearing, physical appearance, conversational ability, fluency, and to some extent maturity. Secondly, the personal interview serves as both a double check on and an amplification of the information contained in the completed application form.

In the application form and the personal interview, guideposts that signal an undesirable candidate are commonly termed "knock-out" factors. A few of the "knock-out" factors and a brief description of why each signals elimination follow:

Marital difficulties: A recent divorce or separation is often a tip-off to emotional instability. Many firms make it a practice not to hire any candidate that has been divorced or separated during the last three years.

Employment record: Working at more than three jobs in the last five years is questionable unless the candidate is in his twenties.

Family responsibility: A large family requires more income than could possibly be earned at least in the crucial beginning years. Family ties might also limit travel.

Financial status: No bank account, excessive debt, or an unsatisfactory payment record indicates a lack of maturity. Income from other sources may reflect a lack of job motivation.

The place of testing in the selection process baffles management. As a result there is a sharp difference of opinion on the benefits to be gained from testing. On the one hand are those who are completely sold on testing, often to the point of slighting the other selection tools. Many such managers are likely to use testing as a crutch. On the other hand there are managements who profess reluctance to use any form of testing. It is their opinion that the acknowledged limitations of testing overshadow all advantages.

In developing a proper perspective toward testing, several points must be kept in mind.

1 The test battery should be constructed along the lines of the vital personality traits constituting the sales profile sought by the firm.
2 The test battery should be an aid to judgment, particularly in pointing out areas for further investigation, rather than the deciding factor.
3 The test battery cannot be expected to reflect motivation.
4 The test battery should be validated insofar as is practical.

Training
Every firm has a sales training program whether it recognizes the

fact or not. Thus, it would seem only logical to formalize the program and orient it toward desirable objectives. The three major questions in setting up a training program are (1) what subject areas should be taught, (2) how the various subject areas should be taught, and (3) when the training should take place.

The four generally recognized areas of sales training are (1) product knowledge, (2) selling skills, (3) work habits, and (4) attitudes. To this list a marketing-oriented firm might conceivably add consumer knowledge. Specific program content in each of these five areas will be determined primarily by the job analysis. The selection profile, a difficulty analysis, and a time and duty study supplement the job description as well as determine the relative emphasis to be placed on subject areas and materials contained within each area. The one overriding principle in selecting subject matter is that the actual needs of salesmen in the field should be the only criteria.

Product knowledge is heavily stressed in training today's industrial salesmen, chiefly because of the tendency to think of his job solely in terms of sales volume. Yet, as one author has found, it is not sales volume which is mentioned as a problem by sales managers, but rather the competence of the salesman to perform all the functions related to his assigned job.[9] This includes analyzing his customer's needs, handling credit, and managing his time.

A serious criticism of the subject matter in product-knowledge training is the preoccupation with the product itself, or the "nuts and bolts" as it is commonly labeled, instead of the product's applications. As part of his initial training, many companies have the apprentice salesman spend up to a year in the plant or mill learning how the product or product line is made. While undoubtedly interesting, it is highly unlikely that this is the sort of information desired by consumers. In other words, consumers will want to know how a particular primary metal or lacquer will satisfy their needs, not its ingredients or how it is made.

The usual methods of imparting product knowledge are lecture, demonstration, film, and specification sheet. Programmed instruction is a recent innovation which appears to be ideally suited to periodic or refresher training in product knowledge. Under this method the material constituting a course of study is presented one step at a time. The difficulty increment between steps is narrowed to facilitate advancement at the student's own pace. Among the industrial-good manufacturers that utilize programmed instruction in dispensing product knowledge are (1) Abbott Laboratories, (2) American

[9] Wilbert J. Miller, "Training Salesmen," *Sales/Marketing Today*, April, 1965, p. 25.

Radiator & Standard Corp., Plumbing & Heating Division, (3) General Electric Co., General Purpose Motor Department, (4) International Business Machines, (5) Charles Pfizer, and (6) Schering Corporation.[10]

With any of the sales training methods, the responsibility for learning rests with the salesman. Therefore, attention should be directed toward ensuring proper motivation. About the best way to accomplish this is to sell the salesman on the personal value of training. It may also be helpful to involve the salesman in the development of the program.

Selling skills are best taught under actual conditions. For this reason on-the-job training is stressed, particularly in respect to men lacking in practical sales experience. On-the-job training is usually conducted by the field sales manager, although a senior salesman or field trainer may be assigned the task initially. Other methods of teaching selling skills as related to a particular firm's products are role playing and conferences. In role playing, two salesmen or a salesman and a field sales manager, assume the roles of seller and buyer in a specific problem situation. Conferences involve group discussions of case problems. The field sales manager may act as discussion leader, or a salesman may present each case. The ideal source for both problem situations and cases is the difficulty analysis. In addition to providing actual circumstantial material regarding the various troublesome selling situations, the difficulty analysis involves the field sales force in the preparation of their own training program.

Work-habit training and attitude training are conducted in conjunction with all of the other three subject areas. Work-habit training is included with on-the-job training in selling skills. Development of proper attitudes toward the company as well as its customers is brought out in every training experience, whether on an individual or a group basis.

In work-habit training, it is not enough that the salesman knows what to do; he must practice conscientiously in his everyday selling activities. One of the best ways of enlisting the cooperation of salesmen is to show the actual value of good work habits. Practical examples of the possible benefits obtainable from effective utilization of time can be drawn from a time and study of the salesmen themselves. Such a study can provide a wealth of information on:[11]

[10] Leon G. Schiffman, "Programed Instruction; Its Use in Sales Training," *Industrial Marketing,* February, 1965, p. 84.

[11] James H. Davis, *Handbook of Sales Training,* 2d ed., New York: Prentice-Hall, Inc., 1954, pp. 28-29.

1   How the salesman spends his time and in what ways it can be utilized to produce better results
2   Which methods of selling are most effective
3   Which types of sales argument produce the best results

The field sales manager occupies a vital position in respect to implementing work-habit and attitude training programs. Not only does he have to be aware of what constitutes proper work habits, he must exercise them as well. The latter requirement is especially important in training neophytes because so much of it is accomplished through leading by example.

If the salesman is to perform at his best, he must have a proper attitude toward his job and his company. Group meetings offer an excellent opportunity, but their occurrence is rather infrequent. As a result the major responsibility falls to the field sales manager. How well he can perform this job depends upon his communicative and human-relations skills.

The principle that all sales training should be continuous applies particularly to the area of consumer knowledge. Indoctrination training alone will no longer suffice; consumer needs are changing too rapidly and the market is becoming too complex. Indeed, training in more than the essentials may be a waste before some work experience. However, the new salesman should be provided with enough consumer data to keep him from floundering and/or losing consumer goodwill.

Home-study courses offer a good approach for the bulk of the training in consumer knowledge. Regular courses can be set up for each of the consumer or industry groups currently being served by the firm. The materials comprised in the regular home-study courses might be presented in such form as to facilitate their use as a reference library upon completion of each study section. To keep the salesman up to date on consumer happenings, a loose-leaf informational service might be maintained on a periodic basis. Two points need to be emphasized in preparing materials for consumer-knowledge training. One is that the materials should be practical enough to assure the salesman ready use of his new knowledge immediately in everyday selling. This will help to ensure his interest in the programs. The other is to write the programs so that they can be understood with normal concentration by the salesman. Any technical jargon associated with a consumer group should be thoroughly defined.

Motivation
The motivation of outside salesmen, regardless of whether they sell

consumer or industrial goods, offers an immense challenge to field sales management. Two complicating factors are the semidetached environment in which the salesman normally functions and the very decided fluctuations his morale is subjected to as he makes or loses a sale. It is interesting to note that many authorities hold that for every ten men failing as salesmen, only one lacks the ability to do the job; the rest fail principally because of a lack of willingness to do the job.

Despite the obvious importance, field sales managers with few exceptions are not sure of what is proper in the way of motivating procedures.[12] Successful motivation starts with understanding the salesman's position. Only then can the manager apply the proper motivational techniques to help the individual fulfill his needs. This places two responsibilities on the field sales manager. First, he must gain an understanding of each individual salesman. This will help him avoid thinking of and treating all subordinates alike. Second, he must know the basic incentives or motivational techniques for satisfying the needs he has uncovered among his subordinates.

As for what incentives are available, a sharp difference can often be found between consumer-goods firms and those marketing industrial goods. Possibilities of satisfaction from financial incentives may be limited for the industrial-goods salesman because fixed salary makes up the greater part of his total pay. Little use is made of extra incentives (e.g. bonus, commission) based on individual performance, for several reasons:

1 The difficulty of equating performance in terms of time periods when consumer education and/or the design cycle extend selling contact over an abnormally long span of time. A field sales manager for a container corporation made the statement that it has taken over two years to sell a company on buying his particular brand of glass bottle.
2 The difficulty or impossibility of determining who should receive credit for a sale when a group or team selling effort was employed.
3 The difficulty of defining individual performance as anything more than customer relations. This might happen when the seller is the only source or some system of allocation is in effect for a firm's output.

Thus, with the motivational stimulus from financial incentives severely limited, the field sales manager for an industrial marketer has

[12] Robert T. Davis, *Performance and Development of Field Sales Managers,* Boston: Division of Research, Graduate School of Business Administration, Harvard University, 1957, pp. 112-113.

to rely more heavily on nonfinancial incentives than his consumer counterpart.

The major categories of nonfinancial motivation are (1) prestige, (2) achievement, (3) opportunity, (4) recognition, (5) loyalty, and (6) security. There are many ways of providing a salesman with prestige or status. One is to call upon a salesman to handle a portion or all of a sales meeting. Another is to assign him to the so-called prestige accounts. Still another, which also involves recognition, is to consult with the salesman to obtain his expert advice on certain sales problems. Achievement is the satisfaction a person obtains from doing things. The salesman can gain greater satisfaction if he is made aware of what he is doing on a more or less continuous basis. There is also a possibility that the sense of achievement is correlated to the amount of money received. Opportunity is thought of as either the chance of organizational advancement or the chance to show selling ability, such as with a particularly difficult account.

Loyalty is related to the salesman's company, to his immediate supervisor, and to his fellow salesmen. It can be equated with the need to belong. Frequently overlooked, recognition is praise for meritorious efforts. The reason recognition is often overlooked is that many sales managers feel it is superfluous. It is their mistaken contention that money is the only means of true recognition for a job well done. Security is the assurance of the continuity of employment. Unlike the other incentives, security can only be supplied by the firm through the salesman's immediate supervisor, the field sales manager.

The practical restriction on financial incentives does not preclude careful consideration of their role in the motivational plan. A good compensation plan should provide direction and stimulus to salesmen's activities without excessive administrative complications. A good pay plan will be able to pass the following tests: [13]

1   Simplicity
2   Flexibility
3   Proportionate reward
4   Controlled incentive
5   Low operating cost
6   Promotion
7   Uniform earnings
8   Promptness
9   Fairness

[13] Harold H. Maynard and James H. Davis, *Sales Management,* 3d ed., New York: The Ronald Press Company, 1957.

Successful motivation of industrial-goods salesmen requires effective integration of financial and nonfinancial incentives, with major emphasis on the latter. A motivational plan so designed will work for the best interests of the consumer, the individual salesman, and the firm. The most important consideration for the field sales manager in applying incentives is understanding. He must understand the salesman's needs as well as the characteristics of the various incentives available to him in satisfying these needs.

SUMMARY

The manufacturer must somehow build a sales and service organization regardless of his size or major marketing channel. Much the same can be said for the middleman in the industrial market.

In structuring sales, the industrial marketer will want to consider the external as well as internal aspects of organization. The status of sales in the firm depends upon whether the marketing management concept has been adopted in its entirety. If it has, a vice-president or director of marketing will have been inserted between the head of sales and top management. Another likely alteration under this concept will be the breaking out of such functions as advertising to give them independence on an organizational level comparable with sales.

Internally, the organization of sales may be based on product, consumer, geographical territory, or function. Typically a geographical base is combined with either a consumer or more likely a product base. The use of a functional base has been seriously hampered by the difficulties inherent in providing line authority to staff officials such as the product manager.

The most obvious difference between an industrial-goods and a consumer-goods sales force is the presence of both inside salesmen and technical counsels in the former. Less obvious are the differences in the roles of product manager and customer service. The main advantage of the product-manager system is that all the responsibility for the technical marketing of a given product can be assigned to one person. Ambiguous authority and profit responsibility are the major disadvantages. The inside salesman has an important role in customer relations—following up orders, solving service problems, and answering complaints. Greater coordination is possible when the inside salesman is assigned to the accounts of a specific outside salesman.

Technical counsels or specialists play an important role when salesmen call upon a heterogeneous group of consumers and/or sell a wide range of products. Although the technical counsel is usually deemed essential to the marketing operation, his true role is seldom evaluated. Questions which might be asked about the technical counsel are: (1) Does the marketer need a specialist? (2) Where can he exert the greatest influence on profits? (3) How shall he be compensated? and (4) What is to be his organizational status?

Customer service for the industrial marketer is performed both before and after the sale. Closely allied to the work of technical counsels, before-sales service has as its objective greater product utilization through customer preparation. After-sales service, on the other hand, is corrective. In planning after-sales service, the major factors to be considered are customer requirements, competitive implications, and costs.

The basic difference between the field sales manager in an industrial-goods firm and his consumer-goods counterpart is the former's interpretation of the management functions rather than the functions themselves. The most discernible differences are to be found in the development and motivation of salesmen. The technical complexities of the industrial market add to the obstacles encountered in developing a sales force. As for motivation, the industrial marketer is much more limited in the use of financial incentives due to the nature of the marketing task.

DISCUSSION QUESTIONS

1   Why would an industrial manufacturer who markets indirectly have to have a sales and service organization?

2   What offsets are there to the breaking out of functions from the sales department?

3   Why is the geographical base used more often than any other base in structuring the sales organization?

4   Why is the product manager a good example of the difficulties inherent in a functional type of organization?

5   What are the normal tasks of a product manager?

6   Do you agree that a firm would not need inside salesmen if its outside salesmen were doing their job? Explain your answer.

7   Where might the technical counsel be positioned in the organization? What would be the reason for each position?

8   Describe in detail the various customer-service philosophies.

9 Outline the steps in formulating a development program for salesmen.
10 Describe the personality traits an industrial salesman should possess.
11 Describe the advantages of programmed instruction.
12 State the reason(s) for relying upon nonfinancial incentives to a great extent in industrial selling.

SUPPLEMENTARY READING

Davis, James H., *Handbook of Sales Training,* 2d ed., New York: Prentice-Hall, Inc., 1954.

Davis, Robert T., *Performance and Development of Field Sales Managers,* Boston: Division of Research, Graduate School of Business Administration, Harvard University, 1957.

Evans, Gordon H., *The Product Manager's Job,* Research Study No. 69, New York: American Management Association, 1964.

Field Sales Management, Experiences in Marketing Management, no. 1, New York: The National Industrial Conference Board, 1962.

Keys to Efficient Selling and Lower Marketing Cost, Studies in Business Policy, New York: The National Industrial Conference Board, 1954.

Luck, David J., and Theodore Nowak, "Product Management—Vision Unfulfilled," *Harvard Business Review,* May-June, 1965, pp. 143-154.

Maynard, Harold H., and James H. Davis, *Sales Management,* 3d ed., New York: The Ronald Press Company, 1957.

Measuring Salesmen's Performance, Studies in Business Policy, no. 114, New York: The National Industrial Conference Board, 1965.

Newgarden, Albert (ed.), *The Field Sales Manager,* Report Series, no. 48, New York: American Management Association, 1960.

The Product Manager System, Experiences in Marketing Management, no. 8, New York: The National Industrial Conference Board, 1956.

Tonning, Wayland A., *How to Measure and Evaluate Salesmen's Performance,* New York: Prentice-Hall, Inc., 1964.

advertising
and sales
promotion

Some idea of the role assigned advertising and sales promotion by the industrial-good manufacturer can be obtained from the findings in Tables 14.1, 14.2, and 14.3. In Table 14.1 it can be seen that median budgets as a percentage of sales for the five selected product groupings show little variation from year to year. Comparing 1953 with 1965 shows that the biggest changes were recorded by manufacturers of electrical machinery, who increased their median budget 0.3 percent, and nonelectrical machinery manufacturers, who reduced their median budget 0.3 percent.

The data in Table 14.2 show that the variance of median budgets in product groupings, while considerable, is not nearly as great as the ranges within any of the product groupings. It is interesting to note that manufacturers of electrical machinery, who have the widest budget range in 1965, showed the largest median budget increase since 1953.

The obvious divergence of opinion among manufacturers within any of the selected product groupings suggests factors in addition to the general type of product as the major determinants of the budget outlay for advertising and sales promotion. These include (1) the competitive status of the manufacturer, (2) the marketing tasks confronting the manufacturer, and (3) the manufacturer's own concept of advertising and sales promotion.

Examination of budgets for industrial-good manufacturers classified in terms of annual sales volume reveals an inverse relationship between the size of the budget and the sales-volume dimensions of the manufacturer (Table 14.3). Also noticeable is the tendency for the budget range to decrease as the sales size of the manufacturer increases. The primary reason for this is the almost progressive reduction in the upper limit.

TABLE 14.1   Median Budget for Advertising and Sales Promotion Expressed as a Percentage of Industrial Sales, by Selected Product Groupings, Biennially, 1953 to 1965

	PERCENTAGE OF INDUSTRIAL SALES						
PRODUCT GROUPING	1953	1955	1957	1959	1961	1963	1965
Instruments, photographic and optical goods	2.0	3.0	2.0	2.5	2.0	2.0	2.0
Machinery (except electrical)	1.8	1.8	1.8	1.8	1.8	1.7	1.5
Fabricated metal products	1.3	1.9	1.5	1.5	1.5	1.5	1.5
Electrical machinery	1.0	2.0	1.5	1.4	1.5	1.4	1.3
Chemicals	1.0	1.0	1.1	1.0	1.0	0.7	0.9

Source: Laboratory of Advertising Performance, McGraw-Hill Research.

TABLE 14.2 Total Budget for Advertising and Sales Promotion Expressed as a Percentage of Industrial Sales, by Selected Product Groupings, 682 Firms Reporting, 1965

| | PERCENTAGE OF INDUSTRIAL SALES | | |
PRODUCT GROUPING	MEDIAN	HIGH	LOW
Instruments, photographic and optical goods	2.0	8.0	0.07
Lumber and wood products	1.69	4.1	0.6925
Fabricated metal products	1.5	16.2[a]	0.003[b]
Machinery (except electrical)	1.5	18.5[c]	0.001[d]
Rubber and plastic products	1.4	8.0	0.1
Electrical machinery	1.285	26.5[e]	0.00143[f]
Stone, clay, and glass products	0.89	5.0	0.09
Chemicals	0.85	9.3[g]	0.003[h]
Paper	0.72	4.0	0.2
Transportation equipment	0.5	5.2	0.001
Primary-metal products	0.4	3.0	0.0004

[a] High occurs in miscellaneous fabricated metal products.
[b] Low occurs in fabricated structural metal products.
[c] High occurs in metal-working machinery.
[d] Low occurs in metal-working machinery.
[e] High occurs in electrical lighting and wiring equipment.
[f] Low occurs in electrical transmission and distance equipment.
[g] High occurs in drugs.
[h] Low occurs in industrial chemicals.

Source: Laboratory of Advertising Performance, McGraw-Hill Research.

The fundamental goal of all advertising and sales promotion is to support and supplement the sales force in bringing about a desirable rate of profitable sales growth. More specifically, the objectives are as follows: (1) promoting the product offerings, (2) building a favorable company image, (3) creating and maintaining communication channels, (4) supporting distribution elements, and (5) reducing the overall cost of selling.

Promoting the Product Offering

The primary objective of all advertising and sales promotion is to promote a firm's product offering. This is too general, however, to be of much practical significance in planning campaigns and creating messages. A list of specific promotion objectives includes:

1 *Building primary demand.* Frequently a marketer will find that he must establish primary demand or the demand for a particular type of product. For example, makers of aluminum, in entering the construction market, traditionally the domain of steel and

TABLE 14.3 Total Budget for Advertising and Sales Promotion Expressed as a Percentage of Industrial Sales by Size of Firm in Terms of Industrial Sales Volume, 1965*

INDUSTRIAL SALES VOLUME	PERCENTAGE OF INDUSTRIAL SALES		
(IN MILLIONS OF DOLLARS)	MEDIAN	HIGH	LOW
Under 0.25	4.0	18.5	0.22
0.25 - 0.50	2.5	13.1	0.2
0.50 - 1.00	2.0	11.8	0.1
1.00 - 5.00	1.8	26.5	0.0004
5.00 - 10.00	1.25	6.2	0.0004
10.00 - 25.00	1.1	9.3	0.001
25.00 - 50.00	0.75	5.2	0.006
50.00 - 100.00	0.686	2.0	0.001
Over 100.00	0.4	3.2	0.015

*Based on reports from 1,059 companies.
Source: Laboratory of Advertising Performance, McGraw-Hill Research.

concrete, find they must promote the concept of aluminum rather than their own brands.

2 *Building selective demand.* In markets where primary demand has been established, promotional effort is directed toward brands in developing awareness, recognition, preference, and insistence.

3 *Informing selected customer targets* about the availability, price, and features of new as well as existing products.

4 *Stimulating buyer action.* Rarely will industrial advertising or sales promotion bring about immediate purchase of the item in question. The buyer action sought is either an inquiry or the placement of a trial order.

5 *Introducing products to new segments of the market.* The new segment might be an untapped geographical area or classification of consumers.

6 *Introducing special events which may take place periodically.* Such events include sales of various types, customer clinics, and service programs.

Building a Favorable Company Image

A favorable company image is of paramount importance to the industrial marketer, for without it any appreciable volume of sales will be difficult and oftentimes impossible to obtain. As stated earlier, a favorable marketing image is a firm large enough to handle the customer's order. In the simplest terms, advertising and sales promotion must be concerned with developing market awareness and recognition of a seller's size or capabilities to do what he says he can.

Publicity which provides information about the marketer and/or his products has been found to be a valuable tool in image development. It has a disarming effect on industrial consumers because the message appears in editorial form and is not readily identifiable as advertising. Of additional value in some cases is the tendency of industrial consumers to focus their attention on the articles rather than the ads appearing in a business publication.

One theory is that every firm by mere virtue of being in business has an image. The image is a composite of facts about the company, inferences made from these facts, and nonrational influences.[1] In industrial marketing, however, the mere existence of a seller does not always suggest an image. The buyer and seller may operate independently of each other in entirely different market spheres. Consequently, the initial step in building a favorable image is determining whether an image exists, and if it does, what traits of corporate personality appear most significant to the market. The best way to do this is to have marketing research or an outside firm conduct an image study or audit.

J. Gordon Lippincott and Walter P. Margulies recommend a periodic image audit structured along the lines of corporate nomenclature, corporate symbols, and corporate graphics.[2]

Corporate nomenclature refers to the company name, division and subsidiary names, product and brand names.
Corporate symbols are the trademark, trade characters, and product symbols used to express the purpose and character of the firm.
Corporate graphics include all corporate communications.

Studies to determine market familiarity with a firm are fairly uncomplicated in design. Typically, the respondent is asked a limited number of questions. For example: (1) What companies are the leaders in this industry? (2) What company has the most R&D competence? (3) What company has the most qualified salesmen? (4) What company has the best service reputation?

The information from image studies can prove useful in two ways. First, institutional advertising campaigns can be planned to take full advantage of the marketer's strong points and to correct wrong im-

[1] Frederick Messner, *Industrial Advertising,* New York: McGraw-Hill Book Company, 1963, p. 43.

[2] Reprinted by permission of the publisher from J. Gordon Lippincott and Walter P. Margulies, "The Care and Grooming of the Corporate Image," *Management Review,* November, 1960. © 1960 by the American Management Association, Inc.

pressions which have led to weaknesses. However, it must be understood that if the facts substantiate the market's impression, no amount of advertising can correct the situation. It is up to management to bring about the indicated change.

Second, the results of the study can serve as a bench mark by which future studies can be compared to evaluate the effectiveness of advertising campaigns. To illustrate, suppose the initial image survey showed that two out of every ten noncustomers and seven out of every ten customers professed awareness of the firm's significant technological advancements. If in a subsequent study it is found that 40 percent of the noncustomers and 90 percent of the customers are now aware of the firm's research advancements, the conclusion is that advertising efforts during the interim period have doubled awareness among noncustomers and increased it by almost 30 percent among customers.

Creating and Maintaining Communication Channels

The industrial marketer must establish communications with the market which are both effective and continuous. Such a communications system will reach buying influences largely inaccessible to salesmen, pave the way for salesmen, introduce new products, establish market contacts, and locate new customers.

It should be further emphasized that continuity is the key to successful accomplishment of this list of tasks. Advertising cannot be turned off and on any more than the efforts of salesmen or the operation of the physical plant can. It is also true that lapses in continuity, even for short periods of time, cause advertising to become a costly drain on the firm's resources rather than an investment.

Supporting Distribution Elements

Although it is more crucial for the manufacturer who markets indirectly, an objective of all industrial marketers, regardless of distribution level, is to direct their advertising and sales-promotional efforts as much as possible toward their elements in the field. To achieve this objective, several different approaches may be taken by advertising. Middlemen, sales branches, and even salesmen may be identified in ads which are to appear nationally or on a regional basis. A similar identification tactic may be used in direct mailings. Cooperative advertising campaigns may be used by manufacturers who market indirectly through middlemen.

Significant support can be obtained from sales-promotional proj-

TABLE 14.4 Advertising and Sales Expenses, 893 Industrial Marketers, 1961

	ADVERTISING EXPENSE	SALES EXPENSE
CLASSIFICATION OF RESPONDENT FIRMS*	AVERAGE PERCENTAGE OF SALES EXPENSE	AVERAGE PERCENTAGE OF SALES
Low advertising budget	7.4	11.6
Medium advertising budget	17.6	9.9
High advertising budget	38.1	8.7

*Respondent firms are divided into thirds on the basis of advertising-to-sales expense: 297 in the low group, 300 in the medium group, and 296 in the high group.
Source: "How Advertising Affects the Costs of Selling," McGraw-Hill Research Study reported in Sim A. Kolliner, Jr., "Business Paper Advertising and the Cost of Selling," *Industrial Marketing*, June, 1964, p. 105.

ects and materials if they are individually designed with the user in mind. An agricultural feed company experienced an abrupt increase in sales after supplying their salesmen with a simplified flip chart dealing with the particulars of livestock feeding. The flip chart was the outgrowth of extensive field investigation of the selling situations faced by their salesmen.

Reducing the Overall Selling Cost

Recently increasing attention has been directed toward the specific objective of reducing overall selling costs through advertising. The assumption is that advertising has a lower cost per consumer contact than personal vists by salesmen.

The McGraw-Hill study "How Advertising Affects the Cost of Selling" provides evidence that industrial marketers who allocate a large amount of money to advertising have a lower sales expense than those who slight advertising financially.[3] A comparison of advertising and selling costs for 893 industrial marketers is summarized in Table 14.4.

It is important to note, however, that this inverse relationship is neither proportionate nor constant. Between the low third and the medium third, an increase in advertising of about 138 percent brought about a 15 percent reduction in sales expense. Between the medium third and the high third, however, a doubling of the average ad budget resulted in only a 12 percent sales expense savings.

Since business publications will have the major responsibility of substituting for the salesman in achieving and maintaining market

[3] Reported in Sim A. Kolliner, Jr., "Business Paper Advertising and the Cost of Selling," *Industrial Marketing*, June, 1964, p. 105.

contacts, it might be well to ask if there is any relationship between the amount of money spent in these media and sales expenses. Further study by McGraw-Hill Research provides one answer.[4] It was found that industrial marketers who gave greater weight to business publications both in terms of sales expense and ad budget experienced lower sales expense.

MEDIA MIX

The conventional media available to the industrial marketers include business publications, catalogs, direct mail, and trade shows or exhibits. The use of such media as TV, radio, general magazines, and outdoor is usually limited to exceptionally large manufacturers, manufacturers that also market consumer products, and special circumstances. The special circumstances are often the result of an industrial marketer's attempting a novel approach. For example, a job stamping shop in Los Angeles used radio commercials successfully to attract new customers.

The yearly budget studies conducted by Advertising Publications, Inc., publishers of *Industrial Marketing,* provide an excellent opportunity to analyze budget composition over a five-year period from 1962 through 1966. The data, presented in Table 14.5, indicate the important position of the four major media. The figures also suggest that after a period of rapid growth from 1962 to 1964, the relative positions of the four major media have leveled off.

PROFILES OF ADVERTISING MEDIA

The essential task in selection is to choose those media which will present the advertising message in the proper perspective to key buying influences in the targeted market segments. The starting point is to define each of the market segments to be targeted. Once this has been done, a listing of key buying influences has to be drawn up. The next step is to determine campaign strategy. In modifying an approach that might be utilized by consumer-good marketers, the following questions should be answered:[5]

---

[4] *Ibid.,* p. 106.

[5] Based in part on six areas developed by Dodds I. Buchanan, "A New Look at 'Old' Advertising Strategy," *Business Horizons,* Winter, 1965, pp. 86-96.

TABLE 14.5 Budget Allocations for Advertising and Sales Promotion, Industrial-good Manufacturers, 1962-1966*

BUDGET COMPONENT	PERCENTAGE OF TOTAL BUDGET					PERCENTAGE OF CHANGE
	1962	1963	1964	1965	1966	1962-1966
Business publications	27.9	33.5	41.9	42.7	40.0	43.4
Catalogs	13.3	17.0	20.0	19.1	20.7	45.4
Direct mail	6.4	10.1	8.5	9.3	9.8	53.1
Exhibits, trade shows, and displays	5.2	5.6	6.1	6.6	6.7	28.8
Subtotal	52.8	66.2	76.5	77.7	77.2	46.4
Administration and/or salaries	6.6	9.7	7.8	8.2	8.3	
Publicity and public relations	....	....	....	3.7	3.5	
Advertising research	....	....	....	1.2	1.0	
All other	40.6	24.1	15.7	9.2	10.0	
Total	100.0	100.0	100.0	100.0	100.0	

*The number of firms surveyed: 1962, 283; 1963, 190; 1964, 250; 1965, 250; and 1966, 312.
Source: Annual Survey of Industrial Advertising Budgets, *Industrial Marketing*, appropriate issues.

1   Should the emphasis be placed on stimulating primary or selective demand? Usually the larger the market share, the greater the benefit from stimulating primary demand. The reasoning is that any enlargement of the total market will be shared on the basis of current market status or possibly siphoned off completely by the larger and better-known marketers.

2   What is to be the duration of the desired response? Generally speaking, industrial advertising seeks to build product and institutional images over a sustained period of time. Immediacy in response is confined to awareness which can be measured in terms of interest inquiries.

3   What product and institutional features are to be emphasized in the advertising messages? Two points should be kept in mind in selecting advertising features. One, it must be assumed that the audience is learned. Therefore, arguments will have to be rational as well as logical. Also it might be foolhardy to ignore competition completely. Two, advertising features should be classified on the basis of how apparent each is to the consumer.

4   Should the spectrum of key buying influences be broad or narrow? Although examples of success can be cited for either approach, it would seem logical in a market dominated by rational motives to concentrate on a smaller number of people.

5   What is to be the desired degree of consumer response? The recognizable degrees of consumer response are (1) awareness, (2) acceptance or recognition, (3) preference, and (4) insistence.

Finally, media profiles have to be drawn up to compare with strategic guidelines and with each other. Elements of a profile for general types of media might include frequency, coverage, continuity, credibility, selectivity, adaptability, impact, and entry cost. The last element refers to the minimum cost incurred in presenting an acceptable ad in a particular medium.

It is usually worthwhile to develop a specific profile for each business publication. An advertiser will normally want to include in this profile breakdowns of circulation by market segment, by job function or title of readers, and by size of establishment. The most readily available sources are the circulation statements of publishers. The Media Data Form is frequently used to disseminate this information (Figure 14.1). Oftentimes, however, what is available will not suffice for critical media analysis. One of the biggest problems is the lack of uniformity in how readers identify themselves or how they are categorized by the reporting publication. Another problem is that an advertiser may wish to consider business publications which will not have all the detailed information desired on coverage of market segments, readers, or the accumulation and duplication of readership.

There are two ways to overcome these handicaps. One is to request from each of the publishers a special circulation report, for which there may be no or very little additional cost. The advertiser will still have to contend with the ambiguities of title nomenclature and rely upon publishers' figures. The other approach is more scientific and will require an outlay of funds. It involves a comprehensive readership survey of targeted market segments, usually by means of a mail questionnaire.

Business Publications

Business publications fall into three general categories: vertical, horizontal, and "umbrella." *Vertical* publications are directed toward one industry or a portion thereof. This direction is supplied by slanting the editorial content toward features that pertain almost exclusively to the one industry. *World Oil,* as an example, is a petroleum-industry publication directed specifically to "exploration, drilling, and producing engineering operations and management." An outline of the topics covered in a representative issue is as follows:

FIGURE 14.1   Media Data Form.

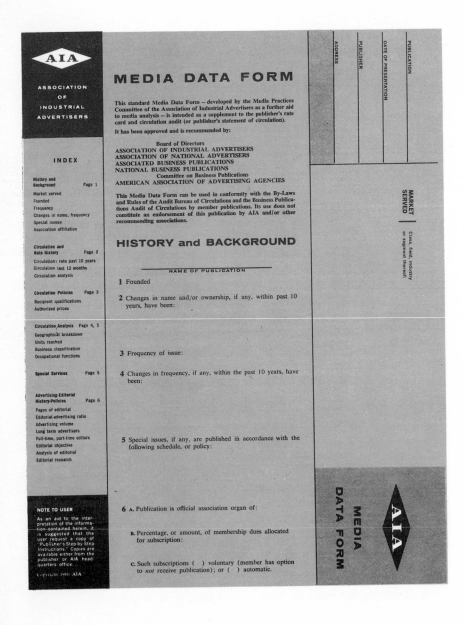

FIGURE 14.1 *(Continued.)*

A I A / **CIRCULATION and RATE HISTORY**

7 A. Average circulation per year for past 10 years.   B. Page or unit advertising rate for the past 10 years.

YEAR ENDING	TOTAL CIRCULATION	PAID See items 9, a, b, c, d	NON-PAID See items 9, f, g, h	12 or 13-time RATE as of Jan. 1

SOURCE of information for Item 7 A

8 Circulation per issue for the last 12-months' period reported in Item 7 A.

ISSUE	TOTAL	PAID	NON-PAID	ISSUE	TOTAL	PAID	NON-PAID

SOURCE of information for Item 8

9 Analysis of circulation of _____ issue.

PAID

A. Subscriptions – addressed to individuals by *personal* name _____

B. Subscriptions – addressed to title or job function (as opposed to A above) _____

C. Subscriptions addressed to firms (as opposed to A and B above) _____

D. All other (such as net single copy sales, and single issue sale in bulk) _____

E. Renewal % of individual subscriptions (excluding ass'n subs) _____

NON-PAID

F. Copies addressed to individuals, by *personal name* _____

G. Copies addressed to title or job function (as opposed to E above) _____

H. Copies addressed to firms (as opposed to E and F above) _____

I. Non-paid rotational circulation is governed by: _____

J. % Direct requests to publishers _____

NOTE that the circulation figures given above *specifically exclude* miscellaneous circulation of no benefit to advertisers — such as correspondents, advertising agencies, exchanges, complimentary samples, advertising departments, etc.

SOURCE of information for Item 9

FIGURE 14.1   *(Continued.)*

CIRCULATION POLICIES

10 To receive publication regularly (as listed under Item 9 above) individual or
company must qualify under the following policies and system:

**NOTE TO
USER**   The above applies *only* to circulation in Item 9. AIA asked publishers the following questions: What functional or occupational qualifications—financial or
business qualifications—must a person meet in order to receive publication?
What is source of names on circulation list—how do you determine number
of copies mailed to a large or small company? How many names added *and*
removed from list during period covered in Item 8?   **NOTE TO
USER**

11 Authorized prices for sale of this publication during period covered in Item 9.

    A. Regular prices: Single copy, regular issue_____Special issue_____
                       Subscription—1 year   _____
                       Subscription—2 years _____
                       Subscription—3 years _____
                               (or more)

    B. Special offers:

SOURCE of information for Item 11_____

FIGURE 14.1 *(Continued.)*

Page 4

AIA / CIRCULATION ANALYSIS

12 A. Geographical Breakdown of Circulation.

B. Units Reached. (This refers to "plants" or "establishments," however, for certain publications it may have a different meaning.) For the purposes of this publication, "units reached" refers to: _____

Issue covered by geographical breakdown_____

Issue covered under "Units Reached" _____

CIRCULATION IN THE FIELD

	PAID COPIES	NON-PAID COPIES	NO. OF UNITS REACHED		PAID COPIES	NON-PAID COPIES	NO. OF UNITS REACHED		PAID COPIES	NON-PAID COPIES	NO. OF UNITS REACHED
N. E.				**S. ATL.**				**MTN.**			
Maine				Del.				Mont.			
N. H.				Md.				Ida.			
Vt.				D. C.				Wyo.			
Mass.				Va.				Col.			
R. I.				W. Va.				N. M.			
Conn.				N. C.				Ariz.			
TOTAL				S. C.				Utah			
				Ga.				Nev.			
MDL. ATL.				Fla.				TOTAL			
N. Y.				TOTAL							
N. J.								**PAC.**			
Penna.								Wash.			
TOTAL								Ore.			
								Cal.			
E. N. C.				**E. S. C.**				Alas.			
Ohio				Ky.				Hawaii			
Ind.				Tenn.				TOTAL			
Ill.				Ala.							
Mich.				Miss.				**U. S.**			
Wis.				TOTAL				**TOTAL**			
TOTAL											
								U. S.			
W. N. C.								Poss. &			
Minn.								Terr.			
Iowa								Canada			
Mo.				**W. S. C.**				Foreign			
N. D.				Ark.				Mil. Serv.			
S. D.				La.				& Civ.			
Neb.				Okla.				Pers.			
Kan.				Texas				Overseas			
TOTAL				TOTAL				**GRAND TOTAL**			

SOURCE of information of Item 12 A_____ 12 B_____

FIGURE 14.1   *(Continued.)*

Page 5

AIA / **CIRCULATION ANALYSIS** Continued

13 Breakdown of circulation by major BUSINESS CLASSIFICATIONS for
_____issue. (PAID, a, b, c, d and NON-PAID, f, g, h of
Item 9, are shown separately.)

SOURCE of information for Item 13_____

14 Breakdown of circulation by recipients' OCCUPATIONAL FUNCTIONS for
_____issue. (PAID, a, b, c, d and NON-PAID, f, g, h of
Item 9, are shown separately.)

SOURCE of information for Item 14_____

SPECIAL SERVICES AVAILABLE TO ADVERTISERS

15 Copy Service _____   Market Analysis _____
Photographic Service _____   Direct Mail List _____
Reader Preference Studies _____   Merchandising Material _____
Split Run _____   Merchandising Services _____
Regional Selection _____   Other Services _____
Market Data _____   _____

FIGURE 14.1   *(Continued.)*

Page 6

ADVERTISING – EDITORIAL HISTORY – POLICIES

16 Average number of pages of *editorial* per issue during the last five years:

YRS.	19	19	19	19	19
PGS.					

17 Average *ratio* of editorial-to-advertising per issue during the last five years:

	19	19	19	19	19
ED.					
ADV.					

20a _____ editors work *full-time* on this publication exclusively.

18 Average number of pages of fully-paid-for *advertising* per issue during the last five years:

YRS.	19	19	19	19	19
PGS.					

19 _____ % of advertisers as of last year (reported above 18) have been advertising in this publication for more than one year. These advertisers represent _____ % of total advertising.

20b _____ other members of the editorial staff work *part-time* on this publication.

21 Editorial objective (i.e., brief statement of publisher's concept of editorial responsibility to readers).

22 Quantitative analysis of editorial *space* during past 12 months. (This is a statistical summary only. It should not be considered as a qualitative measure.)

A. Staff written material		_____ %
B. Material contributed by request	1. Paid	_____ %
	2. Unpaid	_____ %
C. Material contributed, unsolicited	1. Paid	_____ %
	2. Unpaid	_____ %
D. Others, as _____		_____ %
		100%

23 Classification of *type* of editorial material during past 12 months.

_____   _____ %

_____   _____ %

_____   _____ %

_____   _____ %

24 Regular program of reader (editorial) research is conducted in the following manner:

AIA

ASSOCIATION
OF
INDUSTRIAL
ADVERTISERS

The foregoing information is the same as is being supplied to the Headquarters Office of the Association of Industrial Advertisers and has been given with the purpose and intent of selling advertising space. I hereby make solemn oath that it is true to the best of my knowledge and belief.

Signature _____

Title _____

ATTACHED ARE RATE CARD AND CURRENT AUDIT REPORT (OR PUBLISHER'S STATEMENT). THIS MEDIA DATA FORM SUPPLEMENTS THOSE STATISTICS.

1 Nonintegrated firms outpace majors
2 What's new in exploration
3 Photogeology in one easy lesson
4 Needed: Precise stratigraphic terms
5 Do computers aid exploration?
6 Vibratory seismic systems pay off
7 Radiation surveys aid oil search
8 Nomogram for seismic wavelengths
9 New ways to obtain subsurface data
10 Latest logging interpretation ideas
11 How to plan "big holes"
12 Small diameter completions
13 Another major oil area is found
14 Oil know-how tames a steam well

The Engineering and Mining Journal, another vertical publication, devoted a significant portion of its centennial issue to a complex subject that would interest only the members of the industry: namely, new technology for exploration, open-pit mining, underground mining, and mineral processing.

Horizontal publications consider one or several topics which will interest certain individuals in several industries. In contrast to vertical publications, their emphasis is on the specific job or area of concern for an individual regardless of industry affiliations. One example is *Factory,* which, to use the publisher's own words, is directed toward better plant maintenance and engineering, better production, and better plant management. Another example is *Nucleonics,* which covers the field of applied radiation, atomic power, and nuclear engineering. Publications which solicit their prime audience from individuals and firms engaged in the distribution of industrial products are normally categorized as horizontal. These include *Agent & Broker, Distribution Manager, Industrial Distributor News, Industrial Supply Times,* and *Southern Industrial Supplier.*

Umbrella publications are aimed primarily at top management irrespective of industry. A great array of subjects is covered in each issue. For example, a review of the table of contents for an issue of *Dun's Review* shows in addition to regular features eight articles on such a diversity of topics as pyrogenics, plant foremen, and corporate growth. Three monthly umbrella publications are *Dun's Review, Fortune,* and *Nation's Business. Forbes* is semimonthly; *Business Week* is weekly. *The Wall Street Journal,* published five days a week, is typically included under the heading of umbrella publications. It should be noted that even though much of the content from an editorial as well as an advertising standpoint is industrial in nature, umbrella publications manifest an interest in the entire business community.

Regarding business publications as a whole, industrial advertising managers expressed the following opinion in a survey undertaken by *Printers' Ink:*[6]

Conveyors of vital industry information
48 percent excellent, 50 percent good, and 2 percent fair
Means of reaching a segment of an industry
52 percent excellent and 48 percent good
Readability of editorial presentation
9 percent excellent, 66 percent good, and 25 percent fair
Grasp of industries they are intended to serve
10 percent excellent, 80 percent good, and 10 percent fair
Contribution to the industries they cover
5 percent excellent, 75 percent good, 15 percent fair, and 5 percent poor

Before an advertiser can make use of his principal selection tool, the publication profile, he must drastically reduce the staggering volume of well over 2,000 business publications. About the easiest way to do this is to eliminate the obvious unsuitables. In using the publication profile, the advertiser will want to evaluate the differences both quantitatively and qualitatively. One extremely valuable quantitative measurement is the cost-per-thousand concept. This concept relates the size of media audience duly defined to the cost of the media unit. Thus, if the audience is defined as production executives in selected SIC industry groups and the medium is a page in four colors, the formula would be:

$$\text{Cost per thousand} = \frac{\text{4-color page in designated publication}}{\text{defined audience (000 omitted)}}$$

Important qualitative criteria relate to the prestige emanating from editorial content, circulation, and advertising. There is no uniformity in the definition of prestige in any form; consequently, each advertiser will have to develop his own rating scale. In the case of editorial content, for example, a prestige rating scale might run from highly professional articles, often written by noted authorities in the field, to "how to do it" or "we did it this way with success" articles

[6] Steve Blickstein, "Marketing: The Missing Link in Industrial Growth," *Printers' Ink,* Mar. 26, 1965, p. 40. Ratings in terms of percentage of respondents.

written by members of the industry. Parts 21, 22, and 23 of the Media Data Form may be of some assistance in ascertaining editorial prestige. Part 21 is the editorial objective or the publisher's concept of editorial responsibility to readers. Although not intended as a qualitative tool, Part 22 may help the advertiser by a quantitative analysis of editorial space for the last twelve months. Part 23 is a classification of editorial material by type.

To facilitate inquiries about products and services advertised, a great many business publications provide what is called reader service. Several specially prepared postcards are inserted in each magazine for the use of the readers. All that is required of the reader is to circle the numbers of ads he is interested in; fill in his name, title, and company address; and check his primary functional responsibility. The postcards are computer-processed by the publisher, and the resulting mailing lists are distributed to the various advertisers. A typical reader service card is reproduced in Figure 14.2.

Direct Mail

The most selective of all media is direct mail. It allows the advertiser to select his own audience and deliver to it advertising messages that are both individualized and confidential. In regard to the high degree of audience selectivity possible with direct mail, this medium has been likened to a rifle as contrasted with a shotgun for delivering advertising messages. The advantage of selectivity in advertising to the industrial market is undoubtedly responsible for much of the substantial increase in relative budget importance reported over the last few years by respondents to the yearly *Industrial Marketing* studies (Table 14.5).

Other advantages of direct mail that can be cited are:

1 *Flexibility in territorial coverage.* A manufacturer of agricultural chemicals, for example, can adapt his advertising messages to the particular soil condition or pest-control problem prevalent in any geographical area. Flexibility in territorial coverage also means that any industrial advertiser, regardless of size, can make use of direct mail.
2 *Flexibility in cost.* An advertiser can exercise a great deal of discretion in the materials he uses and the size of the mailing list.
3 *Control over timing.* The advertiser is free to adjust his mailings to coincide with the characteristics of his particular market segments. Then, too, there is no need for the advertiser to tie himself down to the schedule set up by a publication.

4   *Competition for reader's attention is minimal.*
5   *Opportunity for self-testing.*

Two significant problems must be dealt with if the advertiser is to obtain maximum effectiveness from direct mail. Foremost is the

FIGURE 14.2   Reader Service Card.

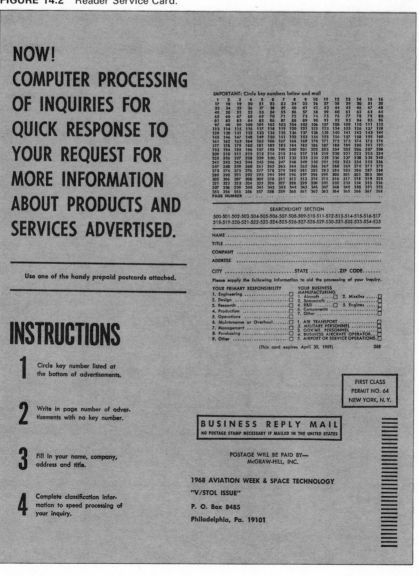

compilation of a mailing list. The whole success of a campaign depends upon developing a list of prospects rather than suspects. An advertiser can purchase, rent, or build his own list. Mailing lists can be purchased or rented from companies known as commercial list houses, publishers of business publications, and trade associations. Unless the advertiser has strong objections to going outside the firm, it would be advisable to rent a list that has been updated by the supplier as part of his regular service.

One publisher offers a mailing service in conjunction with its catalog service. The mailing list is never released, and all submitted mailing materials must bear reference to the fact that the information being mailed supplements data in the designated catalog. Division of the mailing list is by type of company and by geographical location. Approximate costs for this service are as follows:

Personalized automatic typewritten letters—$20 per 100 plus postage and materials

Nonpersonalized letters—$18 per 1,000 plus postage and materials

Printed matter of self-mailer type—$15 per 1,000 plus postage and materials

Postal cards—$15 per 1,000 plus postage and materials

Construction and maintenance of a mailing list is a formidable task. Despite this, many advertisers feel that it is very advantageous to have a list which is especially designed to meet their exact needs. This is particularly true of firms which offer an extensive and diverse product mix. Precise distinctions can be made in terms of product, market, sales personnel, organizational status of the recipient, and marketing status of the account. Generally, mailing lists are converted to punch cards for ready processing.

The second problem is getting the selected audience to read and take note of their direct-mail pieces. An actual check of one buyer's mail for a period of one week revealed that only 12 percent of the direct-mail pieces were read. Of this 12 percent, only one out of every four was referred to someone else or filed.

A brief review of what direct mail can be expected to accomplish and what a technical audience expects from direct mail will help in analyzing this problem. The functions of direct mail include:

1   Developing sales leads. Magnus Chemicals reported that it has been able to supply a sales force of 150 men with an average of more than one lead per week through direct-mail campaigns. The

lead-sales ratio from direct mail was 7 to 1 compared to a ratio of 10 to 1 for other advertising.[7]

2 Disseminating product information.

3 Delivering sales and institutional messages.

4 Communicating on a continuous basis with customers and prospects.

A survey by the Automatic Switch Company indicated the following aspects should be emphasized in performing the above jobs:[8]

1 Direct mail should be strongly product-oriented. New-product information is the most sought-after type of direct mail.

2 Product information should be both complete and concise.

3 Prices are an important part of product information and should be included when possible.

4 "Gimmicks," calendars, and other nontechnical materials are most effective when used as attention getters to introduce factual technical material.

Two other points are worth considering in the preparation of direct mail. One is that product information should be presented from the standpoint of the targeted audience. Superficial knowledge and obsession with product gadgetry are equally disastrous. The other point is that all direct mail should be directed toward obtaining some form of action from the reader. This might be as simple as a return postcard for him to indicate his interest in further information, a catalog, or possibly a visit from a salesman. Some form of incentive may be utilized to stimulate reader action. Du Pont experienced considerable success with incentives in its "Invisible Difference" campaign for plastic pipe. The value of the enclosed Indian arrowhead, postage stamp, or gold could be checked out only by calling the wholesaler salesman, who in the process was able to relate the Du Pont pipe resin story. Provoking reader action also serves as a meaningful measure for evaluating direct-mail campaigns.

SALES-PROMOTIONAL MATERIALS

Sales promotion can be defined as the coordination of personal selling and advertising or nonpersonal selling. Forms which sales pro-

[7]"Using Direct Mail to Spur a Lead a Week," *Printers' Ink,* Dec. 10, 1965, p. 46.

[8]"What Engineers Want in Direct Mail," *Industrial Marketing,* March, 1963, p. 74.

motion may take include catalogs, sales aids, trade shows, exhibits, contests, samples, and novelties. The two predominant forms from a budget standpoint are catalogs and a classification which embraces, under one heading, trade shows, exhibits, and displays. The significance of catalogs is brought out by the fact that their budget importance is second only to business publications.

Catalogs

In the hands of buyers, catalogs constitute continuous sales representation. Basically, catalogs serve as a readily available reference book for engineering and purchasing personnel. Without access to pertinent catalogs, most engineers and purchasing agents would probably feel seriously handicapped. Catalogs will undoubtedly increase in importance in the years to come simply because of the accelerated growth in market complexity. Arthur F. Dires of International Harvester cites several reasons for the growing importance of catalogs to firms marketing indirectly through distributors or dealers. It should be noted that his reasons apply equally well to direct marketers.

1 Catalogs assist dealer salesmen in keeping up with the rapid changes in product lines.
2 Catalogs guide dealer sales presentations by covering the salient sales features of each product.
3 Catalogs provide a sense of security for a new salesman.
4 Catalogs are a source of information for new dealers and new customers gained through increasing sales growth.
5 Catalogs encourage the dealer to do a better selling job for his supplier. This is particularly true of a good catalog.[9]

Standarized and/or large-volume items normally make up a catalog. The following succession of events is fairly typical. A specification sheet and possibly an engineering report are prepared for each new product. As the product enters the growth stage and more units are produced, a brochure is developed. Finally, the product is added to the catalog. The last step is made easier if the catalog is loose-leaf. One exception is the catalog created by Gar Wood Industries of Wayne, Michigan. This catalog, called a "Selectalog," makes it possible for a customer to design his own ditching machine for a particu-

[9] Kathryn Sederberg, "At Harvester Catalogs Do Real Sales Job," *Industrial Marketing*, October, 1964, pp. 104-105.

lar set of circumstances. By going through the "Selectalog" page by page, the customer selects his engine, engine transmission, excavator drive, tractor drive, crawlers, buckets, and any number of other components. The number affixed to each selected component is keyed to the price and weight lists.

There are several types of catalogs—composite, product-line, product, and parts. A composite catalog is a reference book covering all of a firm's products and/or services. A wide diversity in products, which is fairly common for the industrial marketer of today, and the obvious advantages of making a specialized presentation work against the use of a composite catalog. The composite catalog, nonetheless, is suitable for many marketers of industrial services. A typical one is the catalog for an international earth-sciences engineering firm, with a table of contents listing the following: (1) the firm, (2) countries and territories in which the firm has worked, (3) partial list of clients, (4) services offered, (5) capacity, (6) location of offices, (7) representative projects, and (8) exploration and test equipment. Product-line and individual product catalogs can be used either as selling tools or as reference books. The difference is that the emphasis in a reference book is on detailed specifications. The International Harvester line catalog for light construction equipment is described as essentially a bound collection of specification sheets. When a catalog of this type numbers only a few pages, it is often referred to as a brochure. A parts catalog is usually nothing more than a series of descriptions of all available parts and a suggested price list.

To reduce the cumbersome form of catalogs, many firms are experimenting with the use of microfilm. Rather than undertaking the microfilming themselves, firms purchase space in microfilm catalogs much as they would in a business publication. A microfilm catalog service for the aerospace military electronics markets is the Visual Search Microfilm File. This contains over 100,000 pages representing 3,100 suppliers. The publisher, Information Handling Services of Denver, estimates its catalogs are used by 54,250 engineers. Another microfilm catalog is published by Thomas Publishing Company of New York to complement its *Thomas Register.*

Catalogs are distributed by mail, salesmen, distributors, and the so-called "prefiled" method. Catalogs are mailed in response to queries and as part of direct-mail campaigns. Salesmen dispense catalogs during sales calls and when they take part in trade shows and exhibitions. If distribution is effected through distributors, their enthusiastic cooperation is vital. A check on the number of requests received for additional catalogs is one way to measure distributor reaction. Another way is to survey distributors for their opinions about catalogs presently in use.

The prefiled method involves insertion of catalogs from various firms into bound volumes. These volumes may be indexed by firm name, product or end-use classification, or trade name. A single volume serves the machine-tool industry whereas architectural products require eleven volumes. The fee for this service is based on the number of pages in the catalog and the circulation of the bound volume in which it appears. Prefiled catalogs give the seller the assurance of reaching key consumers at a cost which is normally less than for his own distribution. The advantage of such catalogs to the user is that it eliminates at no cost the necessity for maintaining his own system.

Trade Shows, Exhibits, and Displays

Trade shows, now numbering over 3,000, have enjoyed remarkable growth since the end of World War II. Much of the growth is attributable to the fact that participation in trade shows offers marketers the opportunity to show and demonstrate their products to a large number of interested consumers at one time. The marketing tool used to achieve this objective is an exhibit. Located elsewhere, an exhibit is called a display.

Typically, an industrial marketer will participate in at least one and not more than six trade shows during the year.[10] Manufacturers who market indirectly will take part in a greater number of trade shows than those marketing directly. The underlying reason is that trade-show participation in various geographical areas is an excellent way of showing middlemen their vital importance and the desire of the manufacturer to be closely identified with them.

Other objectives of trade-show participation are:

1   To counteract competitive efforts
2   To introduce new products and/or modifications in existing products
3   To enhance the marketer's image
4   To write up sales
5   To hire personnel

[10] Seventy-four percent of the respondents to a survey of company members of the Association of Industrial Advertisers said they used from one to six shows in 1961. The average was 4.26 shows. Ray Kittle, "A Report on the Trends in Industrial Trade Shows," *Industrial Marketing,* June, 1962, p. 101.

6   To investigate new markets
7   To maintain market contacts

Planning is absolutely essential for the successful development of exhibits and displays. The first planning task is to select the show or shows for participation. The best selections are those which cover targeted market segments. It is also wise to review carefully the operational procedures and client list for each trade show under consideration.

Trade shows can be broadly classified as national, regional, and local on the basis of geographical scope. A large proportion of the national trade shows are sponsored by trade associations and are held in conjunction with conventions. The site of a national trade show will normally be shifted around the country.

The next step in planning is to select the theme and type of exhibit. This is followed by preparation of the operational budget. The size of the budget is a reflection of several interrelated factors, of which management effort and competition are predominant. Finally, the objectives for evaluating trade-show participation can be measured in terms of attendance, leads secured, requests for further information, and the degree of recognition secured.

Upon completion of planning, the marketer is ready to develop the necessary procedures for operating the exhibit. These include constructing the exhibit, arranging the products or equipment, preparing the exhibit form, routing physical movement, and manning the exhibit with adequate personnel. To produce a successful exhibit, certain basic rules should be kept in mind:

1   Provide for ample lead time.
2   Appraise trade-show facilities.
3   Design the exhibit to function as an integral unit.
4   Make the exhibit as unique as possible.
5   Plan traffic movement around and within the booth to avoid congestion.
6   Create an appropriate incentive to lure traffic.
7   Use other media, particularly direct mail, both to promote and to control attendance.
8   Decide on the method for distribution of literature.
9   Put salesmen to work and use them effectively.
10 Establish a follow-up program.

The last rule is vital if the promotional value of a trade show is to be maximized. Requested literature should be mailed and leads fol-

lowed up without delay. Evaluation of results may be part of the follow-up program or continuous. The size of the budget appropriation
for trade shows favors the latter.

SIZE AND COMPOSITION OF THE BUDGET

If the marketer takes the view that both advertising and sales promotion make definite contributions to the marketing process, it follows that the outlays for them must be considered investments rather than costs. Then, too, the investment viewpoint is preferable in
that it causes the marketer to focus his attention on maximizing returns from advertising.

The four approaches utilized to determine the overall size of the
budget are (1) flat sum, (2) percentage of sales, either past or future,
(3) competitive parity, and (4) the objective-and-task method.

Flat Sum

A flat-sum allocation for advertising and sales promotion usually
is a result of an arbitrary decision by a top management that is neither advertising- nor marketing-oriented.

It is the least satisfactory approach for several reasons. First, the
sum of money has no relationship to the communications job to be
done. It could be too much as well as too little. Second, it tends to
overemphasize monetary considerations in subdividing the budget.
Third, the advertising program tends to stagnate.

Percentage of Sales

Budgets as a percentage of sales, either past or anticipated, are based
on the assumption that a high degree of positive correlation exists
between sales and the amount of advertising necessary to produce
the given sales volume. There are definite limitations to this approach.
It puts advertising in the position of following rather than preceding sales. It does not take into account the difficulty encountered
in selling. It is inhibiting if based on past sales. The last limitation
is particularly harmful to a growth company or in planning a campaign for a new product. An implicit limitation is the problem of determining the percentage figure which is to be applied to sales.

Substitution of future sales for past sales as a basis eliminates or lessens many of the foregoing limitations. Specifically, it places advertising in its proper role—a generator of sales rather than a resultant. Budgets thus derived should be closely controlled so as to reflect the desired relationship to sales.

Competitive Parity

In using competitive parity the marketer attempts to spend as much for advertising as his major competitor. Two fundamental weaknesses can be noted. One is the difficulty of collecting accurate data on competitor expenditures. This is further complicated by the variances in advertising budget composition among marketers or over a period of time for one marketer. Another weakness is that in using this approach the marketer must assume his status in the marketplace is identical to that of his competition. This is hardly conceivable.

Objective-and-task Method

The objective-and-task method is considered the most desirable approach because:

1 It forces the marketer to focus his attention on setting up objectives and the roles to be played by both advertising and sales promotion.
2 It encourages detailed planning of every division and subdivision of the budget.
3 It is based on a philosophy of what is needed as opposed to availability of funds.
4 It permits a marketer to take full advantage of his strong points.
5 It facilitates measurement and evaluation of effectiveness.

Logically the first step is to determine the objectives of communication. Once this is done, the roles for personal selling, advertising, and sales promotion should be established and a dollar value affixed. The purpose of conversion into dollars is to permit comparative assessment of contribution. When the objectives and advertising's contribution are known, specific tasks can be devised. Advertising, for example, might be assigned 70 percent of the responsibility for searching out qualified prospects and 50 percent of the responsibility for maintaining contact with present customers. The final budget is arrived at by combining the costs of performing each task after making sure duplications have all been pruned.

Budget Composition

Table 14.5 provides some idea of the general categories which are included in the advertising budget. A more exact picture is provided by a study made by McGraw-Hill's Laboratory of Advertising Performance. The findings are presented in Tables 14.6 and 14.7. It is obvious that industrial advertisers are not in agreement as to what is to comprise the budget mix. Only in regard to business publication space is there unanimity. However, there is substantial agreement about not using other media such as television, radio, and consumer publications.

It is interesting to note that the larger the advertiser in terms of industrial sales volume, the greater is the tendency to spend more for production (Table 14.7). None, however, will spend as much as one dollar for every four dollars in space costs.

Budget Submission and Approval

Seemingly, industrial advertisers utilize a calendar year as the temporal basis in budgeting. In Table 14.8, it can be readily seen that September, October, and November are the most common months for submission with approval approximately one month later. November appears to be the most active month, with about three out of ten submissions and approvals.

ORGANIZING THE ADVERTISING AND SALES-PROMOTION FUNCTIONS

Proper organization of the advertising and sales-promotion function embraces three objectives. These are (1) to provide a status within the overall structure of the firm which will be conducive to maximum effectiveness and efficiency in performing the total job; (2) to structure the function internally for maximum effectiveness and efficiency; and (3) to provide for the utmost coordination with outside services, namely, the ad agency.

Position within the Firm

There are three basic methods of locating the advertising and sales-promotion function within the firm's overall structure. One is to position the function in the sales department. The head of advertising

TABLE 14.6   Existence and Importance of Category in Total Advertising and Sales-promotion Budget, 520 Industrial Advertisers, 1965

BUDGET CATEGORY	PERCENTAGE OF COMPANIES WITH CATEGORY IN BUDGET	PERCENTAGE OF BUDGET
Business publication space	99	41
Company catalogs	88	16
Business publication production costs	82	7
Trade shows and exhibits	79	7
Direct mail	78	8
Advertising department administrative expense	62	7
Dealer and distributor helps	43	3
Other media (space or time and production costs)	18	3
All other budget items	73	8

Source: Laboratory of Advertising Performance, McGraw-Hill Research.

will report to the chief sales executive or his line assistant. This plan is extremely popular with industrial marketers who traditionally view advertising and sales promotion as adjuncts to personal selling.

Another organizational plan is to put advertising and sales promotion on the same level as other marketing functions under a chief marketing executive. Such an organization places the function on an equal footing with personal sales and thus follows the marketing management concept. Moreover, it projects into the organizational structure the concept of the marketing mix. Further, this plan supposes an expanded role for both advertising and sales promotion.

The third plan is to have advertising report directly to the president of the firm. This form may result from the chief executive's very personal interest in the function or a personnel entanglement that is best left alone for the time being. A common example of the latter is the firm which has grown without delegating any authority to subordinate executives. In either case it is difficult to conceive of any reason why a chief executive should be concerned directly with advertising and sales promotion.

Internal Organization

The internal structure of the department is affected by the division of work between the firm and outside services and to a lesser extent by top management's attitude toward the function. Industrial advertising departments vary widely in size. For the small marketer the

TABLE 14.7   Share of Business Publication Expense Going to Space and to Production, 427 Industrial Advertisers, 1965

| | PERCENTAGE OF BUSINESS PUBLICATION EXPENSE | |
INDUSTRIAL SALES	SPACE	PRODUCTION
Total	83	17
Under $1 million	87	13
$1 million to $5 million	84	16
$5 million to $10 million	84	16
$10 million to $25 million	83	17
Over $25 million	82	18

Source: Laboratory of Advertising Performance, McGraw-Hill Research.

advertising department is very likely only one man. Large-scale marketers, on the other hand, may employ countless people in advertising especially if extensive use is made of sales-promotional materials.

The established patterns of internal organization are as follows:

1   *By type of media.* Division of the department on the basis of media type might result in sections on business publications, direct mail, catalogs, and trade shows. The advantages are, of course, those of specialization. One drawback is the possibility of overstaffing. The work level in each section may not be great enough to utilize effectively assigned personnel such as copywriters or

TABLE 14.8   Ad Budget Submissions and Approvals, by Month, 1966 (309 industrial advertisers responding)

| | PERCENTAGE OF | |
MONTH	SUBMISSIONS	APPROVALS
January	3.6	6.5
February	2.6	1.9
March	2.3	2.6
April	1.9	3.6
May	4.2	1.6
June	5.2	5.2
July	2.3	2.9
August	7.4	3.2
September	10.7 ⎫	7.1
October	24.9 ⎬ 65.0	10.7 ⎫
November	29.4 ⎭	31.7 ⎬ 65.4
December	5.5	23.0 ⎭

Source: "Annual Survey of Industrial Advertising Budgets," *Industrial Marketing,* February, 1966, p. 68.

artists. Another drawback is the necessity for continuous theme coordination. What is being stressed in publications should be featured in direct mail, and vice versa.

2 *By type of work.* This type of organization places the speciality emphasis on the major activities involved in advertising and sales promotion. A department may be broken down into separate sections on copywriting, art, photography, media, production, distribution, and accounting.

3 *By product or product line.* This form of organization is advantageous to the marketer who has a diverse range of products or product lines, each of which has sufficient volume to merit individual consideration.

4 *By market segment.* Marketers that adhere to a policy of segmentation frequently find it desirable to organize the advertising and sales-promotion function according to the same pattern. The volume of profitable business from each segment will determine whether or not this type of structure is used.

5 *Combinations.* In actuality, advertising departments are likely to be some combination of the above patterns. A typical combination is to have some sections organized on the basis of media type. The primary reason for this is the attention industrial marketers direct toward sales-promotion materials which normally are produced internally.

Relationships with Advertising Agencies

A crucial question for nearly every advertising director is: "How do I select and work with an advertising agency?" To answer the first part of the question, the director must have a full understanding of the functional role of an advertising agency. Basically, this is to provide (1) guidance in media selection, (2) copy and layout competence, (3) advice on insertion timing, and (4) liaison with other specialists such as researchers. Yardsticks can then be developed for rating a prospective or currently retained agency. Some commonly used yardsticks are:

1 Knowledge and past experience
2 Marketing services
3 Creativity
4 Handling of an account

In applying the above criteria, or any other set for that matter, the suggestions of an executive in an advertising agency seem helpful:

1   Look for intelligence, ideational ability, and the bent for problem solving.
2   Judge an agency on the basis of a careful study of the work it has done for other companies.
3   Measure its willingness to mobilize all its resources on your behalf.
4   Determine the concern of the agency in the marketing and advertising problems of its clients.
5   Base the decision on respect rather than personality.
6   Pick an agency for the know-how that will add the most to your priceless store of ideas.
7   Pick an agency for the quality of its human resources.

The bases for working with an agency are teamwork and mutual respect. The reasons most often given for changing agencies are those which should have been looked for during selection. However, only the passage of time is likely to bring out such factors as agency complacency or personality clashes.

Disruption of the client-agency relationship may also result from confusion over billing. There is a multitudinous array of plans, the most common of which are as follows:

1   Commission system—media at gross cost, production plus 15 percent, and miscellaneous charges.
2   Commission system subject to a minimum.
3   Cost-plus-fee system where media is figured at net and no fee is added to production.
4   Guaranteed net profit—client guarantees the agency will make a net profit (both before and after are used) on billings. Any profit above the guarantee is shared by client and agency. This plan is used by Batten, Barton, Durstine & Osborn; Fuller & Smith & Ross; and Paul Klemtner & Company, three agencies which stood third, second, and twenty-third respectively in business publication billings for 1967.[11]
5   Cost plus fixed fee. The fixed fee is tendered by the client in advance.

SUMMARY

Budget appropriations as an indication of the assigned role for advertising and sales promotion show that (1) the relative size of the

[11] According to annual tabulation of 476 agencies in "Marsteller Leads Agencies in Business Press Billings," *Industrial Marketing*, April, 1968, Section Two, pp. 35-39.

budget has tended to stabilize; (2) a greater budget variation exists within a product grouping than between product groupings; and (3) there is an inverse relationship between the size of the budget and the sales-volume dimensions of the manufacturer.

Because of the greater variation within a product grouping, it must be assumed that factors in addition to the general type of product are major determinants of the budget outlay. These include (1) the competitive status of the manufacturer, (2) the marketing tasks confronting the manufacturer, and (3) the manufacturer's own concept of advertising and sales promotion.

In pursuing a desirable rate of profitable sales growth, advertising and sales promotion will seek to promote the product offering, build a favorable image, create and maintain communication channels, support distribution elements, and reduce the overall cost of selling. The conventional media available to the industrial marketer for these tasks include business publications, catalogs, direct mail, and trade shows or exhibits. The use of other media such as TV, radio, general magazines, and outdoor is usually limited to exceptionally large firms, firms which also market consumer goods, and special circumstances.

The job of selection is to choose those media which will present the advertising message in the proper perspective to key buying influences in the targeted market segments. Once this has been done, a listing of key buying influences has to be drawn up. The next step is to determine campaign strategy. Finally, media profiles have to be drawn up for purposes of comparison with strategic guidelines and with each other.

The investment point of view focuses the marketer's attention on maximizing the definite contributions of advertising and sales promotion. In actual practice the approaches utilized to determine the overall size of the budget are (1) flat or set sum, (2) percentage of sales, either past or future, (3) competitive parity, and (4) the objective-and-task method. The last-named approach is the most desirable for several reasons, the most prominent of which is possibly the emphasis on setting up objectives for advertising and sales promotion.

Major budget categories parallel the major media that industrial marketers avail themselves of. Generally, a calendar year is the temporal basis for the industrial advertising budget. The most active month for both submissions and approvals is November.

Properly organized, advertising and sales promotion will achieve the following objectives: (1) status within the firm which is conducive to maximum effectiveness and efficiency, (2) internal effectiveness and efficiency, and (3) utmost coordination with outside services, particularly ad agencies. How to achieve the third objective is a crucial question for nearly every advertising director. Answering requires a full understanding of the functional role of an ad agency. Basically, this is to provide (1) guidance in media selection, (2) copy and layout competence, (3) advice on insertion timing, and (4) liaison with other specialists such as researchers.

DISCUSSION QUESTIONS

1 How would you explain the wide divergence in the size of industrial ad budgets expressed as a percentage of sales?
2 What is an industrial marketer attempting to do in developing a favorable company image?
3 Why is it extremely risky to disrupt the continuity of the advertising effort?
4 Why is it easier to support distribution with sales-promotional projects than with ads?
5 What reasoning is there to support the contention that advertising will reduce the overall cost of selling?
6 What questions should be answered in developing campaign strategy?
7 Define the elements which make up a media profile.
8 Describe in detail the various categories of business publications.
9 What are the advantages of direct mail?
10 What are the reasons advanced for the growing importance of catalogs?
11 Why is planning so absolutely necessary for the successful development of trade shows and exhibits?
12 Discuss the advantages and disadvantages of each of the four approaches to determining the overall size of the budget.
13 What are the various organizational patterns for the internal structure of the ad department?
14 Describe the five most common plans by ad agencies for billing clients.

SUPPLEMENTARY READING

Buchanan, Dodds I., "A New Look at 'Old' Advertising Strategy," *Business Horizons,* Winter, 1965, pp. 86-96.

Freeman, Cyril, "How to Evaluate Advertising's Contribution," in Edward C. Bursk and John F. Chapman (eds.), *Modern Marketing Strategy,* Cambridge, Mass.: Harvard University Press, 1964, pp. 256-270.

Lucas, Darrell Blaine, and Steuart Henderson Britt, *Measuring Advertising Effectiveness,* New York: McGraw-Hill Book Company, 1963.

Messner, Frederick, *Industrial Advertising,* New York: McGraw-Hill Book Company, 1963.

Robinson, Patrick J., and David J. Luck, *Promotional Decision Making,* New York: McGraw-Hill Book Company, 1964.

**marketing
logistics**

Marketing logistics can be defined as the management of systems involved in the physical movement of finished goods from the point of production to the point of consumption. The emphasis in marketing logistics is on linking up manufacturing with sales. Accordingly, the marketer's interest in inventory models is in their application to customer operations and the implementation of the marketing management concept.

ORGANIZATIONAL EVOLUTION OF MARKETING LOGISTICS

Today, marketing logistics is more a state of mind than an organizational actuality. There has been a trend toward merging storage and transportation in what is typically called a physical-distribution department. But as yet, only a handful of firms have attempted to integrate fully this composite functional area into the marketing mix.

Pattern of Internal Development

The internal development of the physical-distribution function has followed a traceable pattern. One author recognizes four phases: shipping, traffic, movement, and physical distribution.[1] In the first phase, shipping, the perspective of the person in charge is limited to the job at hand. Little consideration is given to either shipping charges or inventory control. This, in turn, has led to the second development phase. Here the emphasis shifts to the hiring and routing of transportation facilities. However, inventory management may not interest the typical traffic manager. The result is divided responsibility for inventory among manufacturing, sales, and possibly purchasing.

The third phase is one of transition. Various arrangements are sought for coordinating traffic management and inventory management for maximum efficiency. It is during this phase that transportation and storage are first looked upon as one integrated movement system. Consolidation of all the distribution activities into one department is the final phase of development. Normally, the following activities are included in the physical distribution department: (1) inventory management of finished goods, (2) transportation and traffic management, (3) order processing, (4) warehouse location and

[1] J. L. Heskett, "Ferment in Marketing's Oldest Area," *Journal of Marketing*, October, 1962, pp. 40-45.

operation, (5) package design, (6) materials handling, and (7) customer order service.

Major motivation in the last two developmental phases is the desire to reduce costs. Another important motive, particularly in the final phase, is the desire to eliminate the structural defects due to divided responsibility for various elements of physical distribution. A common example of divided responsibility is the control of warehousing at the plant by manufacturing and in the field by sales management. Such a division is further complicated by the individual views of manufacturing and sales toward inventory. On the one hand, manufacturing tends to view inventory in terms of production requirements without any true evaluation of marketing needs. On the other hand, sales management tends toward a policy of overstocking to avoid back orders.

Fitting Logistics into the Marketing Mix

Dominance of concern for consumer interests signals the emergence of the marketing logistics concept, which in turn relegates cost minimization to a secondary role in favor of profit maximization. As a result, a more positive outlook is placed on logistical activities.

The experiences of both the Witco Chemical Company and the Burroughs Corporation illustrate the key role of consumer service in planning logistics systems.[2] In 1962, the Witco Chemical Company decided to set up a unified physical-distribution system. Their objective was to systemize the flow of a highly diversified range of chemical products emanating from five operating divisions, twelve plants, and more than sixty distribution centers. While the principal concern was to coordinate and improve customer service wherever possible, it was felt that the $8 million bill for physical distribution merited serious investigation. After about two years, with one-third of the job completed, top management was able to report the successful regrouping of distribution activities at both the corporate and regional levels. Notable advances have been the realignment of regional duties, releasing field sales management from the responsibility for physical distribution, and the analytical opportunities provided by the centralized control and systems approach. In regard to the latter, the Distribution and Traffic Department has been able to engage in comprehensive studies on such subjects as transportation rates,

---

[2] The logistics systems of the Witco Chemical Company and the Burroughs Corporation are respectively described in Russ Cornell, "Integrating a P-D System," *Distribution Manager,* March, 1964, pp. 37-42; and L. O. Browne, "Total Distribution," *Distribution Manager,* July, 1964, pp. 33-40.

site locations, transportation services, and public warehouse leasing.

Consolidation of all the physical-distribution activities into one department has brought the Burroughs Corporation improved customer service and significant savings. More specifically, Burroughs established a Distribution Center linked up with the customer on a twenty-four-hour basis, seven days a week. Greater service through a reduction in stock-outs has been brought about by simulation of various patterns of market demand to determine optimum inventory levels. Moreover, a great deal of attention has been given to increased customer satisfaction through the provision of physical-distribution services at the lowest possible cost. After installation of the Distribution Center, the Burroughs Corporation reported annual savings of over $2 million (1 percent) on the distribution of $200 million worth of products. This total savings can be itemized as follows:[3]

1   Finished-goods inventory was reduced 40 percent, which was convertible into a net annual savings of about $1 million in inventory-carrying costs.
2   All eight regional warehouses were closed with a net savings in rent and personnel costs of approximately $200,000.
3   Space requirements were reduced and order-filling efficiency was increased fourfold for service parts and tools. Annual savings are figured at $300,000.
4   Annual transportation bill was cut $175,000.
5   Personal property taxes on inventories were reduced $400,000.
6   A universal standard which helped to simplify inventory stocking and distribution saved $150,000.

These two examples are illustrative of the general trend toward increased emphasis on the customer in the planning of logistics. Contrary to the marketing-logistics concept, however, the organizational solution appears to be a separate department possibly having the status of a fourth organic function rather than inclusion within the marketing area. There are several good reasons why an industrial marketer would possibly want to create a separate entity for logistics. Perhaps the most obvious one is the lack of a formalized marketing department or division. This leaves very little choice between a separate department and either of the other two alternatives—"stepchild" treatment as part of sales or manufacturing, and fragmentation of responsibility between sales and manufacturing.

A second reason is the inclusion and relative importance of inbound

[3] L. O. Browne, "Total Distribution," *Distribution Manager*, July, 1964, p. 34.

shipments. A separate department with corporate status is the best position from which to handle the logistical activities of the firm in their entirety. Another reason is that a new department may not have quite the disruptive effect on morale that results from reassignment and shifting of functional responsibility from one existing area to another.

Arguments in favor of positioning logistics within the marketing structure are: (1) equals such as marketing and logistics seldom achieve the desired degree of coordination with each other; (2) logistics can make vital contributions to the other components of the marketing mix; (3) location of the plant site near major sources of supply, as is the case more often than not with industrial-good manufacturers, lessens appreciably the problems associated with incoming shipments; and (4) fully integrated utilization of logistics as a marketing tool is possible only when logistics is structured as part of marketing.

While there is every indication of a definite trend toward the establishment of the physical-distribution function among industrial marketers—both manufacturer and middleman—the most rapid development is likely among those which have one or more of the following characteristics:

1   Widely dispersed consumer targets
2   Highly diversified product lines
3   Multi-item product lines
4   Irregular demand for products
5   Unrelenting competitive pressures
6   Large physical-distribution bill

THE COST OF LOGISTICS

For purposes of analysis logistics costs can be categorized as *explicit* and *implicit.* Explicit costs are synonymous with operating expenses as recognized by accountants. Examples are common-carrier expenses, public warehouse leasing charges, and payrolls. Implicit costs are inherent though not plainly expressed. As such they are not to be found in the profit and loss statement. The best examples are lost sales or opportunity losses resulting from stock-outs.

Explicit Costs
Industry cost patterns provide an estimate of physical-distribution

TABLE 15.1 Functionalized Physical-distribution Costs as a Percentage of Net Sales, Five Selected Industry Groupings, 1961

	PERCENTAGE OF NET SALES				
EXPENSE FUNCTION	PRIMARY METALS	CHEMICALS*	PAPER	TRANSPOR-TATION EQUIPMENT	MACHINERY†
Common carrier	5.14	9.31	5.60	5.27	5.29
Private trucking	3.53	3.47	2.54	1.83	0.84
Public warehousing	0.58	1.09	1.40	....	0.35
Private warehousing	9.53	2.88	2.01	0.74	0.53
Materials handling	1.51	1.41	1.27	0.80	0.36
Shipping room	2.49	2.41	3.01	1.12	0.95
Over-short and damage	0.02	0.19	0.20	0.01	0.02
Selected administrative	3.63	0.96	0.57	0.45	0.49
Total	26.43	21.72	16.60	10.22	8.83

*Includes chemicals, petroleum, and rubber products.
†Includes electrical and nonelectrical.
Source: Richard E. Snyder, "Physical Distribution Costs," *Distribution Manager,* January, 1963, pp. 46-47.

costs by major function. Data from a survey conducted for *Distribution Manager* are presented in Table 15.1. These statistics indicate, first, the relative significance of physical-distribution costs and, second, a discernible difference in physical-distribution costs as reported in the aggregate by the selected industries. The latter can be partially explained by an analysis of the products involved in terms of value and weight densities. Value density (i.e. the value of the product per cubic unit), being necessarily greater for machinery and transportation equipment than for most of the products of the three other industries, seems to be inversely related to the relative cost level. Weight density refers to the weight of the product per cubic unit. The usual cost pattern is for total costs, influenced greatly by transportation costs, to move downward as weight density increases. This is shown by the following comparison of transportation costs from Memphis to Chicago for iron castings (high weight density) and office stationery (low weight density).

ITEM	SIZE OF TRUCKLOAD	RATE/CWT.
Iron castings	60,000 lb	$0.74
	22,000 lb	1.05
Stationery (Class 70)	24,000 lb	1.37

The wide variance in weight densities within an industry prevents making even a general comment on interindustry differences.

The relative importance of the various major cost elements in the total physical-distribution bill is shown in Table 15.2. It is readily apparent that warehousing is a minor element and transportation a major element of total costs for industries when the tendency is to produce to order rather than to stock. A highly customized industry such as transportation equipment has respondent firms reporting transportation costs almost ten times greater than warehousing cost whereas the cost ratio for paper, generally a mass-produced item, is about 2 1/2 to 1. The chemical and related products industry grouping, typically one which produces to stock, has a cost ratio of approximately 3 to 1, which is very close to the one reported by the paper industry. It is interesting to point out that with the exception of the primary-metals industry, whose warehousing costs are slightly higher than transportation costs, transportation costs are sizably greater than warehousing costs. Finally, it can be noted that if the shipping costs of the paper industry can be excluded from consideration, there is little interindustry variance in the relative importance of costs associated with either materials handling or shipping.

Implicit Costs

The implicit costs of logistics are normally associated with the matching up of the availability of goods with consumer-demand requirements. Failure to accomplish this can mean a lost sale, a lost opportunity to sell, and/or possibly the loss of a customer.

With past experience as the basis for probability assessment, the cost of expected lost sales can be estimated by several different ap-

TABLE 15.2 Major Cost Elements of Physical Distribution in Five Selected Industry Groupings, 1961

| MAJOR COST ELEMENT | PERCENTAGE OF TOTAL PHYSICAL-DISTRIBUTION COSTS | | | | |
	PRIMARY METALS	CHEMICALS*	PAPER	TRANSPOR- TATION EQUIPMENT	MACHINERY†
Transportation	32.8	58.9	49.0	69.5	69.4
Warehousing	38.3	18.2	20.5	7.2	10.0
Materials handling	5.7	6.5	7.6	7.8	4.1
Shipping	9.4	11.1	18.1	11.0	10.8
Subtotal	86.2	94.7	95.2	95.5	94.3

*Includes chemicals, petroleum, and rubber products.
†Includes electrical and nonelectrical.
Source: Computed from the data contained in Table 15.1.

proaches. One is to construct a conditional-loss matrix to reflect the losses which may result from a given inventory level according to consumer demand. This can be shown by the following highly simplified example.

Suppose that an industrial marketer wants to know his costs of lost sales at various inventory levels. He determines that demand will vary throughout the year in 50 unit differentials up to 250 units. The penalty for being out of stock is the gross profit margin which is 30 percent of $10. The net profit margin (gross less variable marketing expense) is 20 percent or $2. The first step is to construct a payoff matrix.

PAYOFF MATRIX

	INVENTORY LEVEL					
DEMAND	0	50	100	150	200	250
0	0*	$ — 100	$ — 200	$ — 300	$ — 400	$ — 500
50	0	+ 100*	— 50	— 150	— 250	— 350
100	0	+ 100	+ 200*	0	— 100	— 200
150	0	+ 100	+ 200	+ 300*	+ 50	— 50
200	0	+ 100	+ 200	+ 300	+ 400*	+ 100
250	0	+ 100	+ 200	+ 300	+ 400	+ 500*

Based on the information thus derived, a lost-sales matrix can be constructed by subtracting each payoff from the best payoff for that particular level of demand. These best payoffs are starred for ready identification. For example, the loss in sales from having only 150 units when demand is 200 units is $100 ($400 less $300). Similarly, a loss of $400 is found when inventory is 50 units and demand is 250 units.

LOST-SALES MATRIX

	INVENTORY LEVEL					
DEMAND	0	50	100	150	200	250
0	$ 0					
50	100	$ 0				
100	200	100	$ 0			
150	300	200	100	$ 0		
200	400	300	200	100	$ 0	
250	500	400	300	200	100	$ 0

The last step is to assign probabilities to the various levels of demand. One way to do this is to set up a probability distribution on the basis of the relative frequency of occurrence during the last year for the specific levels of demand. For purposes of this illustration, suppose the probabilities thus determined are: 0 units—0.05; 50 units—0.20; 100 units—0.20; 150 units—0.25; 200 units—0.20; and 250 units—0.10. The total lost sales which can be expected when the inventory decision is to stock 100 units is computed as follows:

DEMAND	PROBABILITY	CONDITIONAL LOSS	EXPECTED LOSS
0	0.05		
50	0.20		
100	0.20	$ 0	$ 0
150	0.25	100	25
200	0.20	200	40
250	0.10	300	30
			$95

In like manner it is found that total lost sales can be expected to be:

$265	0-unit inventory
170	50-unit inventory
40	150-unit inventory
10	200-unit inventory
0	250-unit inventory

If the order interval plus order cycle is twenty operating days, the marketer can anticipate sustaining the loss from his inventory decision 250/20 or 12.5 times during a given year.

Customer-service levels offer another approach to estimating lost sales. These levels based on a normal probability distribution reflect the number of orders which can be filled during an order period. Using the previous situation, suppose that the mean and standard deviation are found to be 150 units and 34 units respectively. A comparison of estimated lost sales by service level is shown below:

CUSTOMER SERVICE LEVEL (PERCENT)	STANDARD DEVIATIONS FROM THE MEAN	ESTIMATED COST OF LOST SALES
50.0	....	$250.00
60.0	0.25	233.00
70.0	0.52	214.64
80.0	0.84	192.88
85.0	1.04	179.28
90.0	1.65	137.80
95.0	1.96	117.12
100.0	3.00	46.00

It will be noticed that at 100 percent the marketer will still lose $46, (23 units X $2) theoretically. The reason for this is that the demand curve does not conform exactly with the normal curve. Smoothing of the demand curve would help to eliminate much of this deviation.[4] Regardless of which approach is used, it might be wise to calculate lost sales customer by customer, at least for the key accounts. The costs of a lost customer can be based on historical data. The best estimate would be the net marginal contribution of the customer during the last twelve months he was a customer plus or minus a trend increment.

Another implicit logistics cost is the carrying cost of added inventory over and above the amount normally found necessary to satisfy consumer requirements. This additional inventory is frequently the result of a marketing policy or a marketing commitment to a particular customer. Still another implicit cost of logistics is the emergency delivery of goods to a customer; estimates of this type of cost are usually based on prior experience.

LOGISTICS AS A SYSTEM

The systems approach views logistics as an integrated whole in which a change in any one component activity will affect the others. In fact, if any of the other activities are not affected, they are either improperly grouped or superfluous to the system. Developing a logistics system serves to maintain the desired and often competitively necessary consumer-service levels with maximum profitability—a goal of maximum profitability because business is making money rather than spending less. There are several ways a systems approach helps in solving logistics problems:[5]

1   It focuses management attention on product movement. Instead of considering distinct activity spheres as dictated by organizational structure, all affected activities regardless of organizational status are grouped into a movement system.

2   It makes possible the determination of total costs for each alternative system. A lower shipping rate or a new packaging procedure, for example, is viewed not as an isolated problem situation, but in terms of its effects upon all costs.

[4] For an excellent discussion of smoothing, see Robert Schlaifer, *Probability and Statistics for Business Decisions*, New York: McGraw-Hill Book Company, 1959, chap. 6, pp. 95-113.

[5] Adopted in part from Allan Harvey, "Systems Can Be Too Practical," *Business Horizons*, Summer, 1964, pp. 68-69.

3   It provides an opportunity to make use of the more advanced management techniques such as model building and simulation.
4   It facilitates the installation of the most proficient informational and control programs.
5   It is flexible enough to permit gradual redesigning of the entire system.

Marketing logistics can be separated into four identifiable job areas: (1) design and control of movement systems, (2) management of transportation, (3) management of storage or inventory facilities, and (4) packaging. The last-named job area is usually a part of logistics rather than product development or even advertising as it well may be in a consumer-goods organization, because the package rarely sells an industrial product. The emphasis in industrial marketing is on packages which ship the appropriate quantity under the best protection for the money.

DESIGNS OF MOVEMENT SYSTEMS

The first step in designing a movement system is to set up the objectives for logistics. These are usually stated in terms of customer levels. A basic question in setting up objectives concerns the role of logistics in the marketing mix. Is it to be used as a major competitive tool or merely to keep the marketer in competitive equilibrium? The second step is to audit the logistics situation. This will include measurement of the spatial and temporal patterns of demands, characterization of the product's physical properties, and assessment of the existing logistics function.

The third step concerns the determination of alternative systems available to the particular marketer. This is followed in step four by the affixing of total costs to each alternative. For purposes of illustrating the last two steps, suppose a hypothetical machinery manufacturer in St. Louis with a national market wishes to design a movement system. The geographical dispersion of a 3,600-unit sales volume is as follows:

Pacific Coast		900 units
Los Angeles	600 units	
San Francisco	200	
San Diego	100	

Southwest		180 units
Phoenix	180	
Middle West		1,240 units
Chicago	340	
Cincinnati	160	
Cleveland	260	
Detroit	140	
Louisville	100	
St. Louis	240	
Southeast		600 units
Atlanta	300	
Birmingham	120	
Charlotte	180	
Northeast		680 units
Boston	240	
New York	440	

The manufacturer has a regional plant in Los Angeles and one in Cleveland in addition to St. Louis. Annual output for each of the three plants is as follows:

St. Louis	2,000 units
Cleveland	900 units
Los Angeles	800 units

Top management has decided on a customer-service level of twenty-four-hour delivery upon receipt of order. With this limitation, at least two regional warehouses will be necessary. One of these warehouses could be situated in the New York area to serve the New York and Boston markets. The other warehouse could be in Atlanta, where it could reach the Southeastern market areas in Alabama, Georgia, and North Carolina.

For purposes of this hypothetical example, it is further assumed that only one type of machinery is marketed and that the average unit cost of goods sold is $4,000.

Several alternative systems are possible. Cost breakdowns for three of the alternatives are summarized in Table 15.3. The first alternative is to use five warehouses—the minimum number of strategically situated regional warehouses plus warehouses at each of the three plant sites. Excess yearly capacity at the various plant warehouses is limited. As a result the inventory load for Los Angeles is balanced off between Los Angeles and St. Louis, thus contributing to higher than normal inventory levels for St. Louis.

Under the second alternative, a third regional warehouse is added. Located in South Bend, Indiana, this warehouse serves the Chi-

TABLE 15.3 Hypothetical Cost Comparison of Alternative Movement Systems (in thousands of dollars)

COST ELEMENT	NUMBER 1		NUMBER 2		NUMBER 3	
Inventory carrying cost:						
St. Louis	86		21		18	
Los Angeles	90		90		90	
Cleveland	48		28		78	
New York	140		120		120	
Atlanta	148		146		124	
South Bend	. . .	512	160	565	. . .	430
Materials handling:						
Loading and unloading rail cars	. . .	4	. . .	8	. . .	2
Warehousing facilities:						
Depreciation	100		125		100	
Taxes	60	160	75	200	60	160
Transportation (movement) costs:						
Rail (CL only)	60		45		30	
Truck (LTL only)	15		25		20	
Local cartage	9	84	9	79	9	59
Production penalty	....	....	....	....	....	86
Total		760		852		737

cago area as well as Cincinnati, Detroit, and Louisville. Using the South Bend warehouse to serve the latter three market areas frees the Cleveland plant to act as the sole supplier for the Northeast and to fulfill a portion of the demand emanating from the Southeast. The faster delivery to New York and Atlanta allows the reduction of inventory levels in these two warehouses, which in turn lowers carrying costs. However, from an overall standpoint the addition of a third regional warehouse increases total distribution costs $92,000, or 12 percent.

The third alternative proposes an increase in productive capacity at both the Los Angeles and Cleveland plants. The penalty is $40 per unit for the first 1,000 units and $30 per unit for the second 1,000 units. Production is upped 400 units at the Los Angeles plant and 2,000 units at the Cleveland plant. Even with this production penalty, it is obvious that decentralizing production is a better choice than increasing the number of regional warehouses.

These fictitious estimates of cost illustrate two important points. One is that the alternative with the lowest total cost is the one which contains the most favorable cost trade-off. In the third alternative, for example, the decision to decentralize production increased costs

$86,000, but it resulted in significant reductions in inventory carrying charges and transportation expenses. Usually in actual practice, priority is given those cost trade-offs offering the greatest chance for gain. Another important point is that any and every segment of the firm may be involved in costing out a particular movement system.

TOTAL COST APPROACH

The total cost approach is defined as the analysis of movement systems in terms of costs which are normally classified as physical distribution as well as those which are distribution-related. An example of the latter is the production costs associated with the various plants throughout the country. The theory behind this approach is that being interrelated, a change in one cost sets off a chain reaction on all of the other costs of the firm. The most significant types of costs can be roughly divided into two broad categories—physical distribution and distribution-related.

Physical-distribution Costs

Five different costs can be identified in physical distribution. These are warehousing, inventory carrying, transporation, materials handling, and packaging. Warehousing costs are incurred in the operation of private warehouses, or in the leasing of space in public warehouses. Warehouse ownership involves the cost of capital, and as a fixed or semivariable expense, warehousing expenditures are directly proportional to the number, location, and structural characteristics of warehouses. The cost of leasing public warehouse space is a variable expense directly related to the amount used.

The costs of holding an inventory include insurance, taxes, occupancy, interest on investment, opportunity losses, depreciation, deterioration, obsolescence and intrawarehouse service. In aggregate these costs expressed as a percentage of average inventory value will range from about 10 to over 30 percent. American Machine & Foundry Company uses a figure of 24.25 percent, which can be broken down as follows: space costs, 0.25 percent; insurance, 0.25 percent; taxes, 0.50 percent; supplies, 0.25 percent; handling and distribution, 2.00 percent; deterioration, 3.00 percent; interest, 5.00 percent; loss due to inability to invest funds in profit-making ventures (opportunity loss), 8.00 percent; and obsolescence, 5.00 percent.[6]

Movement charges plus the costs associated with special services and terminals are normally included in the transportation category. Consideration is also being given to the costs arising from the differences in service provided by different modes of transportation. This service differential is composed of two parts—one developing from the differences in transit time, the other from the difference in shipment size. In contrasting rail with truck shipments, the generalized data developed by John R. Meyer and his associates show for a distance of 800 miles a service differential of $0.0044 per ton-mile ($0.0043 for time and $0.0001 for size of shipment).[7] This means that in shipping 300 tons by rail, an extra cost of $1,056 will be incurred. If the size of the shipment is 500 tons, the extra costs will increase to $1,760.

Materials-handling costs include the costs of equipment and labor utilized in assembling, manipulating, and dispersing goods. The costs of materials handling are semivariable, varying with the volume of goods handled and the size of the individual orders.

In industrial marketing the costs of packaging and dunnage or external protective materials are generally regarded as logistics costs. These costs vary in relation to the size of container, the mode of transportation, and the particular services supplied by the carrier. Because the purpose of both packaging and dunnage is to supply customers with damage-free goods, the shipper must relate the costs of these services to marketing policy requirements.

Distribution-related Costs

Probably the most obvious distribution-related cost is the one related to production alternatives. Costs will vary from plant to plant; therefore, the decision as to supplying plant will affect cost of goods sold as well as the cost of physical distribution. The plant closest to a customer may have a production cost which more than offsets the savings in movement costs. The major determinant of production cost is the scale of production.

[6] Reprinted by permission of the publisher from John B. Holbrook, "A Simple Tabular Method for Determining Economic Order Quantities," in *Managing the Materials Function*, AMA Management Report No. 35. © 1959 by the American Management Association, Inc.

[7] John R. Meyer, Merton J. Peck, John Stenason, and Charles Zwick, *The Economics of Competition in the Transportation Industries*, Cambridge, Mass.: Harvard University Press, 1959, pp. 190-191.

Also related to distribution are the costs of data processing and communications. These include order processing, stock replenishment, inventory control, and shipping-related activities. These costs are directly proportional to the complexity of the distribution network and the frequency of customer contact. A marketer of operating supplies, for example, with several regional warehouses scattered throughout the nation will sustain greater data processing and communications costs than, say, a marketer of custom machinery.

The requirements imposed on distribution by marketing policies are another cost which must be considered under the total cost concept. Excess inventory to avoid stock-outs, shorten delivery time, supply unusual customer commitments, and maintain status-oriented warehousing locations are examples of such costs. The best approach in determining these expenses is to establish standard costs for each of the various service levels. Using delivery as an illustration, suppose a salesman has promised a good customer six-hour delivery on three pieces of machinery. The customer is located 300 miles from the nearest warehouse and the standard cost for twenty-four-hour delivery of five or less items this distance is $10 per machine. To deliver the machines within six hours, it is necessary to spend $17.50 per item. Thus, the marketing requirement cost would total $22.50. The frequency of such occurrences, based on past sales records or probability predictions, can be used to determine annual requirement costs of each particular distribution network.

Another distribution-related cost category the marketer may want to consider is the one associated with the management of marketing channels. The commitments imposed by the type of marketing channel include the degrees of warehousing and service support as well as the indicated changes in shipping and packaging.

The difficulties in applying the total cost concept are explained by LeKashman and Stolle:[8]

1 The impact of distribution on costs is difficult to unravel.
2 The real cost of distribution is obscured by traditional accounting practices.
3 The problem inherent in having to deal with hundreds of bits of information which can interact in countless different ways.

These three difficulties, particularly the last one, make it obvious that only the most sophisticated techniques of analysis and manipula-

[8] Raymond LeKashman and John F. Stolle, "The Total Cost Approach to Distribution," *Business Horizons*, Winter, 1965, p. 37.

tion can be employed in formulating practical cost data for the development of logistics systems. It is also obvious that without the whole-hearted cooperation of top management, the application of such a program will be impossible.

LOGISTICS MIX—WAREHOUSING

The manufacturer of industrial goods and occasionally the larger industrial distributor are confronted with several problems associated with warehousing. Perhaps the most critical is the determination of exact locations for the optimum logistics network. Another major problem is the choice of private or public warehousing.

Warehouse Location

Before proceeding with a discussion of site location, it should be emphasized that warehousing refers to temporary stoppages in the movement of goods from production to consumption. The purpose of warehousing is to effect an adjustment between supply and demand. When such an adjustment is brought about, it is labeled orderly marketing.

The job of site selection can be divided into several interrelated tasks. A preliminary task is the determination of the right number of warehouses. This is a function of the indicated level of customer service and the spatial location of the market. With a widely scattered market, more warehouses will be necessary for a twenty-four-hour delivery commitment than for delivery promised within a longer period of time. One approach to determining the number of warehouses can be likened to a trial-and-error process. Several promising sites are selected, usually in areas of market concentration. The temporal coverage patterns of transportation media are then plotted for each of the possible sites. If the coverage of one site is in large measure (70 percent or more) duplicated by another site, the number of sites is reduced by one. For duplication of 30 to 70 percent, the number of sites is reduced by one-half site. A final figure involving one-half warehouse is rounded to the next higher whole number.

More scientific is the approach which determines spatial coverage in terms of warehousing efficiency.[9] Area coverage which yields minimum warehousing costs is expressed mathematically as follows:

[9] Edward H. Bowman and John B. Stewart, "A Model for Scale of Operations," *Journal of Marketing*, January, 1956, pp. 243-245.

$$A = (\frac{2b}{ck})^{\frac{2}{3}}$$

where A = area in square miles

   b = fixed costs for the warehouse per unit of time, which divided by the volume will yield the appropriate cost per dollar's worth distributed

   c = the cost of the distribution, which varies with the square root of the area; that is, costs associated with miles covered within the warehouse district such as gasoline, truck maintenance, direct driver expense, etc.

   k = sales or gross profit density in dollars per square mile of designated territory

It is obvious that with both these approaches some thought must be given to the general areas where warehouses are to be located. In the former approach, for example, cost and sales data will necessarily vary from region to region. For this reason, it is essential that the marketer maintain an up-to-date file of pertinent details on possible site locations in various areas throughout the country.

For locating the exact site, the usual approach is analytical. The least-cost site in relation to transportation charges can be determined by application of the grid method. A grid is superimposed over the market area to be served by a proposed warehouse, and each cell is weighted by the result of multiplying the physical volume of actual or potential sales by the freight cost per ton-mile to the center of the cell. The horizontal and vertical axes for the least-cost location are calculated by means of a mathematical formula for finding the point which balances exactly the product summations of cell weightings and grid distances.[10]

If warehousing costs such as land, construction, and operation are approximately the same throughout the designated region, the grid method is appropriate because the only point of differentiation is in transportation charges. However, this rarely happens in actual practice. One very obvious difference is the wide range of taxation rates.

To interject warehousing costs into location selection, a more com-

[10] This method is explained fully in Edward W. Smykay, Donald J. Bowersox, and Frank H. Mossman, *Physical Distribution Management*, New York: The Macmillan Company, 1961, pp. 176-190.

plex approach is indicated. This approach can be called location-transfer analysis. In this approach, the *first step* is to select all the possible warehousing sites in the total market. The *next step* is to collect all the available information about each prospective site and to project warehousing costs over some agreed-upon future period of time. The *third step* is to calculate the aggregate freight costs which would be incurred if each possible warehouse location were to serve each customer. This involves multiplying the physical volume purchased during a year's time by the freight rate applicable to the normal order quantity for the customer. This is expressed as follows:

$$TC_{a,b,\ldots n} = K_1 f_1 + K_2 f_2 + \ldots K_n f_n$$

where TC = transportation costs to all customers from designated warehouse

K = physical volume purchased by a particular customer

f = applicable freight rate; if shipments are sent in different quantities; thus qualifying for different rates, a weighted average is used.

The *fourth step* is to effect the necessary adjustments in line with forecasted changes in market structure. This is accomplished by multiplying the forecasted change in terms of physical volume for each geographical segment by the freight charges to the center of the greatest sales density within the geographical area. The *fifth step* is to sum the costs for each warehouse and then rank all the possible warehouse sites according to their total costs, the lowest total cost first, the next to the lowest cost second, and so forth.

After the total logistics cost for each possible warehouse location is known, the *sixth and final step* is to combine the warehouses into an optimal network. This can be done by trial and error or preferably by simulation. What will evolve from this final step is a series of location combinations which will yield the lowest aggregate cost at each stage of implementation. Suppose, for example, that a marketer wishes to have four warehouses scattered strategically throughout the continental United States. However, full implementation of the plan will take place over a period of five years. In other words, it will be five years before all four warehouses will be operational. Through use of simulation techniques, the marketer will know which location should be his first warehouse as well as the order of the remaining three specified locations.

A heuristic or learning approach to locating warehouses has been suggested by two authors. With this approach, the most profitable arrangement of warehouses is arrived at by a process resembling trial and error.[11]

While the dimension of time is considered in determining the appropriate number of warehouses, in at least two models theorists have attempted to interject time into location models. In one of these, transit time between warehouse and customer in the same metropolitan area was used in constructing a center-of-gravity model.[12] The other model locates a warehouse in a given market area by measuring the service elasticity of demand,[13] service being defined as delivery time.

Nonquantifiable factors which may or may not affect the location of a warehouse include access to major transportation arteries, proximity to a metropolitan area, business climate, community relations, and prestige of address. Such factors as the availability of a labor supply, power facilities, and living conditions tend to be less important than they would be in locating a plant.

Public versus Private Warehousing

To resolve the question of whether to use public or private warehousing, a marketer should review both the advantages and disadvantages of each type in relation to his individual needs. The principal advantage of public warehousing is flexibility, which can be translated into cost savings particularly for the marketer who experiences considerable seasonal variation in sales.

First of all, public warehousing gives the marketer warehousing where he wants it without the necessity of capital investment. Also implied is the opportunity to quickly and easily adjust location to coincide with spatial changes in the market. Although this is a compelling reason for a financially weak marketer, financially strong marketers are finding more and more that utilization of public warehouses tends to minimize opportunity losses on invested capital.

A second advantage is that space costs can be related to temporal needs. Using a public warehouse, the marketer does not have to pay for space which is not being occupied. In building his warehouse, a marketer would undoubtedly want it designed to accommodate the maximum volume plus additional space for anticipated growth,

[11] For a discussion of this approach see Alfred A. Kuehn and Michael J. Hamburger, "A Heuristic Program for Locating Warehouses," *Management Science,* July, 1963, pp. 643-666.

[12] Donald J. Bowersox, "An Analytical Approach to Warehouse Location," *Handling and Shipping,* February, 1962, pp. 17-20.

[13] Frank H. Mossman and Newton Morton, *Logistics of Distribution Systems,* Boston: Allyn and Bacon, Inc., 1965, pp. 248-250.

with the result that during the periods when inventory stocks were not at their peak, the marketer would incur the costs of unused space. The principle of paying only for what is used can be carried over to labor. Using a public warehouse, the marketer has to pay for only his temporal needs. He does not have to contend with the problems of overages or, for that matter, shortages, nor will he have to engage in labor negotiations.

Another advantage of the public warehouse is that it relieves the marketer of much of the paper work associated with shipping and warehousing. A partial list of such services includes:

1   Filing claims
2   Preparing overage, shortage, and damage reports
3   Invoicing
4   Developing freight consolidation plans
5   Back-ordering
6   Taking periodic inventories

Utilization of a public warehouse gives the marketer the advantages of specialized skills at a reduced cost. The personnel of a public warehouse, both executive and operative, possess expertise in matters pertaining to warehousing. In addition to personnel, the public warehouse undoubtedly has specialized equipment. The costs of this specialization are spread among the various clients in relation to individual commitment. Thus, the costs are lower than they would be if the marketer hired the skills and equipment for his own exclusive use. The four basic services in addition to storage which almost every public warehouse offers are:

1   Distribution and transfer of merchandise.
2   Assembly of merchandise, particularly into carloads and truck-loads.
3   Provision of some form of perpetual inventory control.
4   Facilitating transportation of merchandise. Many public warehouses have their own fleet of trucks for area delivery.

Other services which may or may not be offered by a public warehouse include:

1   Bonding
2   Field warehousing
3   Fumigation
4   Packaging from bulk
5   Rental of office and display space
6   Space rental as differentiated from storage
7   Repairing and recoopering

8   Sampling, weighting, and inspection
9   Installing dunnage and bracing materials

A fifth and final advantage is the partial relief of management responsibility, which in turn permits greater concentration on the other aspects of marketing. This keeps management skills from being spread too thin and allows concentration on those areas of marketing where familiarity as well as competence is undoubtedly the greatest.

There are four principal advantages associated with private warehousing. One is the service advantage of having a warehouse specifically designed and located in accordance with customer needs. Many firms have found that the inherent rigidities of the public warehouse limit their service objectives. For example, the public warehouse might not process till the next day orders received after a particular time in the morning. This most certainly would be disastrous to a delivery service policy. A second advantage of private warehouses is the shifting of a portion of costs to a fixed status. This enables a marketer with a fairly consistent pattern of demand to scale his warehouse facility for maximum efficiency, thereby effecting a reduction in total costs.

A third advantage of private warehousing is that it allows the combining of several activities at the same location. These might include sales, service, and fabrication. Combining all these operations under one roof may result in definite economies. However, a warehouse may not be the best location for sales. Finally, the presence of a marketer-owned warehouse is advantageous because of the intangible effect on the local community. Customers are often more kindly disposed toward a marketer that they can identify themselves with in their own locale. Then, too, local warehouses provide excellent opportunities to enhance the company's image.

In summary, public warehousing offers cost savings through its flexibility to the marketer whose sales vary seasonally. The greater the variation, the greater the cost savings. Private warehousing, on the other hand, is more advantageous to the marketer whose sales follow a more or less constant pattern throughout the year and/or who functions in a market where customer service is a decisive competitive tool.

LOGISTICS MIX—INVENTORY MANAGEMENT

Inventory management involves two fundamental decisions—how much should be ordered and how often orders should be placed. How to make these decisions is important not only internally but externally as a service to be merchandised to customers.

Order Quantity

In placing an order, the buyer finds himself in a state of indecision in regard to quantity. If he buys in quantity, he will reduce appreciable unit costs as well as purchasing costs (i.e. the time and effort expended in purchasing). On the other hand, buying too much will have an adverse effect on profits through an increase in carrying charges and will limit his buying maneuverability. A somewhat similar situation confronts the marketer in stocking his own warehouse network. He will want to dispatch the "right" quantities to his various warehouses. To resolve this indecision a basic formula is proposed by theorists to determine optimum quantity or, as it is more commonly labeled, economic order quantity.

Typically four factors are considered in calculating economic order quantity. These are the annual rate of usage (D), the average cost of placing an order (P), the inventory carrying cost (I), and the cost per unity (C), The resultant formula is:

$$Q = \frac{2DP}{IC}$$

Usage or demand can be based on past sales or preferably forecasted sales. The cost of placing an order and inventory carrying charges may be obtained by analyzing company records. Carrying charges are normally expressed as a percentage of average inventory. Where demand tends to be constant throughout the year, average inventory will equal one-half of the amount purchased or transferred during the year. Seasonal variation necessitates averaging monthly or bimonthly balances.

The cost of a product to a purchaser will vary necessarily with the volume ordered. To determine it will require the calculation of economic order quantity at various price levels, which is facilitated by the construction of a nomograph. Cost to the marketer who is transferring goods to his own warehouse network is either manufacturing cost or what he paid for the particular item.

To supplement knowledge of the optimum order quantity, the AMF Company computes penalties incurred by holding other than the optimum quantity,[14] the theory being that quantities near the optimum will yield a zero penalty. The formula used to compute the penalty is:

[14] John B. Holbrook, *op. cit.*, pp. 67-69.

$$P = \frac{cU}{Q} + \frac{iQ}{2} - \sqrt{2ciU}$$

where P = penalty per month in dollars
c = cost of placing the order in dollars
i = cost of carrying the order in inventory as a percentage of the order
U = value of goods used per month in dollars
Q = value of goods ordered per order in dollars

Reconciliation of economic order quantity with the quantity discount structure is of interest to both purchaser and marketer. The question is whether the quantity discount is sufficient to enlarge optimum order quantity to a point where it is at or above the level necessary to obtain the stated discount. Failing this, the quantity discount will not serve its intended purpose—namely, acceleration of purchases.

This question can be answered in at least two ways. One is to compare the AMF penalty incurred in ordering the quantity necessary for the discount with the savings effected by the discount. If the penalty is greater than the savings, it will not be profitable to take the discount. Conversely, the quantity discount should be taken when the penalty is less than savings.

Another way to determine the minimum quantity discount is as follows:[15]

$$D = \frac{I(AI_N - AI_O)}{CS}$$

where D = minimum discount required
I = cost of carrying \$1 of inventory for one year
AI_N = the average value of inventory if a proposed quantity of goods is purchased; this is the quantity to which the minimum discount will be affixed (one-half the value of the purchase).
AI_O = the average value of inventory with present purchasing patterns (one-half the value of the purchase)
CS = the dollar cost of goods sold during a year's time (assumed to be an average of all customers)

For illustrative purposes, suppose the current average order is 100 units with demand fairly constant throughout the year. Suppose

[15] J. L. Heskett, Robert M. Ivie, and Nicholas A. Glaskowsky, Jr., *Business Logistics,* New York: The Ronald Press Company, p. 236.

still further that the average customer buys 400 units which are priced at $30 per unit. Application of the formula to determine the minimum discount necessary to encourage purchases in quantities of 200 yields the following result:

$$D = \frac{.25\,(3,000 - 1,500)}{12,000} = \frac{375}{12,000} = 3.125\%$$

Purchasers may decide to use this formula to solve for the average value of inventory if the proposed quantity discount is taken. Using the preceding situation, suppose a marketer has offered a 2 percent discount for buying in quantities of at least 200 units. The purchaser wants to know whether this is enough of a discount to cover the increased costs of buying in the larger quantity. Rearranging the formula and substituting the necessary information, he finds that the discount is not sufficient for such a purchase quantity:

$$AI_N = \frac{CS\,(D) + I(AI_O)}{I}$$

$$= \frac{\$240 + \$375}{.25} = \$2,460 \text{ or a purchase of 164 units}$$

Order Scheduling

Proper scheduling of orders requires the determination of both the optimum order point and the optimum safety stock. The purpose of the reorder point is to inform management of the need for stock replenishment. The reorder point can be calculated very simply by multiplying usage by lead time. The latter is defined as the number of days necessary for stock replenishment. If usage is 20 units a day and lead time is 10 days, the reorder point is 200 units. However, lead time will necessarily vary, and so to avoid the risk of a stock-out, a safety stock must be provided. Therefore, the formula for reorder point should be amended to read *usage* $\times$ *lead time* + *safety stock.*

To optimize safety stock, consideration must be given to its effect on costs. First, the presence of a safety stock will increase inventory carrying charges. The increase will be fixed because the amount of safety stock will not vary throughout the year. Secondly, the presence of a safety stock will lessen the penalties of lost sales occasioned by stock-outs.

By using probability, the exact amount of safety stock can be determined with a certain degree of accuracy. Past sales records will show the demand pattern during the reorder periods. To illustrate, an analysis of past sales records will allow the assignment of probabilities to usage during the reorder period. The results of this analysis are as follows:

USAGE DURING REORDER PERIOD	CUMULATIVE FREQUENCY	USAGE PROBABILITY
40	9	0.06
80	21	0.14
120	45	0.30
160	120	0.80
200	132	0.88
240	141	0.94
280	147	0.98
320	150	1.00

Assuming annual usage of 7,200 units and a normal lead time of 8 days with the optimum number (10) of orders per year, the costs of being out of stock can be computed.

SAFETY STOCK	STOCK-OUT PROBABILITY	ANNUAL STOCK-OUT COST	
0	0.08—40 units	$640	
	0.06—80	960	
	0.04—120	960	
	0.02—160	640	$3,200
80	0.04—40 units	320	
	0.02—80	320	640
120	0.02—40 units	160	160
160	0	0	0

With a stock-out penalty of $20 per unit, it can be seen that without a safety stock the marketer can expect to suffer a loss of $3,200. Adoption of a safety-stock policy whereby 80 units are retained will reduce these costs by over $2,500. While this shows the obvious desirability of safety stock, it does not provide any information on which level of inventory will be the least costly from an overall standpoint. To do this, it is necessary to consider not only losses from stock-outs but carrying charges as well. If the units are costed out at $100 each and carrying charges are figured at 15 percent, the following comparison can be made of designated safety-stock levels in the hypothetical example:

SAFETY STOCK	ANNUAL STOCK-OUT LOSS	ANNUAL CARRYING CHARGES	TOTAL
0	$3,200	$ 0	$3,200
80	640	1,200	1,840
120	160	1,800	1,960
160	0	2,400	2,400

Selecting the optimum level of safety stock, one finds that the reorder point will be 240 units (20 $\times$ 8 + 80).

LOGISTICS MIX—PACKAGING

Traditionally, the marketer has sought a package at the lowest cost consistent with the goals of increased sales and protection. The emphasis in industrial marketing is on protection, whereas marketers of consumer goods tend to stress the sales goal by utilizing the package as a promotional tool. To a list of packaging goals, the industrial marketer will want to add two more. First, he will want to optimize the package in terms of customer requirements. A manufacturer of industrial shelving, for example, could package his product in kit form or by size of piece.

Secondly, the marketer will want to optimize the functional characteristics of his packaging. The optimum functional package is one which satisfies the requirements of materials handling, warehousing, and transportation. Typically, the goal of optimum functionalization is closely related to lower costs. This is aptly illustrated by the package utilized by the Cummins Engine Company to ship crankshafts.[16] Corrugated containers were specially designed to keep precision-machined crankshafts in top condition from factory to user. Two years after the changeover, Cummins reported significant savings. Providing maximum protection, the corrugated containers not only cost less to purchase, but also facilitated handling and shipping operations.

After the decision on packaging objectives, the next question is who should be involved in the packaging program. Under the direction of logistics, a packaging committee could conceivably include management representatives from manufacturing, purchasing, engineering, and sales. Manufacturing would be interested in the relationship of the container to their operation of the packaging line. They would undoubtedly favor the aforementioned package for crankshafts because in the sealing operation wrapping in special rust-resistant paper eliminated the need for dipping the crankshaft in a corrosion-resistant liquid prior to crating.

The obvious interest of purchasing is in the cost and availability of the packaging material. Engineering will have something to say

[16] "High Powered Packaging," *Package Laboratory News*, Winter, 1962 (quarterly publication of the H&D Division, West Virginia Pulp and Paper Company).

about the functional properties of the package and may become involved in design. Sales will undoubtedly speak for the customer. The job of logistics as coordinator is to synthesize these interests, along with the problems of physical distribution, into an effective packaging program.

What kind of design services will be necessary is the next question to be answered. Corollary to this is the question of who is to supply the design services. Does the marketer have the staff and the facilities, or should the design task be turned over to an outside organization? Finally, the marketer must ask what the competition is doing and how acceptable it is to the market.

The rewards are many to the industrial marketers who install an effective packaging program. Perhaps the most obvious are those which effect cost savings:

1   One marketer reported he was able to reduce the number of package sizes from over 250 to 60, and in doing so cut costs by more than half.
2   A leading optical company claims a 20 percent reduction in packaging costs for air shipments using 125-pound test containers instead of 200-pound test containers.
3   A packaging supplier contends that by switching to corrugated as much as 30 to 50 percent of package weight will be eliminated with a resultant saving in transportation costs.

Here are just a few of the rewards which are not quite as obvious as those associated with cost savings:

1   Creation of a new marketing identity which offered greater advertising and promotional possibilities
2   Enhancement of trade image
3   More careful treatment by freight handlers and truckers

SUMMARY

Marketing logistics has been defined as the management of finished goods from the point of production to the point of consumption. In this context, it has a vital role in the implementation of the marketing management concept.

The trend toward marketing logistics has followed a traceable pattern. The *first* phase is personified by the shipping clerk and his narrow outlook, particularly in relation to transportation and inventory control.

To correct this, many firms have moved into the *second* or traffic-management phase. The apparent weakness in this phase is the neglect of the warehousing function, which results in divided responsibility for warehousing among manufacturing, sales, and purchasing.

During the *third* or transitional phase, transportation and storage are first looked upon as one integrated movement system.

The *fourth* phase, consolidation of all the distribution activities into one department, is as far as industrial marketers have progressed. The guiding motivation in this and the third phase is the desire to reduce costs. Dominance of concern for the consumer interests signals the emergence of the marketing logistics concept. Movement systems are viewed as part of the marketing mix with cost minimization relegated to a secondary role in favor of profit maximization.

The costs of logistics can be categorized as explicit and implicit, or physical distribution and distribution-related. Both bases of categorization are useful in planning and analyzing movement systems. The involvment of every segment of the firm in costing out a particular movement system is called the total cost approach. The theoretical basis for this approach is that because changes are interrelated, a change in one cost sets off a chain reaction on all of the other costs of the firm.

Four steps are involved in designing a movement system. These are:

1   Setting up objectives usually in terms of customer-service levels
2   Audit of the logistics situation in terms of spatial and temporal patterns of demand, characteristics of the physical product, and assessment of the existing logistics function
3   Determination of the alternative systems available to the marketer
4   Affixation of total costs to each alternative

Comparison of the alternatives will reveal that the one with the lowest cost has the most favorable cost trade-off. That is, an increase in the cost of one function is more than offset by a decrease in a related function. In actual practice, highest priority is given to those trade-offs offering the biggest chance of gain.

Certain questions need to be answered in regard to warehousing, inventory, and packaging. As for warehousing, the marketer needs to know the exact locations for an optimum logistics network and whether private or public warehousing would be the more appropriate. Two important questions concern the marketer in managing his inventories. One is the appropriate quantity to be shipped at one time to a customer or warehouse. The other is the proper scheduling of shipments. In packaging, the marketer must determine what he wants to accomplish and how he is going to go about it.

DISCUSSION QUESTIONS

1   Explain the shift in emphasis as the firm passes through the various phases in the organizational evolution of the marketing logistics concept.
2   What are the characteristics of a firm which would be inclined to adopt the marketing logistics concept?
3   Describe the distinguishable effects of weight and value density on transportation costs.
4   Briefly describe the procedure for determining lost sales due to being out of stock.
5   Cite the implicit costs associated with the logistics decision.
6   What are the ways a systems approach can be of assisistance in solving logistics problems?
7   What cost categories are normally included under the general heading of distribution-related?
8   What difficulties would one expect to encounter in applying the total cost approach to logistics?
9   In comparing alternative movement systems, what are known as cost trade-offs become apparent. Explain what is meant by this term and how they should be treated.
10   Explain in detail how a marketer should go about determining the appropriate number of warehouses.
11   How would one summarize the basic differences between private and public warehousing?
12   Give the reasons for including packaging in the logistics mix rather than the promotion mix.

SUPPLEMENTARY READINGS

Bowman, Edward H., and John B. Stewart, "A Model for Scale of Operations," *Journal of Marketing,* January, 1956, pp. 243-245.

Harvey, Allan, "Systems Can Be Too Practical," *Business Horizons,* Summer, 1964, pp. 67-70.

Heskett, J. L., "Ferment in Marketing's Oldest Areas," *Journal of Marketing,* October, 1962, pp. 40-45.

LeKashman, Raymond, and John F. Stolle, "The Total Cost Approach to Distribution," *Business Horizons,* Winter, 1965, pp. 33-46.

Management of the Physical Distribution Function, Management Report No. 49, New York: American Management Association, 1960.

Managing the Materials Function, Management Report No. 35, New York: American Management Association, 1959.

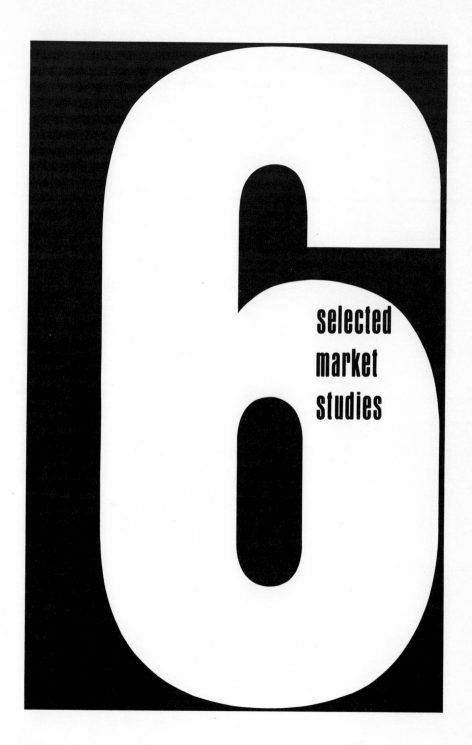

6
selected
market
studies

agricultural and oceanology markets

Both the agricultural and oceanology markets project graphically an implied characteristic of all industrial marketing—a characteristic which was hinted at in the discussion of the foreign flow of capital goods but is much more obvious in either agriculture or oceanology. This characteristic is that in producing and marketing goods and services of an industrial nature, the business units, in turn, represent an industrial market.

The farmer of today, for example, must operate in the dual capacity of marketer and purchaser. As a marketer, he is an initial and vital part of an extremely complex structure which delivers, from over three million farms, products valued at more than $36 billion. As the basic determining element, the farmer is also the key to bringing about any improvement in the efficacy of this structure.

In the role of purchaser the farmer must select from a bewildering array of products—all types of equipment, supplies, fertilizers, chemicals, feeds, seed, and insecticides. Each decision is critical in that it can have a significant effect on yearly earnings. Contingencies such as weather and government action, which are beyond the control of the individual farmer, add to the severity of his purchasing decisions.

With the possible exception of offshore oil wells, the oceanology market of today is predominantly a consumer rather than a dispenser of industrial products. The future potential of the oceanology market should change this condition within the next two decades. For now, however, the market is basically one that supplies the technical means for exploiting the resources to be found in the world's oceans.

AGRICULTURAL MARKETING

The outflow from the agricultural market in the form of either raw materials or supplies is primarily industrial in nature. Using the broadest definition, farm goods which need to be processed or are intended for use as a supply would be classified as industrial. What is meant by processing is subject to some argument. Oranges, for example, are washed and waxed prior to shipment. This would hardly be construed as a process, even if it includes the application of color. On the other hand, oranges which are sold to frozen-juice packers are decidedly raw materials—hence, industrial in nature. Generally, cow's milk is considered a raw material, even when the final product is fluid milk as it is about 45 percent of the time. The reasoning is that any dairy process, even pasteurization or homogenization, brings about a fundamental change in product composition.

The definition of what agricultural goods are industrial in nature can be narrowed by altering the concept of a process. For example, a process may not be considered valid unless it brings about substantial physical change in the product. Such would be the case for either meat packing or flour miling. If this narrow definition is used, approximately 80 percent of farm output can be classified as industrial. Exclusions would include the entire output of vegetable farms (2.5 percent) and fruit and nut farms (4.7 percent), as well as 45 percent of the output of dairy farms (7.1 percent). Therefore, it would seem reasonable to assume that the agricultural market from the standpoint of either input or output has an essentially industrial character.

Structure of the Agricultural Market

The number of farms in the continental United States is steadily decreasing, and the forecasts are that this trend will continue in the foreseeable future. In the period from 1935 to 1964, the number of farms was more than halved, dropping from 6,812,350 to 3,157,857. During the same time, the average farm increased in size by almost 200 acres to about 352 acres. About one-half of the decline in farms and the accompanying increase in average size occurred between 1954 and 1964.

Perhaps the most significant change in the thirty years preceding 1964 has been the increase in farm investment. Indeed, the nation's farms make up its number one industry with assets of nearly $260 billion. The value of buildings and land has swelled ten times per farm and five times per acre (Table 16.1). Present-day capital requirements in machinery and equipment average close to $75,000 for an individual farm with every indication of growing to $100,000 by the early 1970s. An explanation for this upward trend in scale is the desire for volume which, in turn, necessitates large acreage and vast quantities of machinery.

The main item of machinery is the tractor; some 5½ million are in use, or nearly two for every farm. The larger the farm in terms of acreage, the greater is the tendency to have more tractors. In 1964, for example, among farms of 1,000 acres or more, the 134,600 farms with at least one tractor had a total of 529,184, or about five per farm. Conversely, under 100 acres the ratio for farms with tractors was

TABLE 16.1   Value of Land and Buildings for Commercial Farms in the United States, 1935 to 1964

	TOTAL	AVERAGE	
YEAR	(IN MILLIONS)	PER FARM	PER ACRE
1964	$159,931.7	$50,646	$143.81
1959	129,005.4	34,826	115.08
1954	97,582.9	20,405	84.25
1950	75,462.4	14,005	64.97
1945	46,388.9	7,917	40.63
1940	33,788.4	5,532	31.69
1935	32,858.8	4,823	31.16

Source: Adapted from the *Census of Agriculture, 1964—Statistics by Subjects, Chapter 1 Size of Farm,* Washington: Bureau of the Census, 1967, table 3, p. 241.

approximately 1½ tractors per farm. The remainder of the equipment inventory shows an unbelievable 909,691 combines, 751,153 balers, 659,799 corn pickers, and 315,749 harvesters.

Today's farmer relies extensively on agricultural chemicals. Over 800,000 farms report spraying or dusting crops for the control of insects and diseases over 38 million acres. Crops or land treated during 1964 for the control of weeds, grass, and/or brush involved almost 64 million acres. Annually 42 million cattle and 35 million hogs, sheep, and goats are treated for external control of insects.

Roughly one out of every two farms uses some form of commercial fertilizer. Of the nearly 22 million tons consumed in 1964, 90 percent was dry and 10 percent was liquid. The biggest consumers of fertilizer are growers of corn, using one-third of the dry fertilizer and one-half of the liquid fertilizer. The second largest crop for fertilizer consumption is cotton. Heavy users of the 22 million tons of lime or liming materials consumed annually are commercial farms classified as livestock, cash-grain, and dairy.

The total feed bill for livestock and poultry added up to over $5.5 billion in 1964. In Table 16.2, it is apparent that normally less than 50 tons is purchased during the year for a total price which will not exceed $1,000 in two out of every three instances.

This array of statistics demonstrates the seeming insatiability of the farm market for capital goods and supplies. This, in turn, is reflected in a reversing of both labor's and capital's relative input positions (Figure 16.1). Predictions are that capital accumulations will begin to level off. Between 1960 and 1980, capital, real estate, and livestock and machinery are expected to grow at the respective rates

TABLE 16.2   Classification of United States Farms by Dollar Amount and Tonnage of Feed Expenditure, 1964

	COMMERICAL FARMS	
DOLLAR EXPENDITURE	NUMBER	PERCENTAGE OF TOTAL
1 - 199	667,472	29.4
200 - 999	861,003	38.0
1,000 - 1,999	274,425	12.1
2,000 - 4,999	261,371	11.5
5,000 - 9,999	108,482	4.8
10,000 - 19,999	54,837	2.4
20,000 and over	40,652	1.8
TONNAGE		
1 - 49	1,723,531	91.3
50 - 99	80,170	4.2
100 - 199	45,684	2.4
200 - 499	28,231	1.5
500 and over	10,505	0.6

Source: Adapted from *Census of Agriculture, 1964—Statistics by Subjects, Chapter 1 Size of Farm,* Washington: Bureau of the Census, 1967, table 15, p. 274.

of 4, 16, and 13 percent.[1] These rates are considerably below past rates and the projection of future output. In machinery, for example, subsequent purchases are more likely to be replacements than additions. However, the costs will be considerably larger and the productivity greater. Today, there are machines which harvest tomatoes, cube alfalfa, and in a single operation pick and shell peas. Scientists are experimenting with mechanisms to harvest lettuce and shaking-and-catching devices, similar to those already used with certain types of fruit, for such products as apricots and olives. Attempts are even being made to develop strawberry harvesters.

Agricultural output measured in cash receipts increased almost 3½ times between 1920 and 1966. Deflation of cash receipts as shown below reduces this increase to just less than three times. For the principal crops of food grains, feed grains, and oil crops the increase in man-hour productivity during this same period of time was about ten times. The same was true of poultry.

YEAR	VALUE OF CASH RECEIPTS*	ALL FARM PRODUCTS PRICE INDEX (1910-1914 = 100)	DEFLATED CASH RECEIPTS*
1920	$12.6	211	$12.6
1966	42.9	265	34.0

*Billions of dollars.

[1] Earl O. Heady and Luther Tweeten, "Projected Structure of U.S. Agriculture," in Henry Gomez (ed.), *Innovation—Key to Marketing Progress, Proceedings of Forty-sixth National Conference,* Chicago: American Marketing Association, June, 1963, pp. 473-475.

FIGURE 16.1   Percentage Distribution of Agricultural Inputs, 1910–1960.

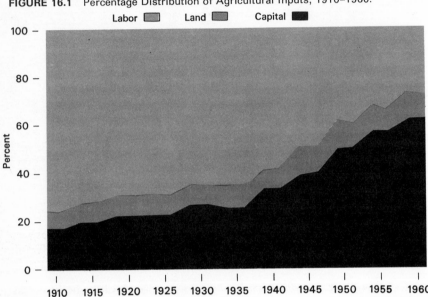

Source: Adapted from Earl O. Heady and Luther Tweeten, "Projected Structure of U.S. Agriculture," in Henry Gomez (ed.), *Innovation—Key to Marketing Progress, Proceedings of Forty-sixth National Conference,* Chicago: American Marketing Association, June, 1963, pp. 473-475.

Today an hour of farm labor produces six times as much as in 1920 and twice as much as in 1955.[2]

Despite the fact that farms are steadily gaining in size, the largest marketers are not always accredited with the biggest share of sales. This is true of three of the more numerous types of farms—dairy, cash-grain, and tobacco. The relative sales importance of the small marketer is most apparent in the case of tobacco farms. Here Economic Class IV farms (annual sales of $5,000 to $9,999) have the largest share, with 29.0 percent of the total value of farm products sold by tobacco farms. The second largest share is accounted for by Class III farms (annual sales of $10,000 to $19,999). Together these two classes sell about 55 percent of the farm products sold by tobacco farms. Among dairy farms, Class III farms market nearly one-third of the total farm products for the largest share. A ranking of states by volume of farm cash receipts shows a drop-off in receipts after California and Iowa as well as a decided reliance on cattle and calves in generating volume. In regard to the latter, cat-

[2] With 1957-1959 as the base period, index numbers of farm output per man-hour were 26 for 1920, 80 for 1955, and 157 for 1966.

TABLE 16.3 The Top Fifteen States in Farm Cash Receipts, 1965

STATE	TOTAL CASH RECEIPTS*	PRINCIPAL PRODUCT AND PERCENTAGE OF TOTAL
California	$3,710.0	Cattle and calves (17.8)
Iowa	3,009.5	Cattle and calves (35.2)
Texas	2,470.3	Cattle and calves (28.1)
Illinois	2,400.6	Corn (24.0)
Minnesota	1,590.3	Cattle and calves (24.9)
Nebraska	1,355.3	Cattle and calves (49.5)
Indiana	1,298.0	Hogs (25.5)
Wisconsin	1,250.0	Dairy products (52.3)
Missouri	1,241.1	Cattle and calves (28.4)
Kansas	1,210.5	Cattle and calves (43.1)
North Carolina	1,189.6	Tobacco (38.3)
Ohio	1,113.4	Dairy products (19.4)
Florida	979.5	Oranges (25.2)
Georgia	945.5	Broilers (21.0)
New York	939.0	Dairy products (51.2)

*Millions of dollars.
Source: U.S. Department of Agriculture.

tle and calves are the most important product for the top three states in cash receipts and seven of the top fifteen states.

Recently there has been a resurgence of business interest in agriculture. This interest has been twofold. In the first place, firms with a proprietary interest in agriculture such as Minute Maid, H. J. Heinz, J. M. Smucker, and Ralston Purina have expanded their activities. Some of the expansion has been in the form of vertical integration backward to the source of supply. As an example, Minute Maid operates a significant number of citrus groves. In another form of activity a supplier integrates forward into a customer segment. In doing this, Ralston Purina has become a major poultry raiser. Vertical integration, whether it is forward or backward, is a major influence in agriculture today. Estimates are that almost all broilers and about 90 percent of the vegetables destined for processing are produced by integrated organizations. Vertical integration has also increased in the production of livestock, sugar beets, nuts, fresh fruits, and turkeys.

Recognizing the potentialities of agriculture, several unrelated firms are engaging in farming operations. Textron, a large conglomerate, is in the poultry business, as is the Gates Rubber Company. The latter is also involved in the growing of sugar beets and cucumbers by irrigation in Colorado. Another company, CBK Industries of Kansas City, has plans to farm at least 1,000 acres.

The merging of business and agriculture into what might be called agribusiness foretokens a new era, one which will see the application of business know-how and money to agricultural problems,

and one too that may see the farmer surrendering his entrepreneur-
ial status for a position in corporate management.

Farms as Industrial Consumers

In the role of an industrial consumer, farms have certain characteristics about which knowledge is vital to those supplying this market. The first and perhaps the most important is the constantly changing internal structure of agriculture. Recognition of such change will
necessarily pervade every decision of the supplier.

A second characteristic is the inferior bargaining position of the
individual farmer in dealing with large suppliers. The purchasing
of farm machinery and equipment is illustrative of this imbalance.
Although there are more than 1,500 manufacturers of farm machinery and equipment, the industry with annual sales of over $3.5 bil-
lion is dominated by a few giants. The two biggest are International Harvester and Deere & Company, both of which have annual sales
of around $900 million. Three other large suppliers are Massey-Fer-
guson, Ltd., J. I. Case, and Allis-Chalmers. The farmer's lack of bargaining strength has led him to join cooperative organizations.

Another characteristic, and one which is possibly an outgrowth
of an inferior bargaining position, is the tendency to shift the responsibility for technical knowledge to the seller. Another reason for this
shift in responsibility is that the farmer, for all practical purposes,
is unable to keep up with agricultural technology. To meet this challenge, suppliers must have specialists to educate the consumer in
all the necessary product-use aspects. Often overlooked is the need
for specialists in the problems associated with a particular region,
such as those dealing with soil and climatic elements.

A fourth characteristic is the trend toward greater segmentation,
which has added to the complexity of the market. One cause has been
a growing tendency toward geographical specialization, examples
of which are poultry in Georgia, citrus products in Florida and south
Texas, rice in Arkansas, and grapes in California. Another cause is
the trend toward specialization in agricultural production rather than
diversification. Today, for example, there is not one formula feed
market but seven highly different market segments. These are (1)
the commercial egg producer, (2) the commercial broilerman, (3)
the commercial turkey grower, (4) the rancher, (5) the cattle feed-
lot operator, (6) the dairyman, and (7) the commercial hogman.[3]

[3] Wren Vinyard, "The Formula Feed Market," in Robert M. Kaplan (ed.), *The Marketing Concept in Action, Proceedings of the 47th National Conference,* Chicago: American Marketing Association, 1964, p. 706.

An erosion of the farm operator's status particularly in regard to decision making is a fifth characteristic. Partially as a result of integration and partially as an outgrowth of membership in a cooperative, an individual farmer has given up his prerogative to choose what to produce, what to buy, and how to use it. Related to this change in status will be the evolution of new ownership patterns. One such arrangement will have the farmer in the dual role of owner-manager, in which he will receive a salary as well as a share of the profits.

A sixth characteristic has to do with the steadily increasing capital and credit needs of the farmer. To illustrate, farm mortgage debt held by selected lenders increased about 75 percent between 1960 and 1966. The predicted growth in the scale of farm operation should accelerate this trend. The credit implications in serving this market are abundantly clear. A marketer must make customer financing an important part of his marketing mix. It is also imperative that the operating financial needs of farms be handled in much the same way as those of any business. Overlapping lines of credit and revolving credit seem to offer the best possibilities at the present time.

The mounting pressures on the prices received for farm produce will cause the farm operator to become highly selective in his purchasing patterns. This, in turn, will squeeze the margins of suppliers, both middlemen and manufacturers. While it is difficult to speculate as to the eventual effects of this price squeeze, it seems safe to say that it will cause a decided change in distribution policies. One doubtful change would be the circumvention of the middlemen. There are just too many farms to be served even in a single market segment. For example, it is unlikely that a manufacturer could market either effectively or efficiently to the more than 15,000 dairy farms with annual cash incomes in excess of $40,000.

Recognizing the essential role of the middlemen, manufacturers will undoubtedly turn their attention toward improving middleman effectiveness and efficiency. The result will be a reduction in the number of middlemen with only the best surviving. In becoming larger, a middleman will tend to specialize in a geographic region rather than a type of farm or a product line. This will allow him to maximize his existing advantages, particularly frequent customer contact and knowledge of local conditions. At the same time, in handling more product lines and a larger volume of goods, his operating costs relative to the sales dollar will be appreciably lower. More lines will also afford the middlemen greater flexibility in pricing and merchandising.

In addition to strengthening their marketing channels, manufacturers will want to take a close look at their products. This will probably involve customer-use product studies and distribution-cost analysis. As John Gillis, Vice-president of Marketing for Monsanto Chemical Company, put it in commenting on the creation of the Agricultural Chemicals Division:

> *Discovering new agricultural chemicals will not be enough for us. Designing plants and making the products will not be enough. Only when our products are channeled into the farmer's hands at reasonable cost . . . and only after the farmer has been shown how to use them profitably . . . will the objective of Monsanto's Agricultural Chemicals Division be fulfilled.*

Farms as Industrial Marketers

Any discussion of agricultural marketing is necessarily a discussion of food marketing. The problems of agricultural marketing are, therefore, inextricably intertwined with the demand for food. The critical decision areas in agricultural marketing can be summarized as follows:

1 *What should be produced and how should it be prepared to promote sales?* Eating habits have tended to shift away from cereal grains and fresh vegetables toward meat products, noticeably beef, poultry products, and frozen vegetables. Within a general food category consumers have displayed a definite preference for certain varieties of a product. For example, the demand for ham is so great that agrotechnicals are experimenting with methods of increasing the portion of the hog from which ham is obtained.

    Preparation for retail sales is becoming increasingly important in agricultural marketing. The implication is either a greater degree of processing or the introduction of processing where none existed previously. In either instance, the volume of industrial trade will be increased: additional processing will require more machinery and equipment; the introduction of processing will increase the volume of agricultural goods which can be classified as raw materials.

2 *What should be done about demand creation?* It has become obvious that agriculture, like the manufacturer of fabricated materials, must bypass the intermediate buyer and concentrate on the retail consumer in expanding demand. Undoubtedly the most common approach has been the organization of cooperative groups to carry out extensive advertising and promotional programs. Cotton farmers, for example, are contributing a fixed fee per bale

to the Cotton Council in an attempt to reverse the shift away from the utilization of cotton in finished fabrics.

3 *How much of the marketing task should be assumed?* This is a decision the farmer must make individually or as a member of a cooperative organization. Basic to any decision about the marketing task, from the simplest such as who is to transport the goods to market to the more complex such as processing and marketing a final product, is the question of whether it will increase the farmer's share of the value generated by his products.

4 *What can be done to adjust supply to demand?* The agricultural community must determine how storage and production can be adjusted to coincide with the demand for products in retail food stores. Not only will this help to stabilize farm prices, but it will take advantage of the demand trend for year-around availability of farm products.

5 *Which of the marketing systems is best?* Because there is so little to base his decision on, the farmer finds it extremely difficult to determine which marketing system is the best for him personally. A possible limiting factor is his inability to cope with what is fundamentally a business problem rather than an agricultural problem. The resulting indecision has slowed the rate of change appreciably. An example is the continued significance of assemblers in certain portions of the United States.

6 *What can be done to correct undesirable marketing practices?* Traditionally, the farmer has sought external help, principally from the federal government. Consequently, much legislation has been enacted, not all of which has achieved its intended purpose. Today, the farmer is looking more and more toward self-help as a better means of accomplishing what is desired.

7 *What is the best way to tap the export markets?* Agricultural exports more than doubled in value during the eleven-year period ending with 1966. This trend plus the seemingly insatiable demand fostered by foreign population growth foretells an ever-increasing export market. To gain profitable entry to this market, farmers must develop means of appraising the various alternative arrangements offered to them.

Cooperative Organizations
The agricultural cooperative organized essentially to perform marketing tasks plays a dominant role in many segments of the agricultural industry. Overall, it is estimated that marketing cooperatives handle

about 20 percent of all the farm commodities sold in the United States and a considerable proportion of the agricultural exports. The proportions of eight commodities which are marketed collectively are shown below:

	PERCENTAGE OF TOTAL
Citrus fruits	60
Butter	58
Milk	45
Grain	40
Rice	30
Apples	25
Cheese	23
Dry beans	20[4]

The dominance of marketing cooperatives cannot always be measured in quantitative terms, however, as witness the market position of such brands as Sun-Maid raisins, Diamond Brand walnuts, Sunsweet prunes, Land-O'Lakes dairy products, and Sunkist oranges.

Marketing cooperatives entered export markets as early as the 1920s. Among the pioneers were cooperatives marketing cotton, citrus fruit, and dried fruit. Two cotton cooperatives, which started exporting in the twenties, are Calcot, Ltd., of Bakersfield, California, which does about 40 percent of its current volume in overseas markets, and Staple Cotton Cooperative Association of Greenwood, Mississippi. Sunkist Growers, Inc., of Los Angeles, California, was the first cooperative to export citrus fruits. A depression at home and bulging productive capacity prompted the largest citrus marketing federation to enter the export market during the 1930s. In 1963, Sunkist exported almost 7 million cartons of fruit. The leading item is lemons, followed by oranges, and then grapefruit. Sunsweet Growers, Inc., of San Jose, California, exports about 25 percent of its dried prunes, apricots, peaches, and pears, mainly to European countries.

Having started export operations before World War II, Land-O'Lakes Creameries, Inc., of Minneapolis, Minnesota, now ships overseas approximately 8 percent of its total sales volume. A large proportion of the exported volume is powdered skim milk. The export market for nonfat dry milk and dry whole milk is important to the Dairymen's League Cooperative Association of New York.

[4] Extracted from unofficial estimates contained in Richard L. Kohls, *Marketing of Agricultural Products,* 2d ed., New York: The Macmillan Company, 1961, table 2, p. 386.

Structure of the marketing cooperative takes several forms. The simplest form is the independent local association. It serves a small area and is limited in the marketing functions it can perform for its members. Usually, a local has only one shipping point. Integration of locals into a larger association is accomplished by either federation or centralization. The difference between the two is that under the federated form, the member belongs to the local which, in turn, is a member of the federated association. In a centralized cooperative, on the other hand, everyone belongs to the centralized organization and exercises control through elected representatives.

Future development of marketing cooperatives is likely to parallel the concepts of Cal-Can (California Canners and Growers). In setting up Cal-Can, the founders believed that cooperation with control of at least 20 percent of the volume, plus good management, production research, public relations, and financing, was a more logical and fruitful way to obtain maximum profits. Components of success are (1) a diversity of products, (2) high volume, (3) efficient, modern low-unit-cost manufacturing plants, (4) aggressive, skilled management of proven ability, and (5) a grower organization willing and able to produce top-quality raw materials.

Structurally, Cal-Can operates in three divisions—production of raw materials, processing (seven canning plants), and marketing. In the first three years, Cal-Can returned to grower members 122 percent, 115 percent, and 117 percent of the commercial value of their raw materials.[5]

An official of one of the nation's giant cooperatives pictures the cooperative of the future as functioning in much the same role as today's Cal-Can. His projections are that:

1   Cooperatives will be called upon to extend the scope of their services, both vertically and horizontally.
2   Cooperatives will undergo organizational changes in order to merge with agricultural-related segments of business.
3   Cooperatives will increase in size.
4   Cooperatives will expand their R&D efforts.
5   Cooperatives will be drawn more and more into the framing of local, state, and national farm policies.

[5] R. R. Mauser, "Coordinating and Integrating Production, Processing, and Marketing in Agriculture—The Cal-Can Story," in George L. Baker, Jr. (ed.), *Effective Marketing Coordination, Proceedings of the Forty-fourth National Conference*, Chicago: American Marketing Association, June, 1961, pp. 43-61.

6   Cooperatives will assume more and more a leadership position in bringing about true industry status in agriculture.[6]

Commodity Exchanges

The importance of commodity exchanges can be traced to the immense volume of raw materials—both agricultural and extractive—which flow through these organized trading facilities. The primary function of an exchange is to make possible the pricing procedure for establishment of a commodity's general or basic price level. The benefit of an organized exchange lies in specialization. What happens is that the exchange brings together the forces of supply and demand for a particular commodity over an extended period of time.[7] This centralized commercial relationship in effect simulates the competitive buying power of total accumulated supply and demand.

The functions of a commodity exchange can be grouped under seven general headings, as follows:

1   Pricing—determined by supply and demand.
2   Protection—lessening of the price risk through hedging.
3   Financing—banking accommodation is afforded.
4   Integrity of contract—credit risk is an inconceivable consideration.
5   Control of speculation—the constructive aspect of speculation is secured; its abuses are curbed.
6   Publicity and information—prices are publicized; vital trade statistics are published.
7   Regulation—uniformity of contracts is assured; inspection, grading, and weighing are supervised and regulated; disputes are settled; rules and regulations are set up and policed.[8]

Two types of traders use exchange facilities—hedgers and speculators. The interest of hedgers is seeking some protection against

[6] J. E. Givens, "Farmer Cooperatives—1980," in Henry Gomez (ed.), *Innovation—Key to Marketing Progress, Proceedings of the Forty-sixth National Conference,* Chicago: American Marketing Association, June, 1963, pp. 488-489.

[7] Reavis Cox, "The Economic Functions of the Commodity Exchanges in a Free Market," *The Problem of the Free Markets and the Role of the Commodity Exchanges in the American Economy, Proceedings of a Symposium,* New York: The Educational Committee of the New York Commodity Exchange, November, 1959, p. 34.

[8] J. A. Higgons, Jr., "The Problem of Free Markets," *The Problem of the Free Markets and the Role of the Commodity Exchanges in the American Economy, Proceedings of a Symposium,* New York: The Educational Committee of the New York Commodity Exchange, November, 1959, p. 10.

unfavorable changes in price. Speculators, on the other hand, wish to profit from changes in price. Typically, trading on a commodity exchange involves two forms of transaction. Cash or spot transactions involve actual commodities which are immediately available for delivery. The normal basis of purchase is a sample of the commodity. Future transactions involve future contracts which require delivery of a commodity described by grade during a stated month in the future. In contrast to cash contracts, futures are highly standardized. For example, the minimum contract for cotton sold through the New York Cotton Exchange is $50,000 or 100 bales. The contract unit set by the London Metal Exchange on copper is 56,000 pounds. The Chicago Board of Trade has set 5,000 bushels for soybeans, 100 tons for soybean meal, and 60,000 pounds for soybean oil.[9]

In addition to minimum quantity, a futures contract has a basic quality in terms of a grade and a designated delivery month. Geographical locations where delivery can be made vary with each exchange. The New York Cotton Exchange has seven official delivery points: Charleston, Galveston, Houston, New Orleans, Mobile, New York, and Savannah.

Another difference between cash and futures transactions is that a report of the latter must be submitted to the clearinghouse at the close of each business day. As an affiliate of the exchange, a clearinghouse simplifies the settlement of member balances by employment of the offsetting principle. With the information supplied by the daily report, the clearinghouse becomes the seller for every buyer, and vice versa. This substitution means that members deal only with the exchange and not the other party to the futures transaction. Members use a settlement price which is usually the day's closing price to determine their net position with the clearinghouse. When a member's purchases exceed his sales, he is said to have an open interest, which must be secured by a specified amount of deposit. The amount of deposit rises and falls according to the amount of open interest.

The legal framework under which commodity exchanges operate is the Commodity Exchange Act passed in 1936 and later amendments. This act created the Commodity Exchange Administration, now called the Commodity Exchange Authority, and gave it broad controls over major commodities in sixteen commodity exchanges specified as contract markets. The major commodities covered are wheat, corn,

---

[9] For a more detailed presentation of facts regarding futures trading, see Theodore N. Beckman and William R. Davidson, *Marketing,* 8th ed., New York: The Ronald Press Company, 1967, table 27-1, pp. 733-735.

oats, barley, rye, flaxseed, cotton, cottonseed meal, cottonseed, grain sorghums, rice, millfeeds, eggs, onions, Irish potatoes, wool, wool tops, peanuts, butter, soybeans, soybean meal, and fats and oils.

The more important controls of the Authority are:

1   Limitations on the daily price movements of individual commodities to prevent unjustified market changes.
2   Limitations on the daily volume of trading by one person. (The one exception is actual hedging transactions.)
3   Preventive measures aimed at protecting the trader in futures from cheating, fraud, and manipulative practices.

Self-regulation is practiced by markets primarily concerned with import commodities, which do not fall under the scope of the Commodity Exchange Act. The operating rules of these "unregulated markets" closely parallel those of "regulated markets." The only difference is that responsibility for administering regulations is vested normally in a group of standing committees which, in turn, are responsible to the board of governors, directors, or managers. The power of "unregulated markets" to enforce self-regulations has been upheld in courts of law.

OCEANOLOGY MARKET

The oceans of the world may indeed be called man's new frontier— a frontier encompassing nearly 70 percent of the earth's surface and so astonishing in its hidden wealth that many insist its economic potential is vastly greater than that of space. For example, it is estimated that suctioning off the deposits found on the surface of a selected square mile of ocean bed would yield 6,000 tons of manganese, 4,000 tons of iron, and 125 tons each of cobalt, copper, and nickel.

Over 300 companies, led by such giants as Bendix, General Dynamics, Litton, North American-Rockwell, and Westinghouse, are directly engaged in oceanology projects. Besides these there are some 700 "outside" firms serving the oceanology market with goods and services. Included in this group are marketers of high-strength steels, anticorrosive compounds, and specialized equipment capable of functioning underwater.

The challenge of the oceans is depth. Men are currently working at depths below 400 feet, but their immediate goal is 1,000 feet. Access to the world's continental shelves at depths of up to 1,000 feet will open up an area roughly equal to the land surface of the African continent.[10] Attainment of a depth of 20,000 feet will reach all but 2 percent of the ocean's bottom. Operational and rescue capabilities at such a depth are the aim of the Navy's Deep Submergence Systems Project. Already Lockheed is building a Deep Submergence Rescue Vehicle (DSRV) large enough for four men.

Depth capabilities of some of the more advanced submersibles are summarized as follows:

NAME	MANUFACTURER	DEPTH CAPABILITY IN FEET
Aluminaut	General Dynamics (Electric Boat Division) and Reynolds Aluminum	15,000
Deep Diver	Perry-Link	1,350
Deep Quest	Lockheed	8,000
Dowb	General Motors (AC Electronics)	6,500
Pisces	International Hydrodynamics Company, Ltd.	4,900

The very vastness of the oceanology market necessitates a cataloging of its branches. These are ocean mining, fish farming, offshore drilling, and saline-water conversion.

Ocean Mining

A great deal of speculation is focused on the ocean mining of minerals. The primary reason is newness—in the type of product, the method of extraction, and the environment. Acceptance of the risks is motivated by the tremendous mineral potential to be found in the world's oceans. Mineral deposits to be found in the oceans can be regionalized as follows:

Marine Beaches: Placer deposits of gold, platinum, diamonds, magnetite, ilmenite, zircon, rutile, columbite, chromite, cassiterite, scheelite, wolframite, monazite, quartz, calcium carbonate, sand, and gravels.

Continental Shelves: Calcareous shell deposits, phosphorite, glauconite, barium sulfate modules, sand, and gravels. Placer deposits in drowned river valleys of tin, platinum, gold, and other minerals.

[10] Mr. Chet Smith, President of Ocean Systems, as quoted in "Business Takes the Deep Plunge," *Business Week,* June 17, 1967, p. 76.

Subsea-floor Rocks: Oil, gas, sulfur, salt, coal, iron ore, and very likely other deposits in veins and other forms as in the rocks in the land.

Seawater: Common salt, magnesium metal, magnesium compounds, bromine, potash, soda, gypsum, and potentially sulfur, strontium, and borax. Potential source of uranium and molybdenum.

Deep-sea Floor: Clays, oozes of a calcareous or siliceous nature, animal remains, zeolities as a source of potash, and manganese modules. The last-named deposit supplies cobalt, copper, nickel, iron, molybdenum, and vanadium, as well as manganese.[11]

Actual mining operations have been undertaken in all of the above regions with the exception of the deep-sea floor. In the Gulf of Mexico, Freeport Sulfur Company is mining sulfur in a molten form from two deposits. One deposit is 1,600 feet below the floor of the Gulf, while the other is slightly deeper, at 1,750 feet. Off the coast of South-West Africa in the vicinity of Chameis Bay, the DeBeers Group is recovering about 1,000 carats of diamonds a day. Approximately 10 million tons of sodium chloride is being taken from the sea by Leslie Salt along the West Coast of the United States, National Bulk Carriers off Baja, California, and other foreign groups. Another fairly large operation throughout the world's oceans is the extraction of limestone shell matter. It is estimated that nearly 10 million tons is mined each year. In seeking out new deposits of minerals, particularly those of an esoteric nature, Australia appears to be a key target area.

Extraction represents a major problem for companies involved in ocean mining today. Not uncommonly the processing facility consumes as much as 80 percent of the capital expenditures. Presently, extraction technology is at the economic threshold for a variety of minerals. The economic status of extraction technology for selected mineral materials is as follows:

Economic: Present Extraction Techniques
Bromine
Magnesium
Potassium chloride
Sodium chloride
Sulfur
Economic: Present Ion-exchange Extraction
Silver
Uranium oxide

---

[11] "Ocean Mining: Here's Where We Stand," *Steel,* May 15, 1967, p. 47.

Possibly Economic: Present Ion-exchange Extraction
Cobalt
Copper
Gold
Molybdenum oxide
Nickel
Tin
Not Economic: Present Conventional Extraction
Borax [12]

For the future, the mining of manganese oxide modules holds tremendous promise. These modules are a source of not only manganese but nickel, copper, and cobalt. They will be found at depths of nearly 10,000 feet, and so present extraction technology must be improved significantly. Some experts estimate it will take at least twenty years to reach full commercialization.

Fish Farming

Many experts feel that the food potential of the world's oceans may go a long way toward solving the Malthusian problems of the population explosion. This is particularly important for underdeveloped nations whose demand for food will all too soon exceed the outflow from conventional agriculture in the more developed nations and the anticipated upgrading of localized agriculture.

In 1964, the total world catch of fish amounted to 114 billion pounds. A large proportion of this catch can be classified as industrial goods in that it is not consumed directly by man. Today, more and more fish are undergoing major processing before reaching the shelves of the local supermarket. Such fish must be considered a raw material. Fish which are processed to make fishmeal and protein concentrate can also be classified as raw materials. It is estimated that 40 percent of the world's catch is used for fishmeal alone. As a high protein source, fishmeal is used in poultry and livestock feeds.

Protein concentrate (85 percent protein) is a white, tasteless, and odorless fish flour. Its greatest potential market seems to be in fighting malnutrition among children in underdeveloped countries. It can be added to foods such as cereals or included in beverages. The cost is surprisingly low. For example, 1 ton of hake yields about 250 pounds of protein, which can be used as a 10-gram daily supplement for thirty people at an annual cost of $2 per person. [13]

[12] *Ibid.,* p. 48.

[13] *Effective Use of the Sea,* Report of the Panel on Oceanography, President's Science Advisory Committee, Washington: Government Printing Office, June, 1966, p. 10.

Fish farming or agriculture faces two enormous problems. The first is restricting the agricultural environment. Fences of bubbles and enemy sounds have been employed, but universality of action is needed. A second problem is controlling the flow of nutrients to simulate deliberate fertilization.

Japan is the world leader in fish farming. However, their efforts have been limited to products of high value such as clams, mollusks, oysters, and shrimp. The Japanese have also pioneered in electric fishing. For the most part, fish farming in the rest of the world has been restricted to isolated experiments.

Offshore Drilling

The main economic impact of the oceanology market has been felt in offshore drilling for oil and gas. Petroleum companies have already invested $6 billion and expect to spend $25 billion in the next ten years. It is estimated that the petroleum industry has invested in and received from their market segment more than the combination of all other industries in oceanology.

Currently, almost 9,000 offshore oil wells are being operated by over a hundred companies in sixty nations. Offshore drilling produces 5 million barrels a day or 15 percent of the free world's daily output.

Investment in explorations and operations consumes many millions of dollars annually. A total of almost $50 million is being added to Canada's offshore oil industry by separate ventures being undertaken by Shell Canada, Ltd., and Mobil Oil of Canada. This combined investment is especially significant when it is compared with an accumulation of $20 million for previous years. On the other side of the Atlantic, North Sea explorations by seventy companies and sixty nations will eventually cost more than $200 million.

The foregoing examples of an upsurge in activity give the impression that offshore drilling is rather youthful. On the contrary, Humble Oil established its first well twenty years ago off the Louisiana coast. Offshore leases were being negotiated as long ago as 1935 by petroleum companies in the Gulf of Mexico off Texas.

In addition to petroleum companies, two other types of firm play a vital marketing role in the offshore drilling segment. One is a contract drilling service company. There are three prominent firms providing this physical service—Globol Marine, Inc., Reading and Bates Offshore Drilling, and Zapata Offshore. The other type of marketer provides an advisory service, namely geophysical and science studies. Examples of such firms are Alpine Geophysics Association,

E.G.G. (Edgeton, Geimeshousen, and Grier), Raytheon, and Texas Instruments.

Depth is the challenge in offshore drilling as it is in mining. Ocean drilling expenses may run thirty times greater than those on land, with giant rigs costing as much as $10 million. The deepest water depth at which a well has been drilled is 632 feet. In accomplishing this feat, Humble Oil made extensive studies of wave action and force, ocean currents, and the ocean bottom.[14] Dr. Charles F. Jones, president of Humble Oil and Refining Company, expressed the urgent need for research in these words:

> Our experiences in offshore work have convinced us that the sea is a challenging and hostile environment that offers little security, but a lot of opportunity. As different industries turn to the sea, they will find themselves faced with new sets of conditions to be handled. The oceans will challenge the imagination and creativity of businessmen. Wholly new concepts will be needed. Industry must make the sea swirl with innovation if its potential is to be harnessed.[15]

Saline-water Conversion

Water is as vital to the world as food. Desalination of our oceans could go a long way toward sustaining our present population and its expected growth as well as bringing life to the barren reaches of the world. It has been speculated that economical desalination would open up such a vast portion of the earth's surface that the diversion of energies to this new frontier would help solve many of our existing problems.

The problem in saline-water conversion is prohibitive cost. Despite a significant reduction in costs from $5 per thousand gallons in the late forties to a present rate of somewhere around $1 per thousand gallons, the level is still too high for commercial use. What is needed is a breakthrough to 20 cents per thousand gallons. It is hoped that this will be made an actuality by the $444 million plant to be built on a man-made island off the coast of southern California. It is expected that this plant will produce 150 million gallons of fresh water a day for 22 cents per thousand gallons. However, this daily output is not nearly enough to sustain a city the size of either San Francisco or Boston.

[14] Charles F. Jones, "High Tides for Business," *New Wealth from the Seas,* New York: National Association of Manufacturers, 1966, p. 18.

[15] *Ibid.*

Another plus, which may help to defray the costs of desalination, is the possible by-products from the sludge which develops as fresh water is brought out of the sea. Undoubtedly, this sludge would be high in mineral content. It could also be used as a source of salt. About ¼ pound of salt can be extracted from 1 gallon of sea water.

Oceanology Projects

A great deal of information is available on the individual roles of United States corporations in oceanology from a study made by *International Science and Technology,* a publication of Conover-Mast Publications, Inc.[16] Classification by amount of annual expenditure in oceanology shows seventeen firms spending over $10 million and eight firms spending about $10 million. Of these twenty-five firms, sixteen or approximately two-thirds, are interested in all three major fields of designated interest—major systems, hardware, and services to include R&D. The other nine are active in hardware and services to include R&D.

ANNUAL EXPENDITURE	NUMBER OF FIRMS
More than $10 million	17
About $10 million	8
Less than $10 million	73

Involvement was keyed to nine categories of goods and services. The firm having the most categories of heavy involvement was North American-Rockwell with four. Lockheed, another aerospace contractor, is extensively involved in three areas. The following shows the pattern of concentration in goods and services for the oceanology market:

CATEGORY OF GOOD OR SERVICE	FIRMS INVOLVED	
	IN ALL AREAS OF CATEGORY	IN MOST AREAS OF CATEGORY
Communications	4	21
Test and analysis	7	15
Survey and research	4	12
Large components	0	16
Structures	0	16
Research vehicles	3	5
Instruments	1	3
Man-in-the-sea	0	3
Heavy construction	0	2

[16] *International Science and Technology,* April, 1967, pp. 58-59.

The number of firms supplying the two advisory services of test and analysis and survey and research is testimony to the comparative newness of the oceanology market. It is also reasonable to expect that the evolutionary character of this market will last for several years. Therefore, firms supplying or possessing adaptable advisory services are the most likely to enter the market.

SUMMARY

Both the agricultural and oceanology markets illustrate dramatically the dual-market character of industrial markets. This is because in producing and distributing industrial goods and services, business units in turn represent an industrial market. The farmer, for example, is both a marketer and a purchaser of industrial goods and services.

What farm goods can be labeled industrial depends upon the definition of processing. The broader the definition of processing, the greater the proportion of farm output which can be classified as industrial. If processing is construed as bringing about a substantial physical change, approximately 80 percent of farm output is industrial.

America's farms make up its number one industry with assets totaling some $260 million. A significant change in agriculture has been the steady reduction in the number of farms coupled with an increase in average size. The seemingly insatiable demand for capital goods and supplies is reflected in the reversing of the relative input positions of labor and capital.

In the forty-six years between 1920 and 1966, cash receipts for agricultural goods increased 3½ times in current dollars, almost 3 times in constant dollars. Man-hour productivity has increased 6 times since 1920, doubled since 1955. Farms which are the largest marketers may not have the largest portion of sales. This is true of dairy, cash-grain, and tobacco farms. Vertical integration, whether it is forward or backward, is a major influence in marketing farm products.

Selling goods and services to today's farm necessitates a knowledge of certain characteristics. These can be listed as follows:

1 The constantly changing internal structure of agriculture
2 The inferior bargaining position of the individual farmer
3 The tendency to shift the responsibility for technical knowledge to the seller
4 The trend toward greater segmentation

5   The erosion of the farm operator's status in regard to decision making
6   The increasing need for capital
7   The tendency for greater selectivity in purchasing
8   The strengthening of middlemen rather than their circumvention

The problems of agricultural marketing are intertwined with the demand for food:

1   What should be produced and how should it be prepared to promote sales?
2   What should be done about demand creation?
3   How much of the marketing task should be assumed?
4   What can be done to adjust supply to demand?
5   Which of the marketing systems is best?
6   What can be done to correct undesirable marketing practices?
7   What is the best way to tap the export markets?

In many segments of the agricultural industry such as citrus fruits, butter, and milk, the marketing cooperative plays a dominant role. This dominance may be measured quantitatively or qualitatively. Cooperatives have not restricted their activities to the domestic market. As early as the 1920s cooperatives were involved in export operations.

In the future, cooperatives will likely expand the scope of their operations, increase their size, and merge with agricultural-related businesses. Other possible changes in the future are an expansion of R&D efforts, the framing of farm policies to be enacted by governmental units, and a leadership position in agriculture.

The importance of commodity exchanges is attributable to the immense volume of raw materials which flows through these organized trading facilities. The normal functions of a commodity exchange are as follows: (1) pricing, (2) protection, (3) financing, (4) integrity of contract, (5) control of speculation, (6) publicity and information, and (7) regulation. Two types of traders—speculators and hedgers—use exchange facilities. Transactions are either cash or futures. "Regulated exchanges" are governed by the Commodity Exchange Authority under provisions of the Commodity Exchange Act of 1936. "Nonregulated exchanges" practice self-regulation.

The oceans of the world as man's newest frontier have an unbelievable potential. Their hidden wealth has led many firms, both large and small, to enter the oceanology market. The challenge of the oceans is depth.

The branches of the oceanology market can be classified under four general headings. The first is the highly speculative mining of the ocean minerals. The primary reason for speculation is newness—in the type of product, the method of extraction, and the environment. A second branch is fish farming. The two problems here are restricting the environment and controlling the flow of nutrients to simulate deliberate fertilization. Offshore drilling for oil and gas is the third branch. It is estimated that the investment plus outflow from offshore drilling is greater than the combination of all other industries in oceanology. In addition to petroleum companies, two other types of firm play a vital marketing role in offshore drilling. One is a contract drilling service, and the other is the advisory service of geophysical and seismic studies.

Desalination of oceans is the fourth and final branch. The major obstacle is prohibitive costs. It is hoped that the by-products of desalination such as the mineral sludge and salt will help defray the costs.

Typically, a firm in the oceanology market will spend less than $10 million annually. Product categories of heavy involvement are communications, test and analysis, and survey and research. The two service categories attest to the comparative newness of oceanology—a newness which will probably last for several years.

DISCUSSION QUESTIONS?

1 Describe the dual functioning of the industrial market.
2 Compare the farm of today with the one of yesterday.
3 What is the basis for classifying agricultural goods as raw materials?
4 What types of business have shown interest in the agricultural market?
5 In marketing to the farm market, what customer characteristics should suppliers be aware of?
6 Certain questions need to be asked by the marketers of farm products. What are they and how can they be satisfactorily answered?
7 How can the future development of the marketing cooperative be characterized?
8 Explain how the functioning of commodity exchanges can be justified from an economic viewpoint.

9   Describe the regulative controls imposed on commodity exchanges.
10   Describe in detail the current status of each of the four branches of the oceanology market.
11   What information is there that the oceanology market is still in the pioneering stages?

SUPPLEMENTARY READINGS

Beckman, Theodore N., and William R. Davidson, *Marketing*, 8th ed., New York: The Ronald Press Company, 1967, chap. 27, pp. 723-759.

Kohls, Richard L., *Marketing of Agricultural Products*, 2d ed., New York: The Macmillan Company, 1961, chaps. 2 and 3.

Mero, John L., *The Mineral Resources of the Sea*, London: Elsevier, 1965.

New Wealth from the Seas, New York: National Association of Manufacturers, 1966.

Panel on Oceanography, President's Science Advisory Committee, *Effective Use of the Sea*, Washington: Government Printing Office, June, 1966.

The Problem of the Free Markets and the Role of the Commodity Exchanges in the American Economy, New York: Educational Committee of the New York Commodity Exchange, November, 1959.

Shepard, Geoffrey S., *Marketing Farm Products*, 4th ed., Ames: The Iowa State University Press, 1962, chaps. 1, 2, 7, and 8.

Thomsen, Frederick Lundy, *Agricultural Marketing*, New York: McGraw-Hill Book Company, 1951, chaps. 1-4 and 20-22.

U.S. Department of Agriculture, *Farmer's World, Yearbook of Agriculture*, Washington: Government Printing Office, current edition.

the
defense
market

Government agencies represent by far the largest customer in the industrial market. Reference to Table 1.4 in Chapter 1 shows that the size of the government segment is staggering. Overall, government purchases of goods and services amounted to $136 billion in 1965. By 1966, this had risen to $154 billion, equally divided between the federal government and state and local agencies.

Any estimate of the swelling of these figures by the multiplier effect emphasizes the importance of the vital economic role played by the government. As an example, subcontracts accounted for 62 percent of the dollar volume of a $1 billion defense contract awarded in 1961 to Lockheed for the C-141 transport. Lockheed made direct contracts with 1,200 companies, of which 33 were major suppliers. The subcontracting did not stop with Lockheed and the first-level suppliers. The Rohr Corporation, one of the prominent first-level suppliers, subcontracted 49 percent of the $85.9 million it received for C-141 engine containers. These suppliers, in turn, subcontracted 40 percent to companies on a third level of suppliers.

The Convair division of General Dynamics, in this instance a major supplier of the tail assembly, spread out its $43.2 million through three more supplier levels. About 25 percent was paid by Convair to the second level. Third-level suppliers earned 20 percent of what the second level received, and the fourth level got 10 percent of the third level's share.

United Aircraft, which did about 63 percent of its 1966 business with the government, placed orders worth $1,359.3 million for delivery in 1966 and later with vendors in forty-seven states and the District of Columbia.[1] Seventy-six percent of the suppliers were classified as small business on the basis of employing fewer than 500 persons. A listing of the top ten states in terms of contract volume is as follows:

Connecticut	$349.1
Ohio	194.2
Pennsylvania	114.7
New York	113.1
Michigan	96.8
Massachusetts	96.0
Indiana	89.3
New Jersey	81.7
Wisconsin	45.6
Texas	43.7

When aggregate government spending is broken down by major category, the Department of Defense emerges as the most important

[1] Extracted from the *1966 Annual Report United Aircraft*, p. 22.

government buyer. The Department of Defense spent around $50 billion in each of the years from 1961 to 1965. In 1966, the requirements of the Vietnam War pushed this to more than $60 billion. To sustain Southeast Asia commitments, a supplemental defense budget for fiscal 1967 showed procurement would be upped approximately $6.3 billion. This total was subdivided as follows:[2]

		MILLIONS OF DOLLARS
Aircraft:		
Combat attrition	1,525	
Training and other	439	
Spares	996	
Other aircraft equipment	775	3,735
Ammunition		677
Vehicles		506
Electronics and communications		581
All other procurement		840
Total		6,339

IMPACT OF DEFENSE EXPENDITURES

The significant effect of defense expenditures can be traced in terms of geographical areas and business institutions. Such an analysis allows a better assessment of the economic spin-off from defense spending.

Geographical Distribution

The sharing of the defense dollar by states is highly disproportionate. This is reflected in terms of contracts and employment. California, for example, receives the lion's share of both prime contracts and subcontracts. The measures of economic impact for California are two to three times greater than those reported for New York, the second leading state. The greater importance of California in subcontracts than in prime contracts furnishes evidence of the tendency for suppliers to cluster like satellites around major industrial buyers. To explain this somewhat further, prime contracts may be awarded to firms or divisions outside the state of California, but much of the subcontracting must be done with California firms because this is where a substantial portion of suppliers are located.

[2] Edward H. Kolcum, "Viet Requirements Boost Budget," *Aviation Week & Space Technology,* Jan. 30, 1967, p. 23.

TABLE 17.1 Ten States Ranked by Defense Prime Contracts and Subcontracts

| STATE | DEFENSE PRIME CONTRACTS | | | | SPECIAL DEFENSE SUBCONTRACT STUDY‡ | | SUBCONTRACTS IN EIS PLANTS§ | |
| | AWARDS* | | EMPLOYMENT† | | | | | |
	RANK	PERCENTAGE OF U.S.	RANK	PERCENTAGE OF U.S.	RANK	PERCENTAGE OF U.S.	RANK	PERCENTAGE OF U.S.
California	1	22.1	1	18.6	1	30.2	1	25.9
New York	2	9.6	2	7.3	2	11.5	2	14.3
New Jersey	9	3.5	9	3.8	3	7.0	4	6.2
Ohio	8	3.7	6	4.8	4	6.0	7	4.4
Connecticut	4	5.1	3	6.0	5	5.6	5	5.2
Pennsylvania	7	4.2	5	4.8	6	5.1	11	2.8
Massachusetts	5	5.1	7	4.7	7	4.2	3	6.4
Florida	11	2.7	10	3.6	8	2.9	8	3.7
Texas	3	6.2	4	5.6	9	2.9	6	4.6
Illinois	17	1.8	13	2.6	10	2.8	18	1.2
Total	..	64.0	..	61.8	..	78.2	..	74.7

*Based on prime contracts in fiscal year 1965.

†Employment on prime contracts as reported by Economic Information System plants.

‡Based on dollars of subcontract awards received.

§Based on June 1966 employment generated by defense subcontracts received by EIS plants.

Source: Adapted from Vernon M. Buehler, "Economic Impact of Defernse Programs," *Statistical Reporter*, no. 68 - 1, July, 1967, table 8, p. 8.

TABLE 17.2 Percentage Distribution of EIS-surveyed Defense Employment by Region and Product Group, June 1966

	DEFENSE PRODUCT GROUPING								
REGION	AIRCRAFT	MISSILES AND SPACE	SHIPS	VEHICLES AND WEAPONS	AMMO	ELECTRONICS AND COMMUNICATION	RDT&E	OTHER	TOTAL
Pacific	15.6	55.0	18.4	12.1	8.5	28.6	68.7	41.5	26.5
Middle Atlantic	13.8	4.1	0.9	7.6	7.7	29.3	9.6	6.7	14.7
New England	16.6	5.7	36.8	24.6	3.5	12.1	6.0	15.3	14.1
South Atlantic	10.4	18.5	28.1	11.2	1.8	11.9	12.1	13.5	12.4
West North Central	15.3	0.7	0.0	9.4	31.8	6.1	0.0	0.0	10.3
East North Central	12.6	1.9	3.7	35.0	19.5	7.0	3.5	12.6	9.5
West South Central	12.1	1.2	1.6	0.0	12.7	3.8	0.0	5.9	6.8
East South Central	2.9	1.4	10.5	0.0	14.0	0.0	0.0	4.2	3.3
Mountain	1.0	11.6	0.0	0.0	0.4	1.0	0.0	0.0	2.6
U.S. Total*	100.0	100.0	100.0	100.0	100.0	100.0	100.0	100.0	100.0
Actual employment (000)	304.5	136.4	65.5	22.3	71.1	228.1	11.5	11.8	851.2

*May not add to 100.0 percent because of rounding.

Source: Adapted from Vernon M. Buehler, "Economic Impact of Defense Programs," *Statistical Reporter*, no. 68-1, July, 1967, table 6, p.7.

Table 17.2 shows the geographical pattern of defense spending by both region and product category. The Pacific region, the largest in terms of defense-generated employment, is particularly significant in the two categories of missiles and space, and research, development, testing, and evaluation. The table also shows that aircraft makers are by far the largest employer in EIS-surveyed plants. Indeed, four out of ten workers in EIS-surveyed plants are aircraft workers.

Another measure of the economic impact of defense dollars is the concept of defense dependency. This concept is defined as the amount of defense-generated employment relative to the civilian labor force in a defined area, usually a state.[3] In June of 1966, the average defense dependency for a state was 3.0 percent. Twenty-two states and the District of Columbia had 3.0 percent or greater dependency. Alaska registered the greatest dependency with 9.7 percent, followed by Utah, Hawaii, the District of Columbia, and Virginia. California, with by far the largest amount of defense-generated employment, was ranked eighth with a dependency of 5.4 percent.

Idaho has the least dependency with only 0.03 percent of its work force attributable to defense generation. In all, seven states have a dependency of less than 1 percent. These states, in order of declining dependence, are Wyoming, Oregon, Iowa, Wisconsin, South Dakota, Montana, and Idaho.

Institutional Distribution

There has been a steady decline in the share of business done by the top defense contractors over the period from fiscal 1958 to fiscal 1966.[4] This continued dilution of market concentration among the top ten contractors was not noticeably felt by the top hundred contractors until fiscal 1965.

Listing of the top fifteen prime defense contractors for each of three fiscal years shows that membership in this select group has remained fairly constant (Table 17.3). Of the top fifteen in 1966, ten were in the top fifteen during 1965, and nine were among the top fifteen during 1964. Only two companies, Lockheed and General Dynamics, were able to hold a position within the top five over the entire three-year

---

[3] Defense-generated employment included employment in 387 EIS plants, all other prime plants, and civil service employment at DOD installations. Data on defense dependency were extracted from Vernon M. Buehler, "Economic Impact of Defense Programs," *Statistical Reporter*, no. 68-1, July, 1967, table 5, p. 5.

[4] "Defense Department Lists 100 Top Contractors," *Aviation Week & Space Technology*, Apr. 12, 1965, Dec. 20, 1965, and Dec. 12, 1966, appropriate pages.

TABLE 17.3   Ranking and Dollar Value of Prime Contracts for Major Defense Contractors, Fiscal Years 1964, 1965, and 1966

	FISCAL 1966		FISCAL 1965		FISCAL 1964	
COMPANY	RANK	MILLIONS OF $	RANK	MILLIONS OF $	RANK	MILLIONS OF $
Lockheed Aircraft Corp.	1	1,531.0	1	1,715.0	1	1,455.4
General Electric Co.	2	1,187.0	4	824.3	6	892.6
United Aircraft Corp.	3	1.138.7	6	632.1	8	625.4
General Dynamics Corp.	4	1,136.0	2	1,178.6	5	986.7
Boeing Co.	5	914.5	8	583.3	2	1,365.2
McDonnell Aircraft Corp.	6	722.2	3	855.8	3	1,157.4
American Telephone & Telegraph Co.	7	672.1	7	587.6	7	635.6
Textron, Inc.	8	554.8	27	195.7	26	216.3
Raymond International, Inc.	9	547.9				
North American Aviation, Inc.	10	520.4	5	745.8	4	1,019.5
General Motors Corp.	11	508.0	19	254.4	19	255.8
Avco	12	506.0	21	234.2	16	278.7
Kaiser Industries Corp.	13	441.4	23	218.8	34	151.7
Ford Motor Co.	14	439.6	12	312.0	27	211.2
Sperry Rand Corp.	15	426.8	10	318.4	12	373.9

Source: "Defense Department Lists 100 Top Contractors," *Aviation Week & Space Technology,* Apr. 12, 1965, Dec. 20, 1965, and Dec. 12, 1966.

period. Lockheed maintained a position of first, while General Dynamics was ranked fourth, second, and fifth.

The most noticeable jump in rankings was recorded by Kaiser Industries. By almost tripling its volume of prime contracts, this firm moved from thirty-fourth to twenty-third, and finally to thirteenth. North American, in losing one-half of its dollar volume of prime contracts between 1964 and 1966, dropped from fourth to fifth to tenth. Another important point is that in 1964 and 1966 each of four firms had a prime contract volume exceeding $1 billion. In 1965, on the other hand, only two firms had contracts totaling $1 billion or more.

Fiscal 1967 saw several changes in the rankings. Of the top fifteen contractors in fiscal 1966, twelve were to be found in this select grouping for 1967. The newcomers were Ling-Temco-Vought, Inc., Grumman Aircraft Engineering Corp., and Westinghouse Electric Corp. They replaced Avco Corp., Kaiser Industries Corp., and Ford Motor Co. The merger in early 1967 of McDonnell Aircraft Corp. and Douglas Aircraft Co. made this company the number one prime contractor. Lockheed, which had been first, dropped to third although its dollar volume was considerably more than in fiscal 1966. The provision of funds for the F-111 variable-geometry fighter helped General Dynamics Corp. move from fourth to second in the rankings. Each of the top five defense contractors in fiscal 1967 received contracts in excess of $1 billion.

Another view of the economic impact of the defense dollar can be obtained by looking at the sales structures of individual companies.[5] The sales of Lockheed, one of the nation's foremost prime contractors, were substantially to the government. In 1966, only $110 billion, or 5 percent of total sales, went to commercial market segments. Commercial sales in 1965 were considerably smaller, amounting to about 3 percent of total sales.

Among the other firms which depend upon defense dollars for at least one-half of their sales are General Dynamics, Collins Radio, United Aircraft, and Martin Marietta. For example, 1966 saw 78 percent of General Dynamics' sales delivered to government services and agencies. This 78 percent was broken down into four major categories as follows: aircraft, 37 percent; marine (including both surface ships and submarines), 20 percent; tactical (including missiles, electronic and support equipment), 10 percent; and space vehicles and support activities, 11 percent.

United Aircraft, a firm which has advanced recently in prime-contract rankings, has nonetheless decreased appreciably its dependence on government sales. Starting in 1962, United Aircraft reduced its dependence by 20 percent over a four-year period. Such was the growth in overall company sales, however, that actual deliveries to the government during this period of time increased over $136 million or about 15 percent.

Thus, the majority of defense business is concentrated among large firms measured in terms of dollar sales and employment. Additional evidence of this is contained in a report published by Arthur D. Little, Inc. It shows that the amount of defense business undertaken by establishments employing fewer than 500 persons is a little less than 2 percent of all United States manufacturing sales.[6] This is extremely small when compared with the 50 percent share of all manufacturing shipments by segments of this size as reported by the *1963 Census of Manufacturing.*

Smaller businesses, however, do have a role in defense marketing, as shown by the plant and employment data compiled by the Economic Information System (EIS).[7] Of the 387 defense plants surveyed by EIS, 192 or 50 percent were under 1,000 in defense employment. These 192 plants, averaging about 473 defense workers each, ac-

---

[5] Information on individual companies was extracted from their annual reports for 1966.
[6] *How Sick Is the Defense Industry?* Cambridge, Mass.: Arthur D. Little, Inc., 1963, p. 15.
[7] Vernon M. Buehler, *op. cit.,* p. 3.

counted for slightly more than 10 percent of total EIS-surveyed employment. For the other 17,000 or so plants receiving prime-contract awards, a breakdown of employment by size of plant, based on Census workers-per-shipment ratios, is shown in Table 17.4.

The role of small business might be better described in terms of subcontracting rather than prime contracting. Lockheed, for example, placed $377 million or 32 percent of all outside purchases with small business firms. Boeing estimates that 74 percent of the firms it deals with directly are small businesses by virtue of having fewer than 500 employees. For the R&D work on the Safeguard antiballistic missile, it is estimated that 12,000 of the 15,000 contractors involved were small businesses. Undoubtedly, the greater proportion of these small businesses functioned as subcontractors.

SEGMENTS OF THE DEFENSE MARKET

Segments of the defense market can be described in three different ways. One way to differentiate the market is by customer grouping. A second way is by type of product, and a third is on the basis of whether the award is a prime contract or subcontract.

Type of Military Customer
There are three principal customers of military goods and services— the Air Force, the Army, and the Navy. The assigned roles and missions of each branch set up their particular purchasing requirements.

Forecasts made prior to the Vietnam War predicted a continuation

TABLE 17.4 Number of Plants and Defense-generated Employment among Prime Contractors Supplying Manufactured Goods, June 1966

PLANT SIZE IN TERMS OF DEFENSE EMPLOYMENT	PLANTS		EMPLOYMENT		AVERAGE EMPLOYMENT
	NUMBER	PERCENT	NUMBER*	PERCENT	
0-99 workers	16,582	95.8	127.9	36.9	77
100-199	401	2.3	56.3	16.3	140
200-299	151	0.9	36.5	10.5	242
300-399	69	0.4	23.4	6.7	339
400 or more	104	0.6	102.2	29.6	983
Total	17,307	100.0	346.3	100.0	200

*In thousands.

Source: Adapted from Vernon M. Buehler, "Economic Impact of Defense Programs," *Statistical Reporter,* no. 68-1, July, 1967, table 3, p. 3.

of the post-Korean trend of a bigger share of the defense dollar for the Air Force and lessening shares for both the Army and the Navy. The basis of this trend was a reshaping of military thinking that emphasized the strategic as opposed to the tactical concepts of modern warfare. In 1951, the Army received the largest share (38 percent) of the combined budget for three services. This dropped to about 25 percent in 1956 and remained around this figure from 1961 until the Vietnam buildup reflected in the 1966 budget.

The dominant customer role of the Air Force has progressively lessened from a high of 46 percent in fiscal 1961 to a little more than 35 percent in 1968. The needs of the Vietnam War have also brought about an additional emphasis on tactical aircraft procurement for the Air Force. With their appropriation increased roughly $10 billion between 1961 and 1968, the Navy has been able to maintain a fairly constant 30 percent share of the combined budget.

The primary authority and responsibility for procurement rests with the Secretary of Defense. Authority for procurement is delegated to the Assistant Secretary of Defense for Supply and Logistics. This official recommends to the Secretary of Defense how contracting responsibilities should be assigned among the three branches. He also acts as a coordinator to reduce unnecessary duplication of effort and expenditures among the three services.

The organization of the actual contracting function differs by branch of service. The Army uses a decentralized system. Seven technical services perform the actual job of purchasing from forty-three offices located in twenty-four different cities in sixteen states. The Air Force,

TABLE 17.5 Dollar and Percentage Distribution of the Combined Budget for the Air Force, the Army, and the Navy, Fiscal Years 1961 to 1968

BRANCH OF SERVICE	1961	1962	1963	1964	1965	1966	1967	1968
				IN BILLIONS OF DOLLARS				
Air Force	19.8	20.2	21.0	20.6	20.1	24.3	25.5	26.0
Army	10.1	12.9	12.2	12.8	12.7	19.1	23.6	24.7
Navy	12.2	15.1	15.1	14.9	15.3	20.0	22.0	22.4
Total	42.1	48.2	48.3	48.3	48.1	63.4	71.1	73.1
			PERCENTAGE OF COMBINED SERVICE BUDGET					
Air Force	47.0	41.9	43.4	42.7	41.8	38.4	35.9	35.6
Army	24.0	26.8	25.3	26.5	26.4	30.1	33.2	33.8
Navy	29.0	31.3	31.3	30.8	31.8	31.5	30.9	30.6
Total	100.0	100.0	100.0	100.0	100.0	100.0	100.0	100.0

Source: Adapted from the budget data contained in the Defense Financial Summary, *Aviation Week & Space Technology,* Jan. 30, 1967, p. 26.

on the other hand, centralizes its procurement in the Air Materiel Command. This Command, located at Dayton, Ohio, is charged with furnishing logistics support for the Air Force on a worldwide basis. Procurement of aircraft is centered at Dayton, Ohio. Procurement of other major items is divided between the Air Materiel Command Headquarters and eight Air Materiel areas. Naval procurement is partially centralized. Purchasing operations are handled by bureaus and agencies located in Washington, D.C., as well as by strategically located field establishments.

Procurement may be accomplished through a coordinated arrangement among the three services. One type is known as Single-Service Procurement. Under this arrangement, a branch of service agency, which has a predominant interest and also experience in purchasing a particular product, buys this product for all three services. The designated agency devotes itself exclusively to purchasing and does not set up requirements, manage inventories, or control issues. Examples of commodity assignments under such an arrangement include:

Autos and trucks—Army Ordnance Corps
Coal—Navy Bureau of Supplies and Accounts
Hand tools—Navy Bureau of Supplies and Accounts
Lumber—Army Corps of Engineers
Paint—Navy Bureau of Supplies and Accounts
Photographic equipment—Air Force Air Material Command

Another type of coordinated procurement is labeled a Single Manager. A Single Manager is a centralized agency which operates under the guidance of one of the service secretaries. Staffed by members from all three services, the agency's duties include the assembly of purchasing requirements, procurement, inventory management, and the issuance of specific supply items or services. The purpose in creating a Single Manager assignment is to eliminate overlapping and duplication of purchasing effort for common-use items. Examples of centralized agencies functioning under the Single Manager concept are:

Military Petroleum Supply Agency
Military Subsistence Supply Agency
Military Medical Supply Agency
Military Clothing and Textile Supply Agency
Military Air Transportation Service
Military Sea Transportation Service
Military Traffic Management Agency

Type of Product

Visualization of the military market in terms of product type is perhaps the most common approach to segmentation. The popularity of the product approach is due in part to the fact that it allows greater precision in pinpointing military demand. Another reason is the traditional product orientation of industrial marketers.

The procurement mix of selected hard goods is shown in Table 17.6. The most obvious shift is the increase in appropriation for missiles between 1955 and 1960. Another noticeable change in this period is the growth in expenditures for electronics and communication. Both of these increases were partially absorbed by a lessening in the aircraft appropriation.

Frost & Sullivan, Inc., a recognized marketing organization which collects and analyzes information on defense contract awards, uses twelve major product categories. These are aircraft; missiles and space; meteorological systems and subsystems; navigation; data processing; electronic warfare; chemical warfare; communication; services; vehicles, ordnance, and vessels; basic research; and mis-

TABLE 17.6   Procurement of Selected Major Hard Goods, Department of Defense, 1955, 1960, 1962 through 1965

MAJOR HARD GOOD	YEAR ENDING JUNE 30					
	1955	1960	1962	1963	1964	1965
	MILLIONS OF DOLLARS					
Aircraft	8,804	6,272	6,400	6,309	6,053	5,200
Missiles	604	3,027	3,442	3,817	3,577	2,096
Ships	944	1,744	1,906	2,522	2,078	1,713
Ordnance, vehicles, and related equipment	1,191	433	1,137	1,665	1,597	1,309
Electronics and communication	441	1,093	1,139	1,427	1,264	897
Other	854	755	507	891	782	625
Total	12,838	13,324	14,531	16,631	15,351	11,840
	PERCENTAGE					
Aircraft	68.6	47.0	44.0	37.9	39.4	43.9
Missiles	4.7	22.7	23.7	22.9	23.4	17.7
Ships	7.4	13.1	13.2	15.2	13.5	14.5
Ordnance, vehicles, and related equipment	9.3	3.2	7.8	10.0	10.4	11.0
Electronics	3.4	8.2	7.8	8.6	8.2	7.6
Other	6.6	5.8	3.5	5.4	5.1	5.3
Total	100.0	100.0	100.0	100.0	100.0	100.0

Source: Report of U.S. Committee on Economic Impact of Defense and Disarmanent, July, 1965.

CHAPTER SEVENTEEN   THE DEFENSE MARKET   **435**

cellaneous components and subassemblies. Each of these major categories is further subdivided to provide greater detail. For example, the data processing category is divided as follows:

Complete systems
Computers
   General purpose, analog—digital
Other systems
   Storage
   Peripheral
   Data conversion and display
Data processing services
   (Software)

Probably the best way to segment the defense market is through use of a dual classification of system-product types by customer. With such a dual classification, the size of various segments can be visualized in terms of total obligational authority or the estimate of total program cost no matter when funds are appropriated or obligated. A summary for the three fiscal years 1966, 1967, and 1968 is contained in Table 17.7.

Market segmentation by a dual classification is also extremely helpful in pinpointing research and development allocations. It is not enough to know that in fiscal year 1968 the total obligational authority for RDT&E related to aircraft is $1,145 million or that the Army is scheduled to spend $1,571 million in RDT&E during fiscal 1968. The marketer must know that $116 million in research funds has been obligated for Army aviation in the fiscal 1968 budget.

Contract Level

A classification of defense spending by prime contract or subcontract shows on what level awards are being made. Cross-indexing by both product type and branch of service pinpoints the segments more accurately. Knowing the contract level, the marketer is in a better position to focus his efforts. As it concerns a prime contractor, the volume of prime contracts awarded by branch of service in the various product categories of interest provides a measurement of potential in each of the market segments. The contractor can then evaluate his marketing efforts and take corrective action. If, on the other hand, the marketer is a subcontractor, he will be interested in the volume of primes as well as subs. The volume of primes indicates the amount of business obtained by his customers. Subcontract vol-

TABLE 17.7 Military Research, Development, Testing, and Evaluation, 1966 to 1968 (in millions of dollars)

CATEGORY	FISCAL YEAR 1966				FISCAL YEAR 1967				FISCAL YEAR 1968			
	TOTAL	ARMY	NAVY	AIR FORCE	TOTAL	ARMY	NAVY	AIR FORCE	TOTAL	ARMY	NAVY	AIR FORCE
Aircraft	1,256	101	292	845	1,171	114	335	711	1,145	116	280	740
Missiles	1,997	699	417	759	2,414	722	715	862	2,499	706	785	890
Astronautics	1,075	23	23	1,025	954	14	18	918	1,119	11	16	1,089
Ships	325	1	324	.....	285	1	284	.....	299	1	298	
Ordnance, vehicles, and related equipment	386	202	184	.....	354	196	158	.....	313	184	130	
Other equipment	901	262	83	314	968	307	110	308	988	309	137	307
Miscellaneous*	1,006	235	259	396	1,029	239	288	369	1,160	245	294	384
Total†	6,946	1,523	1,582	3,339	7,175	1,593	1,908	3,168	7,523	1,571	1,940	3,410

*Includes military sciences, program-wide management and support, and emergency fund.

† Military research, development, testing, and evaluation by other Defense Department agencies: 1966—$501 million; 1967—$508 million; and 1968—$602 million.

Source: *Aviation Week & Space Technology*, Jan. 30, 1967, p. 25.

ume shows the amount of business which requires direct govern-mental contracts.

A hypothetical example might help to illustrate the usefulness of data by contract level. Suppose the following is a first-quarter report of defense-contract awards for navigation systems:

	PRIMES	SUBS
	(IN MILLIONS OF DOLLARS)	
Air Force	38.0	1.0
Navy	15.0	1.5
Army	2.0	0.5
Total	55.0	3.0

Receiving this report, a small subcontractor estimates that the com-ponents he produces account for one out of every ten dollars re-ceived in awards to prime contractors. He also knows that his market share is 5 percent and that subcontracts lag behind prime contracts by about six months. Therefore, he can estimate his potential sales to prime contractors at roughly $275,000 for the last three months of the fiscal year. The size of direct subcontracts indicates that this small marketer must establish direct relationships with the three branches of service, and in particular the Navy, in order to be in a position to evaluate and tap this segment regularly.

PURCHASING PROCEDURES

Defense purchasing procedures can be broken down into three major areas. These are the methods of contract placement, types of con-tract, and procurement policies.

Methods of Contract Placement

Formal advertising and negotiation are the two authorized methods of contract placement. Statistics on defense procurement with United States firms show the extent of reliance on negotiation rather than on formal advertising. (Table 17.8). It is obvious that even though the dollar ratio of negotiated contracts to those brought about by formal advertising declined from 1960 to 1967, it was still a rather formidable 6.1 to 1 in 1967. The popularity of negotiation is attrib-utable to its flexibility.

TABLE 17.8 Value of All New Prime Defense Contracts with United States Firms for Work in the United States by Method of Contract Placement, Selected Years (in millions of dollars)

METHOD OF CONTRACT PLACEMENT	YEAR ENDING JUNE 30						
	1960	1962	1963	1964	1965	1966	1967
Negotiation	18,324	22,732	23,605	22,332	20,621	28,879	34,188
Formal advertising	2,978	3,412	3,538	3,889	4,660	5,147	5,621
Negotiation/formal advertising	6.2/1	6.7/1	6.7/1	5.7/1	4.4/1	5.6/1	6.1/1

Source: *Military Prime Contract Awards and Subcontract Payments or Commitments,* Department of Defense, Office of the Secretary.

Formal advertising is the more economical method of purchasing standardized goods and services and is looked upon by Congress as the accepted method of contracting. Other acknowledged advantages are (1) the tendency to reduce illegalities such as fraud and (2) the widening of opportunity to compete for defense business. For formal advertising to work, two conditions are necessary. One is the availability of complete and definitive product specifications. The other is the existence of competition on the supplier level. Strict procedures are followed in formal advertising. The specific place and time for bids to be publicly opened and recorded is set in advance. Bids must reach the designated office prior to this time. The award is made to the lowest responsible bidder whose bid conforms to the essential requirements of the Invitation to Bids. However, the contracting officer can reject all bids on the basis of the best interests of the government, or for such reasons as the lack of competition between bidders, collusion, bad faith, and lack of reasonableness in submissions. Once the award is made, the accepted bid becomes a legally binding contract.

To provide greater flexibility in procurement, the Armed Services Procurement Act of 1947 sets forth seventeen special conditions permitting negotiation. A brief summary of these conditions is as follows:

1 Necessary to the public interest in a state of national emergency.
2 Criticalness will not permit use of advertising.
3 Amount involved does not exceed $1,000.
4 Services are of a personal or professional nature.
5 Services are to be rendered by an educational institution.
6 Services are to be procured and utilized outside the United States and its possessions.
7 Medicines and medical supplies.
8 Purchases for authorized resale.

9   Perishable subsistence supplies.
10   Impracticalities of securing competition.
11   Experimental, developmental, or research work.
12   Purchase or contract should not be disclosed publicly.
13   Assurance of standardization and interchangeability.
14   Substantial initial investment or an extended period of preparation.
15   Bid prices are not reasonable, or there is evidence of their not being arrived at independently in open competition.
16   Retention of a supplier in the interests of national defense.
17   Otherwise authorized by law.

It is estimated that over 70 percent of procurement by negotiation is brought about by three of the special conditions. These are:

1   The requirements of a substantial initial investment or an extended period of preparation (33 percent)
2   Experimental, developmental, or research work (18.9 percent)
3   Impracticalities of securing competition (18.6 percent)[8]

It should be stressed that negotiation does not indicate a reduction in competition. The testimony of General R. W. Golglazier, Jr., before the House Appropriations Committee was that the great majority of negotiation is on a highly competitive basis.[9] A case in point involved 189 potential suppliers of a piece of equipment.

Normally preaward surveys are made prior to the negotiation of contracts with unknown suppliers. The purpose of the survey is to determine the ability of the supplier to fulfill the terms of the proposed contract. Consideration is given to:

1   Present facilities
2   Manpower skills
3   Production capabilities
4   Internal controls
5   Present financial stability
6   Ethical conduct
7   Percentage of subcontracting contemplated

Preaward surveys of small businesses are governed by special procedures particularly in regard to financial and technical qualifications.

[8] *Background Material on Economic Aspects of Military Procurement and Supply,* Washington: Joint Economic Committee, U.S. Congress, 1960, p. 86.

[9] *Hearings on Department of Defense Appropriations for 1963,* part 4, Washington: Committee on Appropriations, U.S. House of Representatives, 1962, p. 19.

TYPES OF CONTRACT

The types of contract which are used in military purchasing include (1) fixed price, (2) cost plus fixed fee, (3) incentive, (4) cost with no fee, (5) cost sharing, (6) time and materials, and (7) letter of intent. Cost-plus-percentage-fee contracts are not allowable in military purchasing.

Fixed Price

Fixed-price contracts are utilized in either formal advertising or negotiation. A firm fixed-price contract is applicable where costs can be estimated with reasonable accuracy and competition is present. This type of contract carries the highest risk for the supplier because no adjustment is allowable on the basis of his cost experience. This absence of cost adjustment offers the supplier maximun incentive to increase his efficiency. Additionally, the administrative burden is less than normally experienced with other contractual forms.

The usefulness of a firm fixed-price contract is severely limited for long-range projects. For the government, the firm fixed-price contract is disadvantageous in that it does not permit direct and immediate sharing in cost reduction. Because of the limitations, there have developed several variations of the fixed-price contract.

One of these variations is the inclusion of an escalation clause, which allows price revisions based on certain specifically defined contingencies, usually increases in labor and material costs. Normally, escalation clauses are to be found when the performance period is lengthy and when contingencies are likely to be beyond the control of the supplier. Another variation is fixed-price with redetermination at stated intervals during the contract period. At the end of each stated period, the price is reviewed and adjusted up or down in relation to actual cost experience. A ceiling price may be included to limit price increases.

Cost plus Fixed Fee

This type of contract replaced the now illegal cost-plus-a-percentage-of-cost contract. Generally, it is utilized in situations whose scope and feasibility are too uncertain to allow a fixed-price or incentive contract. At the onset, a fee is determined, based on an estimate of total project costs. No variance in fee is allowable if actual costs prove to be higher or lower than the original estimate.

The 1947 Armed Services Procurement Act established the limitation that a fee should not exceed 10 percent of estimated contract costs for projects other than those specifically noted. The limitation on R&D work is 15 percent, while the maximum fee is 6 percent for architectural or engineering services relating to any public works or utility project. In addition to these statutory limitations, administrative orders prohibit fees in excess of 10 percent on R&D work and 7 percent on all other contracts except those with a statutory limit of 6 percent.

The widest use of cost-plus-fixed-fee contracts is made when neither the scope of the task nor the cost structure is known. It is also applicable to large projects in which a small error in cost estimates could mean either excess profits or bankruptcy. Significantly, this type of contract offers no incentive for contractor efficiency and requires constant government surveillance. Another disadvantage is that the whole contract may break down if the initial cost estimates are awry. Faulty cost estimates appear to be the rule rather than the exception in work usually done under a cost-plus-fixed-fee contract. In one study it was discovered that overruns are far more common than underruns, typically 20 percent over target costs. [10]

During the four-year period from 1961 to 1965, cost-plus contracting has dropped from 36.6 percent of the defense dollar to only 9.4 percent. The decline is attributable to the ever-increasing stress on firm fixed-price and incentive awards. This changeover in emphasis has increased the earnings on defense contracts for the efficient contractor. Profits on airframes, for example, which tended to range from 6 to 8 percent for even the most efficient contractor, now have gone as high as 13 percent. However, both fixed-price and incentive contracts are far riskier than cost-plus with the result that the less efficient contractor has been hard-pressed to make anywhere near the profit he would have earned on a cost-plus basis.

Incentive
This type of contract is based on a formula which relates costs, both target and allowable, to contractor profitability. Initial negotiations set up a target cost, a cost ceiling, maximum and minimum profit levels, and a price-adjustment formula. Once a contract is completed and total allowable costs are determined, the final price is set in

[10] Merton J. Peck and Frederick M. Scherer, *The Weapons Acquisition Process: An Economic Analysis,* Cambridge, Mass.: Harvard Graduate School of Business Administration, Division of Research, 1962.

accordance with the predetermined formula. When total allowable costs are less than targeted cost, the formula increases the profit. The contractor and the government share in any amount over the targeted profit at a previously agreed-upon rate. Conversely, an excess over target costs decreases the profit.

The stimulus to contractor efficiency is the major advantage of an incentive contract. Another advantage for the government is immediate participation in any savings forthcoming from efficient contractor performance. Still another advantage is the adaptability of the contract to extended performance periods.

There are several disadvantages, none of which are inherent. Both parties need competent negotiation and administration to bring about the "best" contract for a specific procurement. If target cost has been set tight, the contractor sharing of incentive profit should be liberalized to 20 or 25 percent. On the other hand, a loose target cost should bring about a lowering of contractor share and possibly a profit ceiling. An incentive contract is virtually useless when the contractor lacks an accounting system which will permit price redetermination and formula application. Situations in which cost estimates are not readily available restrict the use of incentive contracts.

A result of what appears to be an ever-increasing use of the incentive awards is a division of defense marketers into two distinct groupings. In one group are the prime contractors and subcontractors who are efficient and hence more profitable. As an example, since the shift away from cost-plus-fixed-fee contracts to either firm fixed-price or incentive awards, Lockheed has increased its earnings after taxes from 1.8 percent of sales in 1961 to 2.8 percent in 1966. Membership in the other group comprises the less efficient contractors. The composition of both groups is in a constant state of flux. The number of changes is determined by the level of competition fostered by the incentive awards.

Cost with No Fee

This contract reimburses only the costs incurred. Its use is restricted to R&D and facilities contracts with educational or other nonprofit organizations.

Cost Sharing

When the marketer stands to gain from a project apart from profits, a cost-sharing contract is frequently used. It may well be that the knowledge gained from a project has greater subsequent value than any amount of fee. Such a situation normally involves R&D work, the results of which may have significant commercial value to the contractor.

A cost-sharing contract is an arrangement whereby the procurement agency reimburses the contractor for all or part of the project costs. Although this type of contract is useful in promoting R&D, it entails excessive administrative overhead. Then, too, there is the problem of allowable costs.

Time and Materials

A time-and-materials contract provides for the reimbursement of contractors at a fixed hourly rate for direct-labor hours plus material cost. This type of contract is used extensively in the purchase of services and during emergencies. In addition to labor and material costs, the contract may include compensation for overhead and a profit based on a predetermined rate. This rate may be firm or subject to readjustment at stated intervals. The period of the contract may be in terms of hours, days, weeks, or months.

Even though there is no built-in incentive, a time-and-materials contract can benefit the contractor as well as the government. Often, it represents an opportunity for the contractor to operate at optimum capacity. The government, on the other hand, pays only for the actual time used. It incurs no developmental or fixed-cost burdens. A hypothetical example might help to illustrate this circumstance. Suppose a time-and-materials contract has been awarded an airline for routine maintenance on Air Force planes. The airline gains from being able to lessen idle capacity without a corresponding reduction in repair personnel. This in turn lowers the fixed-cost burden on each of their own planes. For the Air Force the advantages are several. First of all, they can tap repair capabilities as needed. Repair personnel need not be trained, subsidized, or located. Secondly, the burden of routine maintenance and repair has shifted to a variable cost from a fixed cost. A reassignment of aircraft would not affect the maintenance cost per plane. A third benefit is the availability of highly skilled personnel—individuals the Air Force could not hope to recruit. Finally, a time-and-materials contract would be a good stopgap measure if the airline is in an area where the Air Force assignment is to be short-lived.

Letter of Intent

A letter of intent is not a contract but rather an authorization to start production without delay. It signifies the intention of the procurement agency to enter into a formal contract for certain designated items. Receiving a letter of intent, the contractor is authorized to make commitments and incur costs pending formal contract negotiation. The maximum liability of the government may be included in the letter. The final contract should be negotiated within sixty days after issuance of the letter of intent.

The purposes of the letter are three in number. First, it provides ample time to develop accurate cost estimates. Second, work is started immediately without the delay of negotiation. Third, the contractor is furnished protection for the costs incurred. Generally, the policy of the Defense Department is to refrain from using letters except in emergencies.

CONSIDERATIONS IN DEFENSE CONTRACTING

In defense contracting the marketer should take note of certain considerations. These can be grouped under five major headings as follows: (1) mandatory contract provisions, (2) costing policies, (3) renegotiation, (4) the role of small business, and (5) competitive factors.

Mandatory Contract Provisions

Certain provisions or clauses are a vital part of any government contract in that failure to include them may bring about invalidation. Some of the provisions evolve from congressional statute or executive order. These are:

1 The specification that members of Congress shall not benefit personally by the contract.
2 A formal covenant against contingent fees. This is a warranty by the contractor that he has not employed or retained any person or selling agency to solicit or secure said contract upon an agreement or understanding for a commission, percentage, brokerage, or contingent fee. The contractor may designate bona fide employees or agencies, even though compensated on one of the above bases, as a proper form of representation.
3 The obligation not to discriminate against any employee or applicant for employment because of race, religion, color, or national origin.
4 The adherence to labor conditions as set forth in the Walsh-Healy Public Contracts Act for all awards of over $10,000.

5   The acknowledgment of the said contract's subjectivity to the Renegotiation Act of 1951.
6   The forbidding of any deduction from wages (Davis-Bacon Act) or any kickbacks by employees to contractors (Copeland Act) on construction projects.
7   The forbidding of convict labor.
8   The observance of the Buy American Act.
9   The forbidding of alien employment on aircraft production without written permission of the Secretary of Defense.
10 The requirement of time and a half for overtime (Work Hours Law of 1962).

Another type of contract provision results from Department of Defense directives and generally observed practices. Such provisions include:

1   A gratuities provision prohibiting the practices of offering gifts, granting favors, or entertaining military officers or government employees
2   A schedule of full inspections by the government as various production stages are reached
3   A set of procedures for termination of the contract at government convenience
4   A provision setting forth the procedures for arbitration of disputes
5   A provision dealing with patents, royalties, and copyrights

If a provision is contained in contracts of a limited type, it is referred to as one of special application. Special provisions, such as the following, emanate principally from internal directives.

1   The requirement of immediate notice in the event of a labor dispute
2   A liquidated provision to protect the government in the event that the contractor does not bring the project to completion
3   A statement of policy regarding contractor utilization of government-furnished property
4   An expression of the Department of Defense policy relating to the special tooling furnished by the contractor
5   A provision covering the military security requirements for classified contracts
6   An escalation clause for possible increases in labor and material costs during the life of the contract

In addition to contract provisions, defense marketers must assume other obligations if required by the government. One obligation is concerned with bonds—bid, performance, and payment. Bid bonds represent a guarantee that a bidder will, within the time specified, enter into a contract and give proper bond for its performance. The requirement for a bid bond is specified in the Invitation for Bids. The Miller Act requires that performance bonds be furnished on construction contracts exceeding $2,000 to be performed in the United States. Normally, performance bonds are not required in other procurement areas. Payment bonds which secure the payment of all persons supplying labor and material are usually written in conjunction with performance bonds on fixed-price construction contracts exceeding $2,000.

Certain military specifications contain a qualification test requirement. Products which have passed the qualification tests are included on the Qualified Products List for that specification. This inclusion assures the contractor that his firm will be allowed to compete for future business. When the Invitation for Bids specifies a product in a Qualified Products List, only those bids offering approved products will be considered.

Costing Policies

The primary concern of the government is the reasonableness of the ultimate price. Contractor cost and profit are definitely secondary. In the interpretation of procurement regulations, a report prepared by Arthur D. Little, Inc., specifies two major points at issue between defense contractors and the Department of Defense, particularly the contracting officer.[11]

The first major problem is the manner in which the original fee or profit is set. Defense regulations list nine factors to be considered in establishing the fee or profit.

1 Effect of competition
2 Degree of risk
3 Nature of the work to be performed
4 Extent of government assistance
5 Extent of contractor's investment
6 Character of the contractor's business
7 Contractor's performance
8 Extent of subcontracting
9 Reliability of contractor's previous estimates

---

[11] Discussion of major points at issue is based on *How Sick Is the Defense Industry?*, *op. cit.*, pp. 32-41.

At the outset the most troublesome problem is the inability to gauge asset utilization. This is further complicated by the insular status of the typical contracting officer. Dealing with only a segment of the defense industry, he is not in a position to have an overall view of the defense establishment. Then, too, the contracting officer is well aware that his personal evaluation is based on the fee set rather than his reasons for setting the fee.

The expedient solution is a fee well below the maximum, but high enough to attract contracts. As time goes by, this fee is gradually reduced to establish the image of hard bargaining. The advantages of this "magic number" process are three. First of all, the contractor is dealing with a known entity. Secondly, with a rate which is stable and tending downward, there is little risk of an investigation by the General Accounting office. Finally, the superiors of the contracting officer are pleased with his performance. The disadvantage of the system is the generalizing of profit rates.

The second major problem concerns the allowability of costs. Some of the costs which are not allowable are (1) advertising, (2) bad debts, (3) stock options, (4) contributions and donations, (5) entertainment, (6) excess facility costs, (7) interest, (8) losses on other contracts, (9) plant reconversion, and (10) organization. Contentious areas for the defense industry are the expense of advertising, losses on other contracts, and interest. In regard to interest charges, it is the contention of the government that it should not provide the means by which a contractor can gain entry into the defense business. In other words, the pricing policy is based on equity capital.

If the manufacturer has a high enough "weighted average share" of risk, audits will be eased because the Department of Defense feels that enough risk has been accepted so that he will exercise his own effective cost controls. The threshold at which controls are lessened is 65 percent. Between 50 and 65 is a discretionary range.

To compute the "weighted average share" of risk, the Defense Department places a percentage factor of risk on each type of contract. For four different types of contract, the percentage risk factors are as follows:

Cost plus fixed fee	0%
Cost plus incentive fee	15%
Fixed price incentive	15-90% (depends upon how close the ceiling price accepted by the manufacturer comes to meeting target costs)
Commercial work	100%

Each of these risk factors is then applied to the dollar volume of work under a particular type of contract.

To illustrate, suppose a hypothetical defense manufacturer with total costs of $5 million has the following contract mix:

Cost plus fixed fee	$2.0 million
Cost plus incentive fee	$0.5 million
Fixed price incentive	$2.0 million
Commercial work	$0.5 million

Multiplying each risk factor by the volume of costs for that type of contract, one arrives at a total of $2.175 million or a 43.5 percent "weighted average share" of risk. It is obvious that the manufacturer in question has not accepted a sufficient degree of risk to be considered for a lessening of audit controls. The basic reason is that 40 percent of his costs arise from cost-plus-fixed-fee contracts which carry no element of risk acceptance.

Renegotiation

Established in 1951, the Renegotiation Board directs its activities toward the recovery of "excess profits" on defined contracts and subcontracts with the Department of Defense, the Armed Services, NASA, GSA, and the maritime agencies. The Renegotiation Board is located in Washington, with regional boards in New York, Detroit, Chicago, and Los Angeles.

The 1951 Renegotiation Act provides that in evaluating excessive profits, favorable recognition must be given to efficiency, attainment of quantity and quality production, cost reduction, and economy in the utilization of manpower, materials, and facilities. Other factors to be considered are:

1   Reasonableness of both costs and profits
2   Division of net worth in terms of private and public capital
3   Acceptance of risk
4   Nature and extent of contribution to the defense effort
5   Character of the business in question
6   Requirements of public interest, and fair and equitable dealing

Generally speaking, any contractor who does more than $1 million in renegotiable business yearly must submit a report to the Board. What exactly constitutes yearly business is a very complex subject. Altogether there are nine statutory exemptions covering such areas as standard commercial items, commodities, and products of a nonrelated defense nature.

The significance of renegotiation appears to have lessened appre-

ciably in the last few years. The annual reports of major defense contractors who have been cleared through 1962, 1963, or 1964 state
that the management of the particular company does not feel that any
excessive profits were earned in subsequent years, and thus no provision was made for renegotiation refunds. In fiscal 1962, renegotiation resulted in a gross recovery of something less than $8 million.
This amounted to almost $4.5 million after tax credits.

Role of Small Business

In certain instances preferential treatment for small businesses is
authorized by the Defense Department. In order to be classified as
a small business, a firm must conform to the definition of "small business" as prescribed by the Small Business Administration. The following definition is mandatory for all procurement agencies in the
Defense Department: "A small business concern is a concern that
(1) is not dominant in its field of operations and, with its affiliates,
employs fewer than 500 employees; or (2) is certified as a small
business by the SBA."

Lack of dominance implies that the firm does not exercise a controlling or major influence in an area of business activity. In measuring dominance, consideration is given to such factors as volume
of business, market penetration or share, proprietary rights, and financial resources. The number of employees means the average
number as of the pay period ending the fifteenth of the third month
in each calendar quarter for the preceding four quarters. It is interesting to note that dealers can qualify as small business concerns
by meeting the general definition and by agreeing to furnish products
manufactured in the United States by small businesses.

In addition to an equitable opportunity to compete for defense procurement, small businesses are granted certain preferential treatment. Small businesses may be given exclusive or partial rights to
a contract award. Consideration of small businesses as subcontractors is provided in each fixed-price and cost-reimbursement contract
in excess of $5,000 by contractual clause. Large prime contractors
and major subcontractors have entered into a program designed to
provide small businesses with an equitable opportunity to compete
within their individual capabilities. This is known as the Defense
Small Business Subcontracting Program.

Although negotiation is relied upon more than formal advertising
in procuring defense materials from small businesses, its degree
of popularity is substantially less than that found generally in defense

contracting. Evidence of greater small business participation in defense business is the increase in the ratio of the dollar value of negotiated contracts to that resulting from formal advertising. The ratios in the years 1963 through 1967 are approximately twice the ratio found for 1960 (Table 17.9). By obtaining more negotiated contracts, small businesses have broadened the scope of their activities in the defense market. They should no longer be looked upon as strictly suppliers of standardized goods and services.

Competitive Factors

In awarding defense contracts, especially those of a R&D nature, many factors besides cost are considered. Commenting on the importance of these noncost factors, Brigadiar General Lee W. Fulton, at one time Director of Procurement for the Air Research and Development Command, told a committee of Congress that in awarding a research contract, "The most compelling factor is the technical competence of the individual or firm under consideration. . . . The financial responsibility, facilities available to perform the work, ability to obtain security clearance, and performance experience on previous contracts are also major factors considered."[12]

The following is a list of competitive factors utilized in base-management contracts for a missile program. It can be noted that cost-performance experience has as much relative importance as the projected cost and fee.

COMPETITIVE FACTOR	RELATIVE WEIGHT
Management availability and capability	100
Management philosophy and organizational experience	100
Quality-control organization and controls	100
Resources, skills, and manpower available	100
Labor relations and understanding of human factors	80
Cost and fee	80
Management control in government practices	80
Prior experience and performance on like-type projects	80
Weapons-system knowledge and experience	80
Understanding the scope of work	80
Acceptance of the conditions of contract	70
Acceptance of statement of work	50
Total	1,000[13]

[12] *The Role of Small Business in Defense Missile Procurement—1958,* Washington: Committee on Small Business, U.S. Senate, Apr. 29-May 1, 1958, p. 59.

[13] *Hearings on Department of Defense Appropriations for 1963,* part 4, Washington: Committee on Appropriations, U.S. House of Representatives, 1962, p. 19.

TABLE 17.9 Value of All New Prime Defense Contracts with United States Firms Designated as Small Businesses for Work in the United States by Method of Contract Placement, Selected Years (in millions of dollars)

METHOD OF CONTRACT PLACEMENT	YEAR ENDING JUNE 30						
	1960	1962	1963	1964	1965	1966	1967
Negotiation	2,265	3,533	3,434	3,589	3,885	5,739	6,410
Formal advertising	1,175	1,089	867	930	1,058	1,530	1,663
Negotiation/formal advertising	1.9/1	3.2/1	4.0/1	3.9/1	3.7/1	3.8/1	3.9/1

Source: *Military Prime Contract Awards and Subcontract Payments or Commitments,* Department of Defense, Office of the Secretary.

MARKETING ORIENTATION OF DEFENSE FIRMS

As the defense industry has matured, some outward signs of marketing considerations have come to the forefront in management thinking. Primarily, this is a result of the development of competence that can by and large solve any technical problem which might confront the industry. However, acceptance of marketing has not been easy for defense firms. Sal F. Divita gives the following explanation for the noticeable lack of full understanding.

> *During the formative years (1951 - 1957), the government customer so placed its demands on industry that there was little need for any marketing on the part of any company. It was not until the industry entered a period of over-capacity (1958 - 1960) that most companies set up marketing departments. In the intervening years, while marketing departments have existed, they have had to struggle to gain the acceptance of the key people in the company, and of the customer. In fact, the government, on the one hand, suggests that marketing is simply an extra expense which ought to be abolished. Industry, on the other hand, largely because of lack of knowledge and fear of alienating its customer, has tended to ignore the problem. So, today, the marketing function and those identified with it tend to be "persona non grata."*[14]

Recognizable Marketing Functions

Generally the organizational structure of the marketing department for a defense firm will differ significantly from that of other firms in the industrial market. To begin with, the personal sales function is

[14] Sal F. Divita, "Selling R and D to the Government," *Harvard Business Review,* September - October, 1965, p. 62.

the job of the entire company, not just those designated as sales-men. For salesmen, any title except salesman is utilized—field rep-resentative, customer liaison, applications engineer, or market de-velopment manager. Regardless of title, the salesman is the defense firm's contact with the market. In this role his job comprises three essential tasks: (1) customer relations, (2) order servicing, and (3) marketing research. Customer service entails maintaining a proper state of relations with the customer. One aspect of customer rela-tions is keeping open the communication channels between what are called "like numbers." Customer personnel in engineering, man-ufacturing, and finance want to talk to their company counterparts. Unfortunately, technical personnel are not attuned to the necessity for customer relations. Therefore, it falls to the sales force to make the appropriate arrangements in this realm.

Order servicing in the defense industry does not imply the cleri-cal function of account billing. Rather, it is the administration of the complex array of contract terms and requirements. A common com-plaint is that too few people are assigned to contract administration. In the normal course of his activities, the defense salesman collects large quantity of information relative to the technological require-nts of the customer and the competitive environment.

One author feels that in addition to the normal attributes of a good salesman, the following special characteristics are desirable:

1   He should be knowledgable about the defense market.
2   He should know whom to see and when.
3   He should be strongly customer-oriented.
4   He should be sensitive to changes in customer requirements.
5   He should be enthusiastic about his company and its products.
6   He should have technical comprehension.
7   He should not be reluctant to discuss problems with his supe-riors.
8   He should have the maturity to function as a member of a team.
9   He should possess both physical stamina and personal integrity.
10   He must have strength of character.
11   He must be able to sell.[15]

Perhaps the best description of defense sales is selling without customer awareness. To implement this concept, defense market-ers have had to rely upon a man who is an engineer first and a sales-man second. Obviously, this approach is perilous.

[15] Reprinted by permission of the publisher from Joseph M. Hertzberg, "Defense Marketing in the Next Ten Years: Some Potential Problems," in *Defense Marketing in the 1960's,* AMA Management Report no. 57. © 1961 by the American Management Association, Inc.

The scope of the work done in the marketing research, advertising, and product-development departments is noticeably different from that undertaken in other parts of the industrial market. Marketing research is directed solely toward analyzing customer requirements. To help, many defense marketers have retained consulting firms whose sole function is to provide contract-award information on a regular basis.

Because advertising expenditures do not constitute an allowable expense, defense marketers generally have done little advertising. All or a sizable portion of what ad budget there is goes for trade-show representation. There is also a tendency among many defense contractors to merge public relations with advertising. The job of product development is to customize a product to meet customer requirements. Obtaining customer requirements from marketing research, product development is charged with the responsibility of selecting the projects which are best suited to capabilities.

Potential Marketing Problems

The dynamic pattern of constant change which has characterized the defense market is likely to continue into the future. This means that marketing can anticipate numerous problems. Some of the major problems noted by authorities can be grouped under the following general headings:

1   Improvement of return on investment
2   Adaptability to the ever-increasing changes in the technological mix
3   Projection of a suitable image to the various interest groups
4   Maximizing the efficacy of marketing efforts
5   Coping with the concept of weapons-system procurement
6   Enhancing the profitability of commercial spin-offs
7   Lessening of risk

Acknowledged as the problem which poses the greatest potential threat to the continued healthy existence of the "defense base" is the low rate of return on investment. A comprehensive study by Arthur D. Little, Inc., suggests two ways of enhancing investment return.[16] One way is for management to concentrate on those products which offer the highest return. Presently too much attention is directed toward the identification and follow-up of sales leads. Another way is to make maximum use of suppliers' capital by subcontracting routine

[16] *How Sick Is the Defense Industry?*, *op. cit.*, pp. 85-87.

operations which require high investment. The one danger in this approach is the possibility of charges relative to profit pyramiding.

The ever-increasing rate of technological change has led many defense marketers to overextend their capabilities by attempting to cover every possible product area. Continued observation of this shotgun approach in the face of uncertainty is likely to dissipate profitability. Instead of pursuing every opportunity, defense marketers should concentrate their efforts on a few selected areas and reap the benefits of specialization. What particular areas these are to be should be dictated by the needs of the marketplace. The marketing function is an ideal source of information on this subject. However, in many firms engineering has assumed this job.

Related to the problems attending technological change are those concerned with the concept of weapons-systems procurement. The nature of potential problems is suggested by what one author labels the "five G's of weapons systems." These are (1) greater competition, (2) greater stakes per bid, (3) greater risks per job, (4) greater loss per termination (here loss may be financial or market position), and (5) greater gains per award successfully fulfilled.[17] All of these problems point to a key role for marketing in the future.

To overcome the problems attendant upon obtaining maximum efficacy from marketing output, defense firms must recognize what has been the traditional and seemingly paradoxical role of marketing. Contributing to this state of affairs has been the dominance of engineering in what has tended to be a sellers' market. Coupled with this is a heightened sense of inferiority on the part of sales and marketing personnel. They will go to great lengths to cover up their role, as witness the following example.

A representative of a leading aerospace firm, whose business card reads "program manager," admitted only after hours of intensive interviewing that he was a sales manager.[18]

To enable marketing to achieve maximum efficacy, three proposals deserve attention. The first is to assign the responsibility and authority for all marketing activities to the marketing department. The present division between marketing and engineering is essentially destructive. Second, the status of marketing should be enhanced from both an external and an internal standpoint. The necessary exchange between marketing and technical communities cannot take

[17] Joseph M. Hertzberg, *op. cit.*, p. 52.
[18] Sal F. Divita, *op. cit.*, p. 69.

place unless the two function from comparable communicative levels. The third proposal is the implementation of a program to develop high-caliber marketing personnel. This will involve recruitment, selection, and training.

Above all, defense marketing should take on the job of selling capabilities rather than packaged programs or products. This can be advantageous in three ways. First of all, it keeps the marketer from taking an inflexible position, a position which conveys a "take it or leave it" attitude to the defense agency. Secondly, the marketing of capabilities tends to further return on investment. Finally, selling capabilities parallels the concept that the long-run technical objectives of the marketer and the Defense Department within any specific discipline must necessarily overlap appreciably.

The future will complicate still further the job of public relations for the defense firm. The defense marketer must convey the best image possible to three separate and distinct publics. These are the defense industry and in particular subcontractors, the defense establishment, and the general public. The last-named public presents a problem not encountered in either of the other two publics. This is converting a highly technical language into words and phrases the layman can read and understand without too much difficulty.

Risk comes about in allocating resources to technical areas. Unable to participate to the fullest extent in every area, the defense marketer must decide in which areas he will make commitments. The key to this decision is information. The marketer will need the best available information on the market as well as his own capabilities. The bulk of this task can be assigned to marketing.

SUMMARY

The significance of government purchases is almost unbelievable especially when the multiplier effect is considered. As the biggest government buyer, the Defense Department has concentrated its expenditures geographically as well as institutionally. However, institutional concentration has weakened appreciably in the last nine fiscal years. Listings of the top fifteen prime contractors for fiscal years 1964, 1965, and 1966 shows a fairly fixed membership in this select category.

The defense can be further segmented, using any base or a combination of bases. These are customer grouping, product type, and contract level. Ideally, all three classifications should be used.

Negotiation with its inherent flexibility is used to place six dollars of contract awards for every one dollar obtained through formal advertising. Two conditions are necessary for formal advertising to work. One is the presence of definitive product specifications and the other is competition on the supplier level. The Armed Services Procurement Act of 1947 sets forth seventeen special conditions permitting negotiation. Among the types of contract used in military purchasing are (1) fixed price, (2) cost plus fixed fee, (3) incentive, (4) cost with no fee, (5) cost sharing, (6) time and materials, and (7) letter of intent. Currently, there are strong indications of a shift away from cost plus fixed fee to either fixed price or incentive.

Certain mandatory provisions or clauses are part of any government contract. Some of these evolve from congressional statute or executive order, while others are a result of Defense Department directives or special circumstances surrounding limited-type contracts. In costing out contracts, the primary concern of the government is the reasonableness of the final price. Contractor cost and profit are of secondary importance. The insular view of the contracting tends to create a situation in which the amount of profit is less than might be expected. Government auditing procedures are eased in relation to the degree of risk accepted by the contractor, the assumption being that in accepting risk the contractor will institute effective cost controls.

The purpose of renegotiation is to recover excess profits earned on defense contracts by contractors doing more than $1 million in business defined as renegotiable. The foreknowledge of such action has appeared to lessen appreciably the amount of recoverable profits in recent years. Small businesses, duly defined, are given equal and sometimes preferential treatment by the Defense Department. Although negotiation is relied upon more than formal advertising by small businesses duly defined, its degree of popularity is not nearly as great as among larger firms. The increase in negotiated contracts suggests that small businesses can no longer be looked upon as strictly suppliers of standardized goods and services.

In awarding defense contracts, especially those of an R&D nature, many factors besides cost are weighted. These factors are labeled competitive factors. In base-management contracts for missile programs, the projected cost and fee has as much relative importance as cost performance experience and less relative importance than any of the four factors falling in the category of management capabilities.

With maturity there is some evidence of marketing considerations coming to the forefront in management thinking. Typically, the organization and role of marketing in the defense firm differ from those encountered in other parts of the industrial market. The potential problems foretell both a wider and a changed role for marketing in the future.

DISCUSSION QUESTIONS

1 Explain how the multiplier effect swells the dollar volume of defense awards.
2 Trace the general geographical pattern of defense expenditures.
3 How is the economic impact of defense expenditures measured?
4 What are the advantages of negotiation?
5 Why might an efficient contractor prefer a fixed-price or incentive contract to a cost-plus-fixed-fee contract?
6 What changes are brought about by coordinated procurement?
7 How can a marketer relate mission to procurement requirements?
8 What marketing policies should be developed from defense-contracting considerations?
9 Trace the development of the marketing function in defense firms.
10 What obstacles are there to full recognition of marketing in the defense industry?

SUPPLEMENTARY READINGS

Defense Marketing in the 1960's, New York: American Management Association, Inc., Marketing Division, 1961.

Defense Marketing Reprints, Chicago: American Marketing Association, n.d.

Divita, Sal F., "Selling R and D to the Government," *Harvard Business Review,* September-October, 1965, pp. 62-75.

How Sick Is the Defense Industry? Cambridge, Mass.: Arthur D. Little, Inc., 1963.

Kast, Fremont E., and James E. Rosenzweig, *Management in the Space Age,* New York: Exposition Press, Inc., 1962.

Kennedy, John J., "Defense-Aerospace Marketing: Model for Action," *Business Horizons,* Winter, 1965, pp. 67-74.

Murphy, Russell F., "Selling Aerospace Technology to the Federal Government," *Journal of Marketing,* January, 1968, pp. 46-49.

Peck, Merton J., and Scherer, Frederick M., *The Weapons Acquisition Process: An Economic Analysis,* Cambridge, Mass.: Harvard Graduate School of Business Administration, Division of Research, 1962.

Reynolds, William H., "The Marketing Concept and the Aerospace Business," *Journal of Marketing,* April, 1966, pp. 9-11.

index

Accessory equipment, 7
Accounts receivable:
  definition of, 217–218
  sources of costs, 219
  special dating terms, 218–219
  terms of sale, 218
Administrative pricing, 202–203
Advertising:
  agencies, relationships with,
    359–360
  allowability as defense
    cost, 447
  budgets, 336, 354–358
  business publications, 337,
    344–346
  direct-mail, 346–349
  manufacturer assistance to
    local outlets, 333–334
  media, 335–343
  method of defense contract
    placement, 437–438,
    449–451
  objectives of, 330–335
  organization for, 356–359
  research, 138–139
  selling expense reduction
    by, 334–335

Advertising:
  statistics relating to budgets
    and expenditures, 329–331
Advertising agencies, relation-
  ships with, 359–360
Advertising research, 138–139
Aftermath market (*see*
    Replacement market)
Agribusiness, 403–404
  (*See also* Cal-Can)
Agricultural cooperatives,
    407–410
Agricultural market:
  farms: as industrial
    consumers, 404–406
    as industrial marketers,
      406–407
  structure of, 399–404
Air Materiel Command, 433
Allis-Chalmers Manufacturing
    Company:
  diversification, philosophy of, 78
  industry status of, 404
  New Products Department, 157
Aluminum Company of America
    (Alcoa):
  Alcoa International, Inc., 283

Aluminum Company of
America (Alcoa):
fixed costs allocation in
pricing, 202
American Machine & Foundry
Company (AMF):
inventory carrying costs,
377–378
penalties for excess inventory,
386–387

Barnard, Chester, 72
Basing-point pricing, 196
(*See also* Geographical
pricing)
Battelle Memorial Institute, 158
Bayesian Theory, 162–163
Booz-Allen & Hamilton, Inc.,
152, 167–168, 277–279
Bounded rationality, principle
of, 71
Branches, sales (*see* Manufacturers' sales branches)
Break-even analysis, 103–105
Brokers, 10, 269–270
Brookings Institution, study of
pricing, 201
Budgets:
advertising, 354–358
marketing research, 121–122
use of, with breakeven
analysis, 105
usefulness in control,
102–103
Bundle of services concept,
224–226
Burroughs Corporation, 366–
367
Business publications, 337,
344–346

Cal-Can, 409–410
Cash discounts, 219
Catalogs:
prefiled method, 351–352
purposes of, 350
types of, 351
use of microfilm, 351
Channels, marketing (*see*
Marketing channels)
Chicago Board of Trade, 10
(*See also* Commodity
exchanges)
Clark Equipment Company,
155, 156
Combination export manager,
288–289
Commodity Exchange Act,
411–412
Commodity exchanges, 10,
410–412
Competition, workable, definition
of, 191, 193–194
Component parts, 11–13
Confirming houses, 291–292
Conglomerates, 38, 78–79
(*See also* Diversification,
strategy of)
Consignment, 228–229
Consumer orientation, marketing
management concept, 46–48
Contract administration (*see*
Order servicing, defense
contracts)
Control:
aspects of, 89
comparison of marketing
performance, 100–105
correction and revision of
marketing performance,
106–107
definition of, 89–90

Control:
    measurement of marketing
        performance, 98–100
    objectives of, 90
    standards of marketing
        performance, 90–98
Converters, 11
Cost-per-thousand concept, 345
Costing policies, defense
    contracts, 446–448
Costs:
    break-even analysis, 104–105
    logistics, 368–373
    pricing, 188–190
    standard of marketing
        performance, 96–97
Critical Path Analysis, 163–164
Critical Path Method (CPM), 164
Cummins Engine Company, 390
Customer service, 310–313
Customer-service level, logistics,
    372–373

Defense contracts:
    contract level, 435, 437
    mandatory provisions,
        444–446
    placement of, 437–440
    types of, 440–444
Defense expenditures:
    geographical distribution,
        425–428
    institutional distribution,
        428–431
    multiplier effect, 22–23, 424
Defense marketing:
    potential problems of, 453–455
    recognizable functions of,
        451–453
    role of, 451

Delivered pricing (see
    Geographical pricing)
Delivery rating, suppliers, 32
    (See also Vendor analysis)
Demand for industrial goods:
    derived nature of, 21–23
    fluctuation of, 23–24
    initial elasticity of, 25–26
    inventory sensitivity of, 24–25
    multiplier effect of, 22–23
Design cycle, 33–34
Development corporations, 294
Direct mail, 346–349
Displays (see Trade shows)
Distribution policies (see Market
    coverage policies)
Distribution-related
    costs, 378–380
Distributor discount (see
    Functional discount)
Diversification:
    product line, 176
    strategy of, 77–80
Dow Chemical Company, 157
Drop shippers, 267–268
Dumping in foreign competition,
    55–56
DuPont Chart System, 100–102
DuPont Company:
    geographical pricing, 197
    market manipulator, 149
    structure of research
        function, 83

Economic order quantity (EOQ)
    386–387
Edge Act, 292–293
Elasticity of demand, 25–26
Exclusive distribution, 238
    (See also Limited distribution)

Exhibits (*see* Trade shows)
Expediting factor, 32
  (*See also* Vendor analysis)
Export agent, 288
Export commission house, 289
Export discount house, 292
Export drop shipper, 287–288
Export-Import Bank, 290–291
Export Merchant, 287

Fabricated materials, 10–11
Factoring:
  costs of, 221
  functions of, 220
  maturity, 221
Factory men, 106, 253–254
Fayol, Henri, 73
Fish farming, 415–416
Foreign imports of steel, 55
Free-on-board pricing
    (F.O.B.), 195
  (*See also* Geographical pricing)
Freight absorption, 196–197
  (*See also* Geographical pricing)
Functional discount, 208–209

General-line distributor, 265
General-merchandise
    distributor, 265
Geographical pricing:
  basing-point, 196
  freight absorption, 196–197
  phantom freight, 196
  point-of-origin (F.O.B.), 195
  zone, 197
Government relationships:
  direct, 37–38
  indirect, 38–39

Gross profit:
  definition of, 94, 113
  standard of marketing
    performance, 94

Hedging, 31, 410–411
Hierarchy of objectives, 64–65

Image, company: advertising,
    role, 331–333
  unfavorable to supplier, 29n.
Industrial demand (*see* Demand
    for industrial goods)
Industrial distributors:
  competitive status of, 266–267
  consideration of principals,
    250–251
  definition of, 264
  goods handled by, 9, 12–13, 16
  selection of, 248–249
  trade names of, 264
  types of, 365
Industrial goods:
  definition of, 4–5
  types of, 5–16
  (*See also* Demand for
    industrial goods)
Industrial market, size of, 16–17
Industrial services, 5–6
Information network:
  organization of, 99–100
  requisites of, 98–99
Innovator, new-product
    development, 154–155
Input-output analysis, 21–22
Inside salesmen, 307–308
Installations, 7
Installment contracts, 222–224
Intermerchants, 294

International Business Machines
    Corporation (IBM):
  consent decree, 1956, 228
  market manipulator, 149
  overseas activities, 277–278
  R&D strategy, 80–81
  World Trade Corporation, 283
International company, 282
International division, 282–283
International Harvester
    Company:
  catalogs of, 350
  foreign operations of, 278
  industry status of, 404
International Monetary
    Fund, 291
International subsidiary (*see*
    International division)
Inventory:
  backup, 255
  carrying costs, 377–378

Joint venture, 283–284

Key accounts, 126
Key result areas for
    objectives, 65

Leasing:
  bundle of services concept,
    224–225
  independent leasing
    specialists, 228
  marketing characteristics, 226
  problems involved in, 227–228
  types of, 226–227
Leveling, 165
Licensing, foreign operations,
    284–286

Limited distribution, market
    coverage policy, 238
Little, Arthur D., Inc., 158, 430,
    446–447
Litton Industries:
  diversification, strategy of,
    78–80
  oceanology, 412
Lockheed Aircraft Corporation:
  contract for C-141
    transport, 424
  Deep Quest, 413
  oceanology projects, 418
  status as defense
    contractor, 429
  structure of research
    function, 82
Logistics:
  concept of, 365
  costs of, 368–373
  internal development of,
    365–366
  inventory management,
    385–390
  marketing mix role of,
    366–368
  movement systems, 374–377
  packaging, 390–391
  system of, 373–374
  total cost concept of, 377–380
  warehousing, 380–385

Machinery and equipment, 6–7
Major equipment, 6–7
Management by exception,
    106–107
Manufacturers' agents, 112,
    268–269
Manufacturers' reps (*see*
    Manufacturers' agents)

Manufacturers' sales branches:
with stock, 244–245, 262–263
without stock, 244–245,
263–264
Manufacturers' sales offices,
244–245, 263–264
Manufacturing exporters,
289–290
Market characteristics:
geographical concentration,
27–29
purchasing influences, 35–37
rational buying motives, 29–34
reciprocity, 34–35
types of, 27
Market coverage policies,
237–238
Market potential:
measurement of, 126–131
standard of marketing
performance, 92
Market research, 134–136
Market segmentation, strategy
of, 47–49, 172–173, 435
Market strategy, 48–49, 66
Marketing channels:
assistance to, 252–256
control of, 256–258
coordination with, 252–253
definition of, 236
selection of, 237–252
types of, 239–243
Marketing concept (*see*
Marketing management
concept)
Marketing costs (*see* Costs)
Marketing management concept,
46–57
Marketing managers:
backgrounds of, 59–60
responsibilities of, 58–59

Marketing plans, as standard of
marketing performance,
95–96
Marketing research:
advertising, 138–139
competitor, 136–138
corporate, 139
definition of, 112–114
market, 134-136
product, 131–134
sales, 124–131
for smaller firms, 139–140
statistics on status of,
118–124
Mass distribution, market
coverage policy, 238
Media Data Form, 337–343, 346
Mill supply house, 264
Monopoly, 191
Monopsony, 193
Monsanto Chemical Company:
Advertising and Market-
Development Department,
122–123
Agricultural Chemicals
Division, 406
automated purchasing of, 57
Movement systems, logistics,
374–377
MRO (*see* Operating supplies)

Negotiation, defense contracts,
437–439, 449–451
New-product evolutionary cycle,
166–172
Nonprice competition,
186–187, 192
Nonprofit research corporations,
6

Objectives, 64–65
Obsolescence, planned, 177–178
Ocean mining, 413–415
Offshore drilling, 416–417
Ogden Corporation, 14
Oligopoly, 191–192
Oligopsony, 193
Operating supplies, 15–16
Order quantity, economic,
    386–387
Order scheduling, 388–390
Order servicing, defense
    contracts, 452
Order splitting, purchasing
    policy, 34
Original equipment manufacturer
    (OEM), 11–12

Packaging, 390–391
PERT (*see* Program Evaluation
    and Review Technique)
Phantom freight, 196
    (*See also* Geographical pricing)
Physical-distribution costs,
    368–373, 377–380
"Pittsburgh Plus" pricing, 196
Planned obsolescence, 177–178
Planning:
    benefits from, 67–68
    commitment of, 75–76
    definition of, 64
    features of, 73–75
    organizational placement
        of, 76–77
    steps in, 68–73
    strategies and tactics, 66–67
Planning commitment, 75–76
Point-of-origin pricing
    (F.O.B.), 195
    (*See also* Geographical pricing)

Postage-stamp pricing, 195–196
    (*See also* Geographical pricing)
Preaward survey, 449–450
Prefiled method, catalogs,
    351–352
Price leadership, 192
Pricing:
    decisions in, 187–188
    declining products, 210–211
    goals of, 201–206
    interdivisional, 212
    new products, 209–210
    repair parts, 211–212
Primary demand, 330–331
Prime contract level, defense
    marketing, 435–438, 451
Private warehousing, 383–385
Product development:
    organizational position of,
        180–181
    organizational structure of,
        179–180
    staffing of, 181–182
Product differentiation, strategy
    of, 172–173
Product life cycle, 150–151
Product-line simplification,
    173–176
Product manager, 305–307
Product research, 131–134
Product strategy, 48–49, 66
Productivity, as standard of
    marketing performance,
    92–93
Profit:
    gross profit, 94, 113
    net marketing profit, 94, 113
    standard of marketing
        performance, 94–95
Program Evaluation and Review
    Technique (PERT), 164–165

Programmed instruction, 320–321
Public warehousing, 383–385

Quantity discounts, 207–208

Rational buying motives, 29–35
Raw materials:
  agricultural, 399
  definition of, 7–9
Reciprocity, 34–35
Renegotiation, defense
  contracts, 448–449
Replacement market,
  components, 11–12
Research, marketing (*see*
  Marketing research)
Research & Development (R&D):
  defense, 436
  oceanology, 418–419
  product development, 158
  relationship to research
    goods, 13
  strategy of, 80–84
Research goods, 13
Resource summary, 165
Return on investment, 94–95,
  101–102
Revolving credit, 224
Risk:
  new products, 155–159
  weighted average share,
    defense contracts,
    447–448
Robinson-Patman Act, 38,
  198–201, 208–209

Safety stock, 388–389
Sales force:
  characteristics of, 305–313

Sales force:
  organizational structure of,
    302–305
Sales forecasting, 126–131
Sales management:
  motivation of salesmen,
    322–325
  recruitment and selection of
    salesmen, 314–319
  training of salesmen, 319–322
Sales research, 124–131
Sales training, 319–322
Saline-water conversion,
  417–418
Salvage goods, 13–15
Screw Machine Supply Co.,
  Chicago, Inc., 316
Selective demand, 330
Selective distribution, market
  coverage policy, 238
Selling agents, 10–11, 270–271
Situational audit, 159–161
Small business:
  definition of, 449
  role in defense marketing,
    430–431, 449–450
Speciality distributor, 265
Speculators, 410–411
Strategies, 48–50, 66–67
Subcontract level, defense
  marketing, 431, 435–437
Supplier relations, vendor
  analysis, 32

Tactics, 66–67
Technical counsel, 11, 308–310
Technical specialist (*see*
  Technical counsel)
Testing:
  buying process, part of, 33

Testing:
   new-product evolutionary
      cycle, phase of, 171
Textron, Inc.:
   defense contractor, 429
   diversification, strategy of,
      78–79
   poultry business, 403
Total cost concept, logistics,
   377–380
Trade relations (*see* Reciprocity)
Trade shows, 352–354
Trading company, 287
Trial balloon, use of, in
   planning, 72

United Aircraft Corporation,
   424, 429
United Motor Service Division, 13

United States Steel Corporation,
   196

Value analysis, 30
Vendor analysis, 32–33
Vertical integration:
   agricultural marketing, 403
   definition of, 8–9
   protection, unfavorable price
      fluctuations, 31

Webb-Pomerene Export Trade
   Act, 293
Webb-Pomerene joint export
   operations, 293–294
Witco Chemical Company,
   366–367

Zone pricing, 197
   (*See also* Geographical pricing)